MW01626218

Collingwood, Francis
Woolams, John

The Universal Cook

ISBN: 978-1-948837-17-0

This classic reprint compilation was produced from digital files in the Google Books digital collection, which may be found at http://www.books.google.com. The artwork used on the cover is from Wikimedia Commons and remains in the public domain. Omissions and/or errors in this book are due to either the physical condition of the original book or due to the scanning process by Google or its agents.

Francis Collingwood's and John Woollams's **The Universal Cook** was originally published in 1792 (London).

Townsends
PO Box 415, Pierceton, IN 46562
www.Townsends.us

THE

UNIVERSAL COOK,

AND

City and Country Housekeeper.

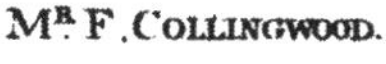

Mr. F. Collingwood.

Mr. J. Woollams.

THE UNIVERSAL COOK,

AND

City and Country Housekeeper.

CONTAINING ALL THE

VARIOUS BRANCHES OF COOKERY:

THE DIFFERENT METHODS OF DRESSING

Butchers Meat, Poultry, Game, and Fish;

AND OF PREPARING

GRAVIES, CULLICES, SOUPS, AND BROTHS;

TO DRESS

ROOTS AND VEGETABLES,

AND TO PREPARE

Little elegant Dishes for Suppers or light Repasts:

TO MAKE ALL SORTS OF

PIES, PUDDINGS, PANCAKES, AND FRITTERS;

CAKES, PUFFS, AND BISCUITS; CHEESECAKES, TARTS, AND CUSTARDS; CREAMS AND JAMS; BLANC-MANGE, FLUMMERY, ELEGANT ORNAMENTS, JELLIES, AND SYLLABUBS.

The various Articles in

CANDYING, DRYING, PRESERVING, AND PICKLING.

THE PREPARATION OF

HAMS, TONGUES, BACON, &c.

DIRECTIONS FOR

TRUSSING POULTRY, CARVING, AND MARKETING.

THE MAKING AND MANAGEMENT OF

Made Wines, Cordial Waters, and Malt Liquors.

Together with

Directions for Baking Bread, the Management of Poultry and the Dairy, and the Kitchen and Fruit Garden; with a Catalogue of the various Articles in Season in the different Months of the Year.

Besides a Variety of

USEFUL AND INTERESTING TABLES.

The Whole Embellished with

The Heads of the Authors, Bills of Fare for every Month in the Year, and proper Subjects for the Improvement of the Art of Carving, elegantly engraved on fourteen Copper-Plates.

By FRANCIS COLLINGWOOD, AND JOHN WOOLLAMS,

Principal Cooks at the Crown and Anchor Tavern in the Strand,

Late from the London Tavern.

LONDON:

PRINTED BY R. NOBLE, FOR J. SCATCHERD AND J. WHITAKER, No. 12, AVE-MARIA-LANE.

1792.

PREFACE.

WE ſhall not attempt to ranſack the Annals of Antiquity, with a View to diſcover what was the Food of our firſt Parents in the Garden of Eden, or in what Manner they performed their culinary Operations: It is ſufficient for us to know at preſent, that Cookery is become a Science, that every Age has contributed its Mite to the Improvement of this Art, which ſeems now to have reached a very high Degree of Perfection.

Complete however as this Science may now be conſidered, it will ever be ſubject to the Variations of Taſte and Faſhion; and from this Source proceeds the great Variety of Books on Cookery now preſented to the Service of the Public. After ſome

Years Practice in two of the most capital Taverns this great Metropolis produces, we have had frequent Occasions to deviate from the printed Directions we found in Books of this Kind, sometimes by altering, but more frequently by reducing the Number of Ingredients, and thereby rendering the Dish more simple and less expensive, though equally salutary to the Constitution, and grateful to the Palate.

It will from hence follow, that we do not presume to arrogate to ourselves the Reputation of having ushered into the World a Work entirely new, which indeed cannot be expected; but we flatter ourselves, that the Alterations we have made in the different Receipts, the new ones we have added, and the methodical Manner in which we have arranged the Whole, will in some Degree entitle us to the Patronage of the Public. Glasse, Mason, Raffald, and Farley, are,

are, like us, equally indebted to the Labours of our Predeceſſors.

It cannot be expected from Men, whoſe Time is wholly employed in the culinary Arts, that they ſhould be much converſant in the Preparation of made Wines, Cordial Waters, and Malt Liquors, or in the Management of Poultry, the Dairy, and the Kitchen and Fruit Gardens; yet theſe being Matters eſſentially neceſſary to be known by every Houſekeeper in the Country, and equally uſeful and amuſing to thoſe, who retire from the Noiſe and Buſtle of the Metropolis to enjoy the calm Retreat of a rural Life, we could not prevail on ourſelves to omit thoſe neceſſary Articles, or be ſatisfied ſolely with our own Judgement thereon. We have therefore engaged different Perſons to treat on thoſe different Subjects; and we doubt not but that, from their known Skill and Experience therein, they will be found to have done no Discredit to the other Parts of the Work.

While we, on our Part, have been particularly careful of improving and amending the different Receipts, and adding such new ones as have occurred to us in the Course of our extensive Practice, the Publishers have been no less attentive to the elegantly Printing of the Work, a bare Inspection into which will give it, in Point of Elegance, a decided Superiority over every other Book of the Kind. The Designs and Engravings of the Plates have been executed at a very great Expence; and we may safely venture to assert, that no Work of *this* Nature ever received such expensive Assistance as THE UNIVERSAL COOK, now humbly submitted to the Perusal and Patronage of the Public.

F. COLLINGWOOD.

J. WOOLLAMS.

CONTENTS.

CHAP. I.

General Observations.

CHAP. II.

The various Methods of dressing Beef.

CHAP.

CONTENTS.

CHAP. III.

The various Methods of dressing Veal.

CHAP.

CONTENTS.

CHAP IV.

The various Methods of dressing Mutton.

CHAP.

CONTENTS.

CHAP. V.

The various Methods of dreſſing Lamb.

CHAP. VI.

The various Methods of dreſſing Pork.

Another

CONTENTS.

CHAP. VII.

Directions for truffing Poultry and Game.

CHAP. VIII.

The various Methods of dreffing Poultry.

To

CONTENTS.

CHAP.

CONTENTS.

CHAP. IX.

The different Methods of dressing Game, small Birds, &c.

CHAP.

CONTENTS.

CHAP. X.

The different Methods of dressing Fish.

CHAP.

CONTENTS.

CHAP. XI.

Sauces, Gravies, and Cullices.

CHAP. XII.

Soups and Broths.

b

Egg

CONTENTS.

CHAP. XIII.

To dreſs Roots and Vegetables.

CHAP. XIV.

Elegant little Diſhes for Suppers or light Repaſts.

To

CONTENTS.

CHAP. XV.

To make Fruit Pies.

(The Reader will find Directions already given for making Meat, Poultry, and Fifh Pies, in the preceding Chapters, on the different Methods of dreffing Beef, Veal, Mutton, Lamb, Pork, Poultry, Game, and Fifh.)

CHAP. XVI.

To make all Sorts of Puddings.

CONTENTS.

CHAP. XVII.

To make Pancakes and Fritters.

CHAP. XVIII.

To make all Sorts of Cakes, Puffs, and Biscuits.

Naples'

CONTENTS.

CHAP. XIX.

To make Cheefecakes, Tarts, and Cuftards.

CHAP. XX.

To make Creams and Jams.

CHAP. XXI.

To make Blanc Mange, Flummery, Jellies, and Syllabubs.

CHAP. XXII.

Candying and Drying.

CHAP. XXIII.

To make all Sorts of Preſerves.

To

CONTENTS.

CHAP. XXIV.

To prepare Pickles of all Sorts.

CHAP. XXV.

The Preparation of Hams, Tongues, Bacon, &c.

To

CONTENTS

CHAP. XXVI.

Directions for Carving.

CHAP. XXVII.

Directions for Marketing.

CHAP.

CONTENTS.

CHAP. XXVIII.

The Preparation of made Wines.

CHAP. XXIX.

The Preparation of Cordial Waters.

CONTENTS.

CHAP. XXX.

Directions for brewing Malt Liquors.

CHAP. XXXI.

Directions for baking Bread.

CHAP. XXXII.

The Breeding, Rearing, and Management of Poultry.

CHAP.

CONTENTS.

CHAP. XXXIII.

The Management of the Dairy.

CHAP. XXXIV.

The Management of the Kitchen Garden.

CHAP. XXXV.

The Management of the Fruit Garden.

CHAP.

CONTENTS.

CHAP. XXXVI.

Articles omitted in the preceding Part of the Work.

THE

THE

UNIVERSAL COOK.

CHAP. I.

General Observations.

BEFORE we enter on the practical part of the Cook's business, it may not be improper to make a few *general observations*, which are as necessary to be attended to as any part of the culinary profession. The first and most important of all these is *cleanliness*, not only in their own persons, but also in every article used in the kitchen. To the want of a due attention to copper vessels badly tinned or decayed, and soups or broths that have been suffered to remain in them all night, many people have unhappily lost their lives, of which the melancholy affair at Salt-hill is a recent proof. To prevent any thing of this kind, the cook should be particularly careful, in families where copper utensils are used, frequently to inspect them, and see that no part of the copper be uncovered with tin; and be careful likewise to wipe them perfectly dry after they have been used, as the least moisture left in them may produce verdigrease, which may affect the health, if not endanger the lives, of some part of the family. A kitchen properly supplied with utensils kept neat and clean is an ornament to a house, and a credit to the cook. But I shall not

 here

here dwell any longer on matters ſo generally known, but proceed to give general directions for Roaſting, Boiling, Made Diſhes, Soups, Puddings and Pies. And firſt of

Roaſting.

THE fire muſt be prepared according to the weight and ſize of what is to be roaſted. If it be any thing ſmall or thin, a briſk fire will be neceſſary, in order that it may be done quick; but if it be a large joint, it will require a ſtrong fire that has lain ſome time to cake. It is a very good cuſtom to put a little ſalt and water in the dripping-pan, with which you may at firſt baſte your meat. As ſoon as the fire has dried it, you may throw a little flour over it, and then baſte it with butter. This will give an agreeable colour to your meat. Take care to keep the meat at a proper diſtance from the fire; becauſe, if it once gets ſcorched, it will make the outſide hard, and will prevent the fire from having a proper effect on the meat, ſo that it will appear to be thoroughly cooked, while it may be nearly raw within ſide. A clear fire, and often baſting the meat, are very eſſential points to be obſerved by the cook. Any kinds of wild-fowl require a briſk fire; but care muſt be taken not to roaſt them too much, as that ſpoils them. Tame fowls require a longer time, as they are not ſo ſoon heated through as the wild ſort; and they muſt be often baſted, as that keeps up the froth, makes them more plump, and gives an addition to their colour. Geeſe and pigs require a good fire, and ſhould turn quick. In order to prevent hares and rabbits from appearing bloody at the neck when they be cut up, when they are about half roaſted, cut the neck ſkin, and the blood will then run out. Theſe require time and care. Every thing will require more roaſting in froſty than in mild weather. It is an improper method, though practised by some cooks, to salt the meat before it be put to the fire, for that draws out the gravy. Take care that the spit be clean, for a spit mark is very disagreeable. When your meat is done, flour and baste it just before you take it up, when it will have a nice froth, and make a better appearance.

Boiling.

MUCH care, nicety, and attention, are required in boiling all sorts of meat, but particularly veal; to boil which properly, you must fill your pot with a proper quantity of soft water. Having dusted your veal with flour, put it in your pot over a strong fire. The custom of putting in milk to make it white is useless, and had perhaps be better left out. Oatmeal has no better effect than milk, and flour is certainly better than either, when dusted on the meat. Be sure to skim it well, for every thing will throw up a scum, and if that be suffered to boil down, it will give a black cast to the meat. The meat must have plenty of water, and boil very slowly, which will give a plump appearance to the veal. To let any sort of meat boil fast is a great error, as it hardens the outside, prevents the water from properly penetrating, and gives a disagreeable colour to the meat. It is a general rule in boiling meat, to allow a quarter of an hour to every pound; but a leg of veal of twelve pounds, will require three hours and a half boiling, for the slower it boils the better. All sorts of fresh meat may be put in when the water boils, but salt meat when the water is warm; though there are many experienced cooks who always put the meat in when the water is cold, as they say it thereby gets warm to the heart before the outside gets hard. To boil a leg of lamb of four pounds weight, you must allow an hour and

 half.

half. Mutton or beef, which you muſt always be careful to dredge well with flour before you put them into the pot, do not require ſo much boiling as lamb, pork, and veal, which, if they are not well boiled, will be unwholeſome; but it is not ſo much thought of, if mutton and beef be not quite ſo well done. A leg of pork will take an hour's boiling more than a joint of veal of the ſame ſize; but never forget to ſcum the pot, let the meat be what ſort it may.

Frying.

TO fry fiſh properly, they muſt be firſt dried in a cloth and then dredged with flour. The dripping or hogſlard, of which you muſt put plenty in your pan, muſt always boil before your fiſh be put in. Hogſlard, for frying, is preferred to butter, as the latter frequently makes the fiſh ſoft, and is apt to burn and blacken them. Your fiſh, when fried, ſhould be put to drain, either in a diſh or hair ſieve, that, when you ſend them up to table, they may not appear or eat greaſy. If you make uſe of parſley, pick it very clean, and waſh it well in cold water, before you throw it into the pan of boiling fat, where you muſt not let it remain too long. It will then be of a fine green, and eat very criſp.

Broiling.

THE principal matter in broiling is to have a clear fire. Turn your meat often while it is broiling, which will prevent its burning or getting ſmokey. You muſt have a diſh placed over ſome hot coals, in order to keep it hot as faſt as it be broiled; for no meat of any kind is good unleſs it be carried hot to table; and for this purpoſe, many cooks ſend up only a ſmall quantity at a time, and that as ſoon as it is broiled.

Made Diſhes.

THOUGH it is not our intention to devote any particular chapter to the article of Made Diſhes of butcher's meat, as we ſhall inſert them under the general heads of Beef, Mutton, &c. yet it may not be amiſs to give ſome general obſervations thereon, as we find them in Raffald, Glaſſe, Maſon, Farley, and other modern books of cookery. As neither eggs nor cream will contribute much to thicken your white ſauce, be careful, before you put your eggs or cream into it, to have all your ingredients well boiled, and the whole of a proper thickneſs. Do not ſtir them with a ſpoon, nor ſet your pan on the fire, after you have put in your eggs and cream, for fear they ſhould gather at the bottom and be lumpy. To prevent this, hold your pan at a proper height from the fire, and keep ſhaking it round one way, which will keep it from curdling; but be ſure that you do not ſuffer it to boil. Remember to take out what you are dreſſing with a fiſh ſlice, and ſtrain your ſauce upon it, which will prevent any ſmall bits of meat mixing with your ſauce, and you will thereby have it clear and fine. Be particularly cautious, in browning diſhes, that no fat floats on the top of the gravy, which may be prevented by its being properly ſkimmed. It ſhould have no predominant taſte, which depends on your juſtly proportioning the different ingredients, and ſhould be of a fine brown. Nothing is more hurtful to the reputation of a made diſh than the taſte of raw wine, or freſh anchovy; in order therefore to avoid this defect, you muſt deprive it of its rawneſs, by putting them in ſome time before your diſh is ready. Fried force-meat balls muſt be put in a ſieve to drain, that the fat may run from them, and never let them boil in your ſauce, as that will ſoften

 them,

them, and give them a disagreeable appearance; the best method therefore is, to put them in after the meat is dished up. Force-meat balls, morels, truffles, artichoke bottoms, and pickled mushrooms, may be used in almost every made dish.

Soups.

IN making any kind of soups, particularly vermicelli, portable, brown gravy soup, or any other in which herbs are used, remember to lay the meat in the bottom of your pan, with a large lump of butter. Having cut the roots and herbs small, strew them over the meat, and set the pan on a very slow fire. This will draw all the virtues out of the different ingredients, will produce a good gravy, and a very different effect in point of flavour, than if at first you had put in the water. Fill your pan with water, as soon as the gravy is almost dried up. Take off the fat as soon as it begins to boil, and then follow the directions for making the sort of soup you wish to have. Green pease, intended for soup, require hard water; but soft water is preferable for old pease soup. In making white soup, let it be taken off the fire before you put in the cream. As soups are soon cold, always dish them up the last thing. Take care that all the greens and herbs you use in soups are well washed and clean picked, and that any one thing has not a predominant taste over another, but that it has a fine agreeable relish, and that all the tastes be united.

Puddings.

WE need not here mention, that the cloth in which you boil puddings should be perfectly clean; but it may not be amiss to tell the cook, that the cloth should be dipped in boiling water, and dredged with flour. A bread pudding may be tied loose; but

but a batter pudding muſt be tied cloſe, and no pudding muſt be put into the pot till the water boils. Puddings may be boiled in a baſon; in which caſe, butter the baſon, and let it have plenty of water, and turn it frequently. As ſoon as you think it is enough, take it out of the pot, and let it ſtand a ſhort time to cool. Then take off the ſtring, wrap the cloth round the baſon, and laying the diſh over it, turn the pudding into it, in doing which you muſt take great care that you do not break the pudding, as every light pudding is very liable to that accident. In making a batter pudding, begin with mixing the flour well with a little milk, after which gradually put in the ingredients, and thus your pudding will be perfectly ſmooth, and without lumps. In making all ſorts of puddings, ſtrain the eggs when you beat them, ſo that they may neither have treadles nor lumps in them. Bread and cuſtard puddings that are to be baked require time, and a moderate oven to raiſe them. If they be put in too great a heat, they will burn, and in courſe be ſpoiled; but batter and rice puddings require a quick oven. Before you put in the pudding, remember to butter the diſh or pan.

Pies.

RAISED pies require a quick oven, and that they ſhould be well cloſed up, otherwiſe they will fall in the ſides. Put no water into them till juſt as you are going to put them into the oven; for, if the water be put in ſooner, it will give the cruſt a ſodden appearance, and may perhaps occaſion it to run. Great judgment is neceſſary in determining what ſhould be the heat of your oven; for light paſte requires a moderate, but not too ſlow a heat, as the latter will occaſion it to look heavy; and too great a heat will catch and burn it, without giving it time to riſe. Iced tarts ſhould be baked in a flow oven, otherwife the icing will become brown before the pafte is properly baked. The pafte neceffary for tarts, we fhall mention hereafter.

Having thus given a few general obfervations, which the young cook fhould always bear in mind, we fhall proceed to defcribe the proper method of dreffing all forts of butchers meat, and fhall then proceed to poultry, game, &c.

CHAP. II.

The various Methods of Dreffing Beef.

Pieces in a Bullock.

THE *Head* includes the tongue and palate. The *Entrails* confift of the fweetbread, kidnies, fkirts, and tripe; as alfo the double, the roll, and the reed-tripe.

The *Fore Quarter* confifts of the haunch, and includes the clod, marrow-bone, fhin, and the fticking-piece, that is the neck end. The leg of mutton piece, which has part of the blade bone. The chuck, the brifket, fore ribs, and middle rib, which is called the chuck-rib.

The *Hind Quarter* confifts of the firloin and rump, the thin and thick flank, the veiny piece, the ifch bone, or chuck bone, buttock, and leg.

To roaft a Bullock's Heart.

AS we have already given general directions for roafting joints of beef, we prefume there is no occafion for repeating it here: we fhall confine ourfelves to the manner of dreffing the fmaller parts

parts of the ox. To roaſt a bullock's heart, mix crumbs of bread with ſome chopped ſuet, or a piece of butter; add ſome chopped parſley, ſweet marjoram, grated lemon peel, pepper, ſalt, and nutmeg, and the yolk of an egg. Stuff the heart with this, and either roaſt or bake it. You may, if you pleaſe, lard it with bacon. Put a little red wine into the gravy, and ſerve it up, with melted butter and currant jelly in boats.

To roaſt Ox Palates.

FIRST boil your palates tender, then blanch them, cut them into pieces about two inches in length, and lard one half with bacon. Have ready two or three pigeons, and two or three chicken-peepers, which muſt be drawn, truſſed, and filled with force-meat. Having larded one half of them, put them on a bird ſpit thus: a bird, a palate, a ſage leaf, and a piece of bacon, and ſo on till you have ſpitted the whole. Parboil and blanch ſome lambs and cocks ſtones, lard them with little bits of bacon, large oyſters parboiled, and each larded with a piece of bacon. Put theſe on a ſkewer, with a little bit of bacon and a ſage leaf between them. Tie them on the ſpit and roaſt them. Beat up the yolks of three eggs, ſome nutmeg, a little ſalt, and crumbs of bread. Baſte them with theſe all the time they are roaſting, and have ready two ſweetbreads, each cut in two, ſome artichoke bottoms quartered and fried, and then rub the diſh with ſhalots. Pile the birds one upon another in the middle, and lay the other things round them all ſeparate by themſelves. Have your ſauce ready, which muſt be made of a pint of good gravy, a quarter of a pint of red wine, an anchovy, the oyſter liquor, and a piece of butter rolled in flour. Boil all theſe together, and pour them

them into the difh, with a little juice of lemon, and the lemon itfelf you may make ufe of as a garnifh.

To ragoo Ox Palates.

BOIL four ox palates till they be tender, clean them well, and cut them fome into long and fome into fquare pieces. Put them into a rich cooley thus made: put a piece of butter into your ftew-pan, and melt it; put a large fpoonful of flour to it, and ftir it till it be fmooth. Put to it a quart of good gravy, a gill of Lifbon, and three fhalots chopped; put in fome lean ham cut very fine, and half a lemon. Let it boil twenty minutes, and then ftrain it through a fieve. Put this and your palates into a pan, with fome force-meat balls, truffles, and morels, and pickled or frefh mufh-rooms ftewed in gravy. Seafon it with pepper and falt to your tafte, and tofs them up five or fix minutes. You may ufe either lemon or beet-root for garnifh.

To boil a Rump of Beef.

BOIL a rump of beef half an hour, and then take it up. Lay it into a large pewter difh or ftew-pan, and cut three or four gafhes all along the fide of it. Rub the gafhes with pepper and falt, and pour into the difh a pint of red wine, as much hot water, two or three onions cut fmall, the hearts of eight or ten lettuces cut fmall, and a large piece of butter rolled in a little flour. Lay the flefhy part of the meat downwards, and cover it clofe. Let it ftew for two hours and a half over a charcoal fire, or a very flow coal fire. When you do it in a pewter difh, it is beft done over a chaffing-difh of hot coals, with a bit or two of charcoal to keep it alive. You muft take care that the bone be chopped

chopped fo clofe, that the meat may lie perfectly flat in the difh. When the beef is enough, take it up, lay it in the difh, and pour the fauce over it. This is a difh cooked in the French manner.

Rump of Beef fmoked.

BONE a rump of beef as well as poffible without fpoiling the fhape, and falt it with a pound of common falt, and two ounces of falt-petre. Put it lengthways into a falting pan, with all forts of fweet herbs, as parfley, fhalots, thyme, bafil, winter favoury, a little coriander, fix cloves, and two cloves of garlic. Leave it about a week or ten days in falt, and then hang it in the chimney. When dried, keep it in a dry place. When you ufe it, boil it in water without falt, with a few onions, cloves, a bundle of fweet herbs, and a little nutmeg. When it is cool in the liquor, ferve it up, and garnifh with parfley. If you apprehend it will be too falt, you may foak it fome time before you boil it.

To bake a Leg of Beef.

LAY your beef at the bottom of a large deep pan, and put in a little piece of bacon, a flice or two of carrot, fome mace, cloves, black and white whole pepper, a large onion cut in flices, and a bundle of fweet herbs; pour in water till the meat be covered, then cover it up, and fend it to the oven. When it is baked, ftrain it through a coarfe fieve, take out all the finews and fat, and put them into a faucepan, with a few fpoonfuls of the gravy, a little red wine, a fmall piece of butter rolled in flour, and fome muftard. Shake your faucepan often, and when the fauce is hot and thick, difh it, and ferve it up.

To broil Beef Steaks.

A rump is generally uſed for ſteaks, which muſt be cut about half an inch thick. Having got a clear fire, rub your gridiron well with beef ſuet, and when it is hot, lay on your ſteaks. As ſoon as they begin to brown, turn them, and when the other ſide is brown alſo, lay them on a hot diſh, with a piece of butter between each ſteak. Sprinkle a little pepper and ſalt over them, and let them ſtand two or three minutes. Then ſlice a ſhalot very thin into a ſpoonful of water. Lay your ſteaks upon the gridiron, and keep turning them till they be enough. Put them on your diſh, pour the ſhalot and water among them, and ſerve them up.

To fry Beef Steaks.

FRY ſome ſteaks, cut out of the middle of the rump, in butter. When they are done, put a little good ſmall beer into the pan, a little nutmeg, a ſhalot, ſome walnut catchup, and a piece of butter rolled in flour. Shake it round the pan till it boils, and pour it over the ſteaks. Pickled muſhrooms, or oyſters, may be added, if you chuſe.

Another Method.

BEAT the lean of a beef ſteak well with the back of a knife, and then fry it in juſt as much butter as will moiſten the pan. Pour out the gravy as it runs from the meat, and turn them often, over a gentle fire. Fry the fat by itſelf, and lay it upon the meat; put to the gravy a glaſs of red wine, half an anchovy, a little nutmeg and beaten pepper, and a ſhalot cut ſmall. Give it two or three gentle boils, and ſeaſon it with ſalt to your taſte. Pour the ſauce over the ſteaks, and ſerve them up.

Beef

Beef Steaks rolled.

TAKE what quantity of beef ſteaks you have occaſion for, and beat them with a cleaver till they be tender. Make a forcemeat with a pound of veal beaten fine in a mortar, the fleſh of a fowl, half a pound of gammon of bacon or cold ham, fat and lean, the kidney fat of a loin of veal, and a ſweet-bread. Cut all theſe very ſmall, and add ſome truffles and morels ſtewed and cut ſmall, two ſhalots, ſome parſley, a little thyme, lemon peel, the yolks of four eggs, a nutmeg grated, and half a pint of cream. Mix theſe well together, and ſtir them over a ſlow fire for eight or ten minutes. Put them upon the ſteaks, and roll them up, and ſkewer them tight. Put them into the frying-pan, and fry them of a nice brown. Take them from the fat, and put them into a ſtew-pan with a pint of good drawn gravy, a ſpoonful of red wine, two of catchup, a few pickled muſhrooms, and let them ſtew for a quarter of an hour. Take up the ſteaks, cut them in two, lay the cut ſide uppermoſt, and garniſh with lemon.

A Rump of Beef rolled.

CUT the meat from the bone as whole as poſſible, ſplit the inſide from top to bottom, and ſpread it open. Take the fleſh of two fowls and ſome beef ſuet, of each an equal quantity, and as much cold boiled ham, a little pepper, an anchovy, a nutmeg grated, ſome thyme, a good deal of parſley, and a few muſhrooms. Chop all theſe together, and beat them in a mortar, with half a pint baſon full of crumbs of bread. Mix all theſe together with four yolks of eggs. Put it into the meat, cover it up, and roll it round. Stick it in one ſkewer, and tie it faſt together with packthread. Put a layer of bacon and a layer of beef, cut in thin ſlices, into a pot

pot or large ſaucepan that will juſt hold it; put in a piece of carrot, ſome whole pepper, mace, ſweet herbs, and a large onion. Lay the rolled beef on it, and put in juſt water enough to cover the top of the beef. Cover it cloſe, and let it ſtew very ſoftly, on a ſlow fire, for eight or ten hours, but not too faſt: as ſoon as you find the meat is tender, which you may know by running a ſkewer into it, take it up, and keep it hot. Boil the gravy till you think it be ſtrong enough, then ſtrain it off, and take ſome chopped muſhrooms, ſome truffles and morels cut ſmall, two ſpoonfuls of red or white wine, and a piece of butter rolled in flour. You may alſo put in the yolks of two eggs; but, as they are apt to curdle, they had perhaps better be omitted. Boil theſe together. Set the meat before the fire, baſte it with butter, and throw crumbs of bread over it. As ſoon as the ſauce is enough, lay the meat in the diſh, and pour the ſauce over it.

To ſtew a Rump of Beef.

HAVING cut the meat clean from the bone, put it into your ſtewpan, and cover it with an equal quantity of gravy and water. Put in a ſpoonful of whole pepper, a bundle of ſweet herbs, two onions, ſome ſalt, and a pint of red wine. Cover it cloſe, and ſet it over a ſtove or ſlow fire for ſome hours, ſhaking and turning it four or five times, and ſtirring it till dinner be ready. Cut ten or twelve turnips into ſlices the broad way, then quarter them, and fry them in beef dripping till they be brown. Take care to let your dripping boil before you put them in, and when done drain them well from the fat. Lay the beef in your ſoup diſh, toaſt a little bread very nice and brown, which cut three corner ways, and lay them and the turnips into the diſh. Skim the fat off clean, ſtrain in the gravy, and ſerve it up, having firſt

firſt ſeaſoned it with pepper and ſalt to your taſte. If you have the convenience of a ſtove, you may put the diſh over it for four or five minutes, which will give the liquor a fine flavour of the turnips, make the bread taſte better, and be a great addition to the whole.

Another Method.

TAKE it up as ſoon as it is boiled a little more than half enough, and peel off the ſkin. Take pepper, ſalt, beaten mace, grated nutmeg, a handful of parſley, a little thyme, winter ſavoury, and ſweet marjoram, all chopped fine and mixed. Make great holes in the fat and lean, and ſtuff theſe into them. Spread the reſt over them, with the yolks of two eggs. To the gravy that runs out, put a pint of claret. Put the meat into a deep pan, pour the liquor in, cover it cloſe, and let it bake two hours. Put it into the diſh, ſtrain the liquor through a ſieve, and, having ſkimmed off the fat very clean, pour it over the meat, and ſerve it up.

To force the Inſide of a Sirloin of Beef.

HAVING ſpitted your ſirloin, cut out from the inſide all the ſkin and fat together, and take off all the fleſh from the bones. Chop the meat very fine, and put to it a little beaten mace, two or three ſhalots, an anchovy, half a pint of red wine, a little pepper and ſalt, and put all on the bones again. Then lay on your fat and ſkin, ſkewer it cloſe, and paper it well. When it is ſufficiently roaſted, take off the fat, and diſh up your meat. Make a ſauce of a little red wine, a ſhalot, an anchovy, and two or three ſlices of horſe-raddiſh. Pour this ſauce over the meat, and ſend it to table.

To

To dreſs a Fillet of Beef.

CAREFULLY cut out the inſide of a ſirloin from the bone, grate ſome nutmeg over it, a few crumbs of bread, a little pepper and ſalt, lemon-peel, and thyme, with ſome parſley ſhred ſmall. Roll it up tight, tie it with packthread, and roaſt it. Put a quart of milk and a quarter of a pound of butter into the dripping-pan, and baſte the meat well. As ſoon as it is enough, take it up, untie it, and leave a ſkewer in it to keep it together. Put ſome good gravy into the diſh, and ſome ſweet ſauce into a cup. Plain butter will do very well to baſte it with; but, if you like it better, you may make uſe of wine and butter.

To dreſs Beef Collops.

TAKE any tender piece of beef, ſuch as the rump, and cut collops rather larger than Scotch collops. Haſh them with a knife, and flour them. Melt a little butter in a ſtewpan, and put in your collops. Having firied them quick for about two minutes, put in a pint of gravy, a little butter rolled in flour, and ſeaſon it with pepper and ſalt. Cut ſome pickled cucumbers into thin ſlices, half a walnut, a few capers, and a little onion ſhred very fine. Stew them five minutes, then put them into a diſh, and ſerve them up. If you chuſe it, you may put into it half a glaſs of wine.

Beef Gobbets.

TAKE any piece of beef, except the leg, cut it into pieces, and put it into a ſtewpan. Cover them with water, and let them ſtew an hour. Then put in a little mace, cloves, and whole pepper, tied looſely in a muſlin rag, with ſome celery cut ſmall. To theſe add ſome ſalt, turnips and carrots pared and cut in ſlices, a little parſley, a bunch of ſweet herbs,

herbs, a large cruſt of bread, and an ounce of barley or rice. Having covered it cloſe, let it ſtew till it be tender. Then take out the herbs, ſpices, and bread, and have ready a French roll toaſted, and cut it into quarters. Put them into your diſh, pour in the meat and ſauce, and ſerve it up hot.

To ſtew Neat's Tongues.

STEW two tongues, for two hours, in water juſt ſufficient to cover them. Take them out and peel them, and then put them in again with a pint of ſtrong gravy, half a pint of white wine, a bundle of ſweet herbs, a little pepper and ſalt, ſome mace, cloves, and whole pepper, tied in a muſlin rag; a ſpoonful of capers chopped, turnips and carrots ſliced, and a piece of butter rolled in flour. Let all ſtew together very ſoftly over a ſlow fire for two hours, and then take out the ſpice and ſweet herbs, and ſend the diſh to table. Some omit the turnips and carrots, and boil the tongues by themſelves.

To make a Mock Hare.

TAKE a large bullock's heart, waſh it, and cut off the deaf ears; then ſtuff it with ſome forcemeat in the ſame manner as a hare. Cover the top of it either with a caul of veal or paper, to keep in the ſtuffing. Roaſt it by a hanging ſpit, and it will take an hour and a half before a good fire. Baſte it with red wine, and when it be roaſted, take the wine out of the dripping-pan, ſkim off the fat, and add a glaſs of wine to it. When it is hot, put in ſome lumps of red currant jelly, and pour it into the diſh. Send it up to table, with ſome red currant jelly cut in ſlices, and placed on a ſaucer.

To ragoo a Piece of Beef.

ANY piece of beef, which is cut ſquare, is free from bones, and has fat at the top, will anſwer this purpofe; either the rump or flank will do very well. Cut the meat from the bones, which laft will make excellent foup. Put the meat into a large ftew-pan with a good piece of butter, and fry it till it be all a little brown; but flour your meat well before you put it into the pan. Then pour into it as much gravy as will cover it. Your gravy muft be thus made: take about a pound of coarfe beef, a little piece of veal cut fmall, a bundle of fweet herbs, an onion, fome whole black and white pepper, two or three large blades of mace, four or five cloves, a piece of carrot, a little piece of bacon, fteeped a little while in vinegar, and a cruft of bread toafted brown. To this add a quart of white wine, and let it boil till it be half wafted. While this is doing, pour a quart of boiling water into the ftewpan, cover it clofe, and let it be ftewing foftly. When the gravy is done, ftrain it, and pour it into the pan in which the beef is. Take an ounce of truffles and morels cut fmall, fome frefh or dried mufhrooms cut fmall, two fpoonfuls of catchup, and cover it clofe. Let all this ftew till the fauce be thick and rich; and then have ready fome artichoke bottoms cut into four, and a few pickled mufhrooms. Give them a boil or two, and when your meat be tender, and your fauce quite rich, lay the meat into a difh, and pour the foup over it. You may add a fweet-bread cut in fix pieces, a palate ftewed tender and cut it into little pieces, fome coxcombs, and a few forcemeat balls. Though it will be very good without this addition, yet it will be much better with it. Some cooks, merely for the fake of variety, when the beef is ready, and the gravy put to it, add a large bunch of celery, cut fmall and wafhed clean, two fpoonfuls of catchup, and a glafs of red wine.

Beef

Beef in Epigram.

HAVING roaſted a ſirloin of beef, take it off the ſpit, raiſe the ſkin carefully off, and cut the lean parts of the beef out; but obſerve not to cut near the ends or ſides. Cut the meat into pieces about as big as a crown-piece, put half a pint of gravy into a toſs-pan, an onion chopped fine, two ſpoonfuls of catchup, ſome pepper and ſalt, ſix ſmall pickled cucumbers cut in thin ſlices, and the gravy that comes from the beef, with a little butter rolled in flour, put the meat in, and toſs it up for five minutes. Then put it on the ſirloin, put the ſkin over, and ſerve it up. You may uſe horſe-radiſh for garniſh.

Buillie Beef.

PUT the thick end of a briſket of beef into a kettle, and cover it quite over with water. Let it boil two hours; then keep ſtewing it cloſe by the fire for ſix hours longer, and fill up the kettle as the water waſtes. At the ſame time that you put in your beef, put in alſo ſome turnips cut into little balls, carrots and ſome celery cut in pieces. About an hour before it be done, take out as much broth as will fill your ſoup-diſh, and boil in it for that hour turnips and carrots cut into balls, or little ſquare pieces, with ſome celery, and ſalt and pepper to your palate. Send it to table in two diſhes, the beef and the ſoup ſeparately. You may, if you pleaſe, put pieces of fried bread into your ſoup, and boil in a few knots of greens. If you apprehend your ſoup will not be rich enough, you may add a pound or two of fried mutton chops to your broth when you take it from the beef, and let it ſtew for that hour in the broth; but be ſure to remember to take out the mutton before you ſend the diſh to table.

Beef Escarlot.

TAKE half a pound of coarse sugar, two ounces of bay salt, one ounce of salt petre, a pound of common salt, and, having mixed them all well together, rub them into a brisket of beef. Then lay it in an earthen pan, and turn it every day. You may let it lie a fortnight in the pickle. Then boil it, and send it to table either with savoys, cabbages, greens, or pease pudding. It eats much better cold, and sent to table cut into slices.

Portugal Beef.

CUT off the meat from the bone of a rump of beef, cut it across, flour it, and fry the thin part brown in butter. Stuff the thick end with suet, boiled chesnuts, an anchovy, an onion, and a little pepper. Stew it in a pan of strong broth, and, when it is tender, lay both the fried and stewed meat together in your dish. Cut the fried in two, and lay it on each side of the stewed. Strain the gravy it was stewed in, put to it some pickled gerkins chopped, and boiled chesnuts. Thicken it with a piece of butter rolled in flour, a spoonful of browning, and give it two or three boils up. Season it with salt to your taste, and pour it over the beef. You may use lemon for garnish.

Beef Tremblant.

TAKE a rump of beef, which is the best of the ox you can use for this purpose, and cut the edge of the bone quite close to the meat, that it may lie flat in your dish. If it be a large rump, cut it at the chump end so as to make it square. Hang it up for three or four days at least, without putting any salt to it. Prepare a pickle, and leave it all night in soak. Fillet it two or three times across, and put it into a pot, the fat uppermost. Put to it a little more water than will cover it, take

care

care to ſkim it well, and ſeaſon it as you would for a good broth, adding about a pint of white wine. Let it ſimmer as long as it will hang together. There are many ſauces for this diſh, as minced carrots, herbs, &c. The carrots muſt be cut an inch long, boiled in a little water, afterwards ſtewed in broth proportionate to your meat. When they are done tender, put in a glaſs of wine, a little minced ſhalot and parſley, and the juice of a lemon. Take your beef out, and put it on a cloth, clean it from the fat and liquor, place it hot and whole in your diſh, and pour your ſauce hot over it.

Beef à la Mode.

TAKE ſome of the veiny-piece, or ſmall round of beef, which is generally called the mouſe buttock. Cut it five or ſix inches thick, and ſlice ſome pieces of fat bacon into long bits. Take an equal quantity of beaten mace, pepper, and nutmeg, with double the quantity of ſalt. Mix them together, dip the bacon into ſome vinegar, (garlick vinegar, if agreeable) and then into the ſpice. Lard the beef with a larding-pin, very thick and even. Put the meat into a pot juſt large enough to hold it, with a gill of vinegar, two large onions, a bunch of ſweet herbs, half a pint of wine, and ſome lemon peel. Cover it down very cloſe, and put a wet cloth round the edge of the pot, to prevent the ſteam evaporating. When it is half done, turn it, and cover it up again. Do it over a ſtove or very ſlow fire. It will require five hours and a half to do it properly. You may add to it truffles and morels.

Beef à la Royal.

TAKE a rump, ſirloin, or briſket of beef, and cut ſome holes in it at a little diſtance from each other. Fill the holes, one with chopped oyſters, another

another with fat bacon, and a third with chopped parfley. Dip each of thefe, before you ftuff your beef, into a feafoning made with falt, pepper, beaten mace, nutmeg, grated lemon peel, fweet marjoram, and thyme. Put a piece of butter into a frying-pan, and, when it has done hiffing, put in the beef. Make it of a fine brown, then put in fome broth made of the bones, with a bay-leaf, a pint of red wine, two anchovies, and a quarter of a pint of fmall beer. Cover it clofe, and let it ftew till it be tender. Then take out the beef, fkim off the fat, and ftrain the gravy. Put in two ox palates ftewed tender and cut into pieces, fome pickled gerkins, truffles, morels, and a little mufhroom powder. Let all thefe boil together. Thicken the fauce with a bit of butter rolled in flour, put in the beef to warm, pour the fauce over it, and fend it up to table.

Beef à la Daube.

BONE a rump of beef, or you may take part of the leg of mutton piece, or a piece of the buttock. Cut fome fat bacon as long as the beef is thick, and about a quarter of an inch fquare. Take eight cloves, four blades of mace, a little all-fpice, and half a nutmeg beat very fine. Chop fine a good handful of parfley, fome fweet herbs of all forts, and put to them fome pepper and falt. Roll the bacon in thefe, and then take a large larding-pin, or a fmall bladed knife, and force the bacon through the beef. Then put the meat into the ftewpan, and cover it with brown gravy. Chop three blades of garlick very fine, and put in fome frefh mufhrooms or champignons, two large onions, and a carrot. Stew it gently for fix hours, then take out the meat, ftrain off the gravy, and fkim off all the fat. Put your meat and gravy again into the pan, put a gill of white wine into it, and

and ſeaſon it with pepper and ſalt, if wanted. Stew them gently for half an hour, and add ſome artichoke bottoms, truffles and morels, ſome oyſters, and a ſpoonful of vinegar. Put the meat into a ſoup-diſh, and the ſauce over it. You may, if you chooſe it, put in turnips and carrots cut in round pieces, ſome ſmall onions, and thicken the ſauce. Then put in the meat, and ſtew it gently for half an hour with a gill of white wine.

Beef Olives.

CUT ſteaks from the rump, or inſide of the ſirloin, half an inch thick, about ſix inches long, and four or five broad; beat them a little, and rub over them the yolk of an egg. Strew on them crumbs of bread, chopped parſley, lemon-peel ſhred fine, pepper and ſalt, chopped ſuet or marrow, and grated nutmeg. Roll them up tight, ſkewer them, and fry or brown them in a Dutch oven. Stew them in beef broth or gravy till tender, thicken the gravy with a little flour, and then add a little catchup or lemon juice. If you wiſh to make it richer, you may add forcemeat balls, hard yolks of eggs, and pickled muſhrooms.

A Fricando of Beef.

TAKE one or more pieces of beef, of what ſize you pleaſe, and lard them with coarſe pieces of bacon ſeaſoned with ſpices. Boil it in broth with a little white wine, a bundle of parſley and ſweet herbs, a clove of garlick, ſhalots, four cloves, whole pepper, and ſome ſalt. When it is tender, ſkim the ſauce well, and ſtrain it, and reduce it to a glaze, with which you may glaze the larded ſide, and ſend it up to table on what ſtewed herbs you pleaſe.

Another

Another Method.

CUT ſome ſlices of beef five or ſix inches long, and half an inch thick. Lard them with bacon, dredge them well with flour, and ſet them before a briſk fire to brown. Put them into a toſſing-pan, with a quart of gravy, a few morels and truffles, half a lemon, and then ſtew them half an hour. Add one ſpoonful of catchup, the ſame of browning, and a little chyan. Thicken your ſauce, and pour it over your fricando. Lay the yolks of hard eggs and forcemeat balls round them.

A Porcupine of the flat Ribs of Beef.

HAVING boned the flat ribs, beat the meat half an hour with a paſte pin, and then rub it over with the yolks of eggs. Strew over it bread crumbs, parſley, leaks, ſweet marjoram, lemon-peel ſhred fine, nutmeg, pepper and ſalt. Roll it up very cloſe, and bind it hard. Lard it acroſs with bacon, then a row of cold boiled tongue, a third row of pickled cucumbers, and a fourth row of lemon-peel. Do it all over in rows till it be larded all round, when it will look like red, green, white, and yellow dice. Then put it in a deep pot, with a pint of water; lay over it a caul of veal to keep it from ſcorching, tie it down with ſtrong paper, and ſend it to the oven. When it comes out, ſkim off the fat, and ſtrain your gravy into a ſaucepan. Add to it two ſpoonfuls of red wine, the ſame of browning, one of muſhroom catchup, half a lemon, and thicken it with a lump of butter rolled in flour. Diſh up your meat, and pour the gravy into the diſh. You may garniſh with forcemeat balls and horſe-radiſh, and then ſend it to table.

A Rib of Beef glaſſé, with Spinach.

TAKE one of the prime ribs, trim it neatly, and lay it in a marinade for an hour or two. Take a ſtew-a ſtewpan that will juſt fit it, put a ſlice or two of bacon at the bottom, lay in your beef, and cover it with the ſame. Seaſon it with an onion or two, ſome bits of carrot, a little ſweet baſil, thyme, and parſley, a little pepper, ſalt, and a blade or two of mace. Let it ſtew gently till it be very tender, then take it out upon a plate, ſtrain your braze, and clean it well from the fat. Put it into a clean ſtewpan, and boil it with a ladle of gravy very faſt, and you will find it come to a ſort of gluey conſiſtence. Then put your beef in, keep it hot till dinner time, and then ſend it up to table with ſpinach. You may ſerve it up with ſavoys or red cabbage, ſtripped fine and ſtewed, after being blanched, only adding a piece of bacon, with a few cloves ſtuck in the ſtewing, but not to ſend to table. A fillet of the ſirloin is done nearly in the ſame manner, marinated and roaſted, with bacon over it, and the ſame ſort of ſauces.

Beef Steak Pie.

BEAT ſome rump ſteaks with a rolling-pin, and then ſeaſon them with pepper and ſalt to your palate. Make a good cruſt, lay in your ſteaks, and then pour in as much water as will half fill the diſh. Put on the cruſt, ſend it to the oven, and let be well baked.

Beef Steak Pudding.

MAKE a good cruſt with dripping, or mutton ſuet, if you have it, ſhred fine. Make a thick cruſt, take a piece of ſalt beef, which has been twenty-four hours in ſoft water. Seaſon it with a little pepper, put it into the cruſt, roll it up cloſe, tie it in a cloth, and boil it. If it be about four or five pounds, boil it five hours.

To

To collar Beef.

BONE a piece of a thin flank of beef, and cut off the ſkin. Salt it with two ounces of ſalt-petre, the like quantity of ſal-prunella, and alſo of bay-ſalt, half a pound of coarſe ſugar, and two pounds of common ſalt. Beat the hard ſalts very fine, and mix all together. Turn it every day, and rub it well with the brine for eight days; then take it out, waſh it, and wipe it dry. Take a quarter of an ounce of cloves, the like quantity of mace, twelve corns of allſpice, and a nutmeg beaten very fine, with a ſpoonful of beaten pepper, a large quantity of chopped parſley, and ſome ſweet herbs ſhred fine. Sprinkle this mixture on the beef, and roll it up very tight; then put a coarſe cloth round it, and tie it very tight with beggars tape. Boil it in a copper of water, and, if it is a large collar, it will take ſix hours boiling, but a ſmall one will be done in five. When it is done, take it out, and put it into a preſs; but, if you have not that convenience, put it between two boards, with a weight on the uppermoſt, and let it remain in that ſtate till it is thoroughly cold. Then take it out of the cloth, cut it into thin ſlices, lay them on a diſh, and ſend them up to table. Raw parſley may be uſed as a garniſh.

To pot Beef.

TAKE twelve pounds of beef, and rub into it a pound of brown ſugar, and an ounce of ſalt-petre. After it has lain twenty-four hours, waſh it clean, and dry it well with a cloth. Having ſeaſoned it to your taſte with pepper, ſalt, and mace, cut it into five or ſix pieces. Then put it into an earthen pot, with a pound of butter in lumps upon it, ſet it in a hot oven, and let it ſtand three hours. Then take it out, cut off the hard outſides, and beat it in a mortar. Add to it a little more pepper, ſalt, and mace. Then oil a pound of butter in the gravy and fat that came from your beef, and put it in as you find neceſſary; but beat the meat very fine. Then put it into your pots, preſs it cloſe down, pour clarified butter over it, and keep it in a dry place.

If you wiſh to pot your beef ſo as to imitate veniſon, proceed in the following manner. Take a buttock of beef, and cut the lean of it into pieces of about a pound weight each. To eight pounds of beef take four ounces of ſaltpetre, the ſame quantity of bay-ſalt, half a pound of white ſalt, and an ounce of ſal-prunella. Beat all the ſalts very fine, mix them well together, and rub them into the beef. Turn it twice a day for four days ſucceſſively. After that put it into a pan, and cover it with pump water, and a little of its own brine. Send it to the oven, and bake it till it is tender; then drain it from the gravy, and take out all the ſkin and ſinews. Pound the meat well in a mortar, lay it in a broad diſh, and mix on it an ounce of cloves and mace, three quarters of an ounce of pepper, and a nutmeg, all beat very fine. Mix the whole well with the meat, and add a little clarified freſh butter to moiſten it. Then preſs it down into pots very hard, ſet them at the mouth of an oven juſt to ſettle, and then cover them two inches thick with clarified butter. When quite cold, cover the pots over with white paper tied cloſe, and ſet them in a dry place. It will keep good a great while, if made agreeable to theſe directions.

CHAP.

CHAP. III.

The various Methods of dreſſing Veal.

Pieces in a Calf.

THE *Head*, and *Inwards* are the pluck, which contains the heart, liver, lights, nut and melt, and what they call the ſkirts, (which eat finely broiled) the throat ſweetbread, and the wind-pipe ſweetbread, which is the fineſt.

The *Fore Quarter* is the ſhoulder, neck, and breaſt.

The *Hind Quarter* is the leg, the knuckle, fillet, and loin.

A Fillet of Veal with Collops.

CUT what collops you want; then take a ſmall fillet of veal, and fill the udder full with force-meat. Roll it round, tie it with packthread acroſs, and roaſt it. Lay your collops in the diſh, and your udder in the middle. Garniſh your diſhes with lemon.

Breaſt of Veal in Hodge Podge.

CUT the briſket off a breaſt of veal into little pieces, and every bone aſunder. Then flour it, and put half a pound of good butter into a ſtew-pan. As ſoon as it is hot, put in the veal, and fry it all over of a fine brown. Have ready a tea-kettle of boiling water, and pour it into the ſtew-pan. Fill it up, ſtir it round, and throw in a pint of green peaſe, a fine whole lettuce clean waſhed, two or three blades of mace, a little whole pepper tied in a muſlin rag, a ſmall bundle of ſweet herbs, a ſmall onion ſtuck with a few cloves, and a little falt. Cover it clofe, and let it ftew an hour, or till it is boiled to your tafte, if you wifh to make foup of it; but, if you only intend to have a fauce to eat with the veal, you muft ftew it till it comes to the quantity you want, and then feafon it with falt to your palate. Take out the fpice, onion, and fweet herbs, and pour it into your difh, which will be a very fine one. If you have no peafe, pare three or four cucumbers, fcoop out the pulp, and cut it into little pieces. Take four or five heads of celery, wafh them clean, and cut the white part fmall; but, for want of lettuces, you may take the little hearts of favoys, or the little young fprouts that grow on the old cabbage ftalks, about the fize of the top of your thumb. If you wifh to make a very fine difh of it, fill the infide of your lettuce with force-meat, tie the top with a thread, and ftew it till there is but juft enough for fauce. Set the lettuce in the middle, the veal round it, and pour the fauce all over it. This difh will ferve a number of people, and it is the cheapeft and beft way of dreffing a breaft of veal.

To ftew a Breaft of Veal in its own Sauce.

PUT a breaft of veal into a ftewpan of its own length, with a little broth, a glafs of white wine, a bundle of fweet herbs, a few mufhrooms, a little coriander tied in a bag, fliced roots, onions, pepper, and falt. Stew it flowly till very tender. When it is done enough, ftrain and fkim the fauce, pour it over the meat, and fend it up to table.

To ftew a Knuckle of Veal.

LAY at the bottom of your faucepan four wooden fkewers, and wafh and clean the knuckle well. Lay it in the pot with two or three blades of mace, a little a little whole pepper, a little thyme, a ſmall onion, a cruſt of bread, and two quarts of water. Cover it down cloſe, make it boil, and then let it only ſimmer for two hours. As ſoon as it is enough, take it up, lay it in a diſh, and ſtrain the broth over it.

Veal Olives à la Mode.

TAKE two pounds of veal, ſome marrow, two anchovies, the yolks of two hard eggs, a few muſhrooms, ſome oyſters, a little thyme, marjoram, parſley, ſpinach, lemon-peel, ſalt, pepper, nutmeg, and mace, finely beaten. Take your veal caul, put a layer of bacon, and a layer of the ingredients: roll them in the veal caul, and either roaſt or bake it. An hour will do either. When it is enough, cut it into ſlices, lay it in your diſh, and pour good gravy over it. You may uſe lemon for a garniſh.

Neck of Veal and ſharp Sauce.

MAKE a marinade with butter and a little flour, ſliced onions, roots, a little coriander ſeed, one clove of garlick, three ſpice cloves, thyme, baſil, pepper, and ſalt. Warm it, and put it in a larded neck of veal. Let it lie in a marinade about two hours, then wrap it in buttered paper, roaſt it, and ſerve it up with a ſharp ſauce.

Neck of Veal à la Royal.

CUT off the ſcrag end of a neck of veal, and part of the chine bone, ſo that it may lie flat in the diſh. Chop very fine a little parſley and thyme, a few ſhalots and muſhrooms, and ſeaſon with pepper and ſalt. Cut middle-ſized lards of bacon, and roll them in the herbs and ſeaſoning. Lard the lean part of the neck, put it in a ſtewpan with ſome bacon, or the ſhank of a ham, the chine bone

bone and ſcrag cut in pieces, with a little beaten mace, a head of celery, onions, and three or four carrots. Pour in as much water as will cover it, ſhut the pan cloſe, and ſtew it ſlowly two or three hours, till it be tender. Then ſtrain half a pint of the liquor through a ſieve, ſet it over a ſtove, let it boil, and keep ſtirring it till it becomes thick, and is of a good brown. Then take the veal out of the ſtewpan, wipe it clean, and put the larded ſide down upon the glaze. Set it five or ſix minutes over a gentle fire to take the glaze, and then lay it in the diſh with the glazed ſide upwards. Put into the ſame ſtewpan as much flour as will lie on a ſixpence, ſtir it well, and add ſome of the braze powder, if any be left. Let it boil till it is of a proper thickneſs, and pour it into the diſh. Squeeze in a little lemon juice, and ſerve it up.

Neck of Veal à la Braiſe.

LARD the beſt end of a neck of veal with bacon rolled in parſley chopped, pepper, ſalt, and nutmeg. Put it into a ſtewpan, and cover it with water. Put in the ſcrag end, with a little lean bacon, or a bit of ham, an onion, two carrots, ſome ſhalots, a head or two of celery, and a little Madeira. Let theſe ſtew gently for two hours, or till tender. Strain the liquor, mix a little butter with ſome flour, and ſtir it in a ſtewpan till it be brown. Lay in the veal, the upper ſide to the bottom of the pan, and let it do a few minutes till it is coloured. Lay it in the diſh, ſtir in ſome more liquor, boil it up, and ſqueeze in orange or lemon juice.

Neck of Veal ſtewed with Celery.

PUT the beſt end of a neck of veal into a ſtewpan with ſome beef broth, or boiling water, ſome ſalt, whole pepper, and cloves, tied in a bit of muſlin;

muſlin; with an onion, and a piece of lemon peel. Stew this till tender; then take out the ſpice and peel, put in a little cream and flour mixed, with ſome celery ready boiled and cut in lengths. Boil it up, diſh it, and ſend it to table.

Neck of Veal ragooed.

CUT a neck of veal into ſteaks, and flatten them with a rolling pin, ſeaſon them with ſalt, pepper, cloves, and mace. Lard them with bacon, lemon peel, and thyme, and dip them in the yolks of eggs. Make a ſheet of ſtrong cap-paper up at the four corners, in the form of a dripping-pan. Pin up the corners, butter the paper and the grid-iron, and ſet it over a charcoal fire. Put in your meat, let it do leiſurely, keep it baſting and turning to keep in the gravy, and have ready a pint of ſtrong gravy againſt it is enough. Seaſon it high, put in muſhrooms and pickles, and force-meat balls dipped in the yolks of eggs, oyſters ſtewed and fried to lay round and at the top of your diſh, and then ſend it to table. If it be for a brown ragoo, put in red wine; if for a white one, put in white wine, with the yolks of eggs beat up with two or three ſpoonfuls of cream.

Breaſt of veal ragooed.

ROAST half the beſt end of a neck of veal, flour it, and ſtew it gently with three pints of good gravy, an onion, a few cloves, whole pepper, and a bit of lemon peel. Turn it while it is ſtewing, and when it is very tender, ſtrain the ſauce. If it be not thick enough, mix a little more flour ſmooth, and add catchup, chyan, truffles, morels, and pickled muſhrooms. Boil it up, and put in hard yolks of eggs.

The Griſtles of a Breaſt of Veal with a white Sauce.

THE half of a breaſt of veal will do for this ſmall diſh. Take off all the upper part of it, and cut the griſtles in ſmall bits, blanch them, and put into a ſtewpan a ladle of broth. Having ſtewed it very tender, put to it a bit of butter mixed with flour, a bunch of parſley and onions, a blade of mace, pepper, and ſalt. For your ſauce, you may procure either peas or aſparagus. Add the juice of a lemon, and ſend it up to table.

Fillet of Veal ſtewed.

STUFF it, and half bake it with a little water in the diſh. Then ſtew it with the liquor and ſome good gravy, and a little Madeira. When it is enough, thicken it with flour, and add catchup, chyan, a little ſalt, and juice of orange or lemon. Then boil it, diſh it up, and ſend it to table.

Leg of Veal marinated.

MARINATE a nice leg of white veal, and roaſt it with four ſlices of bacon over it, cover it with paper. Take four or five heads of endive, cut into bits about an inch in length; blanch it a little, and ſtew it in a little gravy mixed with a ladle full of cullis. Put in a minced ſhalot and ſome parſley, ſqueeze in the juice of a lemon, and ſend it to table with the ſauce under it. For the ſake of a change, you may make uſe of capers, olives, or any other ſort of pickles.

Leg of Veal in Diſguiſe.

TAKE a leg of veal, and lard it with ſlips of bacon, and a little lemon-peel cut very thin. Make a ſtuffing as for a fillet of veal, only mix with it half a pint of oyſters chopped ſmall. Put it into a veſſel, cover it with water, and let it ſtew very gently till quite tender. Then take it up, and ſkim off the fat. Squeeze into it ſome juiceof lemon, put to it ſome muſhroom catchup, the crumb of a roll grated fine, and half a pint of oyſters, with a pint of cream, and a piece of butter rolled in flour. Put the ſauce on the fire to thicken, and having put the veal in the diſh, pour the ſauce over it. You may make uſe of oyſters dipped in butter and fried, and thin ſlices of toaſted bacon, for a garniſh.

Leg of Veal daubed.

LARD and braze it with all ſorts of roots and ſpices, and reduce the ſauce to a jelly. You may ſerve it up either hot or cold.

To dreſs Veal à la Bourgeoiſe.

LARD pretty thick ſlices of veal with bacon, and ſeaſon them with pepper, ſalt, beaten mace, cloves, nutmeg, and chopped parſley. Then cover the bottom of the ſtewpan with ſlices of fat bacon, lay the veal upon them, cover it, and ſet it over a very ſlow fire for eight or ten minutes, juſt to be no more than hot. Then briſk up your fire, and brown your veal on both ſides. Pour in a quart of good broth or gravy, cover it cloſe, and let it ſtew gently till it be enough. Take out the ſlices of bacon, ſkim off all the fat clean, and beat up the yolks of three eggs with ſome of the gravy. Mix all together, and keep it ſtirring one way till it be ſmooth and thick. Then take it up, lay the meat in your diſh, pour the ſauce over it, garniſh with lemon, and ſend it up to table.

Loin of Veal in Epigram.

ROAST a fine loin of veal, take it up, and carefully take off the ſkin from the back part of it without breaking. Cut out all the lean meat; but be ſure to leave the ends whole, in order to hold the

the following mince-meats: Mince all the meat very fine with the kidney part, moiften it with a little veal gravy, and the gravy that comes from the loin. Put in a little pepper and falt, fome lemon-peel fhred fine, the yolks of three eggs, a fpoonful of catchup, and thicken it with a little butter rolled in flour. Give it a fhake or two over the fire, put it into the loin, and then pull the fkin over. If the fkin fhould not quite cover it, give it a brown with a hot iron, or put it into an oven for a quarter of an hour. Garnifh with barberries and lemon, and fend it up to table.

To roaft Sweetbreads with Afparagus.

A couple of good fweetbreads will be fufficient for this fmall difh. Blanch them, and lay them in a marinade. Spit them tight upon a lark-fpit, and tie them to each other, with a flice of bacon upon each, and covered with paper. When the fweetbreads are nearly done, take off the paper, and pour a drop of butter upon them, with a few crumbs of bread, and roaft them of a nice colour. Take two bunches of afparagus, and boil them, but not quite fo much as when boiled to eat with butter. Difh up your fweetbreads, with your grafs between them. Take a little cullis and gravy, with a bit of fhalot and minced parfley, and boil it a few minutes. Squeeze in the juice of a lemon or orange, and fend it up to table. Sweetbreads are very ufeful in many difhes, as in pies, ragoos, fricaffees, &c. And to ufe alone, either fried, roafted, broiled, or otherwife. They muft be foaked in warm water an hour or two, then fcalded about an hour or two in warm water, which is commonly called *fetting* or *blanching*. This will make them keep longer, and prepare them for any ufe you may have occafion to apply them to.

Sweetbreads à la Daube.

PUT three of the fineſt and largeſt ſweetbreads you can get into a ſaucepan of boiling water for five minutes. Then take them out, and, when they are cold, lard them in a row down the middle, with little pieces of bacon, and then a row on each ſide with lemon-peel, cut the ſize of wheat ſtraw. Then a row on each ſide of pickled cucumbers cut very fine. Put them in a toſſing-pan with good veal gravy, a little juice of lemon, and a ſpoonful of browning. Stew them gently a quarter of an hour, and a little before they are ready thicken them with flour and butter. Diſh them up, pour the gravy over them, and lay round them bunches of boiled celery, or oyſter patties. Garniſh with ſtewed ſpinach, green-coloured parſley, and ſtick a bunch of barberries in the middle of each ſweetbread. This is a pretty corner diſh for either dinner or ſupper.

Sweetbreads à la Dauphine.

LARD the fineſt ſweetbreads you can get, and open them in ſuch a manner that you can ſtuff in forcemeat. Three will make a fine diſh. Make your forcemeat with a large fowl or young cock; ſkin it, and pluck off all the fleſh. Take half a pound of fat and lean bacon; cut them very fine, and beat them in a mortar. Seaſon it with an anchovy, ſome nutmeg, a little lemon-peel, a very little thyme, and ſome parſley. Mix them up with the yolks of two eggs, and fill your ſweetbreads, and faſten them with fine wooden ſkewers. Put layers of bacon at the bottom of a ſtewpan, and ſeaſon them with pepper, ſalt, mace, cloves, ſweet herbs, and a large onion ſliced. Upon that lay thin ſlices of veal, and then lay on your ſweetbreads. Cover it cloſe, let it ſtand eight or ten minutes over a

ſlow

ﬂow fire, and then pour in a quart of boiling water or broth. Cover it cloſe, and let it ſtew two hours very ſoftly. Then take out the ſweetbreads, keep them hot, ſtrain the gravy, ſkim off all the fat, boil it till it waſtes to about half a pint, put in the ſweetbreads, and give them two or three minutes ſtew in the gravy. Then lay them in the diſh, pour the gravy over them, garniſh with lemon, and ſend them up to table.

Sweetbreads ragooed.

RUB them over with the yolk of an egg, ſtrew them over with bread crumbs, and parſley, thyme, and ſweet marjoram, all ſhred ſmall, and ſome pepper and ſalt. Make a roll of forcemeat like a ſweetbread, put it in a veal caul, and roaſt them in a Dutch oven. Take ſome brown gravy, and put to it a little lemon pickle, ſome muſhroom catchup, and the end of a lemon. Boil the gravy, and when the ſweetbreads are enough, lay them in the diſh, with the forcemeat in the middle. Take out the end of the lemon, pour the gravy into the diſh, and ſend it up to table.

Sweetbreads as Hedge-Hogs.

HAVING ſcalded your ſweetbreads, lard them with ham and truffles, cut in ſmall pieces. Fry them a ſhort time in butter, and let the pieces ſtick out a little to make the appearance of briſtles. Simmer them in the ſame butter, with broth and a little white wine, and a very little ſalt and pepper. When they are done, ſkim and ſtrain the ſauce, add a little cullis, and ſerve them up. You may uſe any other ſauce that you like better. Sweetbreads being of a very inſipid taſte of themſelves, make it a general rule to ſerve a ſharp reliſhing ſauce with them, ſuch as cullis ſauce, fricaſſee, or ſweet herbs.

Sweetbreads

Sweetbreads forced.

TAKE three ſweetbreads, put them into boiling water for five minutes. Beat the yolk of an egg a little, and rub it over them with a feather. Strew on bread crumbs, lemon peel, and parſley ſhred very fine, nutmeg, ſalt, and pepper, to your palate. Set them before the fire to brown, and add to them a little veal gravy. Put in a little muſhroom powder, caper liquor, or juice of lemon, and browning. Thicken it with flour and butter, boil it a little, and pour it into your diſh. Lay in your ſweetbreads, lay over them lemon-peels in rings, cut like ſtraws, garniſh with pickles, and ſend them up to table.

Shoulder of Veal à la Piedmontoiſe.

HAVING cut the ſkin off a ſhoulder of veal ſo that it may hang at one end, lard the meat with bacon and ham, and ſeaſon it with pepper, ſalt, mace, ſweet herbs, parſley, and lemon-peel. Cover it again with the ſkin, ſtew it with gravy, and when it is juſt tender enough take it up. Then take ſome ſorrel, ſome lettuce chopped ſmall, and ſtew them in butter, with parſley, onions, and muſhrooms. When the herbs are tender, put to them ſome of the liquor, ſome ſweetbread, and ſome bits of ham. Let all ſtew together a little while; then lift up the ſkin, lay the ſtewed herbs over and under, cover it again with the ſkin, wet it with melted butter, ſtrew it over with crumbs of bread, and ſend it to the oven to brown. Serve it up hot, with ſome good gravy in the diſh.

To mince Veal.

CUT your veal as fine as poſſible, but do not chop it. Grate a little nutmeg over it, ſhred a little lemon-peel very fine, dredge a little flour over it, and throw a very little ſalt on it. To a large

large plate of veal, take four or five ſpoonfuls of water, let it boil, and then put in the veal, with a piece of butter as big as an egg. Stir it well together, and it will be done enough as ſoon as it is all thoroughly hot. Have ready a very thin piece of bread toaſted brown, and cut into three-corner ſippets. Lay it round the plate, and pour in the veal. Juſt before you put it in, ſqueeze in half a lemon, or put in half a ſpoonful of vinegar.

A Pillaw of Veal.

HALF roaſt either a neck or breaſt of veal; then cut it into ſix pieces, and ſeaſon it with pepper, ſalt and nutmeg. Put to a pound of rice a quart of broth, ſome mace, and a little ſalt. Do it over a ſtove or very ſlow fire till it is thick; but butter the bottom of the pan or diſh you do it in. Beat up the yolks of ſix eggs, and ſtir them into it. Then take a little round deep diſh, butter it, lay ſome of the rice at the bottom, then lay the veal on a round heap, and cover it all over with rice. Waſh it over with the yolks of eggs, and bake it an hour and half. Then open the top, and pour in a pint of rich good gravy. Send it to table, garniſhed with a Seville orange quartered.

Veal Blanquets.

HAVING roaſted a piece of a fillet of veal, cut off the ſkin and nervous parts, and cut it into little thin bits. Put ſome butter into a ſtewpan over the fire, with ſome chopped onions, and fry them a little. Then add a duſt of flour, ſtir it together, and put in ſome good broth or gravy, and a bundle of ſweet herbs. Seaſon it with ſpice, make it of a good taſte, and then put in your veal, the yolks of two eggs, beat up with cream and grated nutmeg, ſome chopped parſley, a ſhalot, ſome lemon peel grated, and a little juice of lemon.

Keep

Keep it ſtirring one way, and when it is enough, diſh it up, and ſend it to table.

Bombarded Veal.

CUT five lean pieces off a fillet of veal, as thick as your hand. Round them up a little, and lard them very thick on the round ſide with little narrow thin pieces of bacon, and lard five ſheeps tongues, being firſt boiled and blanched; lard then here and there with very little bits of lemon peel, and make a well-ſeaſoned forcemeat of veal, bacon, ham, beef ſuet, and an anchovy beaten well. Make another tender forcemeat of veal, beef ſuet, muſhrooms, ſpinach, parſley, thyme, ſweet marjoram, winter ſavory, and green onions. Seaſon with pepper, ſalt, and mace. Beat it well, make a round ball of the other forcemeat, and ſtuff it in the middle of this; then roll it up in a veal caul, and bake it. What is left, tie up like a Bologna ſauſage, and boil it; but firſt rub the caul with the yolk of an egg. Put the larded veal into a ſtewpan with ſome good gravy, and ſtew it gently till it be enough. Skim off the fat, put in ſome truffles and morels, and ſome muſhrooms. Your forcemeat being baked enough, lay it in the middle, the veal round it, and the tongues fried, and laid between. Cut the boiled into ſlices, fry them, and ſtrew them all over. Put on them the ſauce, garniſh with lemon, and ſend them up to table. You may add ſweetbreads, cockſcombs, and artichoke bottoms, if you think proper.

A Harrico of Veal.

HALF roaſt a neck or breaſt of veal; if the neck, cut the bones ſhort. Put it into a ſtewpan juſt covered with brown gravy, and when it is nearly done, have ready a pint of boiled peas, ſix cucumbers pared, and two cabbage lettuces quartered, ſtewed in brown gravy, with a few forcemeat balls ready fried. Put them to the veal, and let them juſt

juſt ſimmer. When the veal is put into the diſh, pour the ſauce and the peas over it, and lay the lettuce and balls round it.

Veal Rolls.

CUT ten or twelve little thin ſlices of veal; put on them ſome forcemeat, according to your fancy, roll them up, and tie them juſt acroſs the middle with coarſe thread. Put them on a bird-ſpit, rub them over with the yolks of eggs, flour them, and baſte them with butter. Half an hour will do them. Lay them in a diſh, and have ready ſome good gravy, with a few truffles and morels. Garniſh with lemon, and ſend them up to table.

To fry cold Veal.

CUT your veal into pieces of about the thickneſs of half a crown, and of what length you think proper. Dip them in the yolk of an egg, and then in crumbs of bread, with a few ſweet herbs and ſhred lemon-peel; grate a little nutmeg over them, and fry them in freſh butter. The butter muſt be made juſt hot enough to fry them. In the mean time, make a little gravy of the bone of the veal; and when the meat is fried, take it out with a fork, and lay it in a diſh before the fire. Then ſhake a little flour into the pan, and ſtir it round. Then put in a little gravy, ſqueeze in ſome lemon, and pour it over the veal. Garniſh with lemon, and ſerve it up.

A Florentine of Veal.

MINCE two kidnies of veal, fat and all, very fine. Chop a few herbs and put to it, and add a few currants. Seaſon it with cloves, mace, nutmeg, and a little ſalt; four or five yolks of eggs chopped fine, and ſome crumbs of bread; a pippin or two chopped, ſome candied lemon-peel cut ſmall,

ſmall, a little ſack, and orange-flower water. Lay a ſheet of puff paſte at the bottom of your diſh, and put in the ingredients, and cover it with another ſheet of puff paſte. Bake it in a ſlack oven; and ſerve it up hot, with ſugar ſcraped on the top of it.

To boil a Scrag of Veal.

PUT a ſcrag of veal into a ſaucepan, and to each pound of veal put a quart of water. Skim it very clean, then put in a large piece of upper cruſt of bread, a blade of mace to each pound of meat, and a little parſley tied with thread. Cover it cloſe, and let it boil very ſoftly two hours, when both broth and meat will be fit to eat. This is a very good diſh for a ſick perſon.

To mince Veal for a ſick or weak Perſon.

MINCE ſome veal very fine, and take off the ſkin. Juſt boil as much water as will moiſten it, with a very little ſalt; grate a very little nutmeg, throw a little flour over it, and when the water boils put in the meat. Keep ſhaking it about a minute over the fire. Have ready two or three very thin ſippets, toaſted nicely brown; then put them in the plate, and pour the mince-meat over them. A chicken may be done in the ſame manner.

To make Marble Veal.

BOIL a neat's tongue till it be tender; then peel it, cut it in ſlices, and beat it in a mortar with a pound of butter, and a little beaten mace and pepper, till it be like a paſte. Have ready ſome veal ſtewed and beaten in the ſame manner. Put ſome veal in a potting-pot, then ſome tongue in lumps over the veal, then ſome veal over that, tongue over that, and then veal again. Preſs it down hard, pour ſome clarified butter over it, and keep

keep it in a cold dry place. When you ufe it, cut it in flices, garnifh with parfley, and fend it up to table.

Calf's Head Surprife.

WITH a fharp knife raife off the fkin of a calf's head, with as much meat as you can poffibly get from the bones, fo that it may appear like a whole head when ftuffed. Make the following forcemeat. Take half a pound of veal, a pound of beef fuet, the crumb of a twopenny loaf, and half a pound of fat bacon. Beat them well in a mortar, with fome fweet herbs and parfley fhred fine, fome cloves, mace, and nutmeg beat fine; enough falt and chyan pepper to feafon it, the yolks of four eggs beat up, and mixed all together. Stuff the head with this forcemeat, and fkewer it tight at each end. Put it into a deep pot or pan, and put to it two quarts of water, half a pint of white wine, a blade or two of mace, a bundle of fweet herbs, an anchovy, two fpoonfuls of walnut and mufhroom catchup, the fame quantity of lemon pickle, and a little falt and pepper. Lay a coarfe pafte over it to keep in the fteam, and put it for two hours and an half into a fharp oven. When you take it out, lay the head in a foup difh, fkim off the fat from the gravy, and ftrain it through a fieve into a ftewpan. Thicken it in butter rolled in flour, and when it has boiled a few minutes, put in the yolks of four eggs well beaten, and mixed with half a pint of cream. Have ready boiled fome forcemeat balls, half an ounce of truffles and morels; but do not put them into the gravy. Pour the gravy over the head, garnifh with forcemeat balls, truffles, morels, and mufhrooms, and fend it up to table.

The

The best Way to dress a Calf's Head.

SCALD off all the hair of a calf's head, and clean it well. Cut it into two, take out the brains, and boil the head very white and tender. Take one part quite off the bone, and cut it into nice pieces with the tongue; dredge it with a little flour, and let it stew on a slow fire for half an hour, in rich white gravy made of veal, mutton, and a piece of bacon, seasoned with pepper, salt, onion, and a very little mace. It must be strained off before the hash is put in, and then thicken it with a little butter rolled in flour. The other part of the head must be taken off in one whole piece. Stuff it with nice forcemeat, roll it like a collar, and then stew it tender in gravy. Put it into the middle of a dish, and the hash all round it. Garnish it with forcemeat balls, and the brains made into little cakes dipped in butter and fried. You may add wine, morels, truffles, or what else you please, if you choose to add to its richness.

To hash a Calf's Head.

HAVING cleaned the head exceedingly well, boil it a quarter of an hour, and when it is cold cut the meat into thin broad slices. Put it into a tossing-pan with two quarts of gravy. When it has stewed three quarters of an hour, add to it an anchovy, a little beaten mace, chyan to your taste, two spoonfuls of lemon pickle, two meat spoonfuls of walnut catchup, half an ounce of truffles and morels, a slice or two of lemon, a bundle of sweet herbs, and a glass of white wine. Mix a quarter of a pound of butter with flour, and put it in a few minutes before the head is enough. Put the brains into hot water, and beat them fine in a bason. Add to them two eggs, one spoonful of flour, a bit of lemon peel shred fine, a little parsley chopped small, fmall, thyme, and fage. Beat them well together, and ftrew in a little pepper and falt. Then drop them in little cakes into a pan full of boiling hog's lard, and fry them of a light brown. Lay thefe on a fieve to drain, take your hafh out of the pan with a fifh flice, lay it on your difh, and ftrain the gravy over it. Lay upon it a few mufhrooms, force-meat balls, the yolks of four eggs boiled hard, and the brain cakes. Garnifh with lemon and pickles, and fend it up to table.

To grill a Calf's Head.

HAVING wafhed a calf's head clean, and boiled it almoft enough, take it up and hafh one half. Rub the other half over with the yolk of an egg, and a little pepper and falt; ftrew over it bread crumbs, parfley chopped fmall, and a little grated lemon peel. Set it before the fire, and keep bafting it all the time to make the froth rife. When it is of a fine light brown, difh up your hafh, and lay the grilled fide upon it. Blanch your tongue, flit it down the middle, and lay it on a foup plate. Skin the brains, boil them with a little fage and parfley, chop them fine, and mix them with fome melted butter, and a fpoonful of cream. Make them hot, and pour them over the tongue. Serve them up as fauce for the head.

To roaft a Calf's Head.

FIRST wafh the head perfectly clean, then take out the bones, and dry the head well with a cloth. Make a feafoning of pepper, falt, beaten mace, nutmeg, cloves, fome fat bacon cut very fmall, and fome grated bread. Strew this over it, roll it up, fkewer it with a fmall fkewer, and tie it with tape. Roaft it, and bafte it with butter. Make a rich veal gravy thickened with butter and rolled in flour. Some like mufhrooms and the fat part of of oyſters; but you may either uſe or omit theſe, as you pleaſe.

Calf's Head boiled.

HAVING waſhed the head very clean, parboil one half of it. Beat up the yolk of an egg, and rub it over the head with a feather. Then ſtrew over it a ſeaſoning of pepper, ſalt, thyme, parſley chopped ſmall, ſhred lemon peel, grated bread, and a little nutmeg. Stick bits of butter over it, and ſend it to the oven. Boil the other half white in a cloth, and put them both into a diſh. Boil the brains in a piece of cloth, with a little parſley and a leaf or two of ſage. When they are boiled, chop them ſmall, and warm them up in a ſaucepan, with a piece of butter, and a little pepper and ſalt. Lay the tongue, boiled and peeled, in the middle of a ſmall diſh, and the brains round it. Have in another diſh bacon or pickled pork, and in another greens and carrots.

Veal Palates.

BOIL two palates about half an hour; then take off the ſkins, and cut them into pieces, as you do ox palates. Put them into a ſtewpan with a glaſs of white wine, a little minced green onion, parſley, pepper, and ſalt. Toſs it often till the wine is gone, pour in a ladle of your cullis mixed with gravy, and ſtew them ſoftly till very tender. Put in a ſmall glaſs more of wine, add the juice of a lemon or orange, and ſend it up.

Scotch Collops white.

CUT your collops off the thick part of a leg of veal, of the ſize and thickneſs of a crown-piece. Put a lump of butter into a toſſing-pan, and ſet it over a ſlow fire, for a briſk fire will diſcolour your collops.

collops. Before the pan is hot, lay in the collops, and keep turning them over till you ſee the butter is turned to a thick white gravy. Put your collops and gravy into a pot, and ſet them upon the hearth to keep warm. Put cold butter again into your pan every time you fill it, and fry them as above, and ſo continue till you have finiſhed. When you have fried them, pour your gravy from them into your pan, with a tea-ſpoonful of lemon pickle, muſhroom catchup, caper liquor, beaten mace, chyan pepper, and ſalt. Thicken with flour and butter, and when it has well boiled, put in the yolks of two eggs well beaten, and mixed with a tea-ſpoonful of rich cream. Keep ſhaking your pan over the fire till your gravy looks of a fine thickneſs, and then put in your collops, and ſhake them. When they are quite hot, put them on your diſh with forcemeat balls, and ſtrew over them pickled muſhrooms. Garniſh with barberries and pickled kidney-beans, and ſend them up to table.

Scotch Collops brown.

FOR brown collops, cut them in the ſame manner as you did for white collops; but brown your butter before you lay in your collops. Fry them over a briſk fire, ſhake and turn them, and keep them on a fine froth. When they are of a light brown, put them into a pot, and fry them as the white ones. When you have fried them all brown, pour all the gravy from them into a clean toſſing-pan, with half a pint of gravy made of the bones and bits you cut the collops off, two ſpoonfuls of lemon pickle, a large one of catchup, the ſame of browning, half an ounce of morels, half a lemon, a little anchovy, chyan, and ſalt to your taſte. Thicken it with flour and butter, and let it boil five or ſix minutes. Then put in your collops,

lops, and ſhake them over the fire; but take care that they do not boil, as that will make them hard. When they have ſimmered a little, take them out with an egg ſpoon, lay them on your diſh, ſtrain your gravy, and pour it hot on them. Lay over them forcemeat balls, and little ſlices of bacon curled round a ſkewer and boiled. Serve them up with a few muſhrooms over them, and garniſhed with lemon and barberries.

Scotch Collops the French Way.

CUT collops pretty thick, and five or ſix inches long, from a leg of veal. Rub them over with the yolk of an egg, put pepper and ſalt, and grate a little nutmeg on them, and a little ſhred parſley. Lay them on an earthen diſh, and ſet them before the fire. Baſte them with butter, and let them be of a fine brown. Then turn them on the other ſide, rub them as above, and brown them the ſame way. When they are thoroughly enough, make a good brown gravy with truffles and morels, diſh up your collops, lay truffles and morels, and the yolks of hard eggs boiled, over them. Garniſh with lemon and criſp parſley, and ſend them up to table.

Veal Cutlets.

YOUR cutlets muſt be about the thickneſs of a half crown; but the length of them is of no conſequence. Dip them in the yolk of an egg, and ſtrew over them crumbs of bread, a few ſweet herbs, ſome lemon peel, and a little grated nutmeg. Fry them in freſh butter. In the mean time make a little gravy, and when the meat is done, take it out, and lay it in a diſh before the fire. Then ſhake a little flour into the pan, and ſtir it round. Put in a little gravy, ſqueeze in a little

little lemon, and pour it over the veal. Garniſh with lemon, and ſend it up to table.

A Calf's Heart roaſted.

FILL the heart with the following forcemeat. Take the crumb of half a penny loaf, a quarter of a pound of beef ſuet chopped ſmall, a little parſley, ſweet marjoram, and lemon peel, mixed up with a little pepper, ſalt, nutmeg, and the yolk of an egg. Having filled the heart with this forcemeat, lay a veal caul on the ſtuffing, or a ſheet of writing paper, to keep it in its place. Put it into a Dutch oven, and keep turning it till it be thoroughly roaſted. When you diſh it up, lay ſlices of lemon round it, and pour good melted butter over it.

To make a fine ſweet Veal Pie.

SEASON your veal with ſalt, pepper, cloves, mace, and nutmeg, all beaten fine. Cut your meat into little pieces, and having made a good puff-paſte cruſt, lay it into your diſh. Then lay in your meat, ſtrew on it ſome currants and ſtoned raiſins clean waſhed, and ſome ſugar. Then lay on it ſome forcemeat balls made ſweet, and in the ſummer ſome artichoke bottoms boiled, and ſcalded grapes in the winter. Boil Spaniſh potatoes cut in pieces, candied citron, candied orange, and lemon peel, and three or four blades of mace. Put butter on the top, cloſe up your pie, and bake it. Have ready againſt it comes out of the oven, a caudle thus made. Take a pint of white wine, and mix in it the yolks of three eggs; ſtir it well together over the fire one way all the time, till it be thick. Then take it off, ſtir in ſugar enough to ſweeten it, and ſqueeze in the juice of a lemon. Pour it hot into your pie, and cloſe it up again.

A Calf's

A Calf's Head Pie.

LET the head be firſt very well cleaned, and then boil it till it be tender. Take off the meat as whole as you can, take out the eyes, and ſlice the tongue. Make a good puff-paſte cruſt, cover your diſh with it, lay on your meat, throw over it the tongue, and lay the eyes cut in two at each corner, ſeaſon it with a very little pepper and ſalt, pour in half a pint of the liquor it was boiled in, lay on a thin top-cruſt, and bake it an hour in a quick oven. In the mean time, boil the bones of the head in two quarts of liquor, with two or three blades of mace, half a quarter of an ounce of whole pepper, a large onion, and a bundle of ſweet herbs. Let it boil till reduced to about a pint; then ſtrain it off, and add two ſpoonfuls of catchup, three of red wine, a piece of butter as big as a walnut rolled in flour, and half an ounce of truffles and morels. Seaſon it with ſalt to your palate. Boil it, and have half the brains boiled with ſome ſage; beat them and twelve leaves of ſage chopped fine. Then ſtir all together, and give it a boil. Take the other part of the brains, and beat them with ſome of the ſage chopped fine, a little lemon peel minced fine, and half a ſmall nutmeg grated. Beat it up with an egg, and fry it in little cakes of a fine light brown. Boil ſix eggs hard, of which take only the yolks; and when your pie comes out of the oven, take off the lid, lay the eggs and cakes over it, and pour the ſauce all over. Send it hot to table without the lid.

A Veal Suet Pudding.

CUT the crumb of a three-penny loaf into ſlices. Boil and pour two quarts of milk on the bread, and then put to it one pound of melted veal ſuet. Add to theſe one pound of currants, half

half a nutmeg, ſix eggs well mixed together, and ſugar to the taſte. This pudding may be either boiled or baked; but take care to butter well the inſide of the diſh.

Veal Hams.

CUT a leg of veal like a ham; then take a pint of bay-ſalt, two ounces of ſalt-petre, and a pound of common ſalt. Mix them well together with an ounce of juniper berries beaten. Rub the ham well, and lay it on a hollow tray, with the ſkin ſide downwards. Baſte it every day for a fortnight with the pickle, and then hang it in wood ſmoke for a fortnight. You may boil it, or parboil it and roaſt it. In this pickle you may put a piece of pork, or two or three tongues.

To collar a Breaſt of Veal.

BONE the fineſt breaſt of veal you can procure, and rub it over with the yolks of two eggs; ſtrew over it ſome crumbs of bread, a little grated lemon peel, a little pepper and ſalt, and a handful of chopped parſley. Roll it up hard, and bind it tight with packthread. Wrap it in a cloth, boil it an hour and a half, and then take it up, and ſet it to cool. As ſoon as it has cooled a little, take off the cloth, and cut off the packthread carefully, leſt you open the veal. Cut it into five ſlices, lay them on a diſh with the ſweet bread boiled, and cut in thin ſlices, and laid round them with ten or twelve forcemeat balls. Pour your white ſauce over it, and garniſh with barberries or green pickles. Make your white ſauce in the following manner. Take a pint of good veal gravy, put to it a ſpoonful of lemon pickle, half an anchovy, a tea-ſpoonful of muſhroom powder, or a few pickled muſhrooms. Give it a gentle boil, and then put in half a pint of cream, and the yolks of two eggs finely beaten. Shake it over the fire after the eggs and cream are in, but do not let it boil, as that will curdle it.

To collar a Calf's Head to eat like Brawn.

SCALD the head till the hair comes clean off, then cut it into two, and take out the brains and the eyes. Waſh it very clean, put it into a pan of clean water, and then boil it till the bones will come out. Slice the tongue and ears, and lay them all even. Throw a handful of ſalt over them, and roll it up quite cloſe in a collar. Boil it near two hours, and when the head is cold, put it into brawn pickles.

To pot Veal.

TAKE part of a fillet or knuckle of veal that has been ſtewed, or you may bake it on purpoſe for potting. Beat it to a paſte with butter, pepper, ſalt, and mace pounded. Preſs it down in pots, and pour over it clarified butter.

CHAP. IV.

The various Methods of Dreſſing Mutton.

Pieces in a Sheep.

THE *Head*, and *Pluck*, which includes the liver, lights, heart, ſweetbread, and melt.

The *Fore Quarter* is the neck, breaſt, and ſhoulder.

The *Hind Quarter* includes the leg and loin. The two loins together are called a ſaddle or chine of mutton.

To

To roaſt a Haunch of Mutton Veniſon-Faſhion.

CUT a hind quarter of mutton veniſon-faſhion, and let it ſteep in the ſheep's blood five or ſix hours. Then let it hang, in cold dry weather, for three weeks, or as long as it will keep ſweet. Rub it with a cloth, then rub it over with freſh butter, and ſtrew ſome ſalt and a little flour over it. Butter a ſheet of paper, and lay over it, and another over that, or ſome paſte, and tie it round. If it be a large joint, it will take two hours and a half roaſting. Before you take it up, take off the paper, or paſte, and baſte it well with butter and flour it. Let the jack go round quick, that it may have a good froth. Make uſe of gravy and currant jelly for your ſauce.

Another Method.

TAKE the largeſt and fatteſt leg of mutton you can get, cut out like a haunch of veniſon, as ſoon as it is killed, and whilſt it is warm, as it will eat the tenderer. Lay it in a pan with the backſide downwards, and pour a bottle of red wine over it, and there let it lie twenty-four hours. Then ſpit it and roaſt it at a good quick fire, and keep baſting it all the time with the ſame liquor and butter. It will require an hour and an half roaſting; and, when it is done, ſend it up with a little good gravy in one boat, and ſome ſweet ſauce in another. A good fat neck of mutton, dreſſed in this manner, eats exceedingly well.

Gigot of Mutton with Spaniſh Onions.

TAKE a leg of mutton that is cut with part of the loin, that being called by the French a Gigot. Let it hang two or three days, and then put it into a pot juſt big enough to hold it; pour in a little broth, and then cover it with water. Put in about a dozen of Spaniſh onions, with the rinds on, three or four carrots, a turnip or two, ſome parſley, and any other herbs you like. Cover them down cloſe, and ſtew them for three or four hours; but take your onions out after an hour's ſtewing, and take the firſt and ſecond rinds off. Put them into a ſtewpan, with a ladle or two of your cullis, a muſhroom or two, or truffles minced, and a little parſley. Take out your mutton, and drain it clean from the fat and liquor. Then ſeaſon your ſauce and make it hot; ſqueeze in a lemon, pour the ſauce over it, and ſend it up to table with the onions round it.

Leg of Mutton Modina-Faſhion.

BONE a leg of mutton quite to the end, which you muſt leave very ſhort. Boil it in three parts water and one broth, and then take it out. Cut the upper part croſs-ways, into which ſtuff butter and bread crumbs, ſeaſoned with pepper, ſalt, and ſweet herbs chopped. Then put it into a ſtewpan with a little of the broth, and a little white wine. Add the juice of a Seville orange to the ſauce, and when it is done, diſh it, and ſerve it up.

Split Leg of Mutton and Onion Sauce.

SPLIT the leg from the ſhank to the end, and ſtick a ſkewer in to keep the nitch open. Baſte it with red wine till it be half roaſted; then take the wine out of the dripping-pan, and put to it an anchovy. Set it over the fire till the anchovy is diſſolved, rub the yolk of a hard egg in a little cold butter, mix it with the wine, and put it into your ſauce-boat. Put good onion ſauce over the leg when it is roaſted, and ſend it up to table.

Leg of Mutton à la Daube.

LARD a leg of mutton with bacon, half roaſt it, and then put it into a pot that will juſt hold it, with

with a quart of mutton gravy, half a pint of vinegar, ſome whole ſpice, ſweet-marjoram, winter ſavory, and ſome green onions. When it is tender, take it up, and make the ſauce with ſome of the liquor, muſhrooms, ſliced lemon, two anchovies, a ſpoonful of colouring, and a piece of butter. Pour ſome into a boat, and the reſt over the mutton.

Leg of Mutton à la Mode.

LARD a leg of mutton quite through with large pieces of bacon rolled in chopped ſweet herbs and fine ſpices. Braze it on a pan of the ſame ſize with ſlices of lard, onions, and roots, and ſtop the ſteam very cloſe. When it is done, add a glaſs of white wine, and ſtrain the ſauce.

Leg of Mutton à la haut Gout.

HANG up a leg of mutton for a fortnight, and then ſtuff every part of it with ſome cloves of garlick; rub it with pepper and ſalt, and then roaſt it. When it is properly done, put ſome good gravy and red wine into the diſh, and ſend it up to table.

Leg of Mutton forced.

RAISE the ſkin of a leg of mutton, take out the lean part of it, and chop it exceedingly fine, with an anchovy. Shred a bundle of ſweet herbs, grate a penny loaf, half a lemon, ſome nutmeg, pepper, and ſalt, to your taſte. Make them into a forcemeat, with three eggs, and a large glaſs of red wine. Fill the ſkin with the forcemeat, but leave the bone and ſhank in their places, and it will appear like a whole leg. Lay it on an earthen diſh, with a pint of red wine under it, and ſend it to the oven. It will take two hours and an half. When it comes out, take off the fat, ſtrain the gravy over the mutton, lay round it hard yolks of eggs, and pickled mushrooms. Send it up to table, garnished with pickles.

Leg of Mutton ragooed.

TAKE all the skin and fat off a leg of mutton, cut it very thin the right way of the grain, then butter your stewpan, and shake some flour into it. Slice half a lemon and half an onion, cut them very small, a small bundle of sweet herbs, and a little blade of mace. Put all together with your meat into the pan, stir it a minute or two, and then put in six spoonfuls of gravy. Mince an anchovy small, and mix it with some butter and flour. Stir it all together for six minutes, dish it up, and send it to table.

Leg of Mutton à la Royale.

TAKE off the fat, skin, and shank-bone of a leg of mutton. Lard the meat with bacon, and season it with pepper, salt, and a round piece, of about three or four pounds, of beef, or leg of veal, also larded. Have ready boiling some hog's lard, flour your meat, and give it a colour in the lard. Then take out the meat, and put it into a pot, with a bundle of sweet herbs, some parsley, an onion stuck with cloves, two or three blades of mace, some whole pepper, and three quarts of gravy. Cover it close, and let it boil softly for two hours. In the mean time, get ready a sweetbread split, cut into quarters and broiled, a few truffles and morels stewed in a quarter of a pint of strong gravy, a glass of red wine, a few mushrooms, two spoonfuls of catchup, and some asparagus tops. Boil all these together, and then lay the mutton in the middle of the dish. Cut the beef or veal into slices, make a rim round your mutton with the slices, and pour the ragoo over it. When you have taken the meat out of the pot, skim all the fat off the gravy,

gravy, ftrain it, and add as much to the other as will fill the difh. Garnifh with lemon, and fend it up to table.

Leg of Mutton roafted with Oyfters.

MAKE a forcemeat of beef fuet chopped fmall, the yolks of eggs boiled hard, with three anchovies, a fmall bit of onion, thyme, favory, and about a dozen or fourteen oyfters, all cut fine; fome pepper, falt, grated nutmeg, and crumbs of bread, mixed up with raw eggs. Stuff the mutton in the thickeft part under the flap, and at the knuckle. You may make your fauce of fome oyfter liquor, an anchovy, a little red wine, and fome more oyfters ftewed, and laid under the mutton.

Shoulder of Mutton boiled, and Onion Sauce.

PUT in your fhoulder when the water is cold, and when it has boiled enough, cover it with onion fauce, made in the fame manner as for boiled ducks. You may drefs a fhoulder of veal the fame way; but neither of thefe difhes are often ordered.

Shoulder of Mutton in Epigram.

HAVING roafted your fhoulder almoft enough, take off the fkin, about the thicknefs of a crown-piece, very carefully, and with it the fhank-bone at the end. Seafon that fkin and fhank-bone with pepper and falt, a little lemon-peel cut fmall, and a few fweet herbs and crumbs of bread. Lay this on the gridiron, and let it be of a fine brown. In the mean time take the reft of the meat, and cut it like a hafh about the bignefs of a fhilling. Save the gravy, and put it to it, with a few fpoonfuls of ftrong gravy, half an onion cut fine, a little nutmeg, a little pepper and falt, a little bundle of fweet herbs, fome gerkins cut very fmall, a few mufhrooms, muſhrooms, two or three truffles cut ſmall, two ſpoonfuls of either red or white wine, and throw a little flour over the meat. Let all theſe ſtew together very ſoftly for five or ſix minutes; but take care not to let it boil. Take out the ſweet herbs, and put the haſh into the diſh; lay the broiled upon it, and ſerve it up.

Shoulder of Mutton ſurprized.

HALF boil a ſhoulder of mutton, put it into a toſſing-pan, with two quarts of veal gravy, four ounces of rice, a little beaten mace, and a tea-ſpoonful of muſhroom powder. Stew it till the rice is enough, which it will be in about an hour, and then take up your mutton, and keep it hot. Put half a pint of cream to the rice, and a piece of butter rolled in flour. Shake it well, and boil it a few minutes. Lay your mutton in the diſh, and pour your gravy over it. Garniſh with either pickles or barberries, and ſend it up to table.

Breaſt of Mutton collared.

TAKE a breaſt of mutton, ſkin and bone it, and roll it up in a collar like a breaſt of veal. Put a quart of milk and a quarter of a pound of butter in the dripping-pan, and baſte the meat with it well while it is roaſting. Put ſome good gravy into the diſh and into a boat, with ſome currant jelly in another boat, and ſerve it up.

Breaſt of Mutton dreſſed another good Way.

COLLAR a breaſt of mutton as above directed. Roaſt it, and baſte it with half a pint of red wine. When that is all ſoaked in, baſte it well with butter. Have ready a little good gravy, ſet the mutton upright in the diſh, pour in the gravy, prepare ſweet ſauce as for veniſon, and ſend it up to table without any garniſh.

Breaſt

Breaſt of Mutton grilled.

TAKE a breaſt of mutton, half boil it, ſcore it, pepper and ſalt it well, and rub it with the yolk of an egg; ſtrew on chopped parſley and crumbs of bread, and broil it or roaſt it in a Dutch oven. Serve it up with caper ſauce.

To dreſs a Neck of Mutton.

TAKE a neck of mutton, and lard it with lemon peel cut in thin ſmall lengths. Boil it in ſalt and water, with a bunch of ſweet herbs, and an onion ſtuck with cloves. While it is boiling, make a ſauce of a pint of oyſters ſtewed in their own liquor, as much veal gravy, two anchovies diſſolved and ſtrained into it, and the yolks of two eggs beat up in a little of the gravy. Mix theſe together till they come to a proper thickneſs, then pour it over the meat, and ſend it up to table.

Neck of Mutton larded with Ham and Anchovies.

TAKE the fillet of a neck of mutton, and lard it quite through with ham and anchovies, firſt rolled in chopped parſley, ſhalots, ſweet herbs, pepper, and ſalt. Then put it to braze or ſtew in a little broth, with a glaſs of white wine. When done, ſkim and ſtrain the ſauce, and add a little cullis to give it a proper conſiſtence. Squeeze in the juice of half a lemon, pour it upon the meat, and ſend it up to table.

Neck of Mutton, called the Haſty Diſh.

PROVIDE yourſelf with a large pewter or ſilver diſh, made like a deep ſoup-diſh, with an edge about an inch deep on the inſide, with a lid made to fit it, and a handle at top, fixed ſo faſt, that you may lift it up full by that handle without any danger of its falling. This diſh is called a Necromancer. Take a neck of mutton of about ſix pounds, take

take off the ſkin, cut it into chops of a moderate thickneſs, ſlice a French roll thin, peel and ſlice a large onion, pare and ſlice three or four turnips, lay a row of mutton in the diſh, on that a row of roll, than a row of turnips, and then onions; put a little ſalt, then the meat, and ſo on. Put to it a ſmall bundle of ſweet herbs, and two or three blades of mace. Fill the diſh with boiling water, and having covered it cloſe, hang it on the back of two chairs by the rim. Take three ſheets of brown paper, tear each ſheet into five pieces, and draw them through your hand. Light one piece, and hold it under the bottom of the diſh, moving the paper about as faſt as it burns; light another, till all are burnt, and your meat will then be enough. Fifteen minutes will be ſufficient to do it. Send it to table hot in the diſh.

Neck of Mutton dreſſed like Veniſon.

CUT a large neck before the ſhoulder is taken off, rather broader than uſual, and the flap of the ſhoulder with it, to make it look handſome. Stick the neck all over in little holes with a ſharp penknife, and pour a little red wine upon it. Let it lie in the wine four or five days, and turn and rub it three or four times a day. Then take it out, and hang it for three days in the open air out of the ſun, and dry it often with a cloth to keep it from muſting. When you roaſt it, baſte it with the wine it was ſteeped in, if any be left; if not, uſe freſh wine. Put white paper three or four folds to keep in the fat, and roaſt it thoroughly. Then take off the ſkin, froth it nicely, and ſend it up to table.

Fillet of Mutton with Cucumbers.

TAKE a neck of mutton of what ſize you pleaſe, and cut off great part of the ſcrag, and the chine

chine and ſpay-bones cloſe to the ribs. Take off the fat from the great end, and flat it with your cleaver, ſo that it may lie neatly in the diſh. Soak it in a marinade, and roaſt it wrapped up in paper well buttered. For your ſpring and ſummer ſauce, nicely quarter ſome cucumbers, and fry them in a piece of butter, after laying in the ſame marinade. Stew them in a ladle or two of your cullis, a bit of ſhalot or green onion, pepper and ſalt, a little minced parſley, the juice of a lemon, and then ſerve it up. The only difference between this and the celery ſauce is, that inſtead of frying your celery, boil it in a little water till it be tender, or you may ſtew it for a quarter of an hour in broth.

Saddle of Mutton à St. Menehout.

HAVING taken the ſkin off the hind part of a chine of mutton, lard it with bacon, ſeaſon it with pepper, ſalt, mace, beaten cloves, nutmeg, young onions, ſweet herbs, and parſley, all chopped fine. Put layers of bacon in a large oval or gravy pan, and then layers of beef, till the bottom is covered. Put in the mutton, then layers of bacon on that, and a layer of beef. Pour in a pint of wine, and as much good gravy as will ſtew it. Put in two or three ſhalots, and cover it cloſe. Put fire over and under it, if you have a cloſe pan, and let it ſtew for two hours. As ſoon as it is done, take it out, ſtrew crumbs of bread all over it, and put it into the oven to brown, or brown it before the fire. Strain the gravy it was ſtewed in, and boil it till there be only a ſufficient quantity for ſauce. Lay the mutton in a diſh, pour in the ſauce, and ſend it up to table.

Saddle of Mutton frenched.

TAKE the two chumps of the loins, cut off the rump, and carefully lift up the ſkin with a knife. You may begin at the broad end, but muſt be very careful neither to crack it nor take it quite off.

Take

Take ſome ſlices of ham or bacon finely chopped, a few truffles, ſome young onions, ſome parſley, a little thyme, ſweet marjoram, winter ſavory, and a little lemon-peel, all finely chopped; a little mace, and two or three cloves finely beaten, half a nutmeg, and a little pepper and ſalt. Mix all theſe together, and ſtrew them over the meat where you raiſed the ſkin. Lay the ſkin on again, and faſten it with two fine ſkewers on each ſide, and roll it in paper well buttered. It will take two hours roaſting. Then take off the paper, baſte the meat, and when it is of a fine brown, take it up. For ſauce, take ſix ſhalots, cut them very fine, put them into a ſaucepan with two ſpoonfuls of vinegar, and two of white wine. Boil them for a minute or two, pour the ſauce into the diſh, garniſh with horſe-radiſh, and ſend it up to table.

Mutton kebobbed.

JOINT a loin of mutton between every bone, and take off all the fat of the inſide, and the ſkin off the top of the meat, and ſome of the top fat, if there be too much. Seaſon them moderately with pepper and ſalt, and grate a ſmall nutmeg all over them. Dip them in the yolks of three eggs, and have ready crumbs of bread and ſweet herbs. Dip them in, and put them together in the ſame ſhape again. Put them on a ſmall ſpit, and roaſt them before a quick fire. Put under them a diſh; baſte them firſt with a piece of butter, and then with what comes from the meat, and throw ſome crumbs of bread and ſweet herbs all over them while roaſting. When it is enough, take it up, lay it in the diſh, and have ready a pint of good gravy and what comes from the meat; but before you put this into the gravy, take care to pour out all the fat. Take two ſpoonfuls of catchup, mix with it a tea-ſpoonful of flour, and put it to the

gravy.

gravy. Stir it together, give it a boil, and pour it over the mutton.

Mutton the Turkiſh Way.

CUT the meat in ſlices, and waſh it with vinegar. Put it into a pot with ſome whole pepper, rice, and two or three onions. Stew them very ſlowly, and ſkim them frequently. As ſoon as it is tender, take out the onions, put ſippets into the diſh under them, and ſerve them up.

Mutton à la Maintenon.

TAKE a leg of mutton, and cut ſome ſhort ſteaks from it. Make a forcemeat with crumbs of bread, a little chopped ſuet, or a bit of butter, lemon-peel grated, parſley ſhred fine, pepper, ſalt, and nutmeg, mixed up with the yolk of an egg. Pepper and ſalt the ſteaks, and lay on the forcemeat. Butter ſome half ſheets of writing-paper, and in each wrap up a ſteak, twiſting the paper neatly. Fry them, or do them in a Dutch oven. Put a little gravy into the diſh, and ſome in a boat; garniſh with pickles, and ſend them up to table.

A Baſque of Mutton.

TAKE a copper diſh of the ſize of a ſmall punch-bowl, and lay the caul of a leg of veal into it. Chop exceedingly ſmall the lean of a leg of mutton that has been kept a week. Then take half its weight in beef marrow, the crumb of a penny loaf, the rind of half a lemon grated, half a pint of red wine, the yolks of four eggs, and two anchovies. Mix them well together, and lay them in the caul in the inſide of the diſh. Faſten the caul, bake it in a quick oven, and when it comes out, lay your diſh upſide down, and turn the whole out. Pour ſome brown gravy over it, and

and put fome venifon fauce into the difh. Garnifh with pickles, and fend it up to table.

A Harrico of Mutton.

CUT a neck or loin of mutton into thick chops, flour them, and fry them brown in a little butter. Then take them out, and put them on a fieve to drain. Put them into a ftewpan, and cover them with gravy. Put in a whole onion, with a turnip or two, and ftew them tender. Then take out the chops, ftrain the liquor through a fieve, and fkim off all the fat. Put a little butter into the ftew-pan, and mix it with a fpoonful of flour. Stir it well till it is fmooth, then put in the liquor, and ftir it well all the time you are pouring it in, or it will get into lumps. Then put in your chops with a glafs of Lifbon. Have ready fome carrot, about three quarters of an inch long, and cut them round with an apple corer, fome turnips cut with a turnip fcoop, and a dozen fmall onions blanched. Put them to your meat, and feafon with pepper and falt. Stew them gently for a quarter of an hour, and then take out the chops with a fork. Lay them on the difh, and pour the fauce over them. Garnifh with beet root, and fend them to table. This is a very pretty difh for fupper.

Chine of Mutton with Cucumber Sauce.

TAKE two fore-quarters of mutton that are fmall and fat, cut it down the fides, and chop through the fhoulders and breaft fo as to make it lie even in the difh. Raife all the fkin; but take care that you neither cut nor tear it. Scrape a little fat bacon, take a little thyme, favory, fweet marjoram, parfley, three or four large onions, a mufhroom or two, and a fhalot. Cut thefe all very fine, and fry them gently in the bacon. Put to it a little pepper, and when it is nearly cold, put it all

all over the back of your meat with a paſte-bruſh. Then faſten the ſkin on with a ſkewer, ſpit it, and wrap ſome well buttered paper over it. Roaſt it gently till it be enough. In the mean time take ſome cucumbers, quarter them, and nicely fry them in a piece of butter till they be brown. Put them for a minute or two on a ſieve to drain, and then put them into a ladle or two of cullis, and boil them a little time, with ſome minced parſley and the juice of a lemon. For your herb ſauce, prepare juſt ſuch matters as are fried for the firſt part of it, put them into a ſtewpan, with as much cullis as is neceſſary, and boil it about half an hour gently. Then take the paper and ſkin off your chine, pour the ſauce over it, ſqueeze in the juice of a lemon, and ſend it to table.

A Hodge-podge of Mutton.

TAKE off the fat of a neck or loin of mutton, and cut it into ſteaks. Put them into a pitcher, with ſome lettuce, turnips, carrots, two cucumbers quartered, four or five onions, and a little pepper and ſalt. Stop the pitcher very cloſe, but do not put any water into it. Then put the pitcher into a pan of boiling water, and let it boil four hours, and keep the pan ſupplied with freſh boiling water as it waſtes. Take it out of the pitcher, and ſerve it up.

Mutton Rumps à la Braiſe.

TAKE ſix mutton rumps, and boil them for a quarter of an hour. Then take them out and cut them in two, and put them into a ſtewpan, with half a pint of good gravy, a glaſs of white wine, an onion ſtuck with cloves, and a little chyan pepper and ſalt. Cover them cloſe, and ſtew them till they be tender. Then take out the onion, thicken the gravy with a little butter rolled in flour,

 and

and put in a ſpoonful of browning, and the juice of half a lemon. Boil it up till it be ſmooth; but take care not to make it too thick. Put in your rumps, give them a toſs or two, and diſh them up hot. You may garniſh with horſe-radiſh and beet-root. If you chooſe, for variety ſake, you may leave the rumps whole, and lard ſix kidnies on one ſide, and do them the ſame as the rumps, only not boil them. Put the rumps in the middle of the diſh, and the kidnies round them, (or the kidnies will make a pretty ſide-diſh of themſelves) and pour the ſauce over all.

To haſh Mutton.

HAVING cut your mutton into ſmall pieces, and as thin as you can, ſtrew a little flour over it, and put it into ſome gravy, in which ſweet herbs, onion, pepper, and ſalt, have been boiled, and ſtrained. Put in a piece of butter rolled in flour, a little ſalt, a ſhalot cut fine, a few capers and gerkins finely chopped, and a glaſs of red wine, or walnut pickles, if you like it. Toſs all together for a minute or two, and have ready ſome bread toaſted and cut into thin ſippets; lay theſe round the diſh, and pour in your haſh. Garniſh with pickles and horſe-radiſh, and ſend it up to table.

To haſh cold Mutton.

WITH a ſharp knife cut your mutton into little pieces, as thin as poſſible, and then boil the bones with an onion, a little ſweet herbs, a blade of mace, a very little whole pepper, a little ſalt, and a piece of cruſt toaſted very criſp. Let it boil till there be no more than juſt ſufficient for ſauce. Then ſtrain it, and put it into a ſaucepan, with a piece of butter rolled in flour, and as ſoon as the meat is hot, it will be enough. Seaſon it with pepper and ſalt, and have ready ſome thin bread

toaſted

toaſted brown, and cut into any form you beſt like. Lay theſe round the diſh, and pour the haſh upon them. You may put in any kind of pickle you like, and garniſh with ſome of them.

Mutton Cutlets in Diſguiſe.

CUT ſome chops off the loin, and ſimmer them in ſome broth, with a bundle of ſweet herbs. Let the broth waſte till there be no more than ſufficient for ſauce. Put forcemeat round them for a garniſh, which you may make of ſome fillet of veal, ſuet, chopped parſley, ſhalots, pepper, ſalt, and bread crumbs ſoaked in cream, all well pounded. Add three yolks of eggs, and baſte your cutlets with eggs and bread crumbs. Bake it in the oven till it is of a good colour, pour the ſauce over it, and ſend it to table.

Mutton Cutlets Lover's-Faſhion.

LARD ſome cutlets, cut pretty thick, with ham and bacon, and give them a few turns in a little butter, chopped parſley, and a little winter ſavory. Then put them into a ſtewpan, with ſmall pieces of ham, ſliced onions, carrots, and parſnips, which you muſt firſt fry a little in oil or butter. Add a glaſs of wine, and a little cullis. As ſoon as it is done, ſkim the ſauce, pour it over the meat, and ſerve it up.

To broil Mutton Steaks.

CUT ſome ſteaks from the loin, about half an inch thick, and take off the ſkin, and part of the fat. As ſoon as your gridiron is hot, rub it with a little ſuet, lay on your ſteaks, and turn them frequently, leſt the fat that drops from them ſhould occaſion the fire to blaze, which will ſmoke and ſpoil them; but this may in ſome meaſure be prevented by putting your gridiron on a ſlant. When they are enough, put them into a hot diſh, rub

them

them with a little butter, ſlice a ſhalot very thin into a ſpoonful of water, and pour it on them, with the like quantity of catchup. Garniſh with ſcraped horſe-radiſh and pickles, and ſend them up hot to table.

Mutton Steaks baked.

CUT a loin of mutton into ſteaks, as above directed, and ſeaſon them with pepper and ſalt. Lay them in a diſh well buttered, and put in a quart of milk, ſix eggs well beaten, and four ſpoonfuls of flour. Firſt beat the flour and eggs together in a little milk, and then put the reſt to it. Put in a little beaten ginger and ſalt, and pour it over the ſteaks. About half an hour will bake them, and then ſerve them up.

A Mutton Pie.

CUT a loin of mutton into ſteaks, as before directed. Seaſon them well with pepper and ſalt. Then lay your cruſt on the diſh, and fill it with your ſteaks. Then pour in as much water as will nearly fill it, put on your top-cruſt, and ſend it to the oven.

Sheep's Tongues dreſſed in the French Faſhion.

SLICE ſome onions, and fry them in butter. When they are about half done, put to them a little flour, chopped parſley, a clove of garlick, pepper, and ſalt, a little cullis, and a glaſs of white wine. Let it ſtew till the onions be enough, then add as many ſplit tongues, ready boiled, as you chooſe. Stew theſe a quarter of an hour in the ſauce, garniſh with fried bread, and ſerve the whole up all together.

Sheep's Trotters Aſpie.

ASPIE means a ſharp ſauce or jelly, and is generally made with tarragon or elder vinegar, chopped

chopped parfley, fhalots, tarragon leaves, pepper, falt, oil, muftard, and lemon, and may be made ufe of as a fauce for fheep's trotters, or any fort of cold meat. Poultry or game may be ferved up, eithet hot or cold, with this fauce.

Mutton Hams.

CUT a hind quarter of mutton like a ham, and take an ounce of faltpetre, a pound of coarfe fugar, and the like quantity of common falt. Mix them, and rub your mutton well with them. Then lay it in a hollow tray with the fkin downwards, and bafte it every day for a fortnight. Roll it in fawduft, and hang it in wood fmoak for a fortnight. Then boil it, hang it in a dry place, and cut rafhers off it as you want, which eat much bettor broiled than any other way.

CHAP. V.

The various Methods of dreffing Lamb.

Pieces in a Lamb.

THE *Head*, and the *Pluck*, which includes the liver, lights, heart, nut, and melt. There is alfo the fry, which is the fweetbreads, lambs ftones, and fkirts, with fome of the liver.

The *Fore-Quarter* includes the fhoulder, neck, and breaft together.

The *Hind Quarter* includes the leg and loin. This is in high feafon at Chriftmas, but lafts all the year.

Grafs Lamb comes in feafon in April or May, according to the feafon of the year, and holds good till the middle of Auguft.

To force a Quarter of Lamb.

CUT a long flit on the back fide of a large leg of lamb, and take out the meat; but be careful that you do not deface the other fide. Chop the meat fmall with fome marrow, half a pound of beef fuet, fome oyfters, an anchovy wafhed, an onion, fome fweet herbs, a little lemon peel, and fome mace and nutmeg. Beat thefe all together in a mortar, and ftuff up the leg in the fhape it was before. Sew it up, and rub it all over with the yolks of eggs well beaten. Spit it, flour it all over, lay it to the fire, and bafte it with butter, and an hour will roaft it. In the mean time, cut the loin into fteaks, feafon them with pepper, falt, nutmeg, lemon peel cut fine, and a few herbs. Fry them in frefh butter till they are of a fine brown; then pour out all the butter, put in a quarter of a pint of white wine, fhake it about, and then add half a pint of ftrong gravy, in which has been boiled fome good fpice, a quarter of a pint of oyfters and their liquor, fome mufhrooms and a fpoonful of their pickle, a piece of butter rolled in flour, and the yolk of an egg finely beaten. Stir all thefe together till they be properly thick, and then lay your leg of lamb in the difh, and the loin round it. Pour the fauce over them, garnifh with lemon, and fend it up to table.

Two Hind Quarters of Lamb with Spinach.

TRUSS the knuckles of two quarters of lamb in nicely, and lay them to foak two or three hours in fome milk, a little falt, two or there onions, and fome parfley. Put them into boiling water, but do not let there be too much of it. Put in fome flour and

and water well mixed, a lemon or two pared and ſliced, a bit of ſuet, and a ſmall bunch of onions and parſley. Stir it well from the bottom, boil it gently, and theſe ingredients will make it exceedingly white. Prepare your ſpinach, and put to it about a pint of cream, a bit of butter mixed wtth flour, a little pepper, ſalt, and nutmeg. Then ſtir it over a ſlow fire till it is of a nice conſiſtence, ſqueeze in the juice of a lemon, pour it into the diſh, and put your lamb upon it; but take care firſt to drain it from the fat and water, and take off any of the ſeaſoning that may hang to it.

A Shoulder of Lamb Neighbour-Faſhion.

MAKE a forcemeat of roaſted fowls, calf's udder or ſuet, bread crumbs, ſoaked in cream, chopped parſley, ſhalots, pepper, ſalt, and four yolks of eggs finely beaten. Have ready a ſhoulder of lamb half roaſted, fill the ſhoulder with this forcemeat, and make it as round as poſſible. Faſten it well, that the forcemeat may not get out; then lard it, and ſtew it in broth, with a bundle of ſweet herbs. When done, ſtrain the ſauce through a ſieve, reduce it to a glaze, and glaze the larded part. Put to it what other ſauce you pleaſe, and ſend it up to table.

To fry a Neck or Loin of Lamb.

HAVING cut your neck or loin into ſteaks, beat them with a rolling-pin, ſeaſon them with a little ſalt, cover them cloſe, and fry them in half a pint of ale. When they are done enough, take them out of the pan, lay them in a plate before the fire to keep hot, and pour all out of the pan into a baſon. Then put in half a pint of white wine, a few capers, the yolks of two eggs finely beaten, with a little nutmeg and ſalt. Add to this the liquor they were fried in, and keep ſtirring it one way all the

the time till it be thick. Then put in the lamb, keep ſhaking the lamb for a minute or two, lay the ſteaks in the diſh, and pour the ſauce over them. Garniſh with ſome parſley criſped before the fire, and ſend them up to table.

To ragoo Lamb.

CUT the knuckle bone off a fore quarter of lamb, lard it with little thin bits of bacon, flour it, fry it of a fine brown, and then put it into an earthen pot or ſtewpan, put to it a quart of broth or good gravy, a bundle of herbs, a little mace, two or three cloves, and a little whole pepper. Cover it cloſe, and let it ſtew pretty faſt for half an hour. Pour the liquor all out, ſtrain it, keep the lamb hot in the pot till the ſauce be ready. Take half a pint of oyſters, flour them, fry them brown, drain out all the fat clear that you fried them in, and ſkim all the fat off the gravy. Then pour it to the oyſters, put in an anchovy, and two ſpoonfuls of either red or white wine. Boil all together till there be only juſt enough for ſauce, add ſome freſh muſhrooms, if you can get them, and ſome pickled, with a ſpoonful of the pickle, or the juice of half a lemon. Lay your lamb in the diſh, pour the ſauce over it, garniſh with lemon, and ſerve it up.

To force a Leg of Lamb.

TAKE a leg of lamb, and with a ſharp knife cut out all the meat, but leave the ſkin whole, and the fat on it. Make the meat you cut out into the following forcemeat. To two pounds of meat put two pounds of beef ſuet finely chopped. Take away all the ſkin and ſuet from the meat, and mix it with four ſpoonfuls of grated bread, eight or ten cloves, five or ſix large blades of mace dried and finely beaten, half a large nutmeg grated, a little pepper

pepper and ſalt, ſome lemon peel cut fine, a very little thyme, ſome parſley, and four eggs. Mix all together, and put it into the ſkin, as nearly as you can into the ſame ſhape it was before. Sew it up, roaſt it, and baſte it with butter. Cut the loin into ſteaks, and fry it nicely. Lay the leg on the diſh, and the loin round it, with ſtewed cauliflowers, if you like them, all round upon the loin. Pour a pint of good gravy into the diſh, and ſend it up to table.

To boil a Leg of Lamb.

BOIL a leg of lamb an hour, which will be ſufficient to do it. Take the loin and cut it into ſteaks, dip them into a few bread crumbs and egg, and fry them nice and brown. Boil a good deal of ſpinach, and lay it in a diſh. Put the leg in the middle, lay the loin round it, and garniſh with an orange quartered. Put ſome butter in a cup, and ſend the diſh up to table.

To dreſs a Lamb's Head.

HAVING boiled a head and pluck tender, and having taken care not to do the liver too much, take out the head, and cut it in all directions with a knife. Then grate ſome nutmeg over it, and lay it in a diſh before a good fire. Grate ſome crumbs of bread, and ſome ſweet herbs rubbed, a little lemon peel finely chopped, and a very little pepper and ſalt. Strew theſe over the head, and baſte it with a little butter. Then throw a little flour over it, and juſt as it is done baſte it and dredge it. Take half the liver, the lights, the heart, and tongue, and chop them very ſmall, with ſix or eight ſpoonfuls of gravy or water. Firſt ſhake ſome flour over the meat, and ſtir it together; then put into the gravy or water, a large piece of butter rolled in flour, a little pepper and ſalt,

ſalt, and the gravy that runs from the head into the diſh. Simmer them all together a few minutes, and add half a ſpoonful of vinegar. Pour it into your diſh, and lay the head in the middle of the mincemeat. Have ready the other half of the liver cut thin, with ſome ſlices of broiled bacon, and lay them round the head. Garniſh with lemon.

To ſtew a Lamb's Head.

FIRST waſh it and pick it very clean, and then lay it in water for an hour. Take out the brains, and with a ſharp knife carefully extract the tongue and the bones; but take particular care that you do not break the meat. Then take out the eyes. Take two pounds of veal, and two pounds of beef ſuet, a very little thyme, a good piece of lemon peel finely minced, a nutmeg grated, and two anchovies. Chop all theſe well together, grate two ſtale rolls, and mix all with the yolks of four eggs. Save enough of this meat to make about twenty balls. Take half a pint of freſh muſhrooms, clean peeled and waſhed, or pickled cockles. Firſt ſtew your oyſters, and put to them two quarts of gravy, with a blade or two of mace, and then mix all theſe together. Tie the head with packthread, cover it cloſe, and let it ſtew two hours. In the mean time, beat up the brains with ſome lemon peel finely minced, a little chopped parſley, half a grated nutmeg, and the yolk of an egg. Fry the brains in little cakes in boiling dripping, then fry the balls, and keep them both hot. Take half an ounce of truffles and morels, and ſtrain the gravy the head was ſtewed in, put it to the truffles and morels, with a few muſhrooms, and boil all together. Then put in the reſt of the brains that are not fried, and ſtew them together a minute or two. Pour this over the head,

lay

lay the fried brains and balls round it, garniſh with lemon, and ſend it up to table.

A Lamb's Head Condé-Faſhion.

DO a lamb's head in a white braze, and ſerve it up with a ſauce made of verjuice, three yolks of eggs, pepper, ſalt, a piece of butter, chopped parſley ſcalded, and a little nutmeg. Serve theſe up with the head.

Lamb's Head and Pluck.

HAVING ſkinned and ſplit a lamb's head, take the black part out of the eyes, and waſh and clean the head perfectly well. Lay it in warm water till it looks white, and then waſh and clean the pluck, take off the gall, and lay them in water. Boil it half an hour, and then mince your heart, liver, and lights, very ſmall. Put the mince-meat into a toſſing-pan, with a quart of mutton gravy, a little catchup, pepper, and ſalt, and half a lemon. Thicken it with flour and butter, a ſpoonful of good cream, and juſt give it a boil. When your head is enough, rub it over with the yolk of an egg, ſtrew over it bread crumbs, a little ſhred parſley, pepper, and ſalt. Thicken it well with butter, and brown it before the fire, or with a ſalamander. Put the mince-meat, into the diſh, and lay the head over it. You may ſend it up to table, with lemon or pickle for garniſh.

To fry a Loin of Lamb.

CUT a loin of lamb into chops, and rub them over on both ſides with the yolks of eggs; ſprinkle over them ſome bread crumbs, a little parſley, thyme, marjoram, and winter ſavory, and lemon peel very finely chopped. Fry them in butter till they be of a nice brown, garniſh with plenty of criſped parſley, and ſend them up to table.

Lamb

Lamb baked with Rice.

HALF roaſt either a neck or loin of lamb, and then cut it into ſteaks. Boil half a pound of rice ten minutes in water, and put to it a quart of good gravy, with a little nutmeg, and two or three blades of mace. Do it over a ſlow fire or ſtove till the rice begins to thicken. Then take it off, ſtir in a pound of butter, and, when that is quite melted, ſtir in the yolks of ſix eggs finely beaten. Butter a diſh all over, put a little pepper and ſalt to the ſteaks, dip them into a little melted butter, and lay them into the diſh. Pour over them the gravy that comes from them, and then the rice. Pour over all the yolks of three eggs finely beaten, ſend it to the oven, and little more than half an hour will bake it.

Graſs Lamb Steaks.

CUT a loin of lamb into ſteaks, pepper and ſalt, and fry them. When they are enough, put them into a diſh, and pour out the butter. Shake a little flour into the pan, pour in a little beef broth, a little catchup and walnut pickle. Boil this up, and keep ſtirring it all the time. Put in the ſteaks, give them a ſhake round, garniſh with criſped parſley, and ſend them up to table.

Lamb Chops larded.

TAKE the beſt end of a neck of lamb, and cut it into chops. Lard one ſide of them, and ſeaſon them with beaten cloves, mace, nutmeg, and a little pepper and ſalt. Put them into a ſtewpan, the larded ſide uppermoſt, and put in half a pint of gravy, a gill of white wine, an onion, and a bundle of ſweet herbs. Stew them gently till they be tender. Take out the chops, ſkim the fat off clean, and take out the onion and ſweet herbs. Thicken

Thicken the gravy with a little butter rolled in flour, and add a ſpoonful of browning, a ſpoonful of catchup, and one of lemon pickle. Boil it up till it be properly ſmooth, put in the chops the larded ſide downwards, give them a gentle ſtew for a minute or two, and then take them out. Put them in the diſh, with the larded ſide uppermoſt, and pour the ſauce over them. You may garniſh with lemon, or pickles of any ſort.

Lamb Chops en Caſarole.

PUT ſome yolk of eggs on both ſides ſome chops cut off a loin of lamb, and ſtrew bread crumbs over them, with a little cloves and mace, pepper and ſalt mixed. Fry them of a nice light brown, and put them round a diſh as cloſe as you can; but leave a hole in the middle to put in the following ſauce. Take all ſorts of ſweet herbs and parſley finely chopped, and ſtew them a little in ſome good thick gravy. Garniſh with criſped parſley.

To dreſs Lamb's Bits.

TAKE ſome lambs ſtones, and ſkin and ſplit them. Lay them on a dry cloth with the ſweetbreads and liver, and dredge them well with flour. Fry them in boiling lard or butter till they be of a light brown, and then lay them on a ſieve to drain. Fry a good quantity of parſley, and lay your bits in the diſh, and your parſley in lumps over it. Pour melted butter round them, and ſend them up to table.

Lamb's Sweetbreads.

HAVING blanched your ſweetbreads, put them a little time into cold water. Then put them into a ſtewpan with a ladle of broth, ſome pepper, ſalt, a ſmall bunch of green onions, and a blade of mace.

Stir in a bit of butter with ſome flour, and ſtew them all about half an hour. Have ready two or three eggs well beaten in cream, with a little minced parſley and nutmeg. Put in ſome ready boiled tops of aſparagus, and put them into your other articles; but take great care that it does not curdle. Add ſome lemon or orange juice, and ſend it to table. You may make it a pretty diſh by the addition of peas, young gooſeberries, or kidney beans.

Lamb Stones and Sweetbreads fricaſſeed.

BLANCH, parboil, and ſlice ſome lamb ſtones, and flour three or four ſweetbreads; but if they be very thick, cut them in two. Take the yolks of ſix hard eggs whole, a few piſtachio-nut kernels, and a few large oyſters. Fry all theſe till they are of a fine brown, then pour out all the butter, and add a pint of drawn gravy, the lamb ſtones, ſome aſparagus tops about an inch long, ſome grated nutmeg, a little pepper and ſalt, two ſhalots ſhred ſmall, and a glaſs of white wine. Stew all theſe together for ten minutes, and then add the yolks of three eggs finely beaten, with a little cream, and a little beaten mace. Stir all together till it is of a fine thickneſs, then garniſh with lemon, and ſend it up to table.

To fry Lamb's Rumps.

BRAZE or boil your rumps, and make a light batter of flour, one egg, a little ſalt, white wine, and a little oil. Fry them of a good brown colour, and ſerve them up with fried parſley round them. You may put to them any ſauce you like beſt.

Lamb Cutlets fricaſſeed.

TAKE a leg of lamb, and cut it into thin cutlets croſs the grain, and put them into a ſtewpan. Make

Make ſome good broth with the bones, ſhank, &c. enough to cover the cutlets. Put it into the ſtew-pan, and cover it with a bundle of ſweet herbs, an onion, a little clove and mace tied in a muſlin rag, and ſtew them gently for ten minutes. Then take out the cutlets, ſkim off the fat, and take out the ſweet herbs and mace. Thicken it with butter rolled in flour, ſeaſon it with ſalt and a little chyan pepper; put in a few muſhrooms, truffles, and morels, clean waſhed; ſome forcemeat balls, three yolks of eggs beat up in half a pint of cream, and ſome nutmeg grated. Keep ſtirring it one way till it be thick and ſmooth, and then put in your cutlets. Give them a toſs up, take them out with a fork, and lay them in a diſh. Pour the ſauce over them, garniſh with beet-root and lemon, and ſend them up to table.

Lambs Ears with Sorrel.

IN London, ſuch things as theſe, or calves ears, tails, or the ears of ſheep, ready for uſe, as well as in ſome other great market towns, are always to be had of the butchers or tripemen. About a dozen of lambs ears will make a ſmall diſh, and theſe muſt be ſtewed tender in a braze. Take a large handful of ſorrel, chop it a little and ſtew it in a ſpoonful of broth and a morſel of butter. Pour in a ſmall ladle of cullis, grate ſome nutmeg, and put in a little pepper and ſalt. Stew it a few minutes, twiſt up the ears nicely, and diſh it up.

A Lamb Pie.

HAVING cut your lamb into ſmall pieces, ſeaſon it with pepper, ſalt, cloves, mace, and nutmeg, finely beaten. Make a good puff-paſte cruſt, lay it into your diſh, then put in your meat, and ſtrew on it ſome ſtoned raiſins and currants clean waſhed, and add ſome ſugar. Then lay on ſome

forcemeat

forcemeat balls made ſweet, and, if in the ſummer, you may put in ſome artichoke bottoms boiled; but, in the winter time, you may uſe ſcalded grapes. Add to theſe ſome Spaniſh potatoes boiled, and cut into pieces; ſome candied citron and orange, ſome lemon peel, and three or four blades of mace. Put butter on the top, cloſe up your pie, and bake it. Againſt it is done, have ready the following. Mix the yolks of three eggs with a pint of wine, and ſtir them well together over the fire one way, till it is of a proper thickneſs. Then take it off, put in ſugar enough to ſweeten it, and ſqueeze in the juice of a lemon. Raiſe the lid of your pie, put this hot into it, cloſe it up again, and ſend it to table.

A ſavoury Lamb Pie.

CUT your meat into pieces, and ſeaſon it to your palate with pepper, ſalt, mace, cloves, and nutmeg, finely beaten. Having made a good puff-paſte cruſt, put your meat into it, with a few lamb-ſtones and ſweetbreads ſeaſoned like your meat. Then put in ſome oyſters and forcemeat balls, hard yolks of eggs, and the tops of aſparagus two inches long, firſt boiled green. Put butter all over the pie, put on the lid, and ſet it in a quick oven an hour and a half. In the mean time, take a pint of gravy, the oyſter liquor, a gill of red wine, and a little grated nutmeg. Mix all together with the yolks of two or three eggs finely beaten, and keep ſtirring it one way all the time. When it boils pour it into your pie, put on the lid again, and ſend it up to table.

CHAP.

CHAP. VI.

The Various Methods of Dreſſing Pork.

Pieces in a Hog.

THE *Head*, and *Inwards*, including the haſlet, which are the liver and crow, kidney, and ſkirts. Alſo the chitterlins, and the guts, which are cleaned for ſauſages.

The *Fore Quarter* is the fore loin and ſpring. If it be a large hog, you may cut off a ſpare rib.

The *Hind Quarter* conſiſts of only the leg and loin.

A *Bacon Hog* is cut in a different manner, becauſe of making hams, bacon and pickled pork. Here you have fine ſpare-ribs, chines, and griſkins, and fat for hog's lard. The liver and crow are much admired fried with bacon; the feet and ears are both equally good ſouſed.

Pork comes in ſeaſon at Bartholomew-tide, and holds good till about Lady-day.

To ſtuff a Chine of Pork.

HANG up a chine of pork for four or five days, and then make four holes in the lean. Stuff it with a little of the fat leaf chopped very ſmall, ſome parſley, thyme, a little ſage and ſhalot cut very fine, and ſeaſoned with pepper, ſalt, and nutmeg. You may ſtuff it as thick as you chooſe. Put ſome good gravy into the diſh, for ſauce uſe apple-ſauce and potatoes, and ſend it up to table.

Chine of Pork with Poivrade Sauce.

LET a chine lie in ſalt about three days, then roaſt it, and ſerve it up with ſauce poivrade, which is is made in the following manner. Take a little butter, ſliced onion, pieces of carrot, parſley root, two cloves of garlick, and two ſpice cloves. Soak all together till it takes colour, and then add ſome cullis, a little vinegar and broth, ſalt and pepper. Boil it to the conſiſtence of ſauces, and ſkim and ſtrain it for uſe.

To barbacue a Leg of Pork.

ROAST a leg of pork before a good fire, put into the dripping-pan two bottles of red wine, and baſte your pork with it all the time it is roaſting. When it is enough, take up what is left in the pan, put to it two anchovies, the yolks of three eggs boiled hard and finely pounded, with a quarter of a pound of butter and half a lemon, a bunch of ſweet herbs, a tea-ſpoonful of lemon-pickle, and a ſpoonful of catchup. Boil theſe a few minutes, then take up your pork, and cut the ſkin down from the bottom of the flank in rows an inch broad, raiſe every other row, and roll it to the ſhank. Strain your ſauce, and pour it in boiling hot. Garniſh with oyſter patties and green parſley, and ſend it up to table.

To boil pickled Pork.

YOUR pickled pork muſt be put in when the water boils, and if it be a middling piece, an hour will boil it; if it be a very large piece, it will require an hour and a half, or two hours. If you boil pickled pork too long, it will go to a jelly; but you may eaſily know when it is done by trying it with a fork. Pork in general ſhould be well boiled; a leg of ſix pounds will take two hours; the hand muſt be boiled till very tender. Peaſe-pudding, ſavoys, or any ſorts of greens, may be ſerved up with it.

To

To broil Pork Steaks.

WHEN your pork ſteaks are enough, for they require more broiling than mutton chops, put in a little good gravy. Strew over them a little ſage rubbed very fine, which gives them a very agreeable taſte. Remember not to cut them too thick.

Other Methods of dreſſing Pork Steaks.

TAKE a neck of pork that has been kept ſome time, cut it into ſteaks, and pare them properly. You may dreſs them, in every reſpect, as veal cutlets, and in as many different ways, ſerving them up with any ſort of ſtewed greens or ſauces.

Pork Cutlets dreſſed another Way.

HAVING ſkinned a loin of pork, divide it into cutlets. Strew over them ſome parſley and thyme cut ſmall, with ſome pepper, ſalt, and grated bread over them, and fry them of a fine brown. Take ſome good gravy, a ſpoonful of ready-made muſtard, and two ſhalots ſhred fine. Boil theſe together over the fire, thicken with a piece of butter rolled in flour, and a little vinegar, if agreeable. Put the cutlets into a hot diſh, pour the ſauce over them, and ſend them up to table.

To roaſt a Pig.

TAKE a fine young fat pig, and ſtick it juſt above the breaſt bone; but mind that your knife touches the heart of it, otherwiſe it will be a long time in dying. When it is dead, put it a few minutes into cold water, and then rub it over with a little roſin beat exceedingly fine, or with its own blood. Put it for half a minute into a pail of ſcalding water, and then take it out. Lay it on a clean table, and pull off the hair as quick as poſſible; but if it does not come clean off, put it in again. When you have made it perfectly clear of the hair, waſh it in warm water, and then in two or three cold waters, to prevent the rosin tasting. Cut off the fore feet at the first joint, make a slit down the belly, and take out all the entrails. Put the liver, heart, and lights, to the pettitoes, wash it well with cold water, dry it exceedingly well with a cloth, and hang it up. When you roast it, put in a little shred sage, a tea-spoonful of black pepper, two of salt, and a crust of brown bread. Spit your pig, and sew it up. Lay it down to a brisk clear fire, with a pig-plate hung in the middle of the fire. When your pig is warm, put a lump of butter in a cloth, and rub your pig often with it while it is roasting. A large one will require an hour and a half roasting. When your pig is of a fine brown, and the steam draws near the fire, take a clean cloth, rub your pig quite dry, then rub it well with a little cold butter, and it will help it to crisp. Take a sharp knife, cut off the head, take off the collar, and then take off the ears and jaw-bone, which split in two. When you have cut the pig down the back, which must be done before you draw the spit out, lay your pig back to back on the dish, the jaw on each side, the ears on each shoulder, and pour in your sauce, garnish with a crust of brown bread grated, and send it up to table.

To bake a Pig.

WHEN you cannot conveniently roast a pig, but are obliged to bake it, lay it in a dish, flour it well all over, and rub it well with butter. Butter the dish in which you intend to bake it, and put it into the oven. As soon as it is enough, take it out, rub it over with a buttered cloth, and put it into the oven again till it is dry. Then take it out, lay it in the dish, and cut it up. Carefully skim off all the fat from the dish it was baked in, and take care of the good gravy that remains at the

the bottom. To this add a little veal gravy, with a piece of butter rolled in flour, and boil it up. Put it into the diſh, with the brains and ſage in the belly, and ſerve it up.

To barbacue a Pig.

HAVING managed a pig, of nine or ten weeks old, in every reſpect as for roaſting, make a ſtuffing with a few ſage leaves, the liver of the pig, and two anchovies boned, waſhed, and cut very ſmall. Put them into a mortar with ſome crumbs of bread, a quarter of a pound of butter, a very little chyan pepper, and half a pint of Madiera wine. Beat them to a paſte, and ſew it up in the pig. Lay it down at a great diſtance from a large briſk fire, and ſinge it well. Put into the dripping-pan two bottles of Madeira wine, and baſte it well all the time it is roaſting. As ſoon as it is half roaſted, put into the dripping-pan two French rolls, and if there be not wine enough in the dripping-pan, put in more. When the pig is nearly done, take out the rolls and ſauce, and put them into a ſaucepan, with an anchovy cut ſmall, a bunch of ſweet herbs, and the juice of a lemon. Take up the pig, put an apple in its mouth, and a roll on each ſide. Strain the ſauce over it, and ſend it up to table.

Another Method.

TAKE a pig of ten weeks old, and treat it in the ſame manner as for roaſting. Make a forcemeat of two anchovies, ſix ſage leaves, and the liver of the pig; all chopped very ſmall. Put them into a marble mortar, with the crumb of a halfpenny loaf, four ounces of butter, half a tea-ſpoonful of chyan pepper, and half a pint of red wine. Beat them all together to a paſte, put it into the pig's belly, and ſew it up. Put your pig down at a good a good diftance before a brifk fire, and it will take four hours roafting. Singe your pig well, and put into your dripping-pan three bottles of red wine, and bafte it with the wine all the time it is roafting. When it is half roafted, put under your pig two penny loaves, and if there be not wine enough, put in more. When your pig is nearly enough, take the loaves and fauce out of the dripping-pan, and put to it an anchovy chopped fmall, a bundle of fweet herbs, and half a lemon. Boil it a few minutes, draw your pig, put a fmall lemon in its mouth, and a leaf on each fide. Strain your fauce, and pour it boiling hot on the pig. Garnifh with barberries and flices of lemon.

Hind Quarter of a Pig dreffed Lamb Fafhion.

TAKE the hind quarter of a large roafting pig, at the time of the year when houfe-lamb is very dear. Take off the fkin and roaft it, and it will eat like lamb. Half an hour will roaft it. You may ferve up with it either a fallad or mint fauce.

A Pig au Père Duillet.

HAVING cut off the head, and quartered the pig, lard the quarters with bacon, and feafon them with mace, cloves, pepper, nutmeg, and falt. Put a layer of fat bacon at the bottom of a kettle, lay the head in the middle, and the quarters round. Then put in a bay leaf, an onion fliced, lemon, carrots, parfnips, parfley, and chives. Cover it again with bacon, ftew it for an hour, and then take it up. Put your pig into a ftewpan or kettle, pour in a bottle of white wine, cover it clofe, and let it ftew an hour very foftly. If you intend to ferve it up cold, let it ftand till it be cold, then drain it well, and wipe it to make it look white. Lay it in a difh with the head in the middle, and the quarters round, and throw fome green parfley all over it. Indeed,

either

either of the quarters, laid in water-creſſes, is a pretty little diſh. If you intend to ſerve it up hot, while your pig is ſtewing in the wine, take the firſt gravy it was ſtewed in, and ſtrain it; ſkim off all the fat, take a ſweetbread cut in five or ſix ſlices, ſome truffles, morels, and muſhrooms. Stew theſe all together till they are enough, then thicken it with the yolks of two eggs, or a piece of butter rolled in flour, and when your pig is enough, take it out, and lay it in the diſh. Put the wine it was ſtewed in to the ragoo, then pour all over the pig, garniſh with lemon, and ſend it to table.

To dreſs a Pig the French Method.

HAVING ſpitted your pig, lay it down to the fire, and let it roaſt till it be thoroughly warm. Then cut it off the ſpit, and divide it into twenty pieces. Set them to ſtew in half a pint of white wine and a pint of ſtrong broth, ſeaſoned with grated nutmeg, pepper, two onions cut ſmall, and a little ſtripped thyme. When it has ſtewed about an hour, put to it half a pint of ſtrong gravy, a piece of butter rolled in flour, ſome anchovies, and a ſpoonful of vinegar or muſhroom pickle. When it is enough, put it in your diſh, pour the gravy over it, garniſh with orange and lemon, and ſerve it up.

A Pig Matelot.

FIRST gut and ſcald your pig, and cut off the head and pettitoes. Cut your pig into quarters, and put them with the head and toes into cold water. Cover the bottom of a ſtewpan with ſlices of bacon, and put the quarter over them, with the pettitoes, and the head cut into two. Seaſon all with pepper, ſalt, thyme, and onion, and put in a bottle of white wine. Lay over it more ſlices of bacon, put to it a quart of water, and let it boil. Skin and gut two large eels, and cut them into pieces about five or ſix inches long. When your pig is half done, put in your eels; then boil a dozen of large craw-fiſh, cut off the claws, and take off the ſhells of the tails. When the pig and eels are enough, lay your pig in the diſh, and the pettitoes round it; but do not put in the head, as that will be a pretty diſh of itſelf when cold. Then lay your eels and craw-fiſh over them, and take the liquor they were ſtewed in. Skim off all the fat, and add to it half a pint of ſtrong gravy; thicken it with a little piece of butter rolled in flour, and a ſpoonful of browning, and pour it over it. You may fry the brains, and lay them round and all over the diſh. Garniſh with craw-fiſh and lemon, and ſend it up to table.

A Pig in Jelly.

QUARTER a pig, and put it into a ſtewpan, with a calf's foot, the pig's feet, a pint of Rheniſh wine, the juice of four lemons, a quart of water, three or four blades of mace, two or three cloves, ſome ſalt, and a very little piece of lemon-peel. Do theſe for two hours over a ſtove or very ſlow fire, and then take it up. Lay the pig in your diſh, ſtrain the liquor, and when the jelly is cold, ſkim off the fat, and leave the ſettling at the bottom. Beat up the whites of ſix eggs, boil it with the jelly about ten minutes, and ſtrain it perfectly clear. Pour the jelly over your pig, and ſerve it up cold in the jelly.

To collar a Pig.

TAKE a fine young roaſting pig, kill it as before directed, dreſt off the hair, and draw it. Waſh it clean, rip it open from one end to the other, and take out all the bones. Rub it all over with pepper and ſalt, a little cloves and mace finely beaten, ſix

ſix ſage leaves, and ſweet herbs, chopped ſmall. Roll up your pig tight, and bind it with a fillet. Fill the pot you intend to boil it in with ſoft water, a bunch of ſweet herbs, ſome pepper-corns, ſome cloves, mace, a handful of ſalt, and a pint of vinegar. When the liquor boils, put in your pig; boil it till it is tender, and then take it up,. When it is almoſt cold, bind it over again, put it into an earthen pan, pour over it the liquor your pig was boiled in, and always keep it covered. When you want it for uſe, take it out of the pan, untie the fillet as far as you want to cut it, and then cut it into ſlices, and lay them in your diſh. Garniſh with parſley, and ſend it up to table.

To boil Pig's Pettitoes.

BOIL the heart, liver, and lights of one or more pigs ten minutes, and then ſhred them pretty ſmall. Let the feet boil till they are pretty tender, and then take them out and ſplit them. Thicken your gravy with flour and butter, put in your mincemeat, a ſlice of lemon, a ſpoonful of white wine, a little ſalt, and let them boil a little. Beat the yolk of an egg, add to it two ſpoonfuls of good cream, and a little grated nutmeg. Put in your pettitoes, ſhake them over the fire, but do not let them boil. Lay ſippets round your diſh, pour in your mincemeat, lay the feet over them, the ſkin ſide upwards, and ſerve them up.

Another Method to dreſs Pig's Pettitoes.

PUT into a ſaucepan half a pint of water, a blade of mace, a little whole pepper, a bundle of ſweet herbs, an onion, and then put in your pettitoes. After they have boiled five minutes, take out the liver, lights, and heart; mince them very fine, grate a little nutmeg over them, and ſhake a little flour on them. Let the feet do till they are tender,

tender, and then take them out and ſtrain the liquor. Put all together with a little ſalt, and a piece of butter as big as a walnut, into a ſauce-pan. Shake it often, let them ſimmer five or ſix minutes, and then cut ſome toaſted ſippets, and lay them round the diſh. Lay the mincemeat and ſauce in the middle, and the pettitoes ſplit 'round it. Add the juce of half a lemon, or a very little vinegar, and ſerve them up.

Pig's Feet and Ears ragooed.

BOIL the feet and ears, ſplit the feet down the middle, and cut the ears into narrow ſlices. Dip them into butter, and fry them of a nice brown. Put a little beef gravy in a toſſing-pan, with a tea-ſpoonful of lemon-pickle, a large one of muſh-room catchup, the ſame of browning, and a little ſalt. Thicken it with a lump of butter rolled in flour, and put in your feet and ears. Let them boil gently, and when they are enough, lay your feet in the middle of the diſh, and the ears round them. Then ſtrain your gravy, pour it over them, garniſh with criſped parſley, and ſend it up to table.

Another Method.

HAVING taken them out of the ſauce, ſplit them, dip them in egg, and then in crumbs of bread and chopped parſley. Fry them in hog's lard, and drain them. Cut the ears in long narrow ſlips, flour them, and put them into ſome good gravy. Add ſome catchup, morels, and pickled muſh-rooms. Stew them, then pour them into the diſh, and lay on the feet. They are very good dipped in butter and fried, and may be ſerved up with melted butter and muſtard.

A Suck-

A Sucking Pig Pie.

HAVING boned your pig thoroughly, lard the leg and ſhoulders with bacon ſeaſoned with ſpices, and ſweet herbs chopped. Put it in a raiſed cruſt of its own length, and ſeaſon it with ſpices, ſweet herbs chopped, and a pound of butter. Covei it over with thin ſlices of bacon, then finiſh the pie, and bake it about three hours. When it is nearly done, add to it two glaſſes of white wine, and let it be ſerved up cold.

A Cheſhire Pork Pie.

SKIN a loin of pork, cut it into ſteaks, and ſeaſon it with ſalt, nutmeg, and pepper, Make a good cruſt, put a layer of pork, then a layer of pippins pared and cored, and a little ſugar, enough to ſweeten the pie, and then a layer of pork. Put in half a pint of white wine, lay ſome butter on the top, and cloſe your pie. It will take a pint of wine, if your pie be a large one.

Pork Pudding.

HAVING made a good cruſt with dripping or mutton ſuet ſhred fine, take a piece of ſalt pork, which has been twenty-four hours in ſoft water, and ſeaſon it with a little pepper. Put it into the cruſt, roll it up cloſe, tie it in a cloth, and boil it. It will require five hours boiling, if it be about four or five pounds weight. You may make a mutton pudding in the ſame manner, only cut it into thin ſteaks, ſeaſon them with pepper and ſalt, and boil it three hours, if it be large; but if it be ſmall, two hours will do it. Indeed, the time of boiling muſt be regulated by the ſize of it.

CHAP.

CHAP. VII.

Directions for truſſing Poultry and Game.

AS this work is intended for the uſe of the culinary artiſt, as well in the country as in the town, it ſeems indiſpenſably neceſſary to give them ſome inſtructions relative to the properly truſſing of poultry, as it is generally the caſe, that moſt families in the country breed their own poultry, where there is perhaps no poulterer at hand to perform the buſineſs of truſſing, which muſt be done before they can be dreſſed; and this is ſo eſſential a point, that no cook ought to be ignorant of it. In order to prepare them for this buſineſs, we ſhall previouſly ſubmit to their attention the following general directions. Be particularly careful, that you clear the fowl of all the ſtubs; and when you draw any kind of poultry, by all means avoid breaking the gall, as ſhould that happen, it will be impoſſible for you to remove that bitterneſs the breaking of the gall will give to the fowl. Equal care muſt be taken to avoid breaking the gut joining to the gizzard, as that will make the inſide gritty, and ſpoil the whole. Having given theſe general perliminaries, we ſhall now proceed to particulars.

To truſs Chickens.

HAVING properly picked your chickens, cut off the neck cloſe to the back; then take out the crop, and with your middle finger looſen the liver and other matters. Cut off the vent, draw it clean, and beat the breaſt-bone flat with a rolling-pin. If they are to be boiled, cut off the nails, give the ſinews a nick on each ſide of the joint, put the feet in at the vent, and then peel the rump. Draw the ſkin tight over the legs, put a ſkewer in the firſt joint of the pinion, and bring the middle of the leg cloſe. Put the ſkewer through the middle of the legs, and through the body, and do the ſame on the other ſide. Clean the gizzard, and take out the gall in the liver; put them into the pinions, and turn the points on the back. If your chickens are to be roaſted, cut off the feet, put a ſkewer in the firſt joint of the pinions, and bring the middle of the leg cloſe. Run the ſkewer through the middle of the leg, and through the body, and do the ſame on the other ſide. Put another ſkewer into the ſideſman, put the legs between the apron and the ſideſman, and run the ſkewer through. Having cleaned the liver and gizzard, put them in the pinions, turn the points on the back, and pull the breaſt ſkin over the neck.

To truſs Fowls.

PICK, draw, and flatten the breaſts of your fowls in the ſame manner as directed for truſſing chickens. If your fowl is for boiling, cut off the nails of the feet, and tuck them down cloſe to the legs. Put your finger into the inſide, and raiſe the ſkin of the legs; then cut a hole in the top of the ſkin, and put the legs under. Put a ſkewer in the firſt joint of the pinion, bring the middle of the leg cloſe to it, put the ſkewer through the middle of the leg, and through the body; and then do the ſame on the other ſide. Having opened the gizzard, take out the filth, and the gall out of the liver. Put the gizzard and the liver in the pinion, turn the points on the back, and tie a ſtring over the tops of the legs to keep them in their proper place. If your fowl is to be roaſted, put a ſkewer in the firſt joint of the pinion, and bring the middle of the leg cloſe to it. Put the ſkewer through the

the middle of the leg, and through the body, and do the ſame on the other ſide. Put another ſkewer in the ſmall of the leg, and through the ſideſman; do the ſame on the other ſide, and then put another through the ſkin of the feet. Do not forget to cut off the nails of the feet.

To truſs Turkies.

FIRST nicely pick your turkey, break the leg bone cloſe to the foot, and draw out the ſtrings from the thigh, in order to do which you muſt hang it on a hook faſtened againſt a wall. Cut off the neck cloſe to the back; but be ſure to leave the crop ſkin ſufficiently long to turn over the back. Then proceed to take out the crop, and looſen the liver and gut at the throat end with your middle finger. Then cut off the vent, and take out the gut. Pull out the gizzard with a crooked ſharp-pointed iron, and the liver will ſoon follow; but be careful not to break the gall. Wipe the inſide perfectly clean with a wet cloth; and then cut the breaſt-bone through on each ſide cloſe to the back, and draw the legs cloſe to the crops. Then put a cloth on the breaſt, and beat the high bone down with a rolling-pin till it lies flat. If your turkey is to be truſſed for boiling, cut the legs off; then put your middle finger into the inſide, raiſe the ſkin of the legs, and put them under the apron of the turkey. Put a ſkewer into the joint of the wing and the middle joint of the leg, and run it through the body and the other leg and wing. The liver and gizzard muſt be put in the pinions; but be careful firſt to open the gizzard and take out the filth, and the gall of the liver. Then turn the ſmall end of the pinion on the back, and tie a packthread over the ends of the legs to keep them in their places. If the turkey is to be roaſted, leave the legs on, put a ſkewer in the joint of the wing,

wing, tuck the legs cloſe up, and put the ſkewer through the middle of the legs and body. On the other ſide, put another ſkewer in at the ſmall part of the leg. Put it cloſe on the outſide of the ſideſman, and put the ſkewer through, and the ſame on the other ſide. Put the liver and gizzard between the pinions, and turn the point of the pinion on the back. Then put, cloſe above the pinions, another ſkewer through the body of the turkey.

To truſs Turkey Polts.

YOU muſt truſs your turkey polts in the following manner. Take the neck from the head and body, but do not remove the neck ſkin. They are to be drawn in the ſame manner as a turkey. Put a ſkewer through the joint of the pinion, tuck the legs cloſe up, run the ſkewer through the middle of the leg, through the body, and ſo on the other ſide. Cut off the under part of the bill, twiſt the ſkin of the neck round, and put the head on the point of the ſkewer, with the bill-end forwards. Another ſkewer muſt be put in the ſideſman, and the legs placed between the ſideſman and apron on each ſide. Paſs the ſkewer through all, and cut off the toe nails. You may uſe or omit the gizzard and liver, as you like. It is very common to lard them on the breaſt.

To truſs Geeſe.

PICK and ſtub your gooſe clean, then cut the feet off at the joint, and the pinion off the firſt joint. Cut off the neck almoſt cloſe to the back; but leave the ſkin of the neck long enough to turn over the back. Pull out the throat, and tie a knot at the end. With your middle finger looſen the liver and other matters at the breaſt end, and cut it open between the vent and the rump. Having done

done this, draw out all the entrails, excepting the foal. Wipe it clean with a wet cloth, and beat the breaft-bone flat with a rolling-pin. Put a fkewer into the wing, and draw the legs clofe up. Put the fkewer through the middle of the leg, and through the body, and the fame on the other fide. Put another fkewer in the fmall of the leg, tuck it clofe down to the fidefman, run it through, and do the fame on the other fide. Cut off the end of the vent, and make a hole large enough for the paffage of the rump, as by thefe means it will much better keep in the feafoning. Ducks are truffed in the fame manner, except that the feet muft be left on, and turned clofe to the legs.

To trufs a Hare.

CUT off the four legs at the firft joint, raife the fkin of the back, and draw it over the hind legs. Leave the tail whole, draw the fkin over the back, and flip out the fore legs. Cut the fkin off the neck and head; but take care to leave the ears on, and mind to fkin them. Take out the liver and other entrails, and draw the gut out of the vent. Cut the finews that lie under the hind legs, bring them up to the fore legs, put a fkewer through the hind leg, then through the fore leg under the joint, run it through the body, and do the fame on the other fide. Put another fkewer through the thick part of the hind legs and body, put the head between the fhoulders, and run a fkewer through to keep it in its place. Put a fkewer in each ear to make them ftand erect, and tie a ftring round the middle of the body, over the legs, to keep them in their place. A young fawn may be truffed juft in the fame manner, except that the ears muft be cut off. Rabbits are cafed much in the fame manner as hares, only obferving to cut off the ears clofe to the head. Cut open the vent, and

and ſlit the legs about an inch upon each ſide of the rump. Make the hind legs lie flat, and bring the ends to the fore legs. Put a ſkewer into the hind leg then into the fore leg, and through the body. Bring the head round, and put it on the ſkewer. If you would roaſt two together, truſs them at full length with ſix ſkewers run through them both, ſo that they may be properly faſtened on the ſpit.

To truſs Pheaſants and Partridges.

PICK them very clean, cut a ſlit at the back of the neck, and take out the crop. Looſen the liver and gut next the breaſt with your fore finger, and then cut off the vent, and draw them. Cut off the pinion at the firſt joint, and wipe the inſide with the pinion you have cut off. Beat the breaſt bone flat with a rolling pin, put a ſkewer in the pinion, and bring the middle of the legs cloſe. Then run the ſkewer through the legs, body, and the other pinion; twiſt the head, and put it on the end of the ſkewer, with the bill fronting the breaſt. Put another ſkewer into the ſideſman, put the legs cloſe on each ſide the apron, and then run the ſkewer through all. If you wiſh to make the pheaſant, particularly if it be a cock, make a pleaſing appearance on the table, leave the beautiful feathers on the head, and cover them gently with paper to prevent their being injured by the heat of the fire. You may alſo ſave the long feathers in the tail to ſtick in the rump when roaſted. If they are to be boiled, put the legs in the ſame manner as truſſing a fowl. All ſorts of moor game are truſſed in the ſame way.

To truſs Woodcocks and Snipes.

GREAT care muſt be taken in picking theſe birds, as they are exceedingly tender, eſpecially when they happen not to be quite fresh, and you must therefore be very cautious how you handle them, as even the heat of your hand will sometimes take off the skin, which will totally destroy the beautiful appearance of the bird. Pick them clean, cut the pinions of the first joint, and with the handle of a knife beat the breast-bone flat. Turn the legs close to the thighs, and tie them together at the joints. Put the thighs close to the pinions, put a skewer into the pinions, and run it through the thighs, body, and the other pinion. Skin the head, turn it, take out the eyes, and put the head on the point of the skewer, with the bill close to the breast. Do not forget, that these birds must never be drawn.

To truss Wild Fowl.

PICK them clean, cut off the neck close to the back, and with your middle finger loosen the liver and guts next the breast. Cut off the pinion at the first joint, then cut a slit between the vent and the rump, and draw them clean. Clean them properly with the long feathers on the wing, cut off the nails and turn the feet close to the legs. Put a skewer in the pinion, pull the legs close to the breast, and run the skewer through the legs, body, and the other pinion. Cut off the vent, and put the rump through it. Wild fowls of any kind may be trussed in the same manner.

To truss Pigeons.

HAVING picked them clean, cut off the neck close to the back, take out the crop, cut off the vent, and draw out the guts and gizzard, but leave in the liver, for a pigeon has no gall. If they are to be roasted, cut off the toes, cut a slit in one of the legs, and put the other through it. Draw the leg tight to the pinion, put a skewer through the pinions,

pinions, legs, and body, and with the handle of a knife flatten the breaſt. Clean the gizzard, put it in one of the pinions, and turn the points on the back. If you intend to make a pie of them, you muſt cut the feet off at the joint, turn the legs, and ſtick them in the ſides cloſe to the pinions. If they are to be ſtewed or boiled, you muſt do them in the ſame manner.

To truſs Larks.

PICK them perfectly clean, cut off their heads, and the pinions of the firſt joint. Beat the breaſt-bone flat, then turn the feet cloſe to the legs, and put one into the other. Draw out the gizzard, and run a ſkewer through the middle of the bodies. Tie the ſkewer faſt to the ſpit when you put them down to roaſt. In the ſame manner you may treat wheat-ears, and other ſmall birds.

CHAP. VIII.

The various Methods of dreſſing Poultry.

Pullets à la St. Menehout.

TRUSS the legs in the body, ſlit them all along the back, and ſpread them open on a table. Take out the thigh-bones, and beat them with a rolling-pin. Then ſeaſon them with pepper, ſalt, mace, nutmeg, and ſweet herbs. Take a pound and a half of veal cut into thin ſlices, and put it into a ſtewpan of a convenient ſize, to ſtew the pullets in. Cover it, and ſet it over a ſtove or ſlow fire; and when it begins to ſtick to the pan, ſtir in a little flour, and ſhake the pan about till it be a little brown. Then pour in as much broth as will ſtew the pullets, ſtir it together, put in a little whole pepper, an onion, and a little piece of bacon or ham. Put in your pullets, cover them cloſe, and let them ſtew half an hour. Then take them out, lay them on the gridiron to brown on the inſide, ſtrew them over with the yolk of an egg, ſome bread crumbs, and baſte them with a little butter. Let them be of a fine brown, and boil the gravy till there is about enough for ſauce; ſtrain it, put in a few muſhrooms, and a ſmall piece of butter rolled in flour. Lay the pullets in the diſh, pour in the ſauce, garniſh with lemon, and ſend them to table.

Chickens and Tongues.

BOIL half a dozen ſmall chickens very white, boil and peel as many hogs tongues, boil a cauliflower whole in milk and water, and boil a good deal of ſpinach green. Lay your cauliflour in the middle, the chickens cloſe all round, the tongues round them with the roots outwards, and the ſpinach in little heaps between the tongues. Garniſh with with little pieces of toaſted bacon, and lay a ſmall piece on each tongue.

Chicken in Jelly.

LET ſome jelly ſtand in a bowl till it be cold, and then lay in a cold roaſted chicken, with the breaſt downwards. Fill up the bowl with jelly that is a little warm, but as little warm as poſſible ſo as not to be ſet. When it is quite cold, ſet the bowl in warm water, juſt to looſen the jelly, and then turn it out. Put the chicken into the jelly the day before it is wanted.

To

To force Chickens.

HAVING rather more than half roaſted your chickens, take off the ſkin, then the meat, and chop it ſmall with ſhred parſley and crumbs of bread, pepper, and ſalt, and a little cream. Then put in the meat, and cloſe the ſkin. You may brown it with a ſalamander, and ſerve it up with white ſauce.

To fry cold Chickens.

HAVING quartered your chicken, rub the quarters with the yolk of an egg, and ſtrew on them bread crumbs, pepper, ſalt, nutmeg, grated lemon peel, and chopped parſley. Fry them. Thicken ſome gravy with a little flour, and add chyan, muſhroom powder, or catchup, with a little lemon juice. Pour it into the diſh with the chickens.

To broil Chickens.

HAVING ſlit your chickens down the back, ſeaſon them with pepper and ſalt, and lay them on the gridiron over a clear fire, and at a great diſtance. Let the inſide continue next the fire till it is nearly half done; then turn them, taking care that the fleſhy ſides do not burn, and let them broil till they are of a fine brown. Take ſome good gravy ſauce, with ſome muſhrooms, and garniſh with lemon, the liver broiled, and the gizzard cut, ſlaſhed, and broiled, with pepper, and ſalt. Or you may broil your chicken in the following manner; cut it down the back, pepper and ſalt it, and broil it. Put over it white muſhroom ſauce, or melted butter with pickled muſhrooms.

Chicken pulled.

A chicken that has been rather under roaſted is beſt for this purpoſe. Cut off the legs, rumps, and ſide-bones together, and pull all the white part in little flakes, free from any ſkin. Toſs it up with a little cream, thickened with a piece of butter mixed with flour. Stir it till the butter is melted, and add to it mace finely pounded, ſome whole pepper, ſalt, and a little lemon juice. Put this into a diſh, lay the rump in the middle, the legs at each end, peppered, ſalted, and broiled, and ſend them up to table.

To dreſs Chickens the Scotch Way.

YOU muſt firſt ſinge your chickens, waſh, and then dry them in a clean cloth. Quarter them, and put them into a ſaucepan with juſt water enough to cover them. Put in a little bunch of parſley, and ſome chopped, and a blade or two of mace. Cover them cloſe down. Beat up five or ſix eggs with the whites, and pour them into the liquor as ſoon as it boils. As ſoon as they are enough, take out the bunch of parſley, and ſend them to table with the liquor in a deep diſh. While they are doing, take care to properly ſkin them.

Chickens in Aſpic.

TAKE two ſmall chickens, and put into them the pinions, livers, and gizzards, with a piece of butter, and ſome pepper and ſalt. Cover them with fat bacon, then with paper, run a long ſkewer through them, tie them to a ſpit, and roaſt them. When they are cold, cut them up, put them into the following ſauce, ſhake them round in it, and let them lie a few minutes before they are diſhed. Take as much cullis as you ſhall want for ſauce, heat it with ſmall green onions chopped, or ſhalot, a little tarragon and green mint, pepper and ſalt.

Chickens à la Cavalier.

TAKE as many chickens as you want, and truſs them as for boiling. Marinade them two hours in oil, with ſlices of peeled lemon, parſley, ſhalot, a clove of garlic, thyme, ſalt, and ſpices. Tie them up in ſlices of lard and paper, with as much of the marinade as you can, and broil them on a ſlow fire. As ſoon as they are done, take off the paper, lard, and herbs, and ſerve them with any ſauce you think the moſt agreeable.

To ſtew Chickens.

HAVING half boiled two fine chickens, take them up in a pewter diſh, and cut them up, ſeparating every joint one from the other, and taking out the breaſt bones. If the liquor the chickens produce is not ſufficient, add a few ſpoonfuls of of the water in which they were boiled, and put in a blade of mace, and a little ſalt. Cover it cloſe with another diſh, and ſet it over a ſtove or chafing-diſh of coals. Let it ſtew till the chickens are enough, and then ſend them hot to table. This is a pretty diſh for any ſick perſon, or for a lady who lies in. In the ſame manner you may dreſs partridges, moor-game, or rabbits.

Another Method.

CUT a chicken into pieces, and alſo a carp with the roe, a dozen and a half of ſmall onions, a ſlice of ham, a bundle of parſley, ſome thyme, baſil, and four cloves. Put all together in a ſtew-pan with a piece of butter, and ſimmer it a little over a ſlow fire. Put in ſome broth, a little white wine, flour, pepper, and ſalt. Let it ſtew till the chicken is done, and the ſauce properly reduced. Then take out the herbs and ham, put in a chopped anchovy and a few capers, and place the chicken on the diſh. Skim the ſauce, and ſerve it with the meat, uſing fried bread for garniſh.

Artificial Chickens.

HAVING made a rich forcemeat with chickens, veal, or lamb, ſeaſoned with pepper, ſalt, parſley, a ſhalot, a piece of fat bacon, a little butter, and the yolk of an egg, work it up into the ſhape of chickens, putting the foot of the bird you intend to imitate in the middle, ſo as juſt to appear at the bottom. Roll the forcemeat well in the yolk of an egg, then the crumbs of bread, ſend them to the oven, and bake them of a light brown: but in order that they may not touch each other, put them on tin plates well buttered. You may either ſend them to table dry, or with gravy in the diſh. Pigeons may be imitated the ſame way.

Chickens Chiringrate.

CUT off the feet of your chickens, and beat the breaſt-bone flat with a rolling-pin, but take care not to break the ſkin. Flour them, fry them in butter till they are of a fine brown, and then drain all the fat out of the pan, but leave in the chickens. Lay over your chickens a pound of gravy-beef cut very thin, a piece of beef alſo cut thin, a little mace, two or three cloves, ſome whole pepper, an onion, a ſmall bunch of ſweet herbs, and a piece of carrot. Then pour in a quart of boiling water, cover it cloſe, and let it ſtew for a quarter of an hour. Take out the chickens, and keep them hot. Let the gravy boil till it is quite rich and good, and then ſtrain it off, and put it into your pan again, with two ſpoonfuls of red wine, and a few muſhrooms. Put in your chickens again, and as ſoon as they are warm, take them up, lay them in your diſh, and pour your ſauce

ſauce over them. Garniſh with lemon and a few ſlices of ham broiled, and ſend them to table.

Chickens Feet with Forcemeat.

PROCURE as many chickens feet as you want, and ſtrip off the ſkin by ſcalding them; then tie them up in a bundle, and ſtew them in a braze. Boil them till they be tender, with a little ſeaſoning, and then dry them in a cloth. You may make any kind of forcemeat you pleaſe, and fill up the claws with it. Dip them into ſome beaten eggs, and ſtrew over them crumbs of bread. Do it a ſecond time, preſs it well on, and fry them with plenty of lard. Serve them up without any ſauce in the diſh, with a heap of fried parſley under them. Fowls or chickens feet make a pretty ſecond diſh, and may be done various ways, either in a little brown ſauce, with aſparagus tops, peas, artichoke bottoms, or in a fricaſſee, or with any kind of white ſauce.

A Fowl with its own Gravy.

HAVING truſſed a fowl as for boiling, lard it quite through with bacon, ham, and parſley. Put it in a pan of its own ſize, with a little butter, two or three ſlices of peeled lemon, a bundle of ſweet herbs, three cloves, ſliced onions, carrots, pepper, ſalt, a little broth, and a glaſs of white wine. Stew them ſlowly till they be done, ſkim, and ſtrain the ſauce, and ſerve it with the fowl. You may omit the larding, if you have any objection to it.

Fowls ſtuffed.

BONE your fowls, fill them with the following forcemeat, and roaſt them. Take half a pound of beef ſuet, the meat of a fowl cut very ſmall, and beat them in a mortar, with a pound of veal,

ſome

ſome truffles, morels, and muſhrooms, cut ſmall, a' few ſweet herbs, and parſley ſhred fine, ſome grated nutmeg, pepper, ſalt, and grated lemon-peel. Have ready for ſauce, ſome good gravy, with truffles and morels. You may lard the fowls, if you pleaſe.

A Fowl forced, with a Ragoo of Oyſters.

STUFF the craw of a fowl with a forcemeat, in which are a dozen oyſters. Cover the breaſt of the fowl with ſlices of bacon; then put on a ſheet of paper, and roaſt it. Take ſome cullis or good gravy, put in ſome oyſters with their liquor ſtrained, a little muſhroom powder or catchup, lemon-juice, and thicken it with flour. Add ſome chyan and ſalt, if neceſſary, and boil it up. When the fowl is done, take off the bacon, and ſend it to table with the ſauce in the diſh.

To ſtew a Fowl.

HAVING truſſed a fowl as for boiling, put it into a ſtewpan with a piece of butter, chopped parſley, ſhalot, and muſhrooms. Stew it on a ſlow fire about a quarter of an hour, turning it often. Then put it into another ſtewpan, with ſlices of veal and ham, and all the firſt ſeaſoning. Cover it with ſlices of bacon, ſtew it gently for a quarter of an hour longer, and then add a little whole pepper, and ſome ſalt, a little broth and white wine, and, having finiſhed it on a ſlow fire, ſkim and ſtrain the braze. When it is quite ready, ſqueeze in a lemon, wipe the fowl clean from the fat, and ſerve it up.

To force a Fowl.

PICK a large fowl clean, cut it down the back, take out the entrails, and take the ſkin off whole. Cut the fleſh from the bones, and chop it with half a pint of oyſters, an ounce of beef mar-

marrow, and a little pepper and ſalt, mix it up with cream, lay the meat on the bones, draw the ſkin over it, and ſew up the back. Cut large thin ſlices of bacon, lay them over the breaſt of your fowl, and tie the bacon on with a packthread. It will take one hour roaſting before a moderate fire. Make a good brown gravy ſauce, pour it into your diſh, take the bacon off, lay in your fowl, and ſerve it up, garniſhed with oyſters, muſhrooms, or pickles.

A Fowl with ſharp Sauce.

HAVING truſſed a fowl as for roaſting, make a forcemeat with ſcraped lard, or butter, a little tarragon, chervil, burnet, garden-creſs, pepper, ſalt, and the yolks of two or three eggs. Stuff the fowl with it, and make the ſauce with a little cullis, a few of the above herbs pounded, two anchovies, and a few capers. When it is done, ſtrain it, add a little more cullis, and a little muſtard, pepper, and ſalt. Warm it, but do not boil it, and ſend it up with your roaſted fowl.

To marinade a Fowl.

TAKE a large fowl, and with your finger raiſe the ſkin from the breaſt-bone. Cut a veal ſweatbread very ſmall, a few oyſters, a few muſhrooms, an anchovy, ſome pepper, a little nutmeg, ſome lemon-peel, and a little thyme. Chop all together ſmall, and mix it with the yolk of an egg. Stuff it in between the ſkin and fleſh, but take care that you do not break the ſkin, and then ſtuff what oyſters you pleaſe into the body of the fowl. If you chooſe it, you may lard the breaſt of your fowl with bacon. Paper the breaſt, and roaſt it. Make a good gravy, garniſh with lemon, and ſend it up to table.

A Fowl à la Braze.

HAVING truffed your fowl as for boiling, put over it a layer of fat bacon, cut in pretty thin flices. Wrap it round in beet-leaves, then in a veal caul, and put it into a large faucepan with three pints of water, a glafs of Madeira wine, a bunch of fweet herbs, two or three blades of mace, and half a lemon. Stew it till it is quite tender, then take it up, and fkim off the fat. Thicken your gravy with flour and butter, and ftrain it through a hair fieve. Put to it a pint of oyfters, and a teacupful of thick cream. Keep fhaking your toffing-pan over the fire, and when it has fimmered a little, ferve up your fowl with the bacon, beet-leaves, and caul on, and pour your fauce hot upon it. Garnifh with barberries, or red beet-root.

To hafh Fowls.

HAVING cut your fowl into pieces, put to it fome gravy, with a little cream, fome catchup, or mufhroom powder, grated lemon-peel, fome nutmeg, a few oyfters and their liquor, and a piece of butter rolled in flour. Keep it ftirring till the butter is melted, and then lay fippets round the difh.

Another Method.

CUT up your fowl as for eating, and put it into a toffing-pan, with half a pint of gravy, a teafpoonful of lemon pickle, a little mufhroom catchup, a flice of lemon, and thicken it with flour and butter. Juft before you difh it up, put in a fpoonful of good cream, lay fippets round your difh, and fend it up to table.

To ragoo Fowls.

HAVING procured a large capon, or two pullets, cut off their pinions and feet, and tuck in the legs. Prepare your ragoo thus. Get a veal ſweetbread, or two of lambs, the fat liver of a turkey or fowls, ſome cock's ſtones, three or four muſhrooms, and a thin ſlice or two of lemon. Blanch all well with eggs, cut them into ſmall dice, and ſtew them in a ladle of cullis. You may add to it three or four gizzards, and a few coxcombs, boiled till they are tender. Fill up the bellies of your fowls or capon, and ſow them up at both ends, but make a reſerve of ſome of your ragoo to pour over them. Put them acroſs upon a lark-ſpit, and tie them upon another. Lard them with bacon, cover them with paper, and roaſt them gently, that they may be nice and white. Strew in a little minced parſley, and a little ſhalot. Squeeze in the juice of a lemon or orange, and ſerve them up, with the ragoo under them.

A Fowl Servant-Faſhion.

HAVING truſſed a fowl as for roaſting, make a forcemeat with the liver, chopped parſley, ſhalots, butter, pepper, and ſalt. Stuff the fowl with it, cover it with buttered paper, and roaſt it. When it is three parts done, take off the paper, baſte it with yolks of eggs beaten up with melted butter, and a good quantity of bread crumbs. Finiſh the roaſting, when it will be of a fine yellow colour. Make a ſauce with a little butter, an anchovy chopped, a few capers, a little flour, broth, pepper, ſalt, and a little nutmeg. Thicken the ſauce, and ſerve it up under the fowl.

To dreſs a cold Fowl.

CUT your fowl into quarters, and beat up an egg or two. Grate in a little nutmeg, put in a little

little ſauce, ſome chopped parſley, and a few crumbs of bread. Beat them well together, and dip your fowl into this batter. Then put them into a ſtew-pan in hot dripping, and fry them of a fine light brown. Prepare a little good gravy, thickened with a little flour, and put in a ſpoonful of catchup. Lay the fry in the diſh, and pour the ſauce over it. You may garniſh with lemon, or a few muſhrooms.

Another Method.

HAVING peeled off the ſkin of the fowl, and pulled the fleſh off the bones in as large pieces as you could, drudge it with a little flour, and fry it in butter of a nice brown. Toſs it up in rich gravy, well ſeaſoned, and thicken it with a piece of butter rolled in flour. Squeeze in the juice of a lemon, and ſend it up to table.

To roaſt a Fowl with Cheſnuts.

ROAST ſome cheſnuts very carefully, ſo that they may not be burnt, and then take off the ſkins, and peel them. Cut about a dozen of them ſmall, and bruiſe them in a mortar. Parboil the liver of the fowl, bruiſe it, and cut about a quarter of a pound of ham or bacon, and pound it. Then mix them all together, with a good quantity of chopped parſley, ſweet herbs, ſome mace, pepper, ſalt, and nutmeg. Mix theſe together, put it into your fowl, and roaſt it. The beſt way of doing this is to tie the neck, and hang it up by the legs to roaſt with a ſtring, and then baſte it with butter. For ſauce, you may take the reſt of the cheſnuts peeled and ſkinned, put them into ſome good gravy, with a little white wine, and thicken it with a piece of butter rolled in flour. Then lay your fowl in the diſh, pour in the ſauce, garniſh with lemon, and ſend it up to table.

To

To dress a Turkey.

HAVING boned your turkey, make the following forcemeat. Cut the flesh of a fowl small, and beat a pound of veal in a mortar, with half a pound of beef suet, as much crumbs of bread, some mushrooms, truffles, and morels, cut small; a few sweet herbs and parsley, with some nutmeg, pepper, and salt, a little beaten mace, and some lemon peel. Mix all these together with the yolks of two eggs, put it into your turkey, and roast it. Make your sauce of good gravy, and put into it mushrooms, truffles, and morels. You may lard your turkey, if you please.

To roast a Turkey.

HAVING cut your turkey down the back, and boned it with a sharp knife, with a forcemeat, made as above directed, fill up the places where the bones came out, and fill the body, so that it may look just as it did before it was boned. Then sew up the back, and roast it. Be sure to leave the pinions on. Put good gravy into the dish, and garnish with lemon. You may use oyster sauce, celery sauce, or any other sauce you please.

A Turkey roasted with Cray-fish.

TRUSS a young turkey as for roasting, and make a forcemeat with some fat bacon, suet, and the white of a chicken, all cut as fine as possible, with some fresh mushrooms, finely minced. Mix these ingredients well together, with some pepper, salt, the leaves of sweet herbs picked clean from the stalks, and a little grated nutmeg. Mix them and chop them well together. Then boil some crumbs of bread in rich cream, and put it to the forcemeat. Take the yolks of two new-laid eggs, beat them well, and mix them in the forcemeat.

Stuff

Stuff the crop of the turkey, raiſe the ſkin a little above the breaſt, and put as much of the forcemeat as will go in without tearing it. If any be left, put it into the body. Waſh ſome cray-fiſh, boil them in water, and pick out the tails and bodies. Cut ſome muſhrooms, but not ſmall, ſome truffles in thin ſlices, ſome artichoke bottoms and aſparagus tops, boiled and cut in pieces. Mix all theſe together with the cray-fiſh, put them into a ſaucepan, with a piece of butter, ſome nutmeg cut in ſlices, pepper, ſalt, three or four ſlices of lemon, and a little onion cut ſmall. Let all theſe ſimmer over a ſlow fire, and when it is enough, put in ſome cullis of cray-fiſh to thicken it. Put ſome of this ragoo into the body of the turkey, tie it up at both ends, and ſkewer and ſpit it for roaſting. Strew ſome ſtuffing over it, then ſome ſlices of bacon, and cover all with buttered paper. Let it be thoroughly done before a good fire, and then take off the paper and bacon, pour the reſt of the ragoo over it, and ſend it up to table.

Turkey à la Daube.

HAVING cut the turkey down the back juſt enough to enable you to bone it, without ſpoiling the look of it, ſtuff it with forcemeat made of oyſters chopped fine, crumbs of bread, pepper, ſalt, ſhalots, a very little thyme, parſley, and butter. Fill it as full as you like, ſew it up, and tie it up in a clean cloth. Then boil it till it be white; but be careful not to do it too much. You may ſerve it up with oyſter ſauce, or make a rich gravy of the bones, with a piece of veal, mutton, and bacon, ſeaſoned with pepper, ſalt, ſhalots, and a little bit of mace. Strain it off through a ſieve, and ſtew your turkey in it, after it is half-boiled, juſt half an hour. Diſh it up with the gravy after it is well ſkimmed, ſtrained, and thickened

ened with a few muſhrooms ſtewed white, or ſtewed palates, forcemeat balls, fried oyſters, or ſweet-breads, and pieces of lemon.

Turkies and Chickens.

TAKE a turkey, and as many chickens as you like, ſeaſon them with ſalt, pepper, and cloves, and boil them; and to every quart of broth, put a quarter of a pound of rice, or vermicelli. This is eaten with ſugar and cinnamon, though theſe may both be omitted. This is a Dutch diſh.

A Turkey dreſſed the Italian Way.

HAVING minced the liver of a young turkey very fine, with ſome chopped parſley and ſome freſh muſhrooms, ſome pepper, ſalt, and more than an ounce of butter, mix them well together, and put them into the body of the turkey. Put a piece of butter into a ſtewpan, ſome ſhalots, and pepper and ſalt. When it is hot, put in the turkey, turn it often, that it may be of a fine brown, and lay it to cool. Then lap over it ſome ſlices of bacon, and cover it all over with paper; put it upon a ſpit, and lay it down to roaſt. In the mean time, cut ſome large muſhrooms very fine, with twice the quantity of parſley, and a few green onions cut ſmall. Put half a pint of white wine into a ſaucepan, and, as ſoon as it is hot, put in theſe ingredients; add ſome pepper and ſalt, the juice of a lemon, and two cloves of garlic. Let them boil, and then put in a quarter of a pint of rich gravy, and a ſmall teacupful of oil. Let all boil up once or twice, then take out the garlic, and put in a piece of butter rolled in flour. Lay the turkey in the diſh, and pour the ſauce over it.

To ſtew a Turkey.

BONE a ſmall turkey, and fill it with the following forcemeat. Take half a pound of veal, the meat of two pigeons, and a pickled tongue boiled and peeled. Chop theſe all together, and beat them in a mortar, with ſome marrow from a beef bone, or a pound of ſuet from a loin of veal. Seaſon them with two or three cloves, two or three blades of mace, half a nutmeg dried before the fire and pounded, and ſome ſalt. Mix all theſe well together, fill the turkey, and fry it of a fine brown. Put it into a pot that will juſt hold it, lay ſome ſkewers at the bottom of the pot to keep the turkey from ſticking, and put in a quart of good beef gravy. Cover it cloſe, and let it ſtew for half an hour very gently. Then put in a glaſs of red wine, a ſpoonful of catchup, a large ſpoonful of pickled muſhrooms, ſome truffles, morels, and a piece of butter rolled in flour. Cover it cloſe, and let it ſtew half an hour longer. Fry ſome hollow French rolls; then take ſome oyſters, ſtew them in a ſaucepan with their own liquor, a bit of mace, a little white wine, and a piece of butter rolled in flour. Let them ſtew till pretty thick, and then fill the rolls with them. Lay the turkey in the diſh, pour the ſauce over it, lay the rolls on each ſide, and ſend it up to table.

Another Method.

MAKE a good white forcemeat of veal, and ſtuff it into the craw of a large turkey. Having ſkewered it for boiling, boil it in ſoft water till it be almoſt enough. Then take up your turkey, and put it in a pot, with ſome of the water it was boiled in, to keep it hot. Put ſeven or eight heads of celery, well waſhed and cleaned, into the water the turkey was boiled in. As ſoon as they

they are tender, take them up, and put in your turkey with the breaſt downwards, and ſtew it a quarter of an hour. Then take it up, and thicken your ſauce with butter and flour. Then put in your celery, pour the ſauce and celery hot upon the turkey's breaſt, and ſerve it up.

A Turkey with pickled Pork and Onions.

TAKE twenty-four ſmall white onions, and boil them in broth, with half a pound of pickled pork cut into thin ſlices, a bundle of parſley, ſome green ſhalots, ſome thyme, two cloves, and a little whole pepper and ſalt. As ſoon as they be done, drain them, put them into the turkey, and wrap it in ſlices of bacon, and paper over it, and then roaſt it. Make a ſauce with a piece of butter, a ſlice of ham, two ſhalots, and a few muſhrooms. Let them ſoak a little, and then add two ſpoonfuls of broth, and as much cullis. Simmer it about an hour, ſkim it, and drain it. When the whole is ready, add a ſmall ſpoonful of muſtard, a little pepper and ſalt, and ſerve it up.

A Turkey ſtuffed.

MINCE a pound of beef, and three quarters of a pound of ſuet, very ſmall. Seaſon it with pepper, ſalt, cloves, mace, and ſweet marjoram, and mix them with two or three eggs. Looſen the ſkin all round the turkey, and ſtuff it. Then ſpit it and roaſt it. This is the Hambourg method of dreſſing a turkey.

A Turkey in Jelly.

HAVING boiled a turkey properly white, let it ſtand till it be cold, and in the mean time prepare the following jelly. Skin a fowl and take off all the fat; but do not cut it into pieces, nor break the bones. Take four pounds of a leg of veal

veal, without any fat or ſkin, and put it into a well-tinned ſaucepan. Put to it three quarts of water, and ſet it on a very clear fire till it begins to ſimmer; but be ſure to ſkim it well, and take great care that it does not boil. When it is ſkimmed, keep it juſt ſimmering, and put to it two large blades of mace, half a nutmeg, twenty corns of white pepper, and a little piece of lemon-peel the ſize of a ſix-pence. This will require ſix or ſeven hours doing. When you think the jelly is ſtiff enough, which you will know by taking a little out to cool, be ſure to ſkim off all the fat, if there be any, without diſturbing the meat in the ſaucepan. A quarter of an hour before it is done, throw in a large teaſpoonful of ſalt, and ſqueeze in the juice of half a Seville orange or lemon. When you think it is enough, ſtrain it through a ſieve; but do not pour it all quite off to the bottom, for fear of ſettlings. Lay your turkey into the diſh, in which you intend to ſend it up to table, beat up the whites of ſix eggs to a froth, and put the liquor to it. Then boil it five or ſix minutes, run it through a jelly-bag till it is quite clear, and then pour the liquor over the turkey. Let it ſtand till quite cold, and, having given different colours to the jelly, with a ſpoon ſprinkle it over in what forms you pleaſe, and ſend it to table. If you can get a few naſtertium flowers, and ſtick them in different parts, they will have a pretty effect, but all theſe ornaments depend on taſte and fancy.

To glaze a Turkey.

PICK, draw, and ſinge a young turkey, but do not let it be too ſmall. Lay it a little time over a clear charcoal fire, and turn it often. Prepare a ragoo of ſweetbreads, take off the turkey, ſplit it down the back, fill it with the ragoo, ſew it up, up, and lard it with bacon. At the bottom of a deep ſtewpan put ſome ſlices of ham, veal, and beef. Lay the turkey upon theſe, and ſtrew over it ſome ſweet herbs, cover them cloſe, and let them ſtew over a ſlow fire. When they are enough, take off the ſtewpan, take out the turkey, and then pour into the turkey a little good broth. Stir it about, ſtrain off the liquor, and ſkim off the fat. Set it over the fire again, and boil it to a jelly. Then put in the turkey, and ſet the pan over a gentle fire or ſtove, and it will be ſoon well glazed. Pour ſome eſſence of ham into the diſh, and put in the turkey.

Turkey à la Hâte.

HAVING truſſed a turkey with the legs inwards, flatten it as much as you can, and put it into a ſtewpan, with melted lard, chopped parſley, ſhalots, muſhrooms, and a little garlic. Give it a few turns on the fire, and add the juice of half a lemon to keep it white. Then put it into another ſtewpan, with ſlices of veal, a ſlice of ham, the melted lard, and every thing as uſed before, adding whole pepper and ſalt. Cover it over with ſlices of lard, and ſtew it gently about half an hour over a ſlow fire. Then put to it a glaſs of wine, and a little broth, and finiſh the brazing. Skim and ſtrain the ſauce, add a little cullis to it, reduce it to a proper conſiſtence, and then ſend it up to table.

To haſh a Turkey.

STIR ſome flour rolled in a piece of butter into ſome cream and a little veal gravy, and give it a boil. Cut the turkey into pieces of a moderate ſize, and put it into the ſauce, with ſome grated lemon-peel, white pepper, and mace pounded, a little

little muſhroom powder, or catchup. Simmer them up, and add to it ſome oyſters, if you chooſe.

Another Method.

FIRST take the legs of your turkey, and then cut the thighs into two pieces; cut off the pinions, and alſo the breaſt into pretty large pieces; but remember to take off the ſkin, or it will give a greaſy taſte to the gravy. Put it into a ſtewpan with a pint of gravy, a teaſpoonful of lemon-pickle, a ſlice of the end of a lemon, and a little beaten mace. Boil your turkey ſix or ſeven minutes; but, if you boil it longer, it will make it hard. Put it on your diſh, and thicken your gravy with flour and butter. Mix the yolks of two eggs with a ſpoonful of thick cream, and put it into your gravy. Shake it over the fire till it is quite hot, but do not let it boil. Strain it, and pour it over your turkey. Lay ſippets round it, garniſh with lemon or parſley, and ſend it up to table.

Ducks à la Braze.

HAVING larded your duck, put a ſlice or two of beef at the bottom of your ſtewpan, then the duck, a piece of bacon, and ſome more beef ſliced, a carrot, an onion, a ſlice of lemon, ſome whole pepper, and a bunch of ſweet herbs. Cover this cloſe, and ſet it a few minutes over the fire. Then ſhake in ſome flour, pour in near a quart of beef broth or boiling water, and a little red wine heated. Stew it about half an hour, ſtrain the ſauce, ſkim it, put to it chyan, and more wine, if neceſſary, with a ſhalot, and a little lemon juice. Some add artichoke bottoms boiled and quartered.

Ducks

Ducks à la Mode.

TAKE two ducks, ſlit them down the backs, and bone them carefully. Make a forcemeat of the crumb of a penny loaf, four ounces of fat bacon ſcraped, a little parſley, thyme, lemon-peel, two ſhalots or onions ſhred very fine, with pepper, ſalt, and nutmeg, to your taſte, and two eggs. Stuff your ducks with this, and ſew them up. Then lard them down each ſide of the breaſt with bacon, dredge them well with flour, and put them into a Dutch oven to brown. Then put them into a ſtewpan with three pints of gravy, a glaſs of red wine, a teaſpoonful of lemon-pickle, a large one of walnut and muſhroom catchup, one of browning, and an anchovy, with chyan pepper to your taſte. Stew them gently over a ſlow fire for an hour; and when they are enough, thicken your gravy, and put in a few truffles and morels. Strain your gravy and pour it upon them.

A Duck with green Peas.

PUT a piece of freſh butter into a deep ſtewpan, and ſet over the fire. Singe your duck, flour it, and put it into the pan. Turn it two or three minutes, and then pour out all the fat, but let the duck remain in the pan. Put to it a pint of gravy, a pint of peas, two lettuces cut ſmall, a ſmall bundle of ſweet herbs, and a little pepper and ſalt. Cover them cloſe, and let them ſtew for half an hour, now and then giving the pan a ſhake. When they are nearly done, grate in a little nutmeg, put in a very little beaten mace, and thicken it either with a piece of butter rolled in flour, or the yolk of an egg beat up with two or three ſpoonfuls of cream. Shake it all together for three or four minutes, take out the ſweet herbs, lay the duck in the diſh, and pour the ſauce over it.

Macedonian

Macedonian Ducks.

TAKE four artichoke bottoms, and cut them into pieces. Put them into boiling water, with about a pint of garden beans firſt ſcalded and huſked. Boil theſe together till almoſt done, and then drain them. Put the whole into the ſtewpan, with a good piece of butter, chopped muſhrooms, a little winter ſavory, parſley, and ſhalots, all finely chopped. Add a little flour, two ſpoonfuls of veal gravy, and a glaſs of white wine. Simmer them ſlowly till all is well done, and the ſauce reduced to a proper conſiſtence. Laſt of all, add a little cullis, a ſqueeze of a lemon, and a little pepper and ſalt. Serve this ragoo under two ducks quartered, and brazed in a well-ſeaſoned braze, with ſlices of veal and bacon.

To haſh Ducks.

HAVING roaſted two ducks till they be nearly three parts done, take them up, and let them ſtand to cool. Then cut the breaſt into thin ſlices, and take care of the gravy. The legs will ſerve for another diſh, which you may dreſs by wrapping them in a caul with a good forcemeat, and ſerve them up with cullis ſauce. For the fillets, cut cucumbers, and marinade them about an hour, with a little vinegar, ſalt, and an onion ſliced. Then take out the onion, ſqueeze the cucumbers in a cloth, and put them into a ſtewpan with a bit of butter, a ſlice of ham, a little broth, flour, and veal gravy. Boil it ſlowly, ſkim it well, take out the ham, and put the meat to it to warm, without boiling. You may do the ſame with chopped truffles, or muſhrooms, or any thing elſe in ſeaſon. You may haſh a cold roaſted duck in this manner.

To

To boil Ducks the French Way.

TAKE two dozen of roafted chefnuts, and put them into a pint of rich beef gravy, with a few leaves of thyme, two fmall onions, a little whole pepper, and a race of ginger. Then take a fine tame duck, lard it, and half roaft it. Put it into the gravy, let it ftew ten minutes, and put in a quarter of a pint of red wine. When the duck is enough, take it out, and boil up the gravy to a proper thicknefs. Skim it very clean from fat, lay the duck in the difh, pour the fauce over it, garnifh with lemon, and fend it up to table.

Another French Method.

HAVING larded your ducks, and half roafted them, take them off the fpit, and put them into a large earthen pipkin, with half a pint of red wine, a pint of good gravy, fome chefnuts roafted and peeled, half a pint of large oyfters, the liquor ftrained and the beards taken off, two or three little onions minced fmall, a very little ftripped thyme, mace, pepper, and a little ginger finely beaten, with the cruft of a French roll grated. Cover it clofe, and let it ftew half an hour over a flow fire. When they are enough, take them up, and pour the fauce over them.

Ducklings rolled.

CUT a pretty large duckling into two, bone it thoroughly, and lay on a forcemeat made with the breafts of roafted poultry. Roll it up, tie flices of bacon round it, and boil it in a little broth, with a glafs of white wine, a bundle of fweet herbs, and two cloves. When it is done, gently fqueeze out the fat, and wipe the duck clean. Send it up to table with what fauce you like beft.

To

To drefs Wild Ducks.

HAVING half roafted your duck, lay it in a difh, and carve it, but leave the joints hanging together. Throw a little pepper and falt, and fqueeze the juice of a lemon over it. Turn it on the breaft, and prefs it hard with a plate, and add to its own gravy two or three fpoonfuls of good made gravy. Cover it clofe with another difh, and fet it over a ftove ten minutes. Then fend it to table hot in the difh it was done in, and garnifh with lemon.

Goofe à la Mode.

HAVING picked, cleaned, fkinned, and boned your goofe nicely, take off the fat, and boil and peel a dried tongue. Treat a fowl in the fame manner as the goofe, feafon it with pepper, falt, and beaten mace, and roll it round the tongue. Seafon the goofe in the fame manner, and put both tongue and fowl into the goofe. Put it into a little pot that will juft hold it, with two quarts of beef gravy, a bundle of fweet herbs, and an onion. Put fome flices of ham, or good bacon, between the fowl and goofe; then cover it clofe, and let it ftew very flowly for an hour over the fire. Then take up your goofe, and fkim off all the fat. Strain it, and put in a glafs of red wine, two fpoonfuls of catchup, a veal fweetbread cut fmall, fome truffles, mufhrooms, and morels, a piece of butter rolled in flour, and, if wanted, fome pepper and falt. Put in the goofe again, cover it clofe, and let it ftew half an hour longer. Then take it up, pour the ragoo over it, and garnifh with lemon. You muft remember to fave the bones of the goofe and fowl, and put them into the gravy when it is firft fet on. It will be an improvement, if you roll fome beef marrow between the tongue and the

fowl,

fowl, and between the fowl and the goofe, as it will make them mellow, and eat the finer. It may not be improper here to obferve, that the beft method to bone a goofe or fowl of any fort is to begin at the breaft, and take out all the bones without cutting the back; for when it is fewed up, and you come to ftew it, it generally burfts in the back, whereby the fhape of it is fpoiled.

To fmoke a Goofe.

TAKE off all the fat of a large ftubble goofe, and dry it well infide and out with a cloth. Wafh it all over with vinegar, and then rub it over with common falt, faltpetre, and a quarter of a pound of coarfe fugar. Rub the falts well in, and let it lie a fortnight, then drain it well, few it up in a cloth, and let it hang in the chimney for a month. You may then boil it, and ferve it up with onion fauce, greens, &c.

To ragoo a Goofe.

HAVING beat the breaft down with a cleaver, prefs it down with your hand, fkin it, and dip it into fcalding water. As foon as it is cold, lard it with bacon, and feafon it with pepper, falt, and a little beaten mace. Then flour it all over, take a pound of good beef fuet cut fmall, and put it into a deep ftewpan. As foon as it is melted put in your goofe, and let it be brown on both fides. Then put in a quart of boiling gravy, an onion or two, a bundle of fweet herbs, fome whole pepper, and a few cloves. Cover it clofe, and let it ftew foftly till it is tender. An hour will do it, if it be fmall, and an hour and half, if large. In the mean time, boil fome turnips almoft enough, fome carrots and onions quite enough. Cut your turnips and carrots the fame as for a harrico of mutton, and put them into a faucepan with half a pint of good beef gravy,

gravy, a little pepper and ſalt, a piece of butter rolled in flour, and ſtew them all together a quarter of an hour. Take the gooſe and well drain it, then lay it in the diſh, and pour the ragoo over it.

To marinade a Gooſe.

TAKE all the bones out of your gooſe, and make the following forcemeat. Take ten or twelve ſage leaves, two large onions, and two or three large ſharp apples, ſhred very fine. Mix theſe with the crumb of a penny loaf, four ounces of beef marrow, a glaſs of red wine, half a nutmeg grated, pepper, ſalt, and a little lemon-peel ſhred ſmall. Make this into a light ſtuffing, with the yolks of four eggs, about an hour before you want it, and then put it into the gooſe. Fry the gooſe of a good brown, then put it into a deep ſtewpan, with two quarts of good gravy, and cover it cloſe. Having let it ſtew two hours, take it out, and ſkim off the fat. Add to it a large ſpoonful of lemon pickle, one of browning, one of red wine, an anchovy ſhred fine, beaten mace, pepper, and ſalt to your palate. Thicken it with flour and butter, give it a boil, diſh up your gooſe, ſtrain your gravy, and pour it over it.

To ſtew Giblets.

HAVING cut the neck into four pieces, and pinions in two, ſlice the gizzard, clean it well, and ſtew them in two quarts of water, or mutton broth, with a handful of ſweet herbs, an anchovy, a few pepper corns, three or four cloves, a ſpoonful of catchup, and an onion. As ſoon as the giblets are tender, put in a ſpoonful of good cream, and thicken it with flour and butter. Lay ſippets round a ſoup-diſh, pour in the whole, after ſtraining it, and ſend them up to table.

Another Method.

SCALD and clean your giblets well, cut off the bill, divide the head, ſkin the feet, and ſtew all in juſt water enough for ſauce. Put in a ſprig of thyme, ſome whole black pepper, and an onion. Let them do till they are tender, and then ſtrain the ſauce. If the ſauce is not thick enough, add a little catchup and flour. Lay ſippets round the diſh, pour in your giblets and ſauce, and ſerve them up.

Giblets à la Turtle.

CLEAN three pair of giblets well, and cut them as before directed. Put them into a ſtewpan with four pounds of ſcrag of veal, and two pounds of lean beef, covered with water. When they boil, ſkim them very clean. Then put in ſix cloves, four blades of mace, eight corns of allſpice, beat very fine; ſome baſil, ſweet marjoram, winter ſavory, and a little thyme, chopped very fine; three onions, two turnips, and one carrot. Stew them all tender, then ſtrain them through a ſieve, and waſh them clean out of the herbs in ſome warm water. Put a piece of butter into your ſtewpan, melt it, and put in as much flour as will thicken it. Stir it till it is ſmooth, then put in your liquor, and keep ſtirring it all the time, otherwiſe it will go into lumps, and ſhould that happen, you muſt ſtrain it through a ſieve. Then put in a pint of Madeira wine, ſome pepper and ſalt, and a little chyan pepper. Stew it ten minutes, and then put in your giblets. Add the juice of a lemon, ſtew them a quarter of an hour, and ſerve them up in a tureen. Never put your livers in at firſt, but boil them in a ſaucepan of water by themſelves. If you chooſe it, you may put egg-balls into your diſh, made thus. Beat the

the yolks of ſix eggs boiled hard, in a mortar; throw in a ſpoonful of flour, and the yolk of a raw egg, and beat them together till they are ſmooth. Then roll them in little balls, ſcald them in boiling water, and put them in juſt before you ſerve up the giblets.

Pigeons en Compote.

SKEWER ſix young pigeons as for boiling. Grate the crumb of a penny loaf, take half a pound of fat bacon, ſhred ſome ſweet herbs and parſley fine, two ſhalots or a little onion, a little lemon peel, and a little grated nutmeg; ſeaſon it with pepper and ſalt, and mix it up with the yolks of two eggs. Put this forcemeat into the craws and bellies of your pigeons, lard them down the breaſt, and fry them brown with a little butter. Then put them into a ſtewpan, with a pint of ſtrong brown gravy, a gill of white wine, and ſtew them three quarters of an hour. Thicken it with a little butter rolled in flour, ſeaſon it with ſalt and chyan pepper, put the pigeons in the diſh, and ſtrain the gravy over them. Send them up hot to table, with ſome forcemeat balls laid round them.

Pigeons à la Souſſel.

HAVING boned four pigeons, make a forcemeat as above directed. Stuff them, and put them into a ſtewpan with a pint of veal gravy. Stew them very gently half an hour, and then take them out. Wrap them all round with a veal forcemeat, rub them over with the yolk of an egg, and fry them in good dripping of a nice brown. Take the gravy they were ſtewed in, ſkim off the fat, thicken it with a little butter rolled in flour, the yolk of an egg, and a gill of cream beat up. Seaſon it with pepper and ſalt, mix all together, and keep it ſtirring one way till it is ſmooth. Strain it into

into your diſh, and put on the pigeons. Garniſh with plenty of criſped parſley.

Pigeons à la Duxelle.

TAKE four or five pigeons, cut off their feet and pinions, and ſplit them down the breaſt; then take out the livers, and flatten them with a cleaver. Make a hot marinade of ſome ſcraped bacon, ſeaſoned with a muſhroom or two, green onions, pepper, ſalt, thyme, parſley, and a little nutmeg. Fry all for a few minutes, and let the pigeons be heated through in it, and let them remain till you put them upon your gridiron. Take a thin ſlice of ham for each pigeon, and put them with the ham always at top; that is, when you turn your pigeons, turn your ham upon them. For your ſauce, take a ladle of gravy, ſome ſweet baſil, a little thyme, parſley, and ſhalot, minced very fine, and a few ſlices of muſhrooms, boiled all together a few minutes. Diſh them up with their breaſt downwards, let your ham continue upon them, and pour your ſauce over them, with the juice of an orange or lemon.

Pigeons Surtout.

FORCE your pigeons, lay a ſlice of bacon on their breaſts, and a ſlice of veal beaten with the back of a knife, and ſeaſoned with mace, pepper, and ſalt. Faſten it on with two ſmall ſkewers, which will be better than tying it. Roaſt them on a fine bird ſpit, baſte them with a piece of butter, then with the yolk of an egg, and afterwards with ſome crumbs of bread, a little nutmeg, and ſweet herbs. When they are enough, lay them in your diſh, and pour on them ſome good gravy, ſeaſoned with truffles, morels, and muſhrooms.

Pigeons

Pigeons in Savoury Jelly.

HAVING roaſted your pigeons with the heads and feet on, put a ſprig of myrtle in their bills. Make the ſame kind of jelly as directed for chickens, and when it is ſet, lay in the pigeons with their breaſts downwards. Fill up your bowl with the jelly, and turn it out.

Pigeons à la Daube.

STUFF the bellies of your pigeons with the following forcemeat. Take a pound of veal, a pound of beef ſuet, and beat them in a mortar; take an equal quantity of bread crumbs, ſome pepper, ſalt, nutmeg, beaten mace, a little lemon-peel cut ſmall, ſome parſley cut ſmall, and a very little thyme ſtripped. Mix all together with the yolks of two eggs, fill the pigeons, and flat their breaſts down. Then flour them, and fry them a little brown in freſh butter. Then pour the fat clean out of the pan, and put the gravy to the pigeons. Cover them cloſe, and let them ſtew a quarter of an hour, or till you think they are quite enough. In the mean time make the following ſauce. Put a layer of bacon in a large ſaucepan, then a layer of veal, a layer of coarſe beef, and a pound of veal cut very thin, a piece of carrot, a bundle of ſweet herbs, an onion, ſome black and white pepper, a blade or two of mace, and four or five cloves. Cover the ſaucepan cloſe, ſet it over a ſlow fire, and draw it till it is brown, to make the gravy of a fine light brown. Then put in a quart of boiling water, and let it ſtew till the gravy is quite rich and good. Then ſtrain it off, and ſkim off all the fat. When your pigeons are enough, take them up, lay them in your diſh, and pour this ſauce over them. On each pigeon lay a bay-leaf, and a ſlice of bacon on each leaf.

Pigeons à la Royale.

TAKE any number of pigeons you pleaſe that are of an equal ſize, put a peeled truffle in each, and give them a fry in butter, with chopped muſhrooms, parſley, a ſlice of ham, and ſome pepper and ſalt. Put them into a ſaucepan to braze, with a few ſlices of veal firſt ſcalded, and the firſt ſeaſoning over the pigeons. Cover them with thin ſlices of bacon, and put a ſheet of white paper over the whole. Stop the pan cloſe, and let them ſimmer over a ſlow fire till they are quite tender. Take out the pigeons, and clean them from the fat. Strain the braze, and boil it a moment, in order to ſkim it very clean. When it is ready, ſqueeze in a lemon, and pour the ſauce over the pigeons.

Pigeons in Diſguiſe.

HAVING drawn and truſſed your pigeons, ſeaſon them with pepper and ſalt. Make a nice puff paſte, and roll each pigeon in a piece of it. Tie them in a cloth, and take care the paſte does not break. Then boil them an hour and a half in plenty of water; but take care, when you untie them, that they do not break. Put them into a diſh, and pour to them a little good gravy.

Pigeons in Pimlico.

TAKE ſome fat and lean ham or bacon, ſome muſhrooms, truffles, parſley, and ſweet herbs, and the livers of the pigeons. Seaſon with beaten mace, pepper, and ſalt; and beat all this together with two raw eggs, and put it into their bellies. Roll them all in a thin ſlice of veal, and put over them a thin ſlice of bacon. Wrap them up in white paper, and roaſt them on a ſmall ſpit. In the mean time make a ragoo of truffles and muſhrooms chopped ſmall, with ſome parſley alſo cut ſmall. Put to it it half a pint of good veal gravy, and thicken it with a piece of butter rolled in flour. Bafte your pigeons, and about an hour will do them. When they are enough, lay them in your difh, take off the paper, and pour your fauce over them. You may garnifh with patties, which may be thus made. Take veal and cold ham, and an equal quantity of beef fuet, fome mufhrooms, fweet herbs, and fpice. Chop them fmall, fet them on the fire, and moiften them with milk or cream. Then make a little puff-pafte, roll it, and make little patties about an inch deep, and two inches long. Fill them with the above ingredients, cover them clofe, and bake them, and lay fix of them round the difh.

Pigeons à la Charmante.

HAVING fcalded five or fix fmall pigeons, braze them with a few flices of lard and peeled lemon, pepper, falt, a bundle of fweet herbs, and broth. Lard three or four fweetbreads, and put them into a ftewpan by themfelves, with fome broth, a few thin flices of veal fillet, a bundle of fweet herbs, and two cloves. Braze them flowly, and when they are done, ftrain and fkim the braze, and reduce it to a glaze, to rub over the larded fide of the fweetbreads. Strain it again through a fieve, and add a little more pepper and falt, if neceffary, and a good fqueeze of lemon. Put the pigeons and fweetbreads on the difh, and pour the fauce over the pigeons, but not over the fweetbreads, as that would fpoil the colour of the glaze.

A Pupton of Pigeons.

ROLL out a favoury forcemeat like a pafte, and put it into a butter-difh. Put a layer of very thin bacon, fquab pigeons, fliced fweetbreads, afparagus tops, mufhrooms, cokfcombs, a palate boiled tender and cut into pieces, and the yolks of hard

hard eggs. Make another forcemeat, and lay it over like a pie. Bake it, and when it is enough, turn it into a diſh, pour gravy round it, and ſend it up to table.

To broil Pigeons.

IN order to broil pigeons nicely, you muſt take care that your fire is clear. Shred ſome parſley fine, take a piece of butter as big as a walnut, with a little pepper and ſalt, and put it into their bellies. Tie them at both ends, and broil them. Or, having firſt ſeaſoned them with pepper and ſalt, you may ſplit and broil them. Put a little parſley and butter into the diſh, and ſend them up to table.

To ſtew Pigeons.

SEASON your pigeons with pepper and ſalt, a few cloves and mace, and ſome ſweet herbs. Wrap this ſeaſoning up in a piece of butter, and put it into their bellies. Then tie up the neck and vent, and half roaſt them. Put them into a ſtewpan, with a quart of good gravy, a little white wine, a few pepper-corns, three or four blades of mace, a bit of lemon, a bunch of ſweet herbs, and a ſmall onion. Stew them gently, till they are enough. Then take out the pigeons, and ſtrain the liquor through a ſieve. Skim it, and thicken it in your ſtewpan, and put in the pigeons with ſome pickled muſhrooms and oyſters. Stew it five minutes, put the pigeons in a diſh, and pour the ſauce over them.

Pigeons in Fricandeau.

HAVING picked, drawn, and waſhed your pigeons very clean, ſtuff the craws, and lard them down the ſides of the breaſt. Fry them of a fine brown in butter, and then put them into a toſſing-pan with a quart of gravy. Stew them till they are tender, then take off the fat, and put in a tea-ſpoonful of lemon pickle, a large ſpoonful of browning, the ſame of walnut catchup, a little chyan, and ſalt. Thicken your gravy, and add an ounce of morels, and four yolks of hard eggs. Lay the pigeons in your diſh, put the morels and eggs round them, and ſtrain your ſauce over them. Send it up to table, garniſhed with barberries and lemon peel.

Pigeons à la Braize.

TAKE as many large pigeons as you chooſe, and pick, draw, and truſs them. Lay ſome ſlices of bacon, veal, and onions, at the bottom of a ſtewpan; and ſeaſon the pigeons with pepper, ſalt, ſome ſpice finely beaten, and ſome ſweet herbs. Lay them into the ſtewpan, then lay upon them ſome more ſlices of veal and bacon, and let them ſtew very gently over a ſtove, the top of the ſtewpan being put down very cloſe. When they are ſtewed, make a ragoo with veal ſweetbreads, truffles, morels, and champignons. The ſweetbreads muſt be blanched, and put into a ſtewpan with a ladle full of gravy, another of cullis, the truffles, morels, &c. Let them all ſtew together with the pigeons, and when they are enough, put them into a diſh, and pour the ragoo over them.

To bake Pigeons.

SEASON your pigeons with pepper and ſalt, put a piece of butter into each, and mix three eggs, two ſpoonfuls of flour, half a pint of milk, and a little ſalt. Pour this over them, and then ſend them to the oven.

Pigeons in a Hole.

HAVING picked, drawn, and waſhed ſome young pigeons, ſtick their legs in their bellies as you do for boiling, and ſeaſon them with pepper, ſalt,

ſalt, and beaten mace. Put a lump of butter, of the ſize of a walnut, into the belly of each pigeon, and lay them in a pie diſh. Pour over them a batter made of three eggs, two ſpoonfuls of flour, and half a pint of good milk. Bake them in a moderate oven, and ſend them up in the ſame diſh to table.

Pigeons au Soleil.

TAKE half a pound of veal, a quarter of a pound of mutton, and two ounces of beef. Beat them in a mortar with ſome pepper, ſalt, and mace, till they are a paſte. Then take the yolks of three or four eggs, beat them up well, and put them into a plate. Mix a quarter of a pound of grated bread, and two ounces of flour, and put them into another plate. Put on a ſtewpan with a little rich beef gravy, tie up three or four cloves in a bit of muſlin, and put them into the gravy. Put in the pigeons, let them ſtew till they are almoſt enough, then take them up, and ſet them before the fire to keep warm. Then put ſome good beef dripping into a frying-pan, enough to cover them. When it boils, take the pigeons, one at a time, roll them in the meat that was beaten, and then in the yolks of eggs, till they are quite wet. Strew over them the bread and flour, put them into the boiling dripping, and when they are of a fine brown, take them out, and diſh them up.

Boiled Pigeons and Bacon.

WASH and clean ſix young pigeons, turn their legs under their wings, and boil them twenty minutes in milk and water by themſelves. In the mean time boil a ſquare piece of bacon, and take off the ſkin and brown it. Lay the bacon in the middle of the diſh, and the pigeons round it with lumps of ſtewed ſpinach. Pour plain melted butter over them, put parſley and butter in a boat, and ſend them up to table

To boil Pigeons with Rice.

HAVING ſtuffed ſix pigeons with parſley, pepper, and ſalt, rolled in a very little piece of butter, put them into a quart of mutton broth, with a little beaten mace, a bundle of ſweet herbs, and an onion. Cover them cloſe, and let them boil full a quarter of an hour. Then take out the onion and ſweet herbs, and take a good piece of butter rolled in flour; put it in, and give it a ſhake. Seaſon it with ſalt, if it wants it; and, in the mean time, boil half a pound of rice tender in milk. When it begins to be thick, taking great care that it does not burn, take the yolks of two or three eggs, beat up with two or three ſpoonfuls of cream, and a little nutmeg. Stir it together till it is quite thick, and then take up the pigeons, and lay them in a diſh. Pour the gravy to the rice, ſtir it all together, and pour it over the pigeons. Garniſh with hard eggs cut into quarters, and ſerve it up.

Pigeons tranſmogrified.

TAKE ſix ſmall young pigeons, and pick and clean them; but do not cut off their heads. Take off the pinions, and boil them ten minutes in water. Then cut off the ends of ſix large cucumbers, and ſcrape out the ſeeds. Put in your pigeons, and ſtick a bunch of barberries in their bills. Then put them into a toſſing-pan with a pint of veal gravy, a little anchovy, a glaſs of red wine, a ſpoonful of browning, a ſmall ſlice of lemon, and chyan and ſalt to your taſte. Stew them ſeven minutes, take them out, and thicken your gravy with

with a little butter rolled in flour. Boil it up, and ſtrain it over your pigeons.

To roaſt a Rabbit Hare Faſhion.

LARD your rabbit with bacon, and then roaſt it as you do a hare. Make a gravy ſauce; but, if you do not lard it, make the following white ſauce. Take a little veal broth, boil it up with a little flour and butter to thicken it, and add a gill of cream. Keep it ſtirring one way till it is ſmooth, and then put it into a boat.

Rabbits pulled.

HAVING half boiled your rabbits, with an onion, a little whole pepper, a bunch of ſweet herbs, and a lemon-peel, pull the fleſh into flakes, and put to it a little of the liquor, a piece of butter mixed with flour, pepper, ſalt, nutmeg, chopped parſley, and the liver boiled and bruiſed. Boil this up, and keep ſhaking it round.

To florendine Rabbits.

TAKE three young rabbits and ſkin them, but leave on the ears. Waſh and dry them with a cloth. Take out the bones carefully, leaving the head whole, and then lay them flat. Make a forcemeat of a quarter of pound of bacon ſcraped, which anſwers the purpoſe much better than ſuet, as it makes the rabbits look whiter, and eat tenderer. Add to the bacon the crumb of a penny-loaf, a little lemon-thyme, or lemon-peel ſhred fine, parſley chopped ſmall, nutmeg, chyan, and ſalt, to your taſte. Mix them up together with an egg, and ſpread it over the rabbits. Roll them up to the head, ſkewer them ſtraight, and cloſe the ends, to prevent the forcemeat coming out. Skewer the ears back, and tie them in ſeparate cloths, and boil them half an hour. When you

diſh

dish them up, take out the jaw-bones, and stick them in the eyes for ears. Put round them forcemeat balls and mushrooms. In the mean time, prepare a white sauce made of veal gravy, a little anchovy, the juice of half a lemon, or a teaspoonful of lemon pickle. Strain it, and take a quarter of a pound of butter rolled in flour, so as to make the sauce pretty thick. Keep stirring it while the flour is dissolving, and beat the yolk of an egg. Put to it some thick cream, nutmeg, and salt. Mix it with the gravy, and let it simmer a little over the fire; but do not let it boil, as that will curdle the cream. Pour it over the rabbits, and send it up to table.

Rabbits en Casserole.

DIVIDE a couple of rabbits into quarters, flour them, if you do not lard them, and fry them in butter. Put them into a stewpan, with some good gravy, and a glass of white wine. Season them with pepper and salt, and a bunch of sweet herbs. Cover them down close, and let them stew till tender. Then take up the rabbits, strain the sauce, thicken it with flour and butter, and pour it over the rabbits.

Portuguese Rabbits.

TRUSS your rabbits chicken fashion, the heads cut off, and the rabbit turned with the back upwards, two of the legs stripped to the claw-end, and so trussed with two skewers. Lard them, and roast them, and put what sauce you please to them.

To make a Chicken Pie.

HAVING covered the bottom of your dish with a puffpaste, upon that, round the sides, lay a thin layer of forcemeat. Cut two small chickens into

into pieces, and feafon them high with pepper and falt. Put fome of the pieces into the difh, then a fweetbread or two cut into pieces, and well feafoned; a few truffles and morels, fome artichoke bottoms quartered, yolks of eggs boiled hard, chopped a little, and ftrewed over the top. Then put in a little water, and cover the pie. When it comes from the oven, pour in a rich gravy, thickened with a little flour and butter. You may add frefh mufhrooms, afparagus tops, and cockfcombs, if you wifh to make your pie richer.

Another Method.

SEASON your chickens with pepper, falt, and mace. Put a piece of butter into each of them, and lay them in the difh with their breafts upwards. Lay a thin flice of bacon over them, which will give them an agreeable flavour. Then put in a pint of ftrong gravy, and make a good puff-pafte. Put on the lid, and bake it in a moderately heated oven.

Duck Pie.

HAVING fcalded two ducks, and made them very clean, cut off the feet, pinions, necks, and heads. Take out the gizzards, livers, and hearts, pick all clean, and fcald them. Pick out the fat of the infide, lay a good puff-pafte cruft all over the difh, feafon the ducks, both infide and out, with pepper and falt, and lay them in the difh, with the giblets at each end, properly feafoned. Put in as much water as will nearly fill the pie, lay on the cruft, and let it be well baked.

A Goofe Pie.

HAVING quartered your goofe, feafon it well with pepper and falt, and lay it in a raifed cruft. Cut half a pound of butter into pieces, and

and put it in different places on the top. Then lay on the cruſt, and ſend it to a moderately heated oven to bake.

Another Method.

BONE a gooſe and a fowl, and ſeaſon them well. Put forcemeat into the fowl, and then put the fowl into the gooſe. Lay theſe in a raiſed cruſt, and fill the corners with a little forcemeat. Put half a pound of butter cut into pieces on the top, cover it, ſend it to the oven, and let it be well baked. This pie may be eaten either hot or cold.

A Giblet Pie.

CLEAN two pair of giblets well, and put all but the livers into a ſaucepan, with two quarts of water, twenty corns of whole pepper, three blades of mace, a bundle of ſweet herbs, and a large onion. Cover them cloſe, and let them ſtew very gently till they be tender. Cover your diſh with a good cruſt; lay at the bottom a fine rump ſteak, ſeaſoned with pepper and ſalt. Put in your giblets, with the livers, and ſtrain the liquor they were ſtewed in. Then ſeaſon it with ſalt, and pour it into your pie. Put on the lid, and bake it half an hour.

A Pigeon Pie.

HAVING picked and cleaned your pigeons very nicely, and ſeaſoned them with pepper and ſalt, put a large piece of butter, with pepper and ſalt, into each of their bellies. Then cover your diſh with a puff-paſte cruſt, lay in your pigeons, and put between them the necks, gizzards, livers, pinions, and hearts, with the yolk of a hard egg, and a beef ſteak in the middle. Put

as

as much water as will nearly fill the diſh, lay on the top-cruſt, and bake it well.

A Rabbit Pie.

QUARTER a couple of young rabbits; take a quarter of a pound of bacon, and pound it in a marble mortar, with the livers, ſome pepper, ſalt, a little mace, ſome parſley cut ſmall, ſome chives, and a few leaves of ſweet baſil. When theſe are all finely beaten, make the paſte, and cover the bottom of the pie with the ſeaſoning. Then put in the rabbits, pound more bacon in a mortar, and with it ſome freſh butter. Cover the rabbits with this, and lay over it ſome thin ſlices of bacon. Put on the lid, and ſend it to the oven. It will take two hours baking. When it is done, remove the lid, take out the bacon, and ſcum off the fat. If there is not gravy enough in the pie, pour in ſome rich mutton or veal gravy boiling hot.

Another Method.

TAKE two rabbits, cut them into pieces, alſo cut ſmall two pounds of fat pork, and ſeaſon both with pepper and ſalt to your taſte. Then make a good puff-paſte cruſt, cover your diſh with it, and lay in your rabbits. Mix the pork with them; but leave out the livers of the rabbits, parboil them, and beat them in a mortar, with the ſame quantity of fat bacon, a little ſweet herbs, and ſome oyſters. Seaſon with pepper, ſalt, and nutmug, mix it up with the yolk of an egg, and make it into little balls. Scatter them about your pie, with ſome artichoke bottoms cut in dice, and ſome cockſcombs, if you have them. Grate a ſmall nutmeg over the meat, then pour in half a pint of red wine, and half pint of water. Cloſe your pie, and bake it an hour and half in a quick

quick but not too fierce oven. This is the method of making rabbit pies in the county of Salop.

CHAP. IX.

The different Methods of dreſſing Game, ſmall Birds, &c.

To roaſt a Hare.

HAVING caſed your hare, and properly truſſed it for dreſſing, make a ſtuffing of a large ſlice of bread crumbled very fine; put to it a quarter of a pound of beef marrow, or ſuet, the like quantity of butter, the liver boiled and ſhred fine, a ſprig or two of winter ſavory, a bit of lemon-peel, an anchovy, a little chyan pepper, and half a nutmeg grated. Mix theſe well together with a glaſs of red wine and two eggs, put it into the belly of the hare, and ſew it up. When you have ſpitted, and put it down to roaſt, put into your dripping-pan a quart of milk, and keep baſting your hare with it till there is little left. When it is nearly done, dredge it with flour, and baſte it with butter till it is properly frothed. If it is a ſmall hare, it will take about an hour and half; and, if a large one, two hours. When it is done, put it into your diſh, and ſerve it up with plenty of good rich gravy, and ſome currant jelly warmed in a cup. Or, you may take a pint of red wine, and put into it a quarter of a pound of ſugar; ſet it over a ſlow fire, and let it ſimmer for a quarter of an hour; then take it off, and pour it into a baſon or ſauceboat.

Ano-

Another Method of dreſſing a Hare.

CASE your hare, and cut it into two juſt below the ribs. Cut the fore quarters into pieces, and put them into a ſtewpan, with a blade or two of mace, an onion ſtuck with cloves, ſome whole pepper, an anchovy, and a bunch of ſweet herbs. Cover them with water, and let them ſtew gently. Make a pudding, and put it into the belly of the other part; lard and roaſt it, and flour, and baſte it well with butter or ſmall beer. When the ſtew is tender, take it out with a fork into a diſh, and ſtrain off the liquor. Put into it a glaſs of red wine, a ſpoonful of good catchup, and a piece of butter rolled in flour. Shake all together over the fire till it is of a good thickneſs. Then take up the roaſted hare, lay it in the middle of the diſh, with the ſtew round, and ſauce poured over it. Put ſome good gravy into a boat, and ſend it to table.

To ſtew a Hare.

PAUNCH and caſe your hare, cut it as for eating, and put it into a large ſaucepan, with three pints of beef gravy, a pint of red wine, a large onion ſtuck with cloves, a bundle of winter ſavory, a ſlice of horſe-radiſh, two blades of beaten mace, an anchovy, a ſpoonful of walnut catchup, one of browning, half a lemon, and chyan and ſalt to your taſte. Put on a cloſe cover, ſet it over a gentle fire, and ſtew it for two hours. Then take it up into a ſoup diſh, and thicken your gravy with a lump of butter rolled in flour. Boil it a little, and ſtrain it over your hare. Garniſh with lemon cut like ſtraws.

To haſh a Hare.

CUT your hare into ſmall pieces, and if you have any of the pudding left, rub it ſmall, and put

to

to it a gill of red wine, the ſame quantity of water, half an anchovy chopped fine, an anchovy ſtuck with four cloves, and a quarter of a pound of butter rolled in flour. Put theſe all together in a ſaucepan, and ſet it over a ſlow fire, ſhaking it often, ſo that the whole may be equally heated. When it is thoroughly hot, for you muſt take care never to let a haſh boil, as that will harden the meat, take out the onion, lay ſippets in the diſh, and pour your harſh over them.

Hare à la Daube.

CUT a hare into ſix pieces, and bone and lard them with bacon. Seaſon them with pepper, ſalt, and mace, chopped parſley, thyme, ſhalots, and a clove of garlic. Blaze it with ſlices of lard, the bones, a little broth, as much of the blood as you can ſave, a glaſs of brandy, and a quarter of a pound of butter. Stop the pan well, and ſtew it on a very ſlow fire, or in the oven, about four hours. Then take out the bones, put the hare in a tureen, and the ſlices of bacon upon it. Strain the ſauce, and put it to the hare, and let it cool before you uſe it.

To hodge-podge a Hare.

CUT your hare into pieces, as if you intended it for ſtewing, and put it into a pitcher, with two or three onions, a little ſalt and pepper, a bunch of ſweet herbs, and a piece of butter. Stop the pitcher very cloſe, to prevent the ſteam from getting ont, ſet it in a kettle full of boiling water, keep the kettle filled up as the water waſtes, and let it ſtew four or five hours. You may, if you chooſe it, when you put the hare into the kettle, put in a lettuce, cucumbers, turnips, and celery.

To

To jug a Hare.

THIS is done in nearly the ſame manner as the above, with this difference only, that ſome people lard the hare, here and there, with bacon.

A Hare Civet.

HAVING boned your hare, and taken out all the ſinews, cut one half in thin ſlices, and the other half in pieces an inch long. Flour them, and fry them with a little butter. In the mean time, make ſome gravy with the bones of the hare and a little beef. Put a pint of it into the pan to the hare, ſome muſtard, and a little elder vinegar. Cover it cloſe, and let it do ſoſtly till it is as thick as cream, and then diſh it up, with the head in the middle.

To ſcare a Hare.

TAKE a hare and lard it, put a pudding into its belly, and put it into a pot or fiſh-kettle. Put to it two quarts of ſtrong drawn gravy, one of red wine, a whole lemon cut into ſlices, a bundle of ſweet herbs, nutmeg, pepper, ſalt, and ſix cloves. Cover it cloſe, and ſtew it over a ſlow fire till it is three parts done. Then take it up, put it into a diſh, and ſtrew it over wirh crumbs of bread, ſweet herbs chopped fine, ſome lemon-peel grated, and half a nutmeg. Set it before the fire, and baſte it till it is of a fine light brown. In the mean time, take the fat off your gravy, and thicken it with the yolk of an egg. Take ſix eggs boiled hard, and chopped fine, and ſome pickled cucumbers cut very thin. Mix theſe with the ſauce, pour it into the diſh, and ſend it up to table.

Hare

Hare Cake in Jelly.

BONE your hare, and pick out the ſinews. Put to it an equal quantity of beef, and chop and pound them together. Add ſome freſh muſhrooms, ſhalot, ſweet herbs, pepper, ſalt, and two or three eggs. Mix theſe with bacon, pickled cucumbers cut like dice, and put it into a mould ſheeted with ſlices of bacon. Cover it, bake it in a moderate oven, and when cold, turn it out. In the mean time, take a pound and half of ſcrag of veal, a ſlice of ham, two or three cloves, a little nutmeg, ſome ſweet herbs, a carrot or two, ſome ſhalot, an ounce of iſinglaſs, and ſome beef broth. Stew this till it comes to a jelly, then paſs it through a fine ſieve, and then through a bag. Add to it ſome lemon-juice. Then pour this jelly over your hare.

To collar a Hare.

HAVING boned your hare, lard it with thick pieces of bacon, and ſeaſon it with ſpices and ſalt. You may put into it a forcemeat, or not, juſt as you like. Roll it up very tight, and tie it faſt together. Braze it with ſlices of veal, half a pint of white wine, a pint of broth, and cover it over with ſlices of bacon. You may put ſuch meat and ſeaſoning to make jelly of the braze afterwards as you like. Serve up the hare cold with it, either whole or in ſlices.

To pot a Hare.

CASE your hare, and waſh it perfectly clean. Then cut it up as you do for eating, put it into a pot, and ſeaſon it with pepper, ſalt, and mace. Put on it a pound of butter, tie it down cloſe, and bake it in a bread oven. When it comes out, pick the meat clean from the bones, and pound it it very fine in a mortar, with the fat from your gravy. Then put it cloſe down in your pots; and pour clarified butter upon it.

To dreſs a Leveret Kid-Faſhion.

PUT a large leveret, for about three hours, into a warm marinade, made of water, vinegar, butter, flour, pepper, chopped parſley, ſhalots, ſliced onions, thyme, baſil, lemon-peel, and cloves. Then roaſt it, and baſte it with ſome of the marinade. Strain the remainder, mix it with a little cullis, put it into a ſauceboat, and ſerve up the leveret.

To roaſt a Pheaſant.

HAVING ſpitted and laid your pheaſant down to roaſt, duſt it with flour, and baſte it often with freſh butter, keeping it at a good diſtance from the fire, and about half an hour will roaſt it. Make your gravy of a ſcrag of mutton, and put into the ſaucepan with it, a tea-ſpoonful of lemon-pickle, a large ſpoonful of catchup, and the ſame of browning. Strain it, and put a little into the diſh with the bird. Serve it up with the remainder in one baſon, and bread ſauce in another. You may put one of the principal feathers of the pheaſant in the tail, by way of ornament. Partridges are dreſſed in the ſame manner.

Pheaſants à la Mangelas.

CUT the pinions of a large pheaſant as for roaſting, make a good forcemeat, put it into your pheaſant, and ſpit it, with ſome lards of bacon, and paper it. Having nicely roaſted it, prepare the following ſauce. Take ſome fat livers of turkies or fowls, blanch them till they are thoroughly done, and then pound them to a paſte. Put to it ſome gravy and cullis, and mix it well together. Cut off the flesh of the pheasant, slice it very thin, and presceve the carcase hot. Put into your sauce, which you must make of a proper thickness, a little pepper, salt, some minced parsley, and the juice of two or three oranges. Pour this hash over the breast, garnish with oranges quartered, and send it up to table.

To boil a Pheasant.

YOUR pheasant must be boiled in plenty of water; and, if it is a small one, half an hour will do it, but if a large one, it will take three quarters. For sauce, stew some heads of celery cut very fine, thickened with cream, and a small piece of butter rolled in flour. Season it with salt to your palate. When the bird is done, pour the sauce over it, garnish with thin slices of lemon, and serve it up.

Pheasants à l'Italienne.

IF only one pheasant is to be dressed, take only half a dozen oysters, parboil them, and put them into a stewpan, with the liver cut small, a piece of butter, some green onions, some parsley, pepper, salt, sweet herbs, and a little allspice. Let them stand a very little time over the fire, and then stuff the pheasant with it. Put it into a stewpan, with some oil, green onions, parsley, sweet basil, and lemon-juice, for a few minutes. Then take them off, cover the pheasant with slices of bacon, put it on a spit; and tie some paper round it. In the mean time, stew some oysters in their own liquor. Put into a stewpan the yolks of fours eggs beaten up, half a lemon cut into small dice, a little beaten pepper, scraped nutmeg, a little parsley cut small, an anchovy minced, a little oil, a glass of white wine, a piece of butter, and a little ham cullis. Put the sauce

on

on the fire to thicken, but take care it does not burn, then put in the oyſters, and ſeaſon it to your taſte. When your pheaſant is done, lay it in the diſh, pour your ſauce over it, and ſerve it up.

To ſtew Pheaſants.

PUT your pheaſant into a ſtewpan with as much veal broth as will cover it, and let it ſtew till there is juſt enough liquor left for ſauce. Then ſkim it, and put in artichoke bottoms parboiled, a little beaten mace, a glaſs of wine, and ſome pepper and ſalt. If it is not thick enough, put in a piece of butter rolled in flour, and ſqueeze in a little lemon-juice. Take up your pheaſant, pour the ſauce over it, and put forcemeat balls into the diſh.

Pheaſants à la Braze.

COVER the bottom of your ſtewpan with a layer of beef, a layer of veal, a ſmall piece of bacon, part of a carrot, an onion ſtuck with cloves, a blade or two of mace, a ſpoonful of black and white pepper, and a bundle of ſweet herbs. Then put in your pheaſant, and cover it with a layer of beef and veal, and a ſweetbread. Set it on the fire for five or ſix minutes, and then pour in two quarts of boiling gravy. Cover it cloſe, and let it ſtew an hour and a half very gently. Then take up your pheaſant, and keep it hot. Let the gravy boil till it is reduced to about a pint, then ſtrain it off, and put it in again. Put in the veal ſweetbread that was ſtewed with the pheaſant, ſome truffles and morels, the livers of fowls, artichoke bottoms, and ſome aſparagus tops, if you have any. Let theſe ſimmer in the gravy five or ſix minutes, and then add two ſpoonfuls of catchup, a ſpoonful of browning, and a little piece of butter rolled in flour. Shake all together, then put in your pheaſant,

sant, with a few muſhrooms, and let them ſtew about five or ſix minutes more. Take up your pheaſant, pour the ragoo over it, lay forcemeat balls round it, garniſh with lemon, and ſerve it up.

Partridges in Panes.

TAKE two roaſted partridges, and the fleſh of a large fowl, a little parboiled bacon, ſome marrow or ſuet finely chopped, a few muſhrooms and morels cut very fine, ſome truffles, and artichoke bottoms. Seaſon them with beaten mace, ſalt, pepper, a little nutmeg, ſweet herbs chopped fine, and a crumb of a twopenny loaf ſoaked in hot gravy. Mix all well together, with the yolks of two eggs, and make your panes on paper, of a round figure, and the thickneſs of an egg, at a proper diſtance from one another. Dip the point of a knife in the yolk of an egg, in order to ſhape them, bread them neatly, and bake them a quarter of an hour in a quick oven. Obſerve to boil the truffles and morels tender in the gravy you ſoak the bread in.

Partridges à la Braze.

TRUSS the legs into the bodies of two brace of partridges, lard them, and ſeaſon them with pepper, ſalt, and mace. Lay ſlices of bacon at the bottom of a ſtewpan, then ſlices of beef and veal, all cut thin, a piece of carrot, an onion cut ſmall, a bundle of ſweet herbs, and ſome whole pepper. Put in the partridges with their breaſts downwards, lay ſome thin ſlices of beef and veal over them, and ſome parſley finely chopped. Cover them, and let them ſtew eight or ten minutes over a ſlow fire; then give your pan a ſhake, and pour in a pint of boiling water. Cover it cloſe again, and let it ſtew half an hour over a little quicker fire. Then take out your birds, and keep them hot. Pour

Pour into the pan a pint of thin gravy, let it boil till it is about half reduced, then ftrain it off, and fkim off all the fat. In the mean time, cut a veal fweet-bread fmall, take fome truffles and morels, and fowls livers ftewed in a pint of good gravy half an hour, fome artichoke bottoms and afparagus tops, both blanched in warm water, and a few mufhrooms. Then add your other gravy to this, and put in the partridges to heat. If it is not thick enough, put in a piece of butter rolled in flour. When thoroughly hot, put your partridges into the difh, pour the fauce over them, and ferve them up.

Partridges rolled.

HAVING larded young partridges with ham or bacon, ftrew over them fome pepper and falt, fome beaten mace, fhred lemon-peel, and fweet herbs cut fmall. Take fome thin beef fteaks, but without holes in them, and ftrew over them fome of the feafoning. Then fqueeze on them fome lemon juice, lay a partridge upon each fteak, roll it up, and tie it round to keep it together. Set on a ftewpan with fome flices of bacon, and an onion cut into pieces. Lay the partridges carefully in, put to them fome rich gravy, and let them ftew gently till they are done. Then take the partridges out of the beef, lay them in a difh, and pour over them fome rich effence of ham.

To ragoo Partridges.

TRUSS your partridges, and roaft them, without making ufe of any flour. Make a fauce of the livers pounded, and add two or three chickens livers. Put them into a ftewpan with a green onion or two, a mufhroom, fome parfley, pepper, and falt. Boil all in cullis a few minutes, and ftrain them. Cut the partridges as for a fricaffee, and put them to the fauce. Let it boil juft long enough

enough to heat the meat through. Put in a little orange peel, a bit of minced ſhalot, and a little parſley. Squeeze in a good deal of orange juice, diſh it up, and garniſh with oranges quartered.

To boil Partridges.

BOIL them quick in plenty of water, and fifteen minutes will do them. For ſauce, take a quarter of a pint of cream, and a piece of freſh butter about the ſize of a walnut. Stir it one way till it is melted, and then pour it over the birds.

Partridges with Conſommée Sauce.

HAVING truſſed your partridges as for boiling, put them into a ſtewpan, with ſlices of veal and bacon above and below them, a ſlice of ham, a bundle of ſweet herbs, three cloves, and ſliced onions and carrots. Braze on a very ſlow fire, and, when it is done, ſtrain and ſkim the ſauce, and pour it on the partridges.

Partridges en Aſpic.

TAKE ſome ſhalots, parſley, tarragon, chives, garden creſſes, a little baſil, a clove of garlic, and an anchovy, all well chopped. Mix theſe with muſtard, oil, vinegar, pepper, and ſalt. If you ſerve the partridges whole, ſerve the ſauce cold in a ſauceboat. If hot, cut the partridges as for a haſh, and warm them in a little broth. Then put them to the ſauce, and warm them together without boiling. You may alſo mix it in the ſame manner cold. If cold, it will be better mixed an hour or more before uſing.

To ſtew Partridges.

TRUSS your partridges in the ſame manner as for roaſting, ſtuff the craws, and lard them down each ſide of the breaſt. Then roll a piece of butter

ter in pepper, ſalt, and beaten mace, and put it into the bellies of the birds. Sew up the vents, dredge them well with flour, and fry them of a fine light brown. Put them into a ſtewpan with a quart of good gravy, a ſpoonful of Madeira wine, the ſame of catchup, a tea-ſpoonful of lemon-pickle, half the quantity of muſhroom powder, an anchovy, half a lemon, and a ſprig of ſweet marjoram. Cover the pan cloſe, and ſtew them half an hour; then take them out, and thicken the gravy. Boil it a little, and pour it over the partridges. Lay round them artichoke bottoms boiled and quartered, and the yolks of four hard eggs. You may ſtew woodcocks in the ſame way.

Partridges broiled with ſweet Herbs.

HAVING truſſed your partridges as for boiling, ſplit them down the back, and marinade them about an hour, in a little oil, pepper and ſalt, and all ſorts of ſweet herbs chopped. Then roll them in paper, with all the ſeaſoning, and broil them ſlowly. When they are done, take off the paper, mix the herbs with a little good cullis, add the ſqueeze of a lemon, and ſerve it up with the birds.

To roaſt Woodcocks or Snipes.

THESE birds are ſo peculiar from all others, that they muſt never be drawn for roaſting. Having ſpitted them, take the round of a three-penny loaf, and toaſt it nicely brown. Then lay it in a diſh under the birds; and when you put them to the fire, baſte them with a little butter, and let the trail, or gut, drop on the toaſt. When they are done, put the toaſt in the diſh, and lay the birds on it. Pour about a quarter of a pint of gravy into the diſh, and ſet it over a lamp or chafing-diſh for three or four minutes, and ſend them up hot to table. A woodcock will take about twenty minutes roaſting, and a ſnipe fifteen.

To boil Woodcocks or Snipes.

CUT a pound of lean beef into ſmall pieces, and put them into two quarts of water, with an onion, a bundle of ſweet herbs, a blade or two of mace, ſix cloves, and ſome whole pepper. Cover it cloſe, and let it boil till it is half waſted. Then ſtrain it off, and put the gravy into a ſaucepan, with ſalt enough to ſeaſon it. Draw the birds clean; but take particular care of the guts. Put the birds into the gravy, cover them cloſe, and ten minutes will boil them. In the mean time, cut the guts and liver ſmall, take a little of the gravy the birds are boiled in, and ſtew the guts in it with a blade of mace. Take about as much crumb of bread as the inſide of a roll, and rub or grate it very ſmall into a clean cloth; then put it into a pan with ſome butter, and fry it till it is criſp, and of a fine light brown. When your birds are ready, take about half a pint of the liquor they were boiled in, and add to the guts two ſpoonfuls of red wine, and a piece of butter, about the ſize of a walnut, rolled in flour. Set them on the fire, and ſhake your ſaucepan frequently till the butter is melted, but do not ſtir it with a ſpoon. Then put in the fried crumbs, give the ſaucepan another ſhake, take up your birds, lay them in the diſh, and pour your ſauce over them. Garniſh with ſliced lemon, and ſend them up to table.

To haſh a Woodcock.

HAVING cut up your woodcock as for eating, work the entrails very fine with the back of a ſpoon, and mix it with a ſpoonful of red wine, the ſame of water, and half a ſpoonful of allegar. Cut an onion into ſlices, pull it into rings, and roll a little butter

in

in flour. Put them all into your toffing-pan, and ſhake it over the fire till it boils. Then put in your bird, and when it is thoroughly hot, lay it in your diſh, with ſippets round it. Strain the ſauce over the woodcock, and lay the onions in rings. A partridge may be haſhed the ſame way.

Woodcocks or Snipes en Surtout.

MAKE a forcemeat of veal, as much beef ſuet chopped and beaten in a mortar, with an equal quantity of crumbs of bread. Mix in a little beaten mace, pepper and ſalt, ſome parſley, a few ſweet herbs, and the yolk of an egg. Lay ſome of this meat round the diſh, and then put in the birds, being firſt drawn and half roaſted. Take care of the trail, chop it, and ſcatter it all over the diſh. Take ſome good gravy, according to the ſize of your ſurtout, ſome truffles and morels, a few muſhrooms, a ſweetbread cut into pieces, and artichoke bottoms cut ſmall. Let all ſtew together, ſhake them. Take the yolks of two or three eggs, beat them up with a ſpoonful or two of white wine, and ſtir all together one way. When it is thick, take it off, let it cool, and pour it into the ſurtout. Put in the yolks of a few hard eggs here and there, ſeaſon with beaten mace, pepper, and ſalt, to your taſte. Cover it all over with the forcemeat, then rub on the yolks of eggs to colour it, and ſend it to the oven. Half an hour will ſufficiently do it.

Snipes dreſſed with Purſlain Leaves.

DRAW your ſnipes, and make a forcemeat for the inſide; but reſerve your ropes for your ſauce. Put them acroſs upon a lark-ſpit, covered with bacon and paper, and roaſt them gently. For ſauce, take ſome prime thick leaves of purſlain, blanch them well in water, put them into a ladle of cullis and gravy, a bit of ſhalot, pepper, ſalt, nutmeg,

nutmeg, and parfley, and ftew all together for half an hour gently. Have the ropes ready blanched, and put them in, difh up your fnipes upon thin flices of bread fried, fqueeze the juice of an orange into your fauce, and fend them up to table.

Snipes Duchefs-Fafhion.

HAVING fplit the fnipes at the back, make a forcemeat of the infide, with a few chopped capers, parfley, fhalots, mufhrooms, pepper, falt, two chopped anchovies, and a piece of butter. Stuff them with it, few them up clofe, and braze them. While brazing, add a little good cullis and red wine. When done, fkim and ftrain the fauce. If it is not thick enough, add a little butter rolled in flour, and ferve it up with the fnipes.

Snipes in Salmy.

TRUSS them, and half roaft them, without flour. Cut them in pieces as for a fricaffee, and take care to fecure all the infide, except the gizzards and galls, which you muft be careful to take clean away; but pound the ropes, livers, &c. to a pafte, with a little fhalot, green onion and parfley, pepper, falt, and nutmeg. Put in a ladle of your cullis, a glafs of red wine, pafs it through a fieve, and pour it into a ftewpan to your meat. Let it ftew very gently three quarters of an hour; throw in a little minced parfley, the juice of an orange, and ferve it up, garnifhed with fried bread, and fome bits in the difh. All forts of birds, that are not drawn, may be treated in the fame manner.

To drefs Ruffs and Reifs.

THESE birds, which are principally found in Lincolnfhire, may be fatted, like chickens, with bread, milk, and fugar. They fatten very faft, and will die with fat if not killed at the proper time.

Draw

Draw and trufs them crofs-legged, like fnipes, and then roaft them. For fauce, have fome good gravy thickened with butter, and put a toaft under them.

To drefs Plovers.

ROAST green plovers like a woodcock, without drawing, and let the trail run upon a toaft. Have good gravy for fauce. Grey plovers muft be ftewed. Make a forcemeat for them with the yolks of two hard eggs bruifed, fome marrow cut fine, artichoke bottoms cut fmall, and fweet herbs, feafoned with pepper, falt, and nutmeg. Stuff the birds, then put them into a faucepan with good gravy fufficient to cover them; then put in a glafs of white wine, and a blade of mace. Cover them clofe, and let them ftew very gently till they are tender. Then take up the plovers, lay them in a difh, keep them hot, and put in a piece of butter rolled in flour to thicken the fauce. Let it boil till it is fmooth, fqueeze into it a little lemon, fkim it clean, and pour it over the birds.

Plovers dreffed Perigord-Fafhion.

HAVING truffed them as chickens or pigeons for ftewing, braze them in a good braze, and when it is done, fkim and ftrain the braze. You may alfo ftuff and roaft them as partridges, &c. Thrufhes and lapwings may be dreffed in the fame manner, and fent up to table with a cullis fauce.

Quails and Ortolans.

THESE birds may be fpitted fideways, and roafted with a vine leaf between them. Bafte them with butter, and when they are ready, ferve them up with fried crumbs of bread round the difh.

Larks

Larks à la Françoiſe.

TRUSS your larks with the legs acroſs, and put a ſage leaf over their breaſts. Put them upon a long thin ſkewer, and between every lark put a piece of thin bacon. Then tie the ſkewer to a ſpit, and roaſt them at a briſk clear fire. Baſte them with butter, and ſtrew over them ſome crumbs of bread mixed with flour. Fry ſome bread crumbs of a fine brown in butter. Lay the larks round the diſh, and the bread crumbs in the middle.

To ragoo Larks.

HAVING fried your larks with an onion ſtuck with cloves, and a few truffles and muſhrooms, pour off the fat, and ſhake over them a little flour. Put to them ſome good gravy, and ſtew them till they are enough. If there be any fat, ſkim it off. Put to it ſome lemon juice, and pepper and ſalt to your taſte. Other ſmall birds may be dreſſed the ſame way.

Small Birds in ſavoury Jelly.

TAKE eight ſmall birds, with their heads and feet on, and put a good piece of butter into each of their bellies. Put them into a jug, and cover it cloſe with a cloth, and ſet in a kettle of boiling water till the birds are enough. Drain them, and make your jelly as before, and put a little into a baſon. When it is ſet, lay in three birds with their breaſts downwards, and cover them with the jelly. When that is ſet, put in the other five, with their heads in the middle, and proceed in the ſame manner as directed before for chickens.

A Hare Pie.

HAVING cut your hare into pieces, ſeaſon it well with pepper, ſalt, nutmeg, and mace. Then put

put it into a jug with half a pound of butter, clofe it up, and fet it into a copper of boiling water. Make a rich forcemeat with a quarter of a pound of fcraped bacon, two onions, a glafs of red wine, the crumb of a penny loaf, a little winter favory, the liver cut fmall, and a little nutmeg. Seafon it high with pepper and falt, and mix it well up with the yolks of three eggs. Raife the pie, and lay the forcemeat at the bottom of the difh. Then put in the hare, with the gravy that came out of it; put on the lid, and fend it to the oven. It will require an hour and a half baking.

A Partridge Pie.

TRUSS two brace of partridges in the fame manner as you do a fowl for boiling. Put fome fhalots into a marble mortar, with fome parfley cut fmall, the liver of the partridges, and twice the quantity of bacon. Beat thefe well together, and feafon them with pepper, falt, and a blade or two of mace. When thefe are all pounded to a pafte, add to them fome frefh mufhrooms. Raife the cruft for the pie, and cover the bottom of it with the feafoning. Then lay the partridges, without any ftuffing in them, and put the remainder of the feafoning about the fides, and between the partridges. Mix together fome pepper and falt, a little mace, fome fhalots fhred fine, frefh mufhrooms, and a little bacon beat fine in a mortar. Strew this over the partridges, and lay on fome thin flices of bacon. Then put on the lid, fend it to the oven, and two hours will bake it. When it is done, remove the lid, take out the flices of bacon, and fkim off the fat. Pour in a pint of rich veal gravy, fqueeze in the juice of an orange, and fend it hot to table.

To make a Venifon Pafty.

BONE a neck and breaft of venifon, and feafon them well with pepper and falt. Put them into a deep pan, with the beft part of a neck of mutton fliced and laid over them. Pour in a glafs of red wine, put a coarfe pafte over it, and bake it two hours. Then lay the venifon in a difh, pour the gravy over it, and put on it a pound of butter. Make a good puff-pafte, and lay it near half an inch thick round the edge of the difh. Roll out the lid, which muft be a little thicker than the pafte on the edge of the difh, and lay it on. Then roll out another lid pretty thin, and cut it into flowers, leaves, or whatever form you pleafe, and lay it on the lid. It may be eaten either hot or cold.

To roaft Venifon.

AS foon as you have fpitted your venifon, lay over it a large fheet of paper, and then a thin common pafte, with another paper over that. Tie it faft, that the pafte may not drop off; and, if the haunch be a large one, it will take four hours roafting. As foon as it is done enough, take off both paper and pafte, dredge it well with flour, and bafte it with butter. As foon as it becomes of a light brown, difh it up with brown gravy, or currant jelly fauce, and fend up fome in a boat.

CHAP.

CHAP. X.

The different Methods of dreſſing Fiſh.

Salmon à la Braze.

SLIT a large eel open, take out the bone, and the meat quite clean from it. Chop it fine with two anchovies, ſome lemon-peel cut fine, a little pepper and grated nutmeg, with ſome parſley and thyme cut ſmall, and the yolk of an egg boiled hard. Mix them all together, and roll them up in a piece of butter. Then take a large piece of fine ſalmon, or a ſalmon-trout, and put this force-meat into the belly of the fiſh. Sew it up, and lay it in an oval ſtewpan that will juſt hold it. Then put half a pound of freſh butter into a ſtew-pan, and when it is melted, ſhake in a little flour. Stir it till it is a little brown, and then put to it a pint of fiſh broth, and a pint of Madeira. Seaſon it with pepper, ſalt, mace, and cloves, and put in an onion, and a bunch of ſweet herbs. Stir it all together, and put it to the fiſh. Cover it very cloſe, and let it ſtew. When the fiſh is almoſt done, put in ſome freſh and pickled muſhrooms, truffles, or morels, cut in pieces, and let them ſtew till the fiſh is quite done. Take up the ſalmon carefully, lay it in a diſh, and put the ſauce over it.

To broil Salmon.

HAVING cut your ſalmon into thick pieces, flour and broil them. Lay them in your diſh, and ſerve them up with plain melted butter in a boat.

Salmon with ſweet Herbs.

MIX a piece of butter with ſome chopped parſley, ſhalots, ſweet herbs, muſhrooms, pepper, and

and ſalt. Put ſome of this in the bottom of the diſh you intend to ſend to table, then ſome thin ſlices of ſalmon upon it, and the remainder of the butter and herbs upon the ſalmon. Strew it over with bread crumbs, then baſte it with butter, and bake it in the oven. When it is enough, drain the fat from it, and ſerve it up with a clear reliſhing ſauce.

To roll Salmon.

TAKE a ſide of ſalmon, when ſplit, the bone taken out, and ſcalded. Strew over the inſide ſome pepper, ſalt, nutmeg, mace, a few chopped oyſters, parſley, and crumbs of bread. Roll it up tight, put it into a deep pot, and bake it in a quick oven. Make the common fiſh ſauce, and pour over it.

To dreſs dried Salmon.

LAY your dried ſalmon in ſoak two or three hours, then lay it on the gridiron, and ſkake a little pepper over it. Uſe what ſauce you like.

To ſtew a Cod.

Seaſon ſome ſlices of cod with grated nutmeg, pepper, ſalt, a bunch of ſweet herbs, and an onion ſtuck with cloves. Put them into a ſtewpan, with half a pint of white wine, and a quarter of a pint of water. Cover them cloſe, and let them ſimmer five or ſix minutes. Then ſqueeze in the juice of a lemon, put in a few oyſters, and their liquor ſtrained, a piece of butter rolled in flour, and a blade or two of mace. Cover them cloſe, and let them ſtew ſoftly. Shake the pan often, to prevent its burning. When the fiſh is enough, take out the onions and ſweet herbs, lay the cod in a warm diſh, pour the ſauce over it, and ſend it up to table.

Cod's

Cod's Head and Shoulders.

TAKE out the gills, and the blood clean from the bone. Wafh the head very clean, rub over it a little falt and a glafs of allegar, and then lay it on your fifh-plate. Throw a good handful of falt into your water when it boils, with a glafs of allegar; then put in your fifh, and let it boil gently for half an hour; if it be a large one, it will take three quarters of an hour. Take it up very carefully, and ftrip off the fkin very nicely. Set it before a brifk fire, dredge it all over with flour, and bafte it well with butter. When the froth begins to rife, throw over it fome very fine white bread crumbs. You muft keep bafting it all the time to make the froth rife well. When it is of a fine white brown, difh it up, and garnifh it with a lemon cut in flices, fcraped horfe-radifh, barberries, a few fmall fifh fried and laid round it, or fried oyfters. Cut the roe and liver into flices, and lay over it a little of the lobfter in lumps out of the fauce, and then fend it up to table.

To crimp Cod.

HAVING cut a frefh cod into flices, put it into pump water and falt. Almoft fill a fifh-kettle with fpring water, put in falt enough to make it tafte brackifh, and then fet it over a ftove. Make it boil quick, then put in the flices of cod, and keep them boiling, and fkim them very clean. Having let them boil eight or ten minutes, take them out, and lay them on a fifh-plate. You may ferve them up either with fhrimp or oyfter fauce.

To broil Cod.

CUT a cod into flices of about two inches thick, and dry them and flour them well. Make a good clear fire, rub the gridiron with a piece of chalk, and fet it high from the fire. Turn them often till they are quite enough, and of a fine brown; but take very great care that you do not break them. You may fend them up with lobfter or fhrimp fauce.

Frefh Cod with fweet Herbs.

HAVING cut a fmall cod into five or fix pieces, bone it, and marinade it with melted butter, the juice of a lemon, chopped parfley, fhalots, and fweet herbs. Then lay it on the difh you intend for table, with all the marinade both under and over, and ftrew it over with bread crumbs. Bafte it with melted butter, bake it in the oven, and ferve it with any fauce you like beft.

To drefs falt Cold.

PUT your fifh all night into water to foak, and, if you put a glafs of vinegar to it, it will draw out the falt and make it eat frefh. Boil it the next day, and when it is enough, break it into flakes on the difh. Pour over it parfnips boiled and beat fine with butter and cream, though egg fauce is more generally ufed.

To drefs Cod Sounds.

STEEP them as you do the falt cod, and boil them in a large quantity of milk and water. When they are very tender and white, take them up, and drain the water out. Then pour the egg fauce boiling hot over them, and fend them up to table.

To fricaſſee Cod Sounds.

CLEAN them well, and cut them into little pieces. Then boil them tender in milk and water, and ſet them to drain. Then put them into a clean ſaucepan, ſeaſon them with a little beaten mace and grated nutmeg, and a very little ſalt. Pour to them juſt cream enough for ſauce, and a good piece of butter rolled in flour. Keep ſhaking your ſaucepan round all the time, till it is thick enough; then garniſh with lemon, and ſend it up to table.

To dreſs a Turbot with Capers.

HAVING waſhed and dried a ſmall turbot well, put into a ſtewpan ſome thyme, parſley, ſweet herbs, and an onion ſliced. Then lay the turbot into the ſtewpan, which ſhould be juſt large enough to hold it, and ſtrew over the fiſh the ſame herbs that are under it, with ſome chives and ſweet baſil. Then pour in an equal quantity of white wine, and white wine vinegar, till the fiſh is covered. Strew in a little bay ſalt, with ſome whole pepper, and ſet the ſtewpan over a gentle ſtove, encreaſing the heat by degrees, till it is enough. Then take it off the fire, but do not take out the turbot. Set a ſaucepan on the fire with a pound of butter, two anchovies ſplit, boned, and waſhed; two large ſpoonfuls of capers cut ſmall, ſome whole chives, a little pepper, ſalt, grated nutmeg, a little flour, a ſpoonful of vinegar, and a little water. Set the ſaucepan over the ſtove, and keep ſhaking it round for ſome time. Having then put on the turbot to make it hot, put it into a diſh, and pour ſome of the ſauce over it. Lay horſe-radiſh round it, and pour what ſauce remains into a boat. In the ſame way you may dreſs ſoles, flounders, large plaice or dabs.

To bake a Turbot.

RUB butter thick all over a diſh about the ſize of the turbot, and throw in a little ſalt, ſome beaten pepper, half a large nutmeg, and ſome parſley finely mixed. Pour in a pint of white wine, cut off the head and tail, lay the turbot in the diſh, pour another pint of white wine over all, grate the other half of the nutmeg over it, and a little pepper, ſome ſalt, and chopped parſley. Lay a piece of butter in different places, throw on a little flour, and then a good many crumbs of bread. Bake it till it is of a fine brown, then lay it in your diſh. Stir the ſauce all together, pour it into a ſaucepan, ſhake in a little flour, and let it boil. Then ſtir in a piece of butter, and two ſpoonfuls of catchup, and when it has boiled, pour it into your baſons, and ſerve it up.

To fry Trout.

HAVING ſcaled, gutted, and waſhed them well, dry them, and lay them ſeparately on a board before the fire. Duſt them well with flour a few minutes before you fry them, and do them of a fine brown in roaſt dripping, or rendered ſuet. Serve them up with melted butter and criſped parſley. Perch are fried in the ſame manner.

To ſtew Trout.

STUFF a ſmall trout with grated bread, a piece of butter, chopped parſley, lemon-peel grated, pepper, ſalt, nutmeg, ſavoury herbs, and yolks of eggs, all mixed together. Put it into a ſtewpan, with a quart of good boiled gravy, ſome Madeira, an onion, a little whole pepper, a few cloves, and a piece of lemon-peel. Stew it in this gently till it is enough, and then add a little flour

flour mixed with ſome cream, and a little catchup. Give it a boil, and ſqueeze in ſome lemon-juice.

To marinade Trout.

FRY your trout in oil ſufficient to cover them, and put them in when the oil is boiling hot. When they are criſp, lay them to drain till they are cold, and then take ſome white wine and vinegar, of each an equal quantity, with ſome ſalt, whole pepper, nutmeg, cloves, mace, ſliced ginger, ſavory, ſweet marjoram, thyme, roſemary, and two onions. Let theſe boil together a quarter of an hour. Then put the fiſh into a ſtewpan, pour the marianade hot to them, and put in as much oil as white wine and vinegar, which muſt be according to the quantity of your fiſh, as the liquor muſt cover them. Serve them up with oil and vinegar. They will keep a month done in this manner.

To dreſs Carp.

SAVE the blood when you kill your carp, and ſcale and clean them well. Have ready ſome rich gravy made of beef and mutton, ſeaſoned with pepper, ſalt, mace, and onion. Strain it off before you ſtew your fiſh in it, and boil your carp before you ſtew it in the gravy; but take care not to boil them too much before you put them into the gravy. Let it ſtew on a ſlow fire about a quarter of an hour, and thicken the ſauce with a good lump of butter rolled in flour. Garniſh your diſh with fried oyſters, fried toaſts cut into angles, pieces of lemon, ſcraped horſe-radiſh, and the roes of the carp cut into pieces, ſome fried, and others boiled. Squeeze the juice of a lemon into the ſauce juſt before you ſend it up to table.

To fry Carp.

HAVING ſcaled, gutted, and cleaned a brace of carp, dry them well in a cloth, flour them, put them into a frying-pan of boiling lard, and do them of a fine brown. Fry the roes, and fry ſome thin ſlices of bread cut cornerwiſe. Lay the fiſh on a coarſe cloth to drain, then put them into the diſh, with the roes on each ſide, and the toaſt between. You may ſerve them up with anchovy ſauce.

To ſtew Carp.

SCALE, gut, and waſh your carp. Put them into a ſtewpan, with two quarts of water, half a pint of white wine, a little mace, whole pepper, a little ſalt, two onions, a bunch of ſweet herbs, and a ſtick of horſe-radiſh. Cover the pan cloſe, and let it ſtand an hour and a half over a ſlow fire. Then put a gill of white wine into a ſaucepan, with two anchovies chopped, an onion, a little lemon-peel, a quarter of a pound of butter rolled in flour, a little thick cream, and a large teacup of the liquor the carp was ſtewed in. Boil them a few minutes, drain the carp, and add to the ſauce the yolks of two eggs mixed with a little cream. When it boils up, ſqueeze in the juice of half a lemon, diſh up your carp, and pour your ſauce hot on them.

To fricaſſee Carp Roes.

PUT into a ſtewpan a little butter, a dozen ſmall muſhrooms, a ſlice of ham, the ſqueeze of a lemon, and a bundle of ſweet herbs. Stew it a little time on a ſlow fire, then add a little flour, and as many carp roes as you think proper, with a little good broth. Stew them about a quarter of an hour, and ſeaſon them with pepper and ſalt when you put in the broth. When all is ready, thicken

thicken it with the yolks of two or three eggs, ſome cream, and a little chopped parſley.

To fry Tench.

HAVING gutted, waſhed, and dried your tench well in a cloth, ſlit them down the back, ſprinkle a little ſalt over them, dredge them with flour, and fry them of a fine brown in boiling lard. Make your ſauce of an anchovy, muſhrooms, truffles, and capers, all chopped ſmall, and ſtewed in gravy, with the juice of a lemon, and a little fiſh cullis.

To ſtew Tench.

TENCH are ſtewed in the ſame manner as before directed to ſtew carp.

To ſtew Soals.

TAKE the fleſh from the bones of your ſoals, and cut each of them into eight pieces. Put a quart of boiled gravy into a ſtewpan, a quarter of a pint of Madeira or white wine, ſome white pepper pounded, grated nutmeg, and a piece of lemon-peel. Stew theſe together near an hour, and add ſome cream, and a piece of butter mixed in flour. Keep the ſauce ſtirring till it boil, put in the fiſh, and ſtew it a quarter of an hour. Take out the lemon-peel, and ſqueeze in ſome lemon-juice. The fiſh may be ſtewed whole in the ſame ſauce; or they may be cut as before directed, and a little gravy made with the bones and head.

To fry Soals.

HAVING ſcaled and trimmed your ſoals properly, ſkin the black ſide, and mix ſome bread crumbs with a very little flour. Baſte the ſoals with beaten eggs, ſtrew them over with the bread crumbs, and fry them of a good colour in hog's lard.

lard. Serve them up with anchovy fauce, and garnifh with fried parfley.

To marinade Soals.

BOIL them in falt and water, bone and drain them, and lay them on a difh with their bellies upwards. Boil fome fpinach, and pound it in a mortar. Then boil four eggs hard, chop the yolks and whites feparate, and lay green, white, and yellow among the foals, and ferve them up with melted butter in a boat.

Soals à la Françoife.

SKIN and clean a pair of foals, and put them into an earthen difh, with a quart of water, and half a pint of vinegar. Let them lie two hours, and then take them out, and dry them with a cloth. Then put them into a ftewpan with a pint of white wine, a quarter of a pint of water, a very little thyme, a little fweet marjoram, winter favory, and an onion ftuck with four cloves. Put in the foals, fprinkle in a very little bay-falt, cover them clofe, and let them fimmer very gently till they are enough. Then take them out, and lay them in a warm difh before the fire. Strain the liquor, and put into it a piece of butter rolled in flour, and let it boil till of a proper thicknefs. Lay the foals in a difh, and pour the fauce over them. In the fame manner you may drefs a fmall turbot, or any flat fifh.

To drefs Sturgeon.

HAVING wafhed your fturgeon clean, lay it all night in falt and water, and the next morning take it out, rub it well with allegar, and let it lie in it for two hours. Have ready a fifh kettle full of boiling water, with an ounce of bay falt, two large onions, and a few fprigs of fweet marjoram. Boil the

the ſturgeon till the bones will leave the fiſh, then take it up, take the ſkin off, and flour it well. Set it before the fire, baſte it with freſh butter, and let it ſtand till it is of a fine brown. Then diſh it up, and pour into the diſh any ſauce you like.

To boil Sturgeon.

PUT your ſturgeon into as much liquid as will ſtew it, being half fiſh-broth or water, and half white wine, with a little vinegar, ſliced roots, onions, ſweet herbs, whole pepper, and ſome ſalt. When it is done, garniſh with green parſley, and ſerve it up with caper or anchovy ſauce, or any other ſauce you like better.

To ſtew Flounders and Plaice.

THESE fiſh are ſtewed in the ſame manner as before directed to ſtew ſoals. As to frying or boiling them, that buſineſs is too ſimple to need any deſcription here.

To fricaſſee Flounders and Plaice.

HAVING cleaned the fiſh, and taken off the black ſkin, but not the white, cut the fleſh from the bones into long ſlices, and dip them into yolk of egg. Strew over them ſome bread raſpings, and fry them in clarified butter. When they are enough, lay them upon a plate, and keep them hot. To make your ſauce, take the bones of the fiſh, and boil them in ſome water. Then put in an anchovy, ſome thyme, parſley, a little pepper, ſalt, cloves, and mace. Let theſe ſimmer till the anchovy is diſſolved, and then take the butter the fiſh was fried in, and put it into a pan over the fire. Shake ſome flour into it, and keep ſtirring it while the flour is ſhaking in. Then ſtrain the liquor into it, and let it boil till it is thick. Squeeze ſome lemon

juice

juice into it, put the fiſh into a diſh, and pour the ſauce over them.

To broil Mackarel.

FIRST clean your mackarel well, then ſplit them down the back, and ſeaſon them with pepper, ſalt, ſome mint, parſley, and fennel, all chopped very fine. Flour them, and fry them of a fine light brown, and put them on a diſh and ſtrainer. Uſe fennel and butter for ſauce, and garniſh with parſley.

Mackarel au Bouillon.

PUT half a pint of white wine, ſliced roots, onions, ſweet herbs, pepper and ſalt, into a ſtewpan. Boil them about half an hour, and then boil the fiſh in it. Make a ſauce with a piece of butter, a little flour, a ſhalot chopped very fine, ſome ſcalded fennel chopped, and a little of the boiling liquor. When it is ready to ſend up to table, add the ſqueeze of a lemon.

To fry Whitings.

HAVING waſhed, gutted, and ſkinned them, turn their tails into their mouths, dry them in a cloth, and flour them well all over. Fill the frying-pan with lard enough to cover them, and when it boils, put them in, and fry them of a fine brown. Lay them on a coarſe cloth to drain, and then put them on a warm diſh. Make ſhrimp, oyſter, or anchovy ſauce.

To broil Whitings or Haddocks.

GUT, waſh them, dry them well with a cloth, and rub a little vinegar over them, as it will keep on the ſkin better. Duſt them well with flour, rub your gridiron with butter, and let it be very hot when you lay on the fiſh, otherwiſe they will ſtick.

Turn

Turn them two or three times while doing. When they are enough, lay pickles round them, with plain melted butter, and ſend them up to table.

To ſtew Pike.

HAVING made a brown with butter and flour, add a pint of red wine, a bundle of herbs, four cloves, twenty-four ſmall onions half boiled, pepper, and ſalt, and then the pike cut into pieces. Stew it ſlowly till the fiſh is done. Take out the bundle of herbs, and add a piece of butter. When it is ready to ſerve, add two chopped anchovies, and a ſpoonful of capers. Garniſh with fried bread, and pour the ſauce over the fiſh. You may add artichoke bottoms, muſhrooms, &c. if you pleaſe.

To fry Perch.

SCALE, gut, and waſh your perch clean. Score them at ſome diſtance on the ſides, but not very deep. Dry them well, flour them all over, and fry them in oiled butter. When they are of a fine brown, lay ſome criſped parſley round the fiſh, and ſend them up to table with plain butter; or you may make for them the following ſauce. To two ounces of browned butter put ſome flour, a few chives chopped ſmall, ſome parſley, a few muſhrooms cut ſmall, and a little boiling water. Lay the perch in this liquor after they are fried, and let them ſtew gently for four or five minutes. Then lay them in a warm diſh, add two large ſpoonfuls of capers cut ſmall, thicken it with butter and flour, and pour it over them.

To dreſs Perch in Water Souchy.

SCALE, gut, and waſh your perch, and put ſome ſalt into your water. When it boils, put in your fiſh, with an onion cut in ſlices, and ſeparated into round rings, and a handful of parſley. Put in

as

as much milk as will turn the water white. When the perch is enough, put them in a ſoup-diſh, and pour a little of the water over them, with the parſley and the onions. Serve them up with parſley and butter in a boat. If you do not like the onions, they may be omitted. Trout may be boiled in the ſame manner.

To ſtew Eels.

HAVING ſkinned, gutted, and waſhed your eels very clean in ſix or eight waters, cut them in pieces about as long as your finger. Put juſt water enough for ſauce, and put in a ſmall onion ſtuck with cloves, a ſmall bundle of ſweet herbs, a blade or two of mace, and ſome whole pepper in a thin muſlin rag. Cover it cloſe, and let them ſtew very ſoftly. Put in a piece of butter rolled in flour, and a little chopped parſley. When you find they are quite tender, and well done, take out the onion, ſpice, and ſweet herbs. Put in ſalt enough to ſeaſon it, and then diſh them up with the ſauce.

To fricaſſee Eels.

SKIN three or four large eels, and notch them from end to end. Cut them into four or five pieces each, and lay them in ſome ſpring water for half an hour to crimp them. Dry them in a cloth, and toſs them over the fire a few minutes in a bit of freſh butter, a green onion or two, and a little parſley minced; but take care, that the colour of neither is altered by burning your butter. Pour in about a pint of white wine, and as much good broth, ſome pepper, ſalt, and a blade of mace. Stew all together about three quarters of an hour, and thicken it with a bit of butter and flour. Beat the yolks of four or five eggs ſmooth, with two or three ſpoonfuls of broth; grate in a little nutmeg, and put in a little minced parſley. Juſt before you

want

want to ſerve it up, let your eels be boiling hot, and then pour in your eggs, &c. but take care that you do not let it curdle, by keeping it too long on the fire after the eggs are in. Toſs it over the fire for a moment, add the juice of a lemon, and ſerve it up. Tench cut in pieces may be done in the ſame manner.

To broil Eels.

HAVING ſkinned and cleanſed your eels, rub them with the yolk of an egg, ſtrew over them bread crumbs, chopped parſley, ſage, pepper, and ſalt. Baſte them well with butter, and ſet them in a dripping-pan. Roaſt or broil them, and ſerve them up with parſley and butter.

To fry Eels.

CUT one or two eels into pieces, cut out the back-bone, and ſcore it on both ſides. Marinade it about half an hour in vinegar, with parſley, ſliced onions, ſhalots, and four cloves. Then drain it, baſte it with eggs and bread crumbs, and fry it of a good colour. Garniſh with fried parſley, and ſerve it up with a reliſhing ſauce.

To pitchcock Eels.

HAVING ſkinned, gutted, and waſhed your eels, dry them with a cloth. Sprinkle them with pepper, ſalt, and a little dried ſage, turn them backward and forward, and ſkewer them. Rub your gridiron with beef ſuet, broil them of a good brown, put them on your diſh with melted butter, and garniſh with fried parſley.

To fricaſſee Skate or Thornbacks.

CUT the meat from the bones, fins, &c. and make it very clean. Cut it into thin pieces about an inch broad, and two inches long, and lay them in in your ſtewpan. To a pound of fleſh, put a quarter of a pint of water, a little beaten mace, grated nutmeg, a ſmall bundle of ſweet herbs, and a little ſalt. Cover it, and let it boil fifteen minutes. Then take out the ſweet herbs, put in a quarter of a pint of good cream, a piece of butter the ſize of a walnut, rolled in flour, and a glaſs of red wine. Keep ſhaking the pan all the time one way till it is thick and ſmooth, garniſh with lemon, and ſend it up to table.

To fricaſſee Oyſters.

PUT a little butter into a ſtewpan, a ſlice of ham, a bundle of ſweet herbs, and an onion ſtuck with two cloves. Stew it a little on a ſlow fire, then add a little flour, ſome good broth, and a piece of lemon peel. Then put ſcalded oyſters to it, and ſimmer them a little. When it is ready, thicken it with the yolks of two eggs, a little cream, and a bit of good butter. Take out the ham, bundle of herbs, onion, and lemon peel, and ſqueeze in a lemon.

To dreſs Herrings.

THE general method of dreſſing herrings is either to broil or fry them, and ſerve them up with melted butter.

Herrings with Muſtard Sauce.

HAVING gutted and wiped your herrings very clean, melt ſome butter, and put to it chopped parſley, ſhalots, green onions, pepper, and ſalt. Dip the herrings in this, and roll them in bread crumbs. Then broil them, and ſerve them with a ſauce made of melted butter, flour, broth, a little vinegar, pepper, and ſalt. When done, put to them as much muſtard as you think proper.

To

To fry Herrings.

SCALE, gut them, cut off their heads, waſh them clean, dry them in a cloth, flour them, and fry them in butter. Peel and cut thin a good many onions, and fry them of a light brown with the herrings. Lay your herrings in the diſh, and the onions round them, and put butter and muſtard in a cup.

To bake Herrings.

CLEAN your herrings well, lay them on a board, take a little black and Jamaica pepper, a few cloves, a good deal of ſalt, and mix them together. Rub it all over the fiſh, lay them ſtraight in a pot, cover them with allegar, tie ſtrong paper over the pot, and bake them in a moderate oven. If your allegar is good, they will keep two or three months. They may be ſerved up either hot or cold.

To bake Sprats.

HAVING rubbed your ſprats with ſalt and pepper, to every two pints of vinegar put one pint of red wine. Diſſolve a pennyworth of cochineal, and lay your ſprats in a deep earthen diſh. Pour in as much red wine, vinegar, and cochineal, as will cover them. Tie a paper over them, and ſet them in an oven all night. They will keep ſome time, and eat well.

To make an Eel Pie.

SKIN, gut, and waſh your eels very clean, and cut them into pieces about an inch and a half long. Seaſon them with pepper, ſalt, and a little dried ſage rubbed ſmall. Put them into a diſh with as much water as will juſt cover them. Make a good puffpaſte, lay on the lid, and ſend the pie to the oven,

oven, which muſt be quick, but not ſo quick as to burn the cruſt.

Salmon Pie.

MAKE a good cruſt, take a piece of freſh ſalmon, cleanſe it well, and ſeaſon it with pepper, ſalt, mace, and nutmeg. Put a piece of butter at the bottom of your diſh, and then lay in the ſalmon. Melt butter in proportion to the ſize of your pie, and then take a lobſter, boil it, pick out all the fleſh, chop it ſmall, and mix it well with the butter. Pour it over your ſalmon, put on the lid, and bake it well.

Turbot Pie.

PARBOIL your turbot, and then ſeaſon it with a little pepper, ſalt, cloves, nutmeg, and ſweet herbs cut fine. When you have made your paſte, lay the turbot in your diſh, with ſome yolks of eggs, and a whole onion, which laſt muſt be taken out when the pie is baked. Lay plenty of freſh butter on the top, put on the lid, and bake it.

Lobſter Pie.

HAVING boiled two or three lobſters, take the meat out of the tails, and cut it into different pieces. Then take out all the ſpawn, and the meat of the claws; beat it well in a mortar, and ſeaſon it with pepper, ſalt, two ſpoonfuls of vinegar, and a little anchovy liquor. Melt half a pound of freſh butter, with the crumbs of a halfpenny roll rubbed through a fine cullender, and the yolks of ten eggs. Put a fine puff-paſte over the diſh, lay in the tails firſt, and then the reſt of the meat on them. Put on the lid, and bake it in a ſlow oven.

To

To dreſs a Turtle.

KILL your turtle, which we will ſuppoſe to be of about thirty pounds weight, the night before you intend to dreſs it. Cut off the head, and let it bleed three or four hours. Then cut off the fins, and the callapee from the callapaſh, and take care you do not burſt the gall. Throw all the inwards into cold water; but keep the guts and tripe by themſelves, and ſlip them open with a penknife, waſh them very clean in ſcalding water, and ſcrape off all the inward ſkin. As you do them, throw them into cold water, waſh them out of that, and put them into freſh water, and let them lie all night, ſcalding the fins and edges of the callapaſh and callapee. Cut the meat off the ſhoulders, hack the bones, and ſet them over the fire, with the fins, in about a quart of water. Put in a little mace, nutmeg, chyan, and ſalt. Let it ſtew about three hours, then ſtrain it, and put the fins by for uſe. The next morning, take ſome of the meat you cut off the ſhoulders, and chop it ſmall, as for ſauſages, with about a pound of beef or veal ſuet. Seaſon with mace, nutmeg, ſweet marjoram, parſley, chyan, and ſalt, to your taſte, three or four glaſſes of Madeira wine, and ſtuff it under the two fleſhy parts of the meat. If you have any left, lay it over, to prevent the meat from burning. Cut the remainder of the meat and fins in pieces, about the ſize of an egg; ſeaſon it pretty high with chyan, ſalt, and a little nutmeg, and put it into the callapaſh. Take care that it be ſewed or ſecured up at the end, to keep in the gravy. Then boil up the gravy, and add more wine, if required, and thicken it a little with butter and flour. Put ſome of it to the turtle, and ſet it in the oven, with a well buttered paper over it to keep it from burning; and when it is about half baked, ſqueeze in the juice of of one or two lemons, and ftir it up. The callapafh, or back, will take half an hour more baking than the callapee, which two hours will do. The guts muft be cut in pieces two or three inches long, the tripes in lefs, and put into a mug of clear water, and fet in the oven with the callapafh. When it is properly drained from the water, it is to be mixed with the other parts, and fent up very hot to table.

To drefs a Turtle the Weft India Way.

HAVING taken the turtle out of the water the night before you drefs it, lay it on its back. In the morning, cut its head off, and hang it up by its hind fins for it to bleed till the blood is all out. Then cut the callapee, which is the belly, round, and raife it up. Cut as much meat to it as you can, throw it into fpring water with a little falt, cut the fins off, and fcald them with the head. Take off all the fcales, cut out all the white meat, and throw it into fpring water and falt. The guts and lungs muft be cut out. Wafh the lungs very clean from the blood; then take the guts and maw, and flit them open, wafh them very clean, and put them on to boil in a large pot of water till they be tender. Then take off the infide fkin, and cut them in pieces of two or three inches long. In the mean time, make the following good veal broth. Take one large or two fmall knuckles of veal, and put them on in three gallons of water. Let it boil, fkim it well, feafon with turnips, onions, carrots, and celery, and a good large bundle of fweet herbs. Boil it till it is half wafted, and then ftrain it off. Take the fins, and put them into a ftewpan, cover them with veal broth, feafon with an onion chopped fine, all forts of fweet herbs chopped very fine, half an ounce of cloves and mace, and half a nutmeg

nutmeg beat very fine. Stew it very gently till tender, then take out the fins, put in a pint of Madeira wine, and ſtew it a quarter of an hour. Beat up the whites of ſix eggs with the juice of two lemons, put the liquor in, and boil it up; run it through a flannel bag, make it very hot, waſh the fins very clean, and put them in. Put a piece of butter at the bottom of a ſtewpan, put your white meat in, and ſweat it gently till it is almoſt tender. Take the lungs and heart, and cover them with veal broth, an onion, herbs, and ſpice. As for the fins, ſtew them till tender. Take out the lungs, ſtrain off the liquor, thicken it, put in a bottle of Madeira wine, and ſeaſon with chyan pepper and ſalt pretty high. Put in the lungs and white meat, and ſtew them up gently for fifteen minutes. Have ſome forcemeat balls made out of the white part, inſtead of veal, as for Scotch collops. If any eggs, ſcald them; if not, take twelve hard yolks of eggs made into egg balls. Have your callapaſh, or deep ſhell, done round the edges with paſte, ſeaſon it in the inſide with pepper and ſalt, and a little Madeira wine. Bake it half an hour, then put in the lungs and white meat, forcemeat, and eggs over, and bake it half an hour. Take the bones, and three quarts of veal broth, ſeaſon with an onion, a bundle of ſweet herbs, and two blades of mace. Stew it an hour, ſtrain it through a ſieve, thicken it with butter and flour, put in half a pint of Madeira wine, ſtew it half an hour, and ſeaſon it with chyan and ſalt to your taſte. This is the ſoup. Take the callapee, run your knife between the meat and ſhell, and fill it full of forcemeat. Seaſon it all over with ſweet herbs chopped fine, a ſhalot chopped, chyan pepper and ſalt, and a little Madeira wine. Put a paſte round the edge, and bake it an hour and a half. Take the guts and maw, put them in a ſtewpan, with a little broth, a bundle of

ſweet

ſweet herbs, and two blades of mace finely beaten. Thicken with a little butter rolled in flour, ſtew them gently half an hour, and ſeaſon with chyan pepper and ſalt. Beat up the yolks of two eggs in half a pint of cream, put it in, and keep ſtirring it one way till it boils up. Then diſh them up, and put the callapee, ſoup, and callapaſh, in the center; the fricaſſee on one ſide, and the fins on the other. The fins eat fine, when cold, put by in the liquor.

To dreſs a Mock Turtle.

TAKE a calf's head, ſcald off the hair as from a pig, then clean it, and cut off the horny part in thin ſlices, with as little of the lean as poſſible. Chop the brains, and have ready between a quart and three pints of ſtrong mutton or veal gravy, with a quart of Madeira wine, a large ſpoonful of chyan, a large onion cut very ſmall, half the peel of a large lemon ſhred as fine as poſſible, a little ſalt, the juice of four lemons, and ſome ſweet herbs cut ſmall. Stew all theſe together till the head is very tender, which will require about an hour and a half. Then have ready the back ſhell of a turtle, lined with a paſte made of flour and water, which muſt firſt be ſet in the oven to harden, then put in the ingredients, and ſet it in the oven to brown. When that is done, lay the yolks of eggs boiled hard, and forcemeat balls, round the top. Some parboil the head the day before, take out the bones, and then cut it into ſlices.

CHAP. XI.

Sauces, Gravies, and Cullifes.

Ham Sauce.

BEAT fome thin flices of the lean part of a dreffed ham with a rolling-pin to a mafh, and put it into a faucepan, with a teacupful of gravy. Set it over a flow fire, and keep ftirring it to prevent its fticking at the bottom. When it has been on fome time, put in a bunch of fweet herbs, half a pint of beef gravy, and fome pepper. Cover it clofe, let it ftew over a gentle fire, and when it is quite done ftrain it off. This is a very good fauce for any kind of veal.

Effence of Ham.

CUT three or four pounds of lean ham into pieces about an inch thick, and lay them in the bottom of a ftewpan, with flices of carrots, parfnips, and three or four onions cut thin. Let them ftew till they ftick to the pan; but take care that they do not burn. Then, by degrees, pour on fome ftrong veal gravy, fome frefh mufhrooms cut in pieces, or mufhroom powder, truffles, morels, cloves, bafil, parfley, a cruft of bread, and a leek. Cover it down clofe, and when it has fimmered till it is of a good thicknefs and flavour, ftrain it off.

A Sauce for roaft Meat in general.

WASH an anchovy clean, and put to it a glafs of red wine, fome gravy, a fhalot cut fmall, and a little lemon juice. Stew thefe together, ftrain it off, and mix it with the gravy that runs from the meat.

Caper

Caper Sauce.

TAKE ſome capers, chop half of them very fine, and put the reſt in whole. Then chop ſome parſley, with a little grated bread, and put to it ſome ſalt. Put them into butter melted very ſmooth, let them boil up, and then pour them into a ſauce-boat.

Anchovy Sauce.

PUT an anchovy into half a pint of gravy, with a quarter of a pound of butter, rolled in a little flour, and ſtir all together till it boils. If you chuſe it, you may add a little lemon-juice, catchup, red wine, or walnut liquor.

Shalot Sauce.

PUT five or ſix ſhalots, chopped very fine, into a ſaucepan with a gill of gravy, a ſpoonful of vinegar, and ſome pepper, and ſalt. Stew them for a minute, and then pour them into a diſh or ſauce boat.

Egg Sauce.

BOIL two eggs till they are hard. Firſt chop the whites, then the yolks, but neither of them very fine, and put them together. Then put them into a quarter of a pound of good melted butter, and ſtir them well together.

Lemon Sauce.

PARE the rind off a lemon, cut it into ſlices, take the kernels out, and cut it into ſmall ſquare bits. Blanch the liver of a fowl, and chop it fine. Mix the lemon and liver together in a boat, pour on ſome hot melted butter, and ſtir it up.

Bread

Bread Sauce.

PUT a large piece of crumb from a ftale loaf into a faucepan, with half a pint of water, an onion, a blade of mace, and a few pepper-corns in a bit of cloth. Boil them a few minutes, then take out the onion and fpice, mafh the bread very fmooth, and add to it a piece of butter and a little falt.

Fennel Sauce.

BOIL a bunch of fennel and parfley, chop it very fmall, and ftir it into fome melted butter.

Goofeberry Sauce.

PUT fome fcalded goofeberries, a little juice of forrel, and a little ginger, into fome melted butter.

Mint Sauce.

WASH your mint perfectly clean from grit or dirt, then chop it very fine, and put to it vinegar and fugar.

Shrimp Sauce.

PUT half a pint of fhrimps wafhed very clean into a ftewpan, with a fpoonful of anchovy liquor, and half a pound of butter melted thick. Boil it up for five minutes, and fqueeze in half a lemon. Tofs it up, and pour it into a fauce-boat.

Oyfter Sauce.

PRESERVE the liquor of your oyfters as you open them, and ftrain it through a fine fieve. Wafh the oyfters very clean, and take off the beards. Put them into a ftewpan, and pour the liquor over them. Then add a large fpoonful of anchovy liquor, half a lemon, two blades of mace, and thicken it with butter rolled in flour. Then put in half a pound of butter, and boil it up till the butter

butter is melted. Then take out the mace and lemon, and ſqueeze the lemon-juice into the ſauce. Give it a boil, ſtirring it all the time, and pour it into your ſauce-boat.

Sauce for Wild Fowl.

TAKE a proper quantity of veal gravy, with ſome pepper and ſalt, ſqueeze in the juice of two Seville oranges, and add a little red wine, and let the wine boil ſome time in the gravy. This is a good ſauce for wild ducks, teal, &c.

A general Fiſh Sauce.

TAKE ſome mutton or veal gravy, and put to it a little of the liquor that drains from your fiſh. Put it into a ſaucepan, with an onion, an anchovy, a ſpoonful of catchup, and a glaſs of white wine. Thicken it with a lump of butter rolled in flour, and a ſpoonful of cream. If you have no cream, inſtead of white wine you muſt uſe red.

A reliſhing Sauce.

PUT two ſlices of ham, a clove of garlic, and two ſliced onions, into a ſtewpan. Let them heat, and then add a little broth, two ſpoonfuls of cullis, and a ſpoonful of tarragon vinegar. Stew them an hour over a ſlow fire, and then ſtrain it through a ſieve.

Pontiff Sauce.

PUT two or three ſlices of lean veal, and the ſame of ham, into a ſtewpan, with ſome ſliced onions, carrots, parſley, and a head of celery. When it is brown, add a little white wine, ſome good broth, a clove of garlic, four ſhalots, two cloves, and two ſlices of lemon peel. Boil it over a ſlow fire till the juices are extracted from the meat; then ſkim it, and ſtrain it through a ſieve. Juſt before you

you uſe it, add a little cullis, with ſome parſley chopped very fine.

Aſpic Sauce.

INFUSE chervil, tarragon, burnet, garden-creſs, and mint, into a little cullis for about an hour. Then ſtrain it, and add a ſpoonful of garlic vinegar, with a little pepper and ſalt.

Sicilian Sauce.

BRUISE half a ſpoonful of coriander ſeeds, and four cloves, in a mortar. Put three quarters of a pint of good gravy, and a quarter of a pint of eſſence of ham, into a ſtewpan. Peel half a lemon, and cut it into very thin ſlices, and put it in with the coriander ſeeds and cloves. Let them boil up, and then add three cloves of garlic whole, a head of celery ſliced, two bay leaves, and a little baſil. Let theſe boil till the liquor is reduced to half the quantity. Then put in a glaſs of white wine, ſtrain it off, and if not thick enough, put in a piece of butter rolled in flour. This is good ſauce for roaſt fowls.

To make a rich Gravy.

CUT into ſmall bits a piece of lean beef, a piece of veal, and a piece of mutton. Take a large ſaucepan with a cover, lay your beef at the bottom, then your mutton, a very little piece of bacon, a ſlice or two of carrot, ſome mace, cloves, whole black and white pepper, a large onion cut in ſlices, a bundle of ſweet herbs, and then lay on your veal. Cover it cloſe, and ſet it over a ſlow fire for ſix or ſeven minutes, and ſhake the ſaucepan often. Then duſt ſome flour into it, and pour in boiling water till the meat is ſomething more than covered. Cover your ſaucepan cloſe, and let it ſtew till it is rich and good. Then ſeaſon it with ſalt to your taſte,

taſte, and ſtrain it off. This gravy will anſwer almoſt every purpoſe.

To make a common Gravy.

TAKE a piece of chuck or neck beef, and cut it into ſmall pieces. Then ſtrew ſome flour over it, mix it well with the meat, and put it into a ſaucepan, with as much water as will cover it, an onion, a little all-ſpice, a little pepper, and ſome ſalt. Cover it cloſe, and when it boils ſkim it. Then throw in a hard cruſt of bread, or ſome raſpings, and let it ſtew till the gravy is rich and good, and then ſtrain it off.

Brown Gravy.

PUT a piece of butter, about the ſize of a hen's egg, into a ſaucepan, and when it is melted ſhake in a little flour, and let it be brown. Then by degrees ſtir in the following ingredients. Half a pint of water, and the ſame quantity of ale or ſmall beer that is not bitter; an onion, and a piece of lemon peel cut ſmall, three cloves, a blade of mace, ſome whole pepper, a ſpoonful of muſhroom pickle, the ſame quantity of catchup, and an anchovy. Let the whole boil together a quarter of an hour, then ſtrain it off, and it will be a good ſauce for various purpoſes.

To make Browning.

BEAT ſmall four ounces of triple-refined ſugar, and put it into a frying-pan, with an ounce of butter. Put it over a clear fire, and mix it well together. When it begins to be frothy by the ſugar diſſolving, hold it higher over the fire; and when the ſugar and butter is of a deep brown, pour in a little red wine, and ſtir it well together. Then add more wine, about a pint in all, and keep ſtirring it all the time. Put in half an ounce of Jamaica pepper,

pepper, ſix cloves, four ſhalots peeled, two or three blades of mace, three ſpoonfuls of catchup, a little ſalt, and the rind of a lemon. Boil them ſlowly about ten minutes, and then pour it into a baſon. When it is cold, ſkim it very clean, and bottle it up for uſe.

Forcemeat Balls.

CUT fine half a pound of veal and the ſame quantity of ſuet, and beat them in a mortar. Shred fine a few ſweet herbs, a little dried mace, a ſmall nutmeg grated, a little lemon-peel cut very fine, ſome pepper and ſalt, and the yolks of two eggs. Mix all theſe well together, then roll ſome of it in ſmall round balls, and ſome in long pieces. Roll them in flour, and fry them of a nice brown. If they are for the uſe of white ſauce, inſtead of frying, put a little water into a ſaucepan, and when it boils put them in, and they will be done in a few minutes.

To make Lemon Pickle.

GRATE off the outward rinds of a ſcore of lemons, and quarter them, but leave the bottoms whole. Rub on them equally half a pound of bay-ſalt, and ſpread them on a large pewter diſh. Either put them into a cool oven, or let them dry gradually by the fire, till all the juice is dried into the peels. Then put them into a well glazed pitcher, with an ounce of mace, half an ounce of cloves beat fine, an ounce of nutmeg cut into thin ſlices, four ounces of garlic peeled, half a pint of muſtard ſeed a little bruiſed, and tied in a muſlin rag. Pour upon them two quarts of boiling white wine vinegar, cloſe the pitcher well up, and let it ſtand five or ſix days by the fire. Shake it well up every day, then tie it cloſe, and let it ſtand three months to take off the bitter. When you

you bottle it, put the pickle and lemon in a hair ſieve, preſs them well to get out the liquor, and let it ſtand another day. Then pour off the fine, and bottle it. Let the other ſtand three or four days, and it will refine itſelf. Pour it off, and bottle it, let it ſtand again, and bottle it, till the whole is refined. It may be put into any white ſauce, without fear of hurting the colour; and is very good for fiſh-ſauce and made diſhes. A tea-ſpoonful is enough for white, and two for brown ſauce for a fowl. It is a moſt uſeful pickle, and gives an agreeable flavour. Always put it in before you thicken the ſauce, or put in any cream, leſt the ſharpneſs ſhould curdle it.

To make a white Cullis.

HAVING cut a piece of veal into ſmall bits, put it into a ſtewpan, with two or three ſlices of lean ham, and two onions quartered. Put in ſome broth, and ſeaſon it with muſhrooms, parſley, green onions, and cloves. Let it ſtew till the virtues of all are pretty well extracted. Then take out all your meat and roots, put in a few crumbs of bread, and let it ſtew ſoftly. Take the white part of a young fowl, and pound it in a mortar till it is very fine. Put this into your cullis, but do not let it boil; and, if it does not appear properly white, you muſt add to it two dozen of blanched almonds. When it has ſtewed till of a good rich taſte, ſtrain it off.

A rich Cullis.

PUT two pounds of leg of veal, and two ſlices of lean ham, into a ſtewpan, with two or three cloves, a little nutmeg, a blade of mace, ſome parſley roots, two carrots cut in pieces, and ſome ſhalots. Put them over a ſlow fire, cover them cloſe, and let them do gently for half an hour, taking care that they do not burn. Then put in

ſome

ſome beef broth, let it ſtew till it is as rich as required, and then ſtrain it off for uſe. This is a proper cullis for all ſorts of ragoos and rich ſauces.

A Family Cullis.

ROLL a piece of butter in flour, and ſtir it in your ſtewpan till the flour is of a fine yellow colour. Then put in ſome thin broth, a little gravy, a glaſs of white wine, a bundle of ſweet herbs, two cloves, a little nutmeg or mace, a few muſhrooms, and pepper and ſalt. Let it ſtew an hour over a ſlow fire, then ſkim all the fat clean off, and ſtrain it through a fine ſieve.

A Cullis of Roots.

CUT ſome carrots, parſnips, parſley roots, and onions, into ſlices, and put them into a ſtewpan over the fire, and ſhake them round. Take two dozen of blanched almonds, and the crumbs of two French-rolls, ſoaked firſt in good fiſh broth. Pound them with the roots in a mortar, and then boil all together. Seaſon it with pepper and ſalt, ſtrain it off, and uſe it for herb or fiſh ſoups.

A Fiſh Cullis.

BROIL a jack, or pike, till it is properly done, then take off the ſkin, and ſeparate the fleſh from the bones. Boil ſix eggs hard, and take out the yolks. Blanch a few almonds, beat them to a paſte in a mortar, and then add the yolks of the eggs. Mix theſe well with butter, then put in the fiſh, and pound all together. Take half a dozen onions, and cut them into ſlices, two parſnips, and three carrots. Set on a ſtewpan, and put into it a piece of butter to brown, and put in the roots when it boils. Turn them till they are brown, and then pour in a little broth to moiſten them. When it has boiled a few minutes, ſtrain it into another ſaucepan, and then put in a whole leek,

leek, ſome parſley, ſweet baſil, half a dozen cloves, ſome muſhrooms and truffles, and a few crumbs of bread. When it has ſtewed gently a quarter of an hour, put in the fiſh, &c. from the mortar. Let the whole ſtew ſome time longer, but be careful that it does not boil. When it is ſufficiently done, ſtrain it through a coarſe ſieve. This is a very proper ſauce to thicken all made diſhes.

CHAP. XII.

Soups and Broths.

Gravy Soup or Soupe Santé.

PUT at the bottom of a ſtewpan ſix good raſhers of lean ham, then put over them three pounds of lean beef, and cover the beef with three pounds of lean veal, ſix onions cut in ſlices, two carrots, and two turnips ſliced, two heads of celery, a bundle of ſweet herbs, ſix cloves, and two blades of mace. Put a little water at the bottom, draw it very gently till it ſticks, and then put in a gallon of boiling water. Let it ſtew two hours, ſeaſon it with ſalt, and ſtrain it off. Then have ready a carrot cut in ſmall pieces of two inches long, and about as thick as a gooſe quill, a turnip, two heads of leeks, two heads of celery, two heads of endive, cut acroſs, two cabbage lettuces cut acroſs, a little ſorrel, and chervil. Put them into a ſtewpan, and ſweat them gently a quarter of an hour. Then put them into your ſoup, and boil it up gently for ten minutes. Put it into your tureen, with the cruſt of a French roll.

Ver-

Vermicelli Soup.

HAVING put four ounces of butter into a large toſſing-pan, cut a knuckle of veal and a ſcrag of mutton into ſmall pieces about the ſize of walnuts. Slice in the meat of a ſhank of ham, with three or four blades of mace, two or three carrots, two parſnips, two large onions, with a clove ſtuck in at each end. Cut in four or five heads of celery waſhed clean, a bunch of ſweet herbs, eight or ten morels, and an anchovy. Cover the pan cloſe, and ſet it over a ſlow fire, without any water, till the gravy is drawn out of the meat. Then pour the gravy into a pot or baſon, let the meat brown in the ſame pan; but take care it does not burn. Then pour in four quarts of water, and let it boil gently till it is waſted to three pints. Then ſtrain it, and put the gravy to it. Set it on the fire, add to it two ounces of vermicelli, cut the niceſt part of a head of celery, put in chyan pepper and ſalt to your taſte, and let it boil about four minutes. If it is not of a good colour, put in a little browning, lay a French roll in the ſoup-diſh, pour in the ſoup upon it, and lay ſome of the vermicelli over it.

Soup Creſſy.

CUT a pound of lean ham into ſmall bits, and put it at the bottom of a ſtewpan, with a French roll cut and put over it. Cut two dozen heads of celery ſmall, ſix onions, two turnips, one carrot, cut and waſhed very clean, ſix cloves, four blades of mace, and two handfuls of water-creſſes. Put them all into a ſtewpan, with a pint of good broth. Cover them cloſe, and ſweat them gently for twenty minutes; then fill it up with veal broth. and ſtew it four hours. Rub it through a fine ſieve, put it in your pan again, and ſeaſon it with ſalt and a little chyan pepper. Give it a ſimmer

up,

up, and ſend it hot to table, with ſome French roll toaſted hard in it. Boil a handful of creſſes in water till tender, and put it over the bread.

Soup and Bouillie.

PUT into a ſtewpan five pounds of briſket of beef rolled tight with a tape, with four pounds of the leg of mutton piece of beef, and about ſeven or eight quarts of water. Boil theſe up as quick as poſſible, and ſkim it very clean. Add a large onion, ſix or ſeven cloves, ſome whole pepper, two or three carrots, a turnip or two, a leek, and two heads of celery. Cover it cloſe, and ſtew it gently ſix or ſeven hours. About an hour before dinner, ſtrain the ſoup through a piece of dimity that has been dipped in cold water, putting the rough ſide upwards. Have ready boiled carrots, cut like little wheels, turnips cut in balls, ſpinach, a little chervil and ſorrel, two heads of endive, and one or two of celery cut in pieces. Put theſe into a tureen, with a Dutch loaf, or a French roll dried, after the crumb is taken out. Pour the ſoup to theſe boiling hot, and add a little ſalt and chyan. Take the tape off the bouillie, and ſerve it in a ſeparate diſh; maſhed turnips, and ſliced carrots, in two little diſhes. The turnips and carrots ſhould be cut with an inſtrument that may be bought for that purpoſe.

Macaroni Soup.

TAKE three quarts of ſtrong broth, and one of gravy, and mix them. Boil half a pound of ſmall pipe macaroni in three quarts of water, with a little butter in it, till it is tender. Then ſtrain it through a ſieve. Cut it into pieces of about two inches in length, put it into your ſoup, and boil it up ten minutes. Send it to table in a tureen, with the cruſt of a French roll toaſted.

Dauphin

Dauphin Soup.

PUT a few ſlices of lard at the bottom of a ſaucepan, ſome ſliced ham and veal, three onions ſliced, and a carrot and parſnip. Soak it over the fire till it catches, then add weak broth or boiling water, and boil it on a ſlow fire till the meat is done. Pound the breaſt of a roaſted fowl, ſix yolks of hard eggs, and as many ſweet almonds. Strain your broth. Soak your bread in broth till it is tender, warm your cullis without boiling, and mix it with as much broth as will give it a pretty thick conſiſtence.

Soupe à la Reine.

TO a knuckle of veal, and three or four pounds of lean beef, put ſix quarts of water, with a little ſalt. Skim it well as ſoon as it boils, and then put in ſix large onions, two carrots, a head or two of celery, a parſnip, one leek, and a little thyme. Boil them all together till the meat is boiled quite down, then ſtrain it through a hair ſieve, and let it ſtand about half an hour. Then ſkim it well, and clear it off gently from the ſettlings into a clean pan. Boil half a pint of cream, and pour it on the crumb of a halfpenny loaf, and let it ſoak well. Blanch and beat half a pound of almonds as fine as poſſible, putting in now and then a little cream to prevent them oiling. Then take the yolks of ſix hard eggs, and the roll that is ſoaked in the cream, and beat them all together quite fine. Then make your broth hot, and pour it to your almonds. Strain it through a fine hair ſieve, rubbing it with a ſpoon till all the goodneſs is gone through into a ſtewpan, and add more cream to make it white. Set it over the fire, keep ſtirring it till it boils, ſkim off the froth as it riſes, and ſoak the tops of two French rolls in melted butter, in a ſtewpan, till they are criſp, but not brown.

brown. Then take them out of the butter, and lay them in a plate before the fire. A quarter of an hour before you ſend it to table, take a little of the hot ſoup, and put it to the roll in the bottom of the tureen. Put your ſoup on the fire, keep ſtirring it till ready to boil, then put it into your tureen, and ſerve it up hot. Be careful to take all the fat off the broth before you put it to the almonds, or it will ſpoil it, and take care it does not curdle.

Tranſparent Soup.

TAKE a leg of veal, cut the meat from it into ſmall pieces, and break the bone into ſeveral bits. Put the meat into a large jug, and the bones at top, with a bunch of ſweet herbs, a quarter of an ounce of mace, and half a pound of Jordan almonds finely blanched and beaten. Pour on it four quarts of boiling water, and let it ſtand all night, covered cloſe, by the fire ſide. The next day put it into a well-tinned ſaucepan, and let it boil ſlowly till it is reduced to two quarts. Be careful, all the time it is boiling, to ſkim it, and take off the fat as it riſes. Strain it into a punch-bowl, and, when it has ſettled two hours, pour it into a clean ſaucepan, clear from the ſediments, if any, at the bottom. Add three ounces of rice or two ounces of vermicelli, boiled in water.

Soup au Bourgeois.

CUT four or five bunches of celery, and ten or a dozen heads of endive, into ſmall bits. Waſh them, let them be well drained from the water, and put them into a large pan. Pour upon them four quarts of boiling water. Then ſet on three quarts of beef gravy, made for ſoup, in a large ſaucepan. Strain the herbs very dry from the water, and, when the gravy boils, put them in. Cut off the cruſt of two French rolls, break them, and put them into the reſt. The ſoup will be enough

enough as ſoon as the herbs are tender. A boiled fowl may be put into the middle; but it will be good enough without it. If you like white ſoup better, you may make uſe of veal gravy.

Calf's Head Soup.

HAVING waſhed a calf's head clean, ſtew it with a bunch of ſweet herbs, an onion ſtuck with cloves, mace, pearl barley, and Jamaica pepper. When it is very tender, put to it ſome ſtewed celery. Seaſon it with pepper and ſalt, diſh it up with the head in the middle, and ſend it to table.

Hare Soup.

CUT a large old hare into ſmall pieces, and put it into a mug, with three blades of mace, a little ſalt, two large onions, a red herring, ſix morels, half a pint of red wine, and three quarts of water. Bake it three hours in a quick oven, and then ſtrain it into a toſſing-pan. Have ready, boiled in water, three ounces of French barley, or ſago. Then put the liver of the hare two minutes into ſcalding water, and rub it through a hair ſieve with the back of a wooden ſpoon. Put it into the ſoup with the barley or ſago, and a quarter of a pound of butter. Set it over the fire, and keep it ſtirring, but do not let it boil.

Almond Soup.

HAVING blanched a quart of almonds, beat them in a marble mortar, with the yolks of ſix hard eggs, till they become a fine paſte. Mix them by degrees with two quarts of new milk, a quart of cream, and a quarter of a pound of double refined ſugar beat fine. Stir all well together, and when it is well mixed, ſet it over a ſlow fire, and keep it ſtirring quick all the time, till you find it is thick enough; but take great care that it does not curdle. Then pour it into your diſh, and ſerve it up.

Partridge Soup.

TAKE two old partridges and ſkin them. Cut them into ſmall pieces, with three ſlices of ham, two or three onions ſliced, and ſome celery. Fry them in butter till they are as brown as they can be made without burning, and then put them into three quarts of water with a few pepper corns. Boil it ſlowly till a little more than a pint is conſumed. Then ſtrain it, and put in ſome fried bread and ſtewed celery.

Giblet Soup.

PUT about two pounds of ſcrag of mutton, the ſame quantity of ſcrag of veal, and four pounds of gravy beef, into two gallons of water, and let it ſtew very ſoftly till it is a ſtrong broth. Then let it ſtand till it is cold, and ſkim off the fat. Scald and clean two pair of giblets, put them into the broth, and let them ſimmer till they are very tender. Take out the giblets, and ſtrain the ſoup through a cloth. Put a piece of butter rolled in flour into a ſtewpan, and make it of a light brown. Chop ſmall ſome parſley, chives, a little pennyroyal, and a little ſweet marjoram. Put the ſoup over a very ſlow fire. Put in the giblets, fried butter, herbs, a little Madeira wine, ſome ſalt, and a little chyan pepper. Let them ſimmer till the herbs are tender, put the giblets into the diſh, and ſend them and the ſoup up to table.

Green Peas Soup.

SHELL a peck of peas, and boil them in ſpring water till they are ſoft. Then work them through a hair ſieve. Put into the water the peas were boiled in a knuckle of veal, three ſlices of ham,

ham, two carrots, a turnip, and a few beet-leaves cut ſmall. Add a little more water to the meat, ſet it over the fire, and let it boil an hour and an half. Then ſtrain the gravy into a bowl, mix it with the pulp, and put in a little juice of ſpinach, which muſt be beaten and ſqueezed through a cloth. Put in as much as will make it look of a pretty colour, and then give it a gentle boil, which will take off the taſte of the ſpinach. Slice in the whiteſt part of a head of celery, put in a lump of ſugar the ſize of a walnut, cut a ſlice of bread into little ſquare pieces, a little bacon in the ſame manner, and fry them of a light brown in freſh butter. Cut a large cabbage lettuce into ſlices, fry it after the other, and put it into the tureen with the fried bread and bacon. Have ready boiled, as for eating, a pint of young peas, and put them into the ſoup, with a little chopped mint.

Common Peas Soup.

TO a quart of ſplit peas put a gallon of ſoft water, and a little lean bacon, or roaſt-beef bones. Waſh a head of celery, cut it, and put it in with a turnip. Boil it till it is reduced to two quarts, and then work it through a cullender with a wooden ſpoon. Mix a little flour and water, boil it with the ſoup, and ſlice in another head of celery, chyan pepper, and ſalt to your taſte. Cut a ſlice of bread into ſmall dice, fry them of a light brown, put them into your diſh, and pour the ſoup over them.

Portable Soup.

TAKE three large legs of veal, one of beef, and the lean part of half a ham, and cut them into ſmall pieces. Put a quarter of a pound of butter at the bottom of a large cauldron, then lay in the meat and bones, with four ounces of anchovies, and two ounces of mace. Cut off the green leaves of of five or fix heads of celery, wafh them very clean, cut them fmall, and put them in, with three large carrots cut thin. Cover the cauldron clofe, and fet it over a moderate fire. When you find the gravy begins to draw, keep taking it up till you have got it all out, and then put in water fufficient to cover the meat. Set it on the fire again, and let it boil flowly four hours. Then ftrain it through a hair fieve into a clean pan, and let it boil three parts away. Then ftrain the gravy that you drew from the meat, into the pan, and let it boil gently, obferving to fkim the fat off as it rifes, till it looks thick like glue. Great care muft be taken, when it is nearly enough, that it does not burn. Put in chyan pepper to your tafte, then pour it on flat earthen difhes a quarter of an inch thick, and let it ftand till the next day. Cut it out with round tins a little larger than a crown piece; lay the cakes on difhes, fet them in the fun to dry, and take care to turn them often. Frofty weather is the beft feafon for making this foup. When the cakes are dry, put them in a tin box, with writing-paper between every cake, and keep them in a dry place. Gentlemens families fhould not be without this foup; for by pouring a pint of boiling water on one cake, and a little falt, it will make a good bafon of broth, and alfo gravy for turkies or fowls. As it will keep a great while, it is extremely ufeful to travellers.

Afparagus Soup.

CUT four or five pounds of beef into pieces, and fet it over a fire, with an onion or two, a few cloves, fome whole black pepper, a calf's foot or two, a head or two of celery, and a fmall piece of butter. Let it draw at a diftance from the fire. Put in a quart of warm beer, and three quarts of warm beef broth, or water, and let them ftew till enough. Strain it, take off the fat very clean, put in fome afparagus aſparagus heads cut ſmall, and the cruſt of a toaſted French roll. You may add palates, boiled very tender, if you chooſe them.

Soupe Lorraine.

BLANCH and beat a pound of ſweet almonds in a mortar, with a very little water to keep them from oiling. Put to them all the white part of a large roaſt fowl, the yolks of four poached eggs, and pound all together as fine as poſſible. Take three quarts of ſtrong veal broth, let it be very white, and ſkim off the fat. Put it into a ſtewpan with the other ingredients, mix them well together, and boil them ſoftly over a ſtove, or on a clear fire. Mix the white part of another roaſt fowl pounded very fine, and ſeaſon with pepper, ſalt, nutmeg, and a little beaten mace. Put in a bit of butter as big as an egg, a ſpoonful or two of the ſoup ſtrained, and ſet it over the ſtove till it is quite hot. Cut two French rolls into thin ſlices, and ſet them before the fire to criſp. Take one of the hollow rolls, which are made for oyſter loaves, and fill it with the mince. Lay on the top as cloſe as poſſible, and keep it hot. Strain the ſoup through a piece of dimity into a clean ſaucepan, and let it ſtew till it is of the thickneſs of cream. Put the criſped bread in the diſh or tureen, pour the ſauce over it, and put in the middle the minced meat and the roll.

Soup Maigre.

HAVING put half a pound of butter into a deep ſtewpan, ſhake it about, and let it ſtand till it has done making a noiſe. Peel and cut ſmall ſix middling-ſized onions, throw them into the pan, and ſhake them about. Take a bunch of celery, clean waſhed and picked, and cut in pieces about two inches long; pick and waſh clean a large handful of ſpinach, waſh and cut ſmall a good lettuce, and

and chop fine a bundle of parſley. Shake all theſe well together in the pan for a quarter of an hour, and then ſhake in a little flour. Stir all together, and pour two quarts of boiling water into the ſtew-pan. Put in a handful of dry hard cruſt, a tea-ſpoonful of beaten pepper, three blades of mace beat fine; ſtir them all together, and let them boil ſoftly for half an hour. Then take it off the fire, beat up the yolks of two eggs, and ſtir them in, with a ſpoonful of vinegar. Pour it into the ſoup-diſh, and ſerve it up.

Egg Soup.

HAVING beat the yolks of two eggs in a diſh, with a piece of butter the ſize of a common egg, take a tea-kettle of boiling water in one hand, and a ſpoon in the other. Pour in, by degrees, about a quart of water, and keep ſtirring it well all the time, till the eggs are well mixed, and the butter melted. Then pour it into a ſaucepan, and keep ſtirring it till it begins to ſimmer. Take it off the fire, and pour it out of one veſſel into another, till it is quite ſmooth, and has a good froth. Then put it on the fire again, keep ſtirring it till it is quite hot, and then pour it into your ſoup-diſh.

Rice Soup.

TO two quarts of water put a pound of rice and a little cinnamon; then cover it cloſe, and let it ſimmer very ſoftly till the rice is quite tender. Then take out the cinnamon, and ſweeten it to your palate, grate in half a nutmeg, and let it ſtand till it is cold. Beat up the yolks of three eggs with half a pint of white wine, mix them well, and ſtir them into the rice. Set them on a ſlow fire, and keep conſtantly ſtirring them, to prevent their curdling. When it boils, and is of a good thickneſs, take it up, and ſend it to table.

Onion

Onion Soup.

BROWN half a pound of butter with a little flour; but take care it does not burn. When it has done hiffing, flice a dozen of large white onions, fry them very gently till they are tender, and then pour to them, by degrees, two quarts of boiling water, fhaking the pan well round as it is pouring in. Put in a cruft of bread, let it boil gently half an hour, and feafon it with pepper and falt. Take the top of a French roll, dry it at a fire, put it into a faucepan with fome of the foup to foak it, and then put it into the tureen. Let the foup boil fome time after the onions are tender, as it will add much to the richnefs of the foup. Strain it off, and pour it on the French roll.

Muffel Soup.

HAVING wafhed an hundred of muffels very clean, put them into a faucepan till they open, and then take them from the fhells, beard them, and ftrain the liquor through a lawn fieve. Beat a dozen craw-fifh very fine, with as many blanched almonds, in a mortar. Take a carrot and a fmall parfnip fcraped, cut them into flices, and fry them in butter. Take the muffel liquor, with a fmall bunch of fweet herbs, a little parfley and horfe-radifh, with the crawfifh and almonds, a little pepper and falt, and half the muffels, with a quart of water, or more. Let it boil till all the goodnefs is extracted from the ingredients, and then ftrain it off to two quarts of white fifh-ftock. Put it into a faucepan, and put in the reft of the muffels, a few truffles and mufhrooms, and a leek wafhed and cut fmall. Cut out the crumb of two French rolls, fry it brown, cut it into little pieces, and put it into the foup. Let it boil together a quarter of an hour, with the fried carrot and parfnip, and at the fame ſame time, fry the cruſt of the roll criſp. Take the other half of the muſſels, a quarter of a pound of butter, and a ſpoonful of water. Shake in a little flour, and ſet them on the fire till the butter is melted. Seaſon it with pepper and ſalt, then beat the yolks of three eggs, put them in, ſtir them conſtantly to prevent their curdling, and grate in a little nutmeg. When it is thick and fine, fill the rolls, pour the ſoup into the tureen, and ſet the rolls in the middle.

Oyſter Soup.

TAKE a proper quantity of fiſh ſtock, and two quarts of oyſters bearded. Beat the hard part in a mortar, with the yolks of ten hard eggs, put them to the fiſk ſtock, and ſet it over the fire. Seaſon it with pepper, ſalt, and grated nutmeg. When it boils, put in the eggs, and let it boil till it is of a good thickneſs, and like a fine cream.

Eel Soup.

A pound of eels will make a pint of good ſoup; or take any greater quantity of eels, in proportion to the quantity of ſoup you intend to make. To every pound of eels put a quart of water, a cruſt of bread, two or three blades of mace, a little whole pepper, an onion, and a bundle of ſweet herbs. Cover them cloſe, and let them boil till half the liquor is waſted. Then ſtrain it, toaſt ſome bread, cut it ſmall, lay the bread into your diſh, and pour in the ſoup. If you find your ſoup is not rich enough, you may let it boil till you think it is properly thick.

Scate Soup.

SKIN and waſh two pounds of ſcate, and boil it in ſix quarts of water. When it is boiled, take the meat from the bones. Take two pounds of flounders,

flounders, waſh them clean, put them into the water the ſcate was boiled in, with ſome lemon peel, a bunch of ſweet herbs, a few blades of mace, ſome horſe-radiſh, the cruſt of a penny loaf, a little parſley, and the bones of the ſcate. Cover it very cloſe, and let it ſimmer till it is reduced to two quarts. Then ſtrain it off, and put to it an ounce of vermicelli. Set it on the fire, and let it boil very ſoftly. Take one of the hollow rolls, which are made for oyſters, and fry it in butter. Take the meat of the ſcate, pull it into little ſlices, and put it into a ſaucepan with two or three ſpoonfuls of the ſoup. Shake into it a little flour, and put in a piece of butter, and ſome pepper and ſalt. Shake them together in a ſaucepan till it is thick, and then fill the roll with it. Pour the ſoup into the tureen, put the roll into it, and ſerve it up.

Milk Soup.

PUT two ſticks of cinnamon, two bay-leaves, a very little baſket ſalt, and a very little ſugar, into two quarts of milk. Blanch half a pound of ſweet almonds, beat them up to a paſte in a marble mortar, and mix ſome milk with them by degrees. Grate the peel of a lemon with the almonds and a little of the juice. Then ſtrain it through a coarſe ſieve, mix it with the milk that is heating in the ſtewpan, and let it boil up. Cut ſome ſlices of French bread, and dry them before the fire. Soak them a little in the milk, lay them at the bottom of the tureen, and pour in the ſoup.

Chicken Broth.

FLAY an old cock, or a large fowl, pick off all the fat, and break it to pieces with a rolling pin. Put it into two quarts of water, with a good cruſt of bread, and a blade of mace. Let it boil ſoftly till it is as good as you would have it, and it

will

will take five or ſix hours doing. Then pour it off, put a quart more boiling water to it, and cover it cloſe. Let it boil ſoftly till it is good, and then ſtrain it off. Seaſon it with a very little ſalt. When you boil the chicken, ſave the liquor, and when the meat is eaten, take the bones, break them, and put them to the liquor in which you boiled the chicken, with a blade of mace, and a cruſt of bread.

Veal Broth.

STEW a knuckle of veal in about a gallon of water, two ounces of rice, or vermicelli, a little ſalt, and a blade of mace.

Strong Beef Broth to keep for Uſe.

TAKE the ſcrag end of a neck of mutton, and part of a leg of beef, and break the bones in pieces. Put to it as much water as will cover it, and a little ſalt. When it boils, ſkim it clean, and put into it a whole onion ſtuck with cloves, a bunch of ſweet herbs, ſome pepper, and a nutmeg quartered. Let theſe boil till the meat is boiled in pieces, and the ſtrength boiled out of it. Strain it off, and keep it for uſe.

Common Beef Broth.

BREAK the bone of a leg of beef in two or three places, put it into a gallon of water, with two or three blades of mace, a little parſley, and a cruſt of bread. Boil the beef very tender, ſtrain the broth, and pour it into a tureen; if you chooſe it, the meat may be put along with the broth. Put into a plate ſome bread toaſted, and cut into ſquares.

Mutton

Mutton Broth.

PUT a ſcrag of mutton into three or four quarts of water, and boil it. Skim it as ſoon as it boils, and put to it a carrot, a turnip, a cruſt of bread, an onion, and a ſmall bundle of herbs, and let them ſtew. Put in the other part of the neck, that it may be boiled tender, and when it is enough, take out the mutton, and ſtrain the broth. Put in the mutton again, with a few dried marigolds, chives, or young onions, and a little chopped parſley. Boil theſe about a quarter of an hour. The broth and mutton may be ſerved together in a tureen, or the meat in a ſeparate diſh. The broth may be thickened with either crumbs of bread, or oatmeal. Send up maſhed turnips in a little diſh.

Scotch Barley Broth.

HAVING chopped a leg of beef to pieces, boil it in three gallons of water, with a piece of carrot, and a cruſt of bread, till it is half boiled away. Then ſtrain it off, and put it into the pot again with half a pound of barley, four or five heads of celery waſhed clean and cut ſmall, a large onion, a bundle of ſweet herbs, a little parſley chopped ſmall, and a few marigolds. Let it boil an hour. Take an old cock, or a large fowl, clean picked and waſhed, and put it into the pot. Boil it till the broth is quite good. Then ſeaſon it with ſalt, take out the onion and ſweet herbs, and ſerve it up.

CHAP.

CHAP. XIII.

To dreſs Roots and Vegetables.

To dreſs Cabbages.

HAVING cut your cabbage into quarters, boil it in plenty of water, with a handful of ſalt. When it is tender, drain it on a ſieve, but never preſs it. Savoys and greens are boiled in the ſame manner; but they ſhould be always boiled by themſelves.

To dreſs Brocoli.

STRIP off all the little branches till you come to the top one, and then carefully peel off the hard outſide ſkin that is on the ſtalks and little branches, and throw them into water. Throw a little ſalt into a ſtewpan, and put in your brocoli as ſoon as it boils. When the ſtalks are tender, it will then be enough. Put in a piece of toaſted bread, dipped in the water the brocoli was boiled in, at the bottom of your diſh, and put your brocoli on the top of it. Send it up to table laid in bunches, with butter in a boat.

To dreſs Cauliflowers.

CUT off the ſtalks, but leave a little green on. Boil them in ſpring water and ſalt, and about a quarter of an hour will do them; but take care that they do not boil too faſt, as that will ſpoil them. Some people boil them in milk and water, without ſalt.

To dreſs Spinach.

SPINACH muſt be clean picked, and waſhed in ſeveral waters. Put it into a ſaucepan that will juſt hold it, throw a little ſalt over it, and cover the pan cloſe; but put no water in, and ſhake the pan often. When the ſpinach is ſhrunk, and fallen to the bottom, and the liquor that comes out of it boils up, it is enough. Throw it into a clean ſieve to drain, and give it a ſqueeze between two plates. Put it on a plate, and ſerve it up with butter in a boat, but never pour any over it. Sorrel is ſtewed in the ſame manner.

To dreſs French Beans.

IF your French beans are not very ſmall, ſplit and quarter them, and throw them into ſalt and water. Boil them in plenty of water, with ſome ſalt, and take them up as ſoon as they are tender. All ſorts of greens ſhould boil as quick as poſſible, as it preſerves their colour.

To dreſs Aſparagus.

HAVING ſcraped your aſparagus, tie them in bundles, cut them even, and throw them into water. Tie them up into little bundles, and put them into a ſtewpan of boiling water with ſome ſalt. Let the water keep boiling, and when they are a little tender, take them up; for, if you boil them too much, you will ſpoil both their colour and flavour. Lay them on a toaſt that has been dipped in the water the aſparagus was boiled in. Pour over them melted butter, or put butter into a baſon, and ſend them up to table.

To dreſs Peas.

DO not ſhell your peas till juſt before you want them. Put them into boiling water with a little ſalt, and a lump of loaf ſugar, and when they begin to dent in the middle, they are enough. Strain them into a ſieve, put a good lump of butter into your diſh, and ſtir them till the butter is melted. Boil a ſprig of mint by itſelf, chop it fine, and lay it in lumps round the edge of your diſh.

To dreſs Garden Beans.

BEANS muſt be boiled in plenty of water; and, like peas, ſhould be ſhelled only juſt before they are wanted. Put a good quantity of ſalt into the water, and boil them till they are tender. Boil and chop ſome parſley, put it into good melted butter, and ſerve them up with boiled bacon, and the butter and parſley in a boat. The bacon muſt not be boiled with the beans.

To dreſs Artichokes.

HAVING twiſted the ſtalks off your artichokes, put them into cold water, and waſh them well. Put them into boiling water with the top downwards, in order that all the grit and ſand may boil out. They will require an hour and a half, or two hours boiling. Put melted butter into little cups, and ſerve them up.

To fricaſſee Artichoke Bottoms.

TAKE either dried or pickled artichoke bottoms; but, if you uſe dried, you muſt put them in warm water three or four hours, ſhifting the water two or three times. Have ready a little cream, and a piece of freſh butter, ſtirred together one way till it is melted. Then put in the artichokes, and diſh them up as ſoon as they are hot.

To dreſs Turnips.

PARE your turnips thick, and when they are boiled, ſqueeze them, and maſh them ſmooth. Heat them with a little cream, and a piece of butter.

butter. Put to them ſome pepper and ſalt, and ſerve them up. It will be perhaps better to omit the pepper and ſalt, and leave the company to pleaſe their own palates.

To dreſs Carrots.

IF your carrots are young, you need only wipe them after they are boiled; but, if they are old, you muſt ſcrape them before they are boiled. Slice them into a plate, and pour melted butter over them. Young ſpring carrots will be boiled in half an hour, large ones in an hour, and old Sandwich carrots will take two hours.

To dreſs Potatoes.

COVER the ſaucepan cloſe, boil them in very little water, and when the ſkin begins to crack, they will be enough. Drain out all the water, and let them ſtand covered a little.

To dreſs Parſnips.

THEY muſt be boiled in plenty of water, and when you can run a fork into them eaſily, they will be enough. They may be ſerved up either whole with melted butter, or beat ſmooth in a bowl, heated with a little cream, butter, and flour, and a little ſalt.

To fricaſſee Skirrets.

WASH the roots well, and boil them till they are tender. Take the ſkin off the roots, and cut them into ſlices. Have ready a little cream, a piece of butter rolled in flour, the yolk of an egg beaten, a little nutmeg grated, two or three ſpoonfuls of white wine, a very little ſalt, and ſtir them all together. Put your roots into the diſh, and pour the ſauce over them.

To fricassee Mushrooms.

HAVING peeled your mushrooms, and scraped the inside of them, throw them into salt and water. If they are buttons, rub them with flannel; take them out, and boil them with fresh salt and water. When they are tender, put in a little shred parsley, and an onion stuck with cloves, and toss them up with a good lump of butter rolled in a little flour. You may put in three spoonfuls of thick cream, and a little nutmeg cut in pieces; but be sure to take out the nutmeg and onion before you send it to table.

CHAP. XIV.

Elegant little Dishes for Suppers or light Repasts.

To ragoo Asparagus.

TAKE one hundred grass, scrape and clean them, and throw them into cold water. Cut them as far as they are good and green, and pick and wash clean, and cut very small, two heads of endive; take a young lettuce clean washed and cut small, and a large onion peeled and cut small. Put a quarter of a pound of butter into a stewpan, and when it is melted, throw in the above ingredients. Toss them about, and fry them ten minutes. Season them with a little pepper and salt, shake in a little flour, toss them about, and pour in half a pint of gravy. Let them stew till the sauce is very thick and good, and then pour all into

into your diſh. You may make uſe of a few of the ſmall tops of the graſs for garniſh.

Eggs and Brocoli.

WHEN you boil your brocoli, which will be enough as ſoon as it is tender, ſave a large bunch for the middle, and ſix or eight little ſprigs to ſtick round. Toaſt a bit of bread, of what ſize you pleaſe, but proportion it to the ſize of your diſh. Take as many eggs as you have occaſion for, beat them well, and put them into a ſaucepan with a good piece of butter, and a little ſalt. Keep beating them with a ſpoon till they are thick enough, and then pour them on the toaſt. Set the largeſt bunch of brocoli in the middle, and the other little pieces round them, and garniſh the diſh with ſprigs of brocoli.

To ragoo Cauliflowers.

PICK a large cauliflower, or two ſmall ones, in the ſame manner as for pickling. Stew them in a brown cullis till they are enough, and ſeaſon them with pepper and ſalt. Put them into a diſh, and pour the cullis over them. Lay round them ſome ſprigs of the cauliflower boiled very white.

To ſtew Peas with Lettuces.

SHELL your peas, and boil them in hard water, with ſome ſalt in it, and drain them in a ſieve. Slice your lettuces, and fry them in freſh butter. Then put your peas and lettuces into a toſſing-pan, with a little good gravy, pepper, and ſalt. Thicken it with flour and butter, put in a little ſhred mint, and ſerve it up.

To ragoo Cucumbers.

SLICE two cucumbers and two onions, fry them in a little butter, and drain them in a ſieve. Put

Put them into a ſaucepan, with ſix ſpoonfuls of gravy, two of white wine, and a blade of mace. Let them ſtew five or ſix minutes, and then take a piece of butter, as big as a walnut, rolled in flour, a little ſalt, and chyan pepper. Shake them together, and when it is thick diſh them up.

Artichoke Bottoms with Eggs.

BOIL them in hard water, but, if dry bottoms, in ſoft water. Put a good lump of butter into the water, which will make them boil much ſooner, and look more white and plump. When you ſerve them up, put the yolk of a hard egg in every bottom.

To ragoo Artichoke Bottoms.

IF your artichoke bottoms are dry, let them lie in warm water two or three hours, changing the water. Put to them ſome good gravy, muſhroom catchup or powder, chyan, and ſalt. Thicken with a little flour, and boil all together.

To ſtew Muſhrooms.

PUT your muſhrooms into ſalt and water, then wipe them with a flannel, and put them in again. Put them into a ſaucepan by themſelves, and let them boil as quick as poſſible. Then put in a little chyan pepper and mace, and let them ſtew in this a quarter of an hour. Put in a teaſpoonful of cream, with a little flour and butter the ſize of a walnut, and when they are done, ſerve them up.

To ragoo Muſhrooms.

HAVING procured ſome large muſhrooms, ſcrape the inſides of them, and broil them. As ſoon as they are a little brown, put them into ſome gravy thickened with a little flour, a very little Madeira, ſalt, and chyan, and a little lemon-juice. Give them a boil all together.

To

To make Muſhroom Loaves.

WASH ſome ſmall buttons as for pickling, and boil them a few minutes in a little water. Put to them a little cream, a piece of butter rolled in flour, and ſome ſalt and pepper. Boil theſe up, and fill ſome ſmall Dutch loaves, or French rolls, with the crumb taken out; but Dutch loaves are better, if they are to be had.

Aſparagus and Eggs.

HAVING toaſted a piece of bread of what ſize you pleaſe, butter it, and lay it in your diſh. Take as many eggs as you want, beat them well, and put them into a ſaucepan, with a good piece of butter, and a little ſalt. Keep beating them with a ſpoon till they are thick enough. In the mean time, boil ſome graſs tender, cut it ſmall, pour the eggs over the toaſt, and lay the graſs upon it.

Spinach and Eggs.

HAVING picked, and waſhed your ſpinach very clean in ſeveral waters, put it into a ſaucepan with a little ſalt, cover it cloſe, and ſhake the pan often. When it is ſtewed tender, and while it is green, throw it into a ſieve to drain, and then lay it in your diſh. Break as many eggs into cups as you intend to poach, and put them into boiling water. When they are done, take them out with an egg ſlice, and lay them on the ſpinach. Serve it up with melted butter in a cup, and garniſh with an orange quartered.

To make an Amulet.

TAKE ſix eggs, beat them, ſtrain them through a ſieve, and put them into a frying-pan, in which is a quarter of a pound of hot butter. Put in a little boiled ham, ſcraped fine, ſome ſhred parſley, and ſeaſon them with pepper, ſalt, and nutmeg. Fry it brown on the under ſide, and lay it on your diſh, but do not turn it. Hold a hot ſalamander over it half a minute, to take off the raw look of the eggs, ſtick in it ſome curled parſley, and ſend it up to table.

To force Eggs.

HAVING ſcalded two cabbage lettuces with a few muſhrooms, parſley, ſorrel, and chervil, chop them very ſmall, with the yolks of hard eggs, ſeaſoned with ſalt and nutmeg. Stew them in butter, and when they are enough, put in a little cream, and then pour them into the bottom of a diſh. Chop the whites very fine, with parſley, nutmeg, and ſalt. Lay this round the rim of the diſh, and brown it with a ſalamander.

To ragoo Celery.

CUT the white part of the celery into lengths, and boil it till it is tender. Then fry and drain it, flour it, and put to it ſome rich gravy, a very little red wine, ſalt, pepper, nutmeg, and catchup. Give it a boil, and then ſend it up to table.

To fry Celery.

FIRST boil it, then dip it into batter, and fry it of a light brown in hog's lard. Put it on a plate, and pour melted butter over it.

To fry Chardoons.

HAVING cut them about ſix inches long, ſtring them, and boil them till tender. Then put them into a ſtewpan, in melted butter, flour them, and fry them brown. Send them up in a diſh, with melted butter in a cup. You may, if you pleaſe, dreſs and diſh them up like aſparagus.

To scallop Potatoes.

FIRST boil your potatoes, and then beat them in a bowl with some good cream, and a lump of butter and salt. Put them into scollop shells, make them smooth on the top, score them with a knife, lay thin slices of butter upon the top of them, and put them in a Dutch oven to brown.

To mash Potatoes.

BOIL and peel them, and put them into a saucepan. Mash them well, and put a pint of milk to two pounds of potatoes. Add a little salt, stir them well together, and take care that they do not stick to the bottom. Then take a quarter of a pound of butter, stir it in, and send them up to table.

To fry Potatoes.

HAVING cut your potatoes into thin slices, as large as a crown piece, fry them brown, lay them in a plate or dish, and pour melted butter, and sack and sugar over them.

CHAP. XV.

To make Fruit Pies.

To make Paste for large Pies.

BEFORE we enter on the making of pies, it may not be improper to give some instructions for making the different sorts of paste. The method of making Meat, Poultry, Game, and Fish

Fiſh Pies, will be found in the preceding chapters, under the heads of beef, mutton, &c. &c.

To make a good paſte for large pies, put the yolks of three eggs to a peck of flour, pour in ſome boiling water, then put in half a pound of ſuet, and a pound and a half of butter. Skim off the butter and ſuet, and as much of the liquor as will make it a light good cruſt. Work it up well, and roll it out.

To make a Puff-paſte.

RUB a pound of butter into a quarter of a peck of flour, and make it up in a light paſte with cold water, juſt ſtiff enough to work it up. Then roll it out about as thick as a crown piece, and put a layer of butter all over. Sprinkle on a little flour, double it up, and roll it out again. Double it, and roll it out three times, and it will then be a good puff-paſte.

To make a ſhort Cruſt.

PUT ſix ounces of butter into eight of flour, and mix it up with as little water as poſſible, ſo as to have it a ſtiffiſh paſte. Beat it well, and roll it thin. This is the beſt cruſt for all tarts that are to be eaten cold, and for preſerved fruit. Bake it in a moderate oven.

To make a Paſte for Cuſtards.

PUT ſix ounces of butter to half a pound of flour, the yolks of two eggs, and three ſpoonfuls of cream. Mix them together, and let them ſtand a quarter of an hour. Then work it up and down, and roll it very thin.

To make a Paſte for Tarts.

MIX three quarters of a pound of butter with one pound of flour, and beat it well with a rolling pin.

To make a crifp Pafte for Tarts.

BEAT the white of an egg to a ftrong froth, put in by degrees four ounces of double refined fugar, with about as much gum as will lie upon a fixpence, beaten and fifted fine. Beat it half an hour, and it will then be fit for ufe.

To make an Apple Tart.

SCALD eight or ten large codlings, and fkin them as foon as they are cold. Beat the pulp very fine with a fpoon, and then mix the yolks of fix eggs, and the whites of four. Beat all together as fine as poffible, and put in grated nutmeg and fugar to your tafte. Melt fome frefh butter, and beat it till it is like a fine cream. Then make a fine puff-pafte, cover a tin patty-pan with it, and pour in the ingredients, but do not cover it with the pafte. Bake it a quarter of an hour, then flip it out of the patty-pan on a difh, and ftrew over it fome fugar finely beaten and fifted.

To make an Apple Pie.

HAVING laid a good puff-pafte round the fides of the difh, pare and quarter your apples, and take out the cores. Lay a row of apples thick, throw in half the fugar you intend to ufe, throw over it a little lemon-peel minced fine, and fqueeze over them a little lemon; fprinkle in a few cloves, and then put in the reft of your apples and your fugar. Sweeten to your palate, and fqueeze a little more lemon. Boil the peelings of the apples and the cores in water, with a blade of mace, till it is very good. Strain it, and boil the fyrup with a little fugar, till it is confiderably reduced in quantity. Pour it into your pie, put on the upper cruft, and bake it. You may beat up the yolks of two eggs, and half a pint of cream, with a little nutmeg and ſugar. Put it over a ſlow fire, and keep ſtirring it till it is ready to boil. Then take off the lid, and pour in the cream. Cut the cruſt into little three corner-pieces, ſtick them about the pie, and ſend it to table cold. You may, if you think proper, when you make your pie, put in a little quince or marmalade. A pear pie may be made in the ſame manner; but you muſt omit the quince.

To make a Codling Pie.

TAKE ſome ſmall codlings, put them into a pan with ſpring water, lay vine leaves on them, and cover them with a cloth, wrapped round the cover of the pan to keep in the ſteam. As ſoon as they grow ſoft, peel them, and put them in the ſame water as the vine leaves. Hang them high over the fire to green, and, when you ſee them of a fine colour, take them out of the water, and put them into a deep diſh, with as much powder or loaf ſugar as will ſweeten them. Make the lid of a rich puff-paſte, and bake it. When it comes from the oven, take off the lid, and cut it into little pieces, like ſippets, and ſtick them round the inſide of the pie, with the points upwards. Then make a good cuſtard, and pour it over your pie. Make your cuſtard thus. Boil a pint of cream with a ſtick of cinnamon, and ſugar enough to make it a little ſweet. As ſoon as it is cold, put in the yolks of four eggs well beaten, ſet it on the fire, and keep ſtirring it till it grows thick; but take care not to let it boil, as that will curdle it. Pour this into your pie, pair thin a little lemon, cut the peel like ſtraws, and lay it on the top of your pies.

To make a Cherry Pie.

HAVING made a good cruſt, lay a little of it round the ſides of the diſh, and throw ſugar at the bottom. Then lay in your fruit, and ſome ſugar at the top. You may, if you pleaſe, add ſome red currants, which will give an additional flavour to your pie. Then put on your lid, and bake it in a ſlack oven. You may make plumb or gooſeberry pies in the ſame manner.

Orange or Lemon Tarts.

HAVING rubbed half a dozen large oranges or lemons with ſalt, put them into water, with a handful of ſalt in it, for two days. Then change them every day with freſh water, without ſalt, for a fortnight. Boil them till they are tender, and then cut them into half quarters corner-wiſe as thin as poſſible. Take half a dozen pippins, pared, cored, and quartered, and put them into a pint of water. Let them boil till they break, then put the liquor to your oranges or lemons, half the pulp of the pippins well broken, and a pound of ſugar. Boil theſe together a quarter of an hour, then put it into a pot, and ſqueeze into it the juice of either an orange or a lemon, according to which of the tarts you intend to make. Two ſpoonfuls will be ſufficient to give a proper flavour to your tart. Put fine thin puff-paſte into your patty-pans, which muſt be ſmall and ſhallow. Before you put your tarts into the oven, take a feather or bruſh, and rub them over with melted butter, and then ſiſt ſome double-refined ſugar over them, which will form a pretty icing, and make them have a very agreeable appearance.

To make a Tart de Moi.

HAVING made a puff-paſte, lay it round your diſh, and then put in a layer of biſcuit, a layer of butter and marrow, and then a layer of all ſorts of ſweetmeats, or at leaſt as many as you have, and continue to do ſo till your diſh is full. Boil a quart of cream, and thicken it with four eggs, and a ſpoonful of orange-flower water. Sweeten it with ſugar to your palate, and pour it over the reſt. It will be ſufficiently baked in half an hour.

To make a Mince Pie.

BOIL a neat's tongue two hours, then ſkin it, and chop it as ſmall as poſſible. Chop alſo very ſmall three pounds of beef ſuet, three pounds of good baking apples, four pounds of currants, clean waſhed, picked, and well dried before the fire, a pound of jar-raiſins ſtoned and chopped ſmall, and a pound of powder ſugar. Mix them all together with half a pound of mace, as much nutmeg, a quarter of an ounce of cloves, the ſame quantity of cinnamon, and a pint of French brandy. Make a rich puff-paſte, and as you fill up the pie, put in a lttle candied citron and orange cut into ſmall pieces.

Another Method.

TAKE three pounds of ſuet, and ſhred and chop it as ſmall as poſſible; ſtone and chop very fine three pounds of raiſins, and the ſame quantity of currants, nicely picked, waſhed, rubbed, and dried at the fire. Pare half a hundred of fine pippins, core them, and chop them ſmall; take half a pound of fine ſugar, and pound it fine, a quarter of an ounce of mace, the ſame quantity of cloves, and two large nutmegs, all finely beaten. Put all together into a large pan, and mix it well together with half a pint of brandy, and the like quantity of ſack. Put it down cloſe in a ſtone pot, and it will keep good three or four months. When you make your pies, take a little diſh, ſomething larger than a ſoup-plate, and lay a very thin cruſt all over it. Lay a thin layer of meat, and then a thin layer of citron cut very thin, then a layer of mince meat, and a layer of orange-peel cut thin; over that a little meat, ſqueeze in the juice of half a fine Seville orange or a lemon, lay on your cruſt, and bake it nicely. Theſe pies eat very fine cold. If you make them in little patties, mix your meat and ſweetmeats accordingly.

CHAP. XVI.

To make all Sorts of Puddings.

To make a Hunting Pudding.

BEAT up the yolks of ten eggs, and the whites of ſix, with half a pint of cream, ſix ſpoonfuls of flour, a pound of beef ſuet chopped ſmall, a pound of currants well waſhed and picked, a pound of jar raiſins ſtoned and chopped ſmall, two ounces of candied citron, orange and lemon, ſhred fine, two ounces of fine ſugar, a ſpoonful of roſe-water, a glaſs of brandy, and half a nutmeg grated. Mix all well together, tie it up in a cloth, and boil it four hours. Remember to put it in when the water boils, and keep it boiling all the time.

A

A Custard Pudding.

BOIL a pint of thick cream, with a bit of cinnamon in it, and put to it a quarter of a pound of ſugar. When it is cold, put to it the yolks of five eggs well beaten, and ſtir it over the fire till it is pretty thick; but take care not to let it boil. When it is quite cold, butter a cloth well, duſt it with flour, tie the cuſtard up in it very cloſe, and boil it three quarters of an hour. When you take it up, put it into a baſon to cool a little, untie the cloth, lay the diſh on the baſon, and turn it up. You will break the pudding, if you do not take off the cloth carefully. Grate over it a little ſugar, put melted butter and a little wine in a boat, and ſend it up to table.

A boiled Almond Pudding.

TAKE a quart of cream, a penny loaf grated, one nutmeg, ſix ſpoonfuls of flour, half a pound of almonds blanched and beat fine, half a dozen bitter almonds, ſtrain into them two eggs well beaten, put in ſugar to your taſte, and add a little brandy. Boil it half an hour, pour round it melted butter and wine, and ſtick it with ſlit and blanched almonds.

An Almond Pudding baked.

BOIL the ſkins of two lemons till they are very tender, and then beat them very fine. Beat half a pound of almonds in roſe-water, and a pound of ſugar, very fine. Then melt half a pound of butter, and let it ſtand till it is quite cold. Beat the yolks of eight eggs, and the whites of four. Mix them, and beat them all together, with a little orange-flower water, and ſend it to the oven to bake.

A Rice Pudding.

HAVING put a quarter of a pound of rice into a ſaucepan, with a quart of new milk, and a ſtick of cinnamon, ſtir it often to prevent it ſticking to the pan. When it has boiled to a proper thickneſs, pour it into a pan, ſtir in a quarter of a pound of freſh butter, and ſweeten it to your taſte. Grate in half a nutmeg, add three or four ſpoonfuls of roſe water, and ſtir them all well together. When it is cold, beat all up eight eggs, with half the whites. Then butter a diſh, pour it in, and bake it, with a puff-paſte all over the diſh.

A plain cheap Rice Pudding.

TIE in a cloth a quarter of a pound of rice, half a pound of raiſins ſtoned, and boil them two hours; but take care, when you tie it, that you give the rice a good deal of room to ſwell. When it is enough, turn it into a diſh, and pour over it melted butter and ſugar, with a little nutmeg grated in it.

A ground Rice Pudding.

HAVING boiled a quarter of a pound of ground rice in water till it is ſoft, beat the yolks of four eggs, and put to them a pint of cream, a quarter of a pound of ſugar, and a quarter of a pound of butter. Mix them all well together, and either boil or bake it. You may put in currants and ſweetmeats, if you pleaſe.

An Apple Pudding baked.

BOIL and pound well half a pound of apples, and mix half a pound of butter well beaten with them before they are cold. Put to them ſix eggs with their whites, well beaten and ſtrained, half a pound of ſugar pounded and ſifted, and the rinds of two lemons well boiled and beaten. Shift the

peel

peel into clean water twice in the boiling; then put a thin cruſt at the bottom and rims of your diſh, and bake it half an hour.

A Bread Pudding.

BOIL half a pint of milk with a little cinnamon, four eggs well beaten, the rind of a lemon grated, half a pound of ſuet chopped fine, and as much bread as neceſſary. Pour your milk on the bread and ſuet, keep mixing it till cold, then put in the lemon-peel, the eggs, a little ſugar, and ſome nutmeg grated fine. You may either boil or bake this pudding.

An Italian Pudding.

SLICE ſome French rolls into a pint of cream, and when you have put in as much roll as will make it thick enough, beat ten eggs fine, grate a nutmeg, butter the bottom of the diſh, ſlice a dozen pippins into it, throw over it ſome orange-peel and ſugar, and put in half a pint of red wine. Then pour your cream, bread, and eggs, over it, lay a puff-paſte at the bottom of the diſh, and round the edges. Half an hour will bake it.

A Plain Pudding.

BEAT the yolks and whites of three eggs together, with two large ſpoonfuls of flour, a little ſalt, and half a pint of milk or cream. Make it the thickneſs of a pancake batter, and beat all well together. Half an hour will boil it.

A Batter Pudding.

BEAT up the yolks of ſix eggs and the whites of three, and mix them with a quarter of a pint of milk. Put to it the remainder of a quart of milk, ſix ſpoonfuls of flour, a teaſpoonful of ſalt, and one of beaten ginger. Mix them all together, boil

boil them an hour and a quarter, and pour melted butter over the pudding. You may, if you pleaſe, put in half a pound of prunes or currants, and two or three more eggs.

A Marrow Pudding.

HAVING grated a penny loaf into crumbs, pour on them a pint of boiling hot cream. Cut very thin a pound of beef marrow, beat four eggs well, and then put in a glaſs of brandy, with ſugar and nutmeg to your taſte. Mix them all well together, and either boil or bake it. Three quarters of an hour will do it. Cut two ounces of citron very thin, and, when you ſerve it up, ſtick them all over it.

An Orange Pudding.

BOIL the rind of a Seville orange very ſoft, and beat it in a marble mortar, with the juice. Put to it two Naples biſcuits grated wery fine, half a pound of butter, a quarter of a pound of ſugar, and the yolks of ſix eggs. Mix them well together, lay a good puff-paſte round the edge of the diſh, and bake it half an hour in a gentle oven. A lemon pudding is made in the ſame manner, only uſing lemon inſtead of orange.

An Apricot Pudding.

HAVING coddled ſix large apricots very tender, break them very ſmall, ſweeten them to your taſte, and when they are cold add the yolks of ſix eggs, and the whites of two, well beaten. Mix them all well together, with a pint of good cream, lay a puff-paſte all over your diſh, and pour in your ingredients. Bake it half an hour in a moderate oven, and when it is enough, throw a little fine ſugar all over it.

A Goofeberry Pudding.

SCALD a pint of green goofeberries, and rub them through a fieve. Put to them half a pound of fugar, an equal quantity of butter, two or three Naples bifcuits, and four eggs well beaten. Mix it well, and bake it half an hour.

A green Codling Pudding.

GREEN about a quart of codlings as for a pie, and rub them through a hair fieve, with as much of the juice of beets as will green your pudding. Put in the crumb of a halfpenny loaf, half a pound of butter, and three eggs well beaten. Beat them all together, with half a pound of fugar, and two fpoonfuls of cyder. Lay a good pafte round the rim of the difh, and pour in the pudding.

A Quaking Pudding.

BOIL a quart of cream, and let it ftand till almoft cold. Beat four eggs a full quarter of an hour, with a fpoonful and a half of flour, and then mix them with your cream. Add fugar and nutmeg to your palate, tie it clofe up in a cloth well buttered, let it boil an hour, and then turn it carefully out.

A Spoonful Pudding.

TO a fpoonful of flour, and a fpoonful of cream or milk, put an egg, a little nutmeg, ginger, and falt. Mix all together, with a few currants, if you choofe, and boil it in a wooden difh half an hour.

A Yorkfhire Pudding.

BEAT up five eggs in a quart of milk, and mix them with flour till it is of a good pancake batter, and very ſmooth. Put in a little ſalt and ſome grated nutmeg and ginger. Butter a dripping or frying-pan, and put it under a piece of beef, mutton, or a loin of veal, that is roaſting, and then put in your batter. When the top-ſide is brown, cut it in ſquare pieces, turn it, and let the under ſide be brown. Put it in a hot diſh, as clear from fat as you can, and ſend it hot to table.

A Potatoe Pudding.

HAVING boiled a quarter of a pound of potatoes till they are ſoft, peel them, and maſh them with the back of a ſpoon, and rub them through a ſieve to have them fine and ſmooth. Then take half a pound of butter melted, half a pound of fine ſugar, and beat them well together till they are ſmooth. Stir ſix eggs, well beaten, into a glaſs of ſack or brandy; and, if you think proper, you may put in half a pint of currants. Boil it half an hour. Pour over it melted butter, with a glaſs of wine in it, and ſweeten it with ſugar.

Apple Dumplings.

PARE and take out the cores of your apples, fill the hole with quince, orange marmalade, or ſugar, which you like beſt. Then take a piece of cold paſte, and make a hole in it, as if you were going to make a pie. Lay in your apple, and put another piece of paſte in the ſame form, and cloſe it up round the ſide of your apple. This is much preferable to the method of gathering it in a lump at one end. Tie it in a cloth, and boil it three quarters of an hour.

Damaſcene Dumplings.

MAKE a good hot paſte cruſt, roll it pretty thin, lay it in a baſon, and put in as many damaſcenes as you pleaſe. Wet the edge of the paſte,

and

and close it up. Boil it in a cloth an hour. Pour melted butter over it, grate sugar round the edge of the dish, and send it up to table whole.

Hard Dumplings.

MAKE a little salt, flour, and water, into a paste, and roll them in balls the size of a turkey's egg. Roll them in a little flour, throw them into boiling water, and half an hour will boil them. If you choose it, you may put into them a few currants. They are best boiled with a good piece of beef.

Norfolk Dumplings.

MAKE half a pint of milk, two eggs, and a little salt, into a good thick batter with flour. Drop your batter into a saucepan of boiling water, and two or three minutes will boil them. Be particularly careful that the water boils fast when you put the batter in. Then throw them into a sieve to drain, turn them into a dish, and stir a piece of fresh butter into them.

A Millet Pudding.

SPREAD a quarter of a pound of butter at the bottom of a dish, and lay into it six ounces of millet, and a quarter of a pound of sugar. Pour over it three pints of milk, and send it to the oven.

A Plum Pudding.

OF suet, currants, and raisins stoned, take one pound of each; the yolks of eight eggs, and the whites of four; the crumb of a penny loaf grated, one pound of flour, half a nutmeg, a teaspoonful of grated ginger, a little salt, and a small glass of brandy. First beat the eggs, and then mix them with some milk. Add the flour and other ingredients by degrees, and as much more milk as may be be neceſſary. It muſt be very thick and well ſtirred, and will take five hours boiling.

A Suet Pudding.

SHRED a pound of ſuet fine, take a quart of milk, four eggs, two teaſpoonfuls of grated ginger, a little ſalt, and flour enough to make it a thick batter. It muſt be boiled two hours. They may be alſo made into dumplings, when half an hour will be ſufficient to boil them.

Yeaſt Dumplings.

HAVING made a light dough, as for bread, with flour, water, yeaſt, and ſalt, cover it with a cloth, and ſet it half an hour before the fire. Make the dough into little round balls, as big as a large hen's egg, flatten them with your hand, put them into a ſaucepan of boiling water, and a few minutes will do them. Take care that they do not fall to the bottom of the pot or ſaucepan, as that will make them heavy, and be ſure to keep the water boiling all the time. When they are enough, take them up, and lay them in your diſh, with melted butter in a boat. The dough you get at the baker's will do as well, and ſave you the trouble of making it yourſelf.

Almond Hog's Puddings.

CHOP fine a pound of beef marrow, blanch and beat fine a pound of ſweet almonds, with a little orange-flower or roſe-water; grate fine half a pound of white bread, clean waſh and pick half a pound of currants; take a quarter of a pound of ſugar, a quarter of an ounce of mace, nutmeg, and cinnamon together, of each an equal quantity, and half a pint of ſack or mountain. Mix all well together, with half a pint of good cream, and the yolks of four eggs. Fill the guts half full, tie them up, and boil them a quarter of an hour, and prick them as they boil to keep the guts from breaking. If you choose it, you may leave out the currants; but, in that case, a quarter of a pound more of sugar must be added.

To make Black Puddings.

BOIL a peck of groats half an hour in water, then drain them, and put them into a clean tub or large pan. Then kill your hog, and save two quarts of the blood; and keep stirring the blood till it is quite cold. Then mix it with your groats, and stir them well together. Season with a large spoonful of salt, a quarter of an ounce of cloves, mace, and nutmeg together, an equal quantity of each. Dry them, beat them well, and mix all together. Take a little winter savory, sweet marjoram, thyme, and penny royal, stripped of the stalks and chopped very fine; just enough to season them, and give them a flavour, but no more. The next day, take the leaf of the hog, and cut it into dice, wash the guts very clean, then tie one end, and begin to fill them. Mix in the fat as you fill them, and be sure to put in plenty of fat. Fill the skins three parts full, tie the other end, and make your pudding what length you please. Prick them with a pin, and put them in a kettle of boiling water. Boil them softly an hour, and then put them on clean straw to drain and dry.

A Carrot Pudding.

SCRAPE and grate a raw carrot very clean; take half a pound of the grated carrot, and a pound of grated bread. Beat up the yolks of eight eggs and the whites of four, and mix them with half a pint of cream. Stir in the bread and carrot, half a pound of fresh butter melted, half a pint of sack, three spoonfuls of orange-flower water,

ter, and a nutmeg grated. Sweeten to your palate. Mix all well together, and if it be not thin enough, ſtir in a little new milk or cream. Let it be of a moderate thickneſs, lay a puff-paſte all over the diſh, and pour in the ingredients. It will take an hour's baking; but, if you boil it, you muſt melt butter, with ſugar and white wine.

An Herb Pudding.

WASH, ſcald, and ſhred very fine, of ſpinach, beet, parſley, and leeks, each a handful. Have ready a quart of groats ſteeped in warm water half an hour, and a pound of hog's lard cut in little bits, three large onions chopped ſmall, and three ſage leaves hacked fine. Put in a little ſalt, mix all well together, and tie it cloſe up. While it is boiling, you muſt take it up, and looſen the ſtring a little, in order to give it room to ſwell.

Peas Pudding.

AS ſoon as the peas are boiled tender, take them up, untie them, and ſtir in a good piece of butter, a little ſalt, and a good deal of beaten pepper. Then tie it up again, boil it an hour longer, and it will be ready to ſerve up.

A Haſty Pudding.

TO a pint of cream, and the ſame quantity of milk, put a little ſalt, and ſweeten it with loaf ſugar. Make it boil, and then put in ſome fine flour, and keep it continually ſtirring while you are putting in the flour, till it is thick enough, and ſufficiently boiled. Pour it out, and ſtick the top full of little bits of butter.

An Oatmeal Pudding.

HAVING boiled a pint of fine oatmeal in three pints of new milk, ſtirring it till it is as thick as a haſty pudding, take it off, and ſtir in half

half a pound of fresh butter, a little beaten mace and nutmeg, and a gill of sack. Then beat up the yolks of eight eggs, and the whites of four, and stir all well together. Lay a puff-paste all over the dish, pour in the pudding, and bake it half an hour. If you please, you may put in a few currants, and boil it.

A Sago Pudding.

BOIL two ounces of sago with some cinnamon, and a bit of lemon-peel, till it is soft and thick. Grate the crumb of a halfpenny roll, put to it a glass of red wine, four ounces of chopped marrow, the yolks of four eggs well beaten, and sugar to your taste. When the sago is cold, put these ingredients to it, and mix it all well together. Bake it with a puff-paste; and, when it comes from the oven, cut citron into pieces, and blanched almonds into slips, and stick them over the pudding.

A Vermicelli Pudding.

HAVING boiled a quarter of a pound of vermicelli in a pint of milk till it is soft, with a stick of cinnamon, take out the cinnamon, and put in half a pint of cream, a quarter of a pound of butter melted, and a quarter of a pound of sugar, with the yolks of four eggs well beaten. Bake it, without a paste, in an earthen dish.

A grateful Pudding.

TO a pound of white bread grated, put a pound of fine flour; take eight eggs with half the whites, beat them up, and mix them with a pint of milk, Then stir in the bread and flour; a pound of raisins stoned, a pound of currants, half a pound of sugar, and a little beaten ginger. Mix all well to-

together, and either bake or boil it. It will take three quarters of an hour baking.

A Tansey Pudding.

GRATE four Naples biscuits, and put as much boiling cream to them as will wet them, and beat up the yolks of four eggs. Chop a few tansey leaves, but not too many, with as much spinach as will make it a pretty green. Mix all together when the cream is cold, with a little sugar, and thicken it over a slow fire. When it is cold, put it into a cloth well buttered and floured, tie it up close, and let it boil three quarters of an hour. Serve it up with white wine sauce.

CHAP XVII.

To make Pancakes and Fritters.

Pancakes.

HAVING beat six or eight eggs well together, leaving out half the whites, stir them into a quart of milk. Mix your flour first with a little of the milk, and then put in the rest by degrees. Add two spoonfuls of beaten ginger, a glass of brandy, and a little salt, and stir all well together. Put some butter into a stewpan, and then pour in a ladleful of batter, which will be sufficient to make a pancake, and keep moving the pan round, that the batter may spread properly. Shake the pan, and turn the pancake, as soon as you think one side is done enough. When both sides are done, lay it in a dish before the fire, and pro-

proceed in the fame manner till you have fried as many as you choofe. Strew a little fugar over them, and fend them up to table.

Cream Pancakes.

PUT the yolks of two eggs into half a pint of cream, with two ounces of fugar, and a little beaten cinnamon, mace, and nutmeg. Proceed in every other refpect, as above directed.

Clary Pancakes.

TO three fpoonfuls of fine flour, put three eggs, and a little falt. Beat them well together in a pint of milk. Fry them in lard, and pour in your batter as thin as poffible. Then lay in fome clary leaves wafhed and dried, and pour a little more batter over them. Take care to fry them of a nice brown.

Rice Pancakes.

MIX three fpoonfuls of flour of rice with a quart of cream, fet it on a flow fire, and keep ftirring it till it is as thick as pap. Pour into it half a pound of butter, and a nutmeg grated. Put it into an earthen pan, and as foon as it is cold, ftir in three or four fpoonfuls of flour, a little falt, fome fugar, and nine eggs well beaten. Mix all well together, and fry them nicely. New milk muft be ufed, when you cannot get cream; but, in that cafe, a fpoonful more of rice muft be added.

Pink-coloured Pancakes.

HAVING boiled a large beet-root till it is tender, beat it fine in a marble mortar. Put to it the yolks of four eggs, two fpoonfuls of flour, and three fpoonfuls of cream. Sweeten it to your tafte, grate in half a nutmeg, and add a glafs of brandy. Mix all well together, and fry them as before directed.

rected. Garniſh with green ſweetmeats, green ſprigs of myrtle, or preſerved apricots.

To make Almond Fraze.

BLANCH a pound of Jordan almonds, and ſteep them in a pint of cream, ten yolks of eggs, and four whites. Then take out the almonds, and pound them fine in a mortar. Mix them again in the cream and eggs, and add ſome grated white bread and ſugar. Stir them all well together, and fry them as before directed.

To make plain Fritters.

PUT the crumb of a penny-loaf grated into a pint of milk, and mix it very ſmooth. When it is cold, put in the yolks of five eggs, three ounces of ſifted ſugar, and a little grated nutmeg. Fry them in the ſame manner as pancakes, and ſerve them up with melted butter, wine, and ſugar.

Apple Fritters.

PARE and core ſome of the largeſt apples you can get, and cut them into round ſlices. Take half a pint of ale, and two eggs, and beat in as much flour as will make it rather thicker than a common pudding, with nutmeg and ſugar to your taſte. Let it ſtand three or four minutes to riſe. Dip your ſlices of apple into the batter, fry them criſp, grate over them ſome ſugar, put wine ſauce in a boat, and ſend them up to table.

Cuſtard Fritters.

HAVING beat up the yolks of eight eggs with a ſpoonful of flour, half a nutmeg, a little ſalt, and a glaſs of brandy, add a pint of cream, ſweeten it, and bake it in a ſmall diſh. When it is cold, cut it into quarters, and dip them in batter made of half a pint of cream, a quarter of a pint

pint of milk, four eggs, a little flour, and a little ginger grated. Fry them in good lard or dripping, and when done, ſtrew grated ſugar over them.

Royal Fritters.

PUT a quart of new milk into a ſaucepan, and pour in a pint of ſack or wine as ſoon as it begins to boil. Then take it off, and let it ſtand five or ſix minutes, ſkim off the curd, and put it into a baſon. Beat it up well with ſix eggs, and ſeaſon it with nutmeg. Then beat it with a whiſk, and add flour ſufficient to give it the uſual thickneſs of batter. Put in ſome ſugar, and fry them quick.

Bibloquet Fritters.

HAVING broken five eggs into a handful of fine flour, and put milk enough to make it work well together, then put in ſome ſalt, and work it again. When it is well made, put in a teaſpoonful of powder of cinnamon, the ſame quantity of lemon-peel grated, and half an ounce of candied citron cut very ſmall. Put on a ſtewpan, rub it over with butter, and put in the paſte. Set it over a ſlow fire, and let it do gently, without ſticking to the bottom or ſides of the pan. When it is in a manner baked, take it out, and lay it on a diſh. Set on a ſtewpan with a large quantity of lard; when it boils, cut the paſte the ſize of a finger, and then cut it acroſs at each end, which will riſe and be hollow, and have a very good effect. Put them into the boiling lard; but great care muſt be taken in frying them, as they riſe ſo much. When they are done, ſift ſome ſugar on a warm diſh, lay on the fritters, and ſift more ſugar over them.

German Fritters.

PARE, quarter, and core, ſome well-taſted criſp apples; take the core quite out, and cut them into

into round pieces. Put into a ſtewpan a quarter of a pint of French brandy, a table ſpoonful of fine ſugar pounded, and a little cinnamon. Put the apples into this liquor, and ſet them over a gentle fire, ſtirring them often; but take care not to break them. Set on a ſtewpan with ſome lard, and when it boils, drain the apples, dip them in ſome fine flour, and put them into the pan. Strew ſome ſugar over the diſh, and ſet it on the fire. Lay in the fritters, ſtrew a little ſugar over them, and glaze them over with a red hot ſalamander.

Water Fritters.

TO five or ſix ſpoonfuls of flour, put a little ſalt, eight eggs well beaten, and a glaſs of brandy, and mix them all well together. The longer they are made before dreſſing, the better. Juſt before you do them, melt half a pound of butter, and beat it well in. Fry them in hog's lard.

Rice Fritters.

HAVING boiled a quarter of a pound of rice in milk till it is pretty thick, mix it with a pint of cream, four eggs, ſome ſugar, cinnamon and nutmug, ſix ounces of currants waſhed and picked, a little ſalt, and as much flour as will make it a thick batter. Fry them in little cakes in boiling lard, and ſerve them up with white ſugar and butter.

White Fritters.

WASH two ounces of rice clean in water, and dry it before the fire; then beat it very fine in a mortar, and ſift it through a lawn ſieve. Put it into a ſaucepan, juſt wet it with milk, and put to it another pint of milk as ſoon as it is thoroughly moiſtened. Set the whole over a ſtove, or very ſlow fire, and take care to keep it always moving. Put in a little ginger, and ſome candied lemon

mon-peel grated. Keep it over the fire, till it come almoſt to the thickneſs of a fine paſte. When it is quite cold, ſpread it out with a rolling-pin, and cut it into little pieces, taking care that they do not ſtick to each other. Flour your hands, roll up your fritters handſomely, and fry them. Strew on them ſome ſugar, and pour over them a little orange-flower water.

Tanſey Fritters.

HAVING poured a pint of boiling milk on the crumb of a penny loaf, let it ſtand an hour, and then put in as much juice of tanſey to it as will give it a flavour. Add to it a little juice of ſpinach, to give it a green colour. Put to it a ſpoonful of ratafia-water, or brandy, ſweeten it to your taſte, grate the rind of half a lemon, beat the yolks of four eggs, and mix them all together. Put them in a ſtewpan, with a quarter of a pound of butter, and ſtir it over a ſlow fire till it is quite thick. Take it off, and let it ſtand two or three hours. Then drop a ſpoonful at a time into boiling lard. When they are done, grate ſugar over them, and put wine ſauce in a boat, and ſend them up to table.

Raſpberry Fritters.

GRATE two Naples biſcuits, or the crumb of a French roll, and put to it a pint of boiling cream. When it is cold, add to it the yolks of four eggs well beaten up. Mix all well together with ſome raſpberry juice, and drop them into a pan of boiling lard in very ſmall quantities. Stick them with blanched almonds ſliced, and ſerve them up.

Strawberry Fritters.

HAVING made a batter with flour, a ſpoonful of ſweet oil, another of white wine, a little raſped lemon-

lemon-peel, and the whites of two or three eggs, make it pretty ſoft, ſo as juſt to drop with a ſpoon. Mix it with ſome large ſtrawberries, and drop them with a ſpoon into the hot fritters. When they are of a good colour, take them out, and drain them on a ſieve. When they are done, ſtrew ſome ſugar over them, and glaze them.

Currant Fritters.

STIR into half a pint of ale that is not bitter as much flour as will make it pretty thick, and put in a few currants. Beat it up quick, have the lard boiling, and put a large ſpoonful at a time into the pan.

Haſty Fritters.

HEAT ſome butter in a ſtewpan; take half a pint of good ale, and ſtir a little flour into it by degrees. Put in a few currants, or chopped apples, beat them up quick, and drop a large ſpoonful at a time all over the pan. Take care they do not ſtick together, turn them with an egg ſlice, and when they are of a fine brown, lay them on a diſh, ſtrew ſome ſugar over them, and ſend them up hot to table.

CHAP. XVIII.

To make all Sorts of Cakes, Puffs, and Biſcuits.

To make a Plum Cake.

TO three pounds of flour put an equal quantity of currants, three quarters of a pound of almonds, blanched and a little beat, half an ounce of them bitter; a quarter of a pound of ſugar, the yolks

yolks of ſeven eggs, and the whites of ſix; a pint of cream, two pounds of butter, and half a pint of good ale yeaſt. Mix the eggs and the yeaſt together, and ſtrain them. Set the cream on the fire, and melt the butter in it. Stir in the almonds, and half a pint of ſack, part of which muſt be put to the almonds while beating. Mix together the currants, flour, and ſugar, with nutmeg, cloves, and mace, to your palate. Stir theſe to the cream, and put in the yeaſt.

Shrewſbury Cakes.

HAVING beat half a pound of butter to a cream, put in half a pound of flour, an egg, ſix ounces of loaf ſugar beaten and ſifted, half an ounce of carraway ſeeds, mixed into a paſte, and roll them thin. Cut them round with little tins, or a ſmall glaſs, prick them, lay them on ſheets of tin, and bake them in a ſlow oven.

A Bride Cake.

TO four pounds of fine flour well dried, put the like quantity of freſh butter, two pounds of loaf ſugar, a quarter of an ounce of mace, and the ſame quantity of nutmeg, both finely pounded and ſifted. To every pound of flour put eight eggs; waſh and pick four pounds of currants, and dry them before the fire; blanch a pound of ſweet almonds, and cut them lengthways very thin; of citron, candied orange, and candied lemon, a pound each, and half a pint of brandy. Firſt work the butter with your hand to a cream, then beat in your ſugar a quarter of an hour, beat the whites of your eggs to a very ſtrong froth, and mix them with your ſugar and butter. Beat your yolks at leaſt half an hour, and mix them with your cake. Then put in your flour, mace, and nutmeg, and keep beating it till your oven is ready. Put in your

your brandy, and beat in lightly your currants and almonds. Tie three ſheets of paper round the bottom of your hoop, to keep it from running out, and rub it well with butter. Put in your cake, and lay in your ſweetmeats in three layers, with cake between every layer. After it is riſen and coloured, cover it with paper before your oven is ſtopped up, and bake it three hours.

Portugal Cakes.

BEAT and ſift a pound of loaf ſugar, and mix it with a pound of fine flour. Then rub it into a pound of good ſweet butter, till it is as thick as grated white bread. Put to it two ſpoonfuls of roſe-water, two of ſack, and ten eggs. Whip them well with a whiſk, then put into it eight ounces of currants, and mix all well together. Butter the tin pans, fill them half full, and bake them. If you do not put currants into them, they will keep half a year. Add a pound of almonds blanched, and beat with roſe-water, as above, and leave out the flour. Theſe are better than the ſort firſt mentioned.

A Pound Cake.

BEAT a pound of butter, in an earthen pan, with your hand, one way, till it reſembles a fine thick cream. Then beat up with the butter twelve eggs, with only half their whites; and beat in alſo a pound of ſugar, a pound of flour, and a few carraways. Beat all well together with your hand, or with a large wooden ſpoon, for an hour. Then butter a pan, put it in, and bake it an hour in a quick oven. You may, if you think proper, put in a pound of clean-waſhed and picked currants.

Little

Little Currant Cakes.

DRY well a pound and an half of fine flour before the fire; take a pound of butter, half a pound of fine loaf ſugar well beaten and ſifted, four yolks of eggs, four ſpoonfuls of roſe-water, the like quantity of ſack, a little mace, and a nutmeg grated. Beat the eggs well, and put them to the roſe-water and ſack. Then put to them the ſugar and butter, work them all together, and ſtrew in the currants and flour, having warmed them both together before. This will be ſufficient to make ſix or eight cakes. Bake them of a fine brown, and let them be pretty criſp.

Little fine Cakes.

BEAT a pound of butter to a cream; take a pound and a quarter of flour, a pound of fine ſugar finely beaten, a pound of clean-waſhed and picked currants, ſix eggs, uſing only two of the whites. Beat them fine, mix the flour, ſugar, and eggs, by degrees into the batter, and beat it all well with both hands. This may be baked in one cake, or made into ſeveral little ones.

Heart Cakes.

WITH your hand work a pound of butter to a cream; then put to it twelve eggs, with only ſix of the whites, well beaten, a pound of dried flour, a pound of ſifted ſugar, four ſpoonfuls of good brandy, and a pound of currants waſhed, and dried before the fire. As the pans are filled, put in two ounces of candied orange and citron, and continue beating the cake till you put it into the oven. This quantity will be ſufficient to fill three dozen of middling-ſized pans.

A Common

A Common Seed Cake.

TAKE a pound of butter beat to a cream with the hand, a pound and a quarter of flour, three quarters of a pound of lump ſugar pounded, the yolks of ten eggs, and the whites of four. Mix theſe well together, and put to them an ounce of carraway ſeeds bruiſed. Butter the pan or hoop, and ſift ſugar on the top.

A rich Seed Cake.

TAKE a pound of butter, a pound of flour well dried, a pound of loaf ſugar beaten and ſifted, eight eggs, two ounces of carraway ſeeds, one nutmeg grated, and its weight of cinnamon. Having beaten your butter to a cream, put in your ſugar, beat the whites of your eggs half an hour, and mix them with the ſugar and butter. Then beat the yolks half an hour, and put to them the whites. Beat in your flour, ſpices, and ſeeds, a little before it goes to the oven. Put it in the hoop, and bake it two hours in a quick oven. The ingredients will take two hours, in order to be beaten up properly together.

A good Family Cake.

TAKE rice and wheat flour, of each ſix ounces, the yolks and whites of nine eggs, half a pound of lump ſugar pounded and ſifted, and half an ounce of carraway-ſeeds. Having beaten this one hour, bake it for the ſame time in a quick oven. This is a very light cake, and is very proper for young people and delicate ſtomachs.

Royal Cakes.

BEAT and ſift a pound of ſugar; then take a pound of well-dried flour, a pound of butter, eight eggs, half a pound of waſhed and picked currants, grate a nutmeg, and the ſame quantity of mace and

and cinnamon. Having worked your butter to a cream, put in your ſugar. Beat the whites of your eggs near half an hour, and mix them with your ſugar and butter. Then beat your yolks near half an hour, and put them to your butter. Theſe muſt be well beaten together, and when it is ready for the oven; put in your flour, ſpices, and currants. Sift a little ſugar over them, and bake them in tins.

Orange or Lemon Cakes.

QUARTER as many Seville oranges, or lemons, as you pleaſe, but they muſt have good rinds, and boil them in two or three waters till they be tender, and have loſt their bitterneſs. Then ſkin them, and lay them in a clean napkin to dry. With a knife take out all the ſkins and ſeeds out of the pulp, ſhred the peels fine, put them to the pulp, weigh them, and put rather more than their weight of fine ſugar into a toſſing-pan, with juſt as much water as will diſſolve the ſugar. Boil it till it becomes a perfect ſugar, and then by degrees put in your peels and pulps. Stir them well before you ſet them on the fire, boil it very gently till it looks clear and thick, and then put them into flat-bottomed glaſſes. Set them in a ſtove, and keep them in a conſtant and moderate heat, and turn them out upon glaſſes, as ſoon as they are candied on the top.

Almond Cakes.

BLANCH and beat two ounces of bitter, and one pound of ſweet almonds; take a little roſe or orange-flour water, and the white of an egg; half a pound of loaf-ſugar ſifted, eight yolks and three whites of eggs, the juice of half a lemon, and the rind grated. Bake it in one large pan, or in ſeveral ſmall ones.

Bath

Bath Cakes.

RUB half a pound of butter into a pound of flour, and put to it a ſpoonful of good barm, and, with ſome warm cream, make it into a light paſte, and ſet it to the fire to riſe. When you make them up, take four ounces of carraway comfits, work part of them in, and ſtrew the reſt on the top. Make them into round cakes, about the ſize of a French roll, bake them on ſheet tins, and ſend them in hot for breakfaſt.

Icings for Cakes.

POUND and ſift fine a pound of double-refined ſugar, and mix with it, in an earthen pan, the whites of twenty-four eggs. Whiſk them well for two or three hours, till it looks white and thick, and then, with a bunch of feathers, ſpread it all over the top and ſides of the cake. Set it at a proper diſtance before a clear fire, and keep turning it continually that it may not change colour; but a cool oven is beſt, in which an hour will harden it. You may alſo make your icing in the following manner. Beat the whites of three eggs to a ſtrong froth, beat a pound of Jordan almonds very fine with roſe-water, and mix your almonds and eggs lightly together. Then beat a pound of loaf ſugar very fine, and put it in by degrees. When your cake is enough, take it out, lay on your icing, and proceed as above directed.

Almond Puffs.

BLANCH and beat very fine two ounces of ſweet almonds with orange-flower water. Beat the whites of three eggs to a very high froth, and then ſtrew in a little ſifted ſugar. Mix your almonds with your ſugar and eggs, and then add more ſugar till

till it is as thick as paſte. Lay it in cakes, and bake it on a paper in a cool oven.

Lemon Puffs.

HAVING beaten and ſifted a pound of double-refined ſugar, put it into a bowl, with the juice of two lemons, and beat them well together. Then, having beaten the white of an egg to a very high froth, put it alſo into your bowl, and beat it half an hour. Put in three eggs, and two rinds of lemons grated. Mix it well up, duſt ſome ſugar on your papers, drop on the puffs in ſmall drops, and bake them in a moderately-heated oven.

Sugar Puffs.

BEAT the whites of ten eggs till they riſe to a high froth; put them into a ſtone mortar or wooden bowl, and add as much double-refined ſugar as will make them thick. Put in a little ambergris to give them a flavour, rub them round the mortar for half an hour, and put in a few carraway ſeeds. Take a ſheet of wafers, lay them on as broad as a ſixpence, and as high as they can be laid. Put them into a moderately-heated oven for ſix or ſeven minutes, and they will look of a beautiful white.

To make Wafers.

BEAT the yolks of two eggs in a pint of cream, and mix it as thick as a pudding with well-dried flour, and ſugar and orange-flower water to your taſte. Put in a ſufficient quantity of warm water to make it as thin as fine pancakes. Mix them very ſmooth, and bake them over a ſtove. Butter the irons when they ſtick.

To make common Biſcuits.

BEAT eight eggs half an hour, and put to them ·nd of ſugar beaten and ſifted, with the rind of of a lemon grated. Whiſk it an hour, or till it looks light, and then put in a pound of flour, with a little roſe-water. Sugar them over, and bake them in tins, or on paper.

Drop Biſcuits.

TAKE the yolks of ten eggs and the whites of ſix, and beat them with a ſpoonful of roſe-water half an hour. Then put in ten ounces of loaf ſugar finely beaten and ſifted. Whiſk them well for half an hour, and then add an ounce of carraway-ſeeds, bruiſed, and ſix ounces of fine flour. Whiſk in your flour gently, drop them on wafer-paper, and bake them in an oven moderately heated.

Naples Biſcuits.

MIX a pound of ſoft ſugar finely ſifted with three quarters of a pound of very fine flour. Sift it three times, and then add ſix eggs well beaten, and a ſpoonful of roſe-water. When the oven is almoſt hot, make them, but take care that they are not made up too wet.

Savoy Biſcuits.

HAVING beaten the whites of eight eggs till they bear a ſtrong froth, put the yolks to them, with a pound of ſugar, and beat them all together a quarter of an hour. When the oven is ready, add a pound of fine flour to the other ingredients. Stir them till they be well mixed, lay the biſcuits upon the paper, and ice them. Bake them in a quick oven.

French Biſcuits.

TAKE three new laid eggs, and an equal weight of dried flour. Mix the flour with an equal quantity of fine powdered ſugar. Firſt beat the whites of of the eggs up well with a whisk, till they are of a fine froth. Then whip in half an ounce of candied lemon-peel cut very thin and fine, beat them well up. Then, by degrees, whip in the flour and sugar; then put in the yolks, and with a spoon temper it well together. Shape your biscuits on fine white paper with your spoon, and throw powdered sugar over them. Bake them in a moderately heated oven, and give them a fine colour at the top. When they are baked, cut them from the paper with a thin knife, and put them into boxes till wanted.

To make Gingerbread.

MIX three quarts of fine flour, two ounces of beaten ginger, a quarter of an ounce of nutmeg, cloves, and mace, beat fine, then add three quarters of a pound of fine sugar, two pounds of treacle, and set it over the fire, but do not let it boil. Melt three quarters of a pound of butter in the treacle, put in some candied lemon and orange-peel cut fine. Mix these well together, and let it stand in a quick oven one hour.

CHAP. XIX.

To make Cheesecakes, Tarts, and Custards.

To make common Cheesecakes.

BEAT eight eggs well, while a quart of milk is on the fire, and when it boils, put in the eggs, and stir them till they come to a curd. Then pour it out, and when it is cold, put in a little salt, two spoonfuls of rose-water, and three quarters of a pound of currants, well washed. Put it into puff-paste, and bake it. If you use tin patties to bake

bake in, butter them, or you will not be able to take them out; but if you bake them in glafs or china, only an upper cruft will be neceffary, as you will not want to take them out when you fend them to table.

Elegant Cheefecakes.

WARM a pint of cream, and put to it five quarts of milk warm from the cow. Then put runnet to it, and ftir it well. As foon as it is curdled, put the curd in a linen bag or cloth, and let the whey properly drain from it, but do not fqueeze it much. Then put it into a mortar, and break the curd as fine as butter. Put to the curd half a pound of fweet almonds blanched, and half a pound of mackaroons, both finely beaten. Put in nine eggs well beaten, a whole nutmeg grated, two perfumed plums diffolved in rofe or orange-flower water, and half a pound of fine fugar. Mix all well together; then melt a pound and a quarter of butter, and ftir it well in. Make a puff-pafte as follows: Wet a pound of fine flour with cold water, and roll it out. Put into it by degrees a pound of frefh butter, and fhake a little flour over each coat as you roll it. Make it juft before you want to ufe it. If you choofe it, you may put in a little tincture of faffron to give them a high colour.

Rice Cheefecakes.

HAVING boiled a quarter of a pound of rice till it be tender, drain it, and put in four eggs well beaten, half a pound of butter, half a pint of cream, fix ounces of fugar, a nutmeg grated, and a glafs of ratafia-water or brandy. Beat them all together, and bake them in raifed crufts.

Almond Cheefecakes.

BLANCH four ounces of Jordan almonds, and put them into cold water. Beat them with rofe-

rofe-water in a marble mortar or wooden bowl, with a wooden peftle: Put to it four ounces of fugar, and the yolks of four eggs finely beaten. Work it in the mortar or bowl till it becomes white and frothy. Then make the following rich puff-pafte: Take half a pound of flour, and a quarter of a pound of butter; rub a little of the butter into the flour, mix it ftiff with a little cold water, then roll your pafte ftraight out, ftrew over it a little flour, lay over it, in thin bits, one third of your butter; throw a little more flour over the butter; do fo for three times; then put your pafte in your tins, fill them, and grate fugar over them. Bake them in a moderately-heated oven.

Citron Cheefecakes.

HAVING boiled a quart of cream, let it ftand till it is cold, and then mix it with the yolks of four eggs well beaten. Then fet it on the fire, and let it boil till it curds. Blanch fome almonds, beat them well with orange-flower water, put them into the cream, with a few Naples bifcuits and green citron fhred fine. Sweeten it to your tafte, and bake them in teacups.

Lemon and Orange Cheefecakes.

BOIL the peel of two large lemons till they be quite tender, and then pound it well in a mortar with four or five ounces of loaf fugar, the yolks of fix eggs, half a pound of frefh butter, and a little curd beat fine. Pound and mix all together, lay a puff-pafte in your patty-pans, fill them half full, and bake them. Orange cheefecakes are made in the fame method, only with this difference, that the bitternefs muft be taken out of the peel by boiling it in two or three waters.

A Rafpberry Tart with Cream.

LAY fome thin puff-pafte in a patty-pan, put in fome rafpberries, and ftrew over them fome very fine fugar. Put on the lid, and bake it. Then cut it open, and put in half a pint of cream, the yolks of two or three eggs well beaten, and a little fugar. Let it ftand to cool before you fend it to table.

A Spinach Tart.

SCALD fome fpinach in boiling water, drain it well and chop it. Then ftew it in butter and cream, with a little falt, fugar, a few pieces of fried comfit citron, and a few drops of orange-flower water. Make it into tarts.

Rhubarb Tarts.

CUT the ftalks of the rhubarb that grows in the garden into pieces of the fize of a goofeberry, and make it in the fame manner as a goofeberry tart.

To make apple tarts, lemon tarts, and tarts de moi, fee Chapter XV.

A common Cuftard.

SWEETEN a quart of new milk to your tafte, grate in a fmall nutmeg, beat up eight eggs with only four whites, ftir them into the milk, and add a little rofe-water. Bake it in china bafons, or put them in a deep china difh. Prepare a kettle of boiling water, fet the cups into it, and let the water come above half way; but do not let it boil too faft, for fear of its getting into the cups. Colour them at top with a hot iron.

Cuftards to bake.

HAVING boiled a pint of cream with mace and cinnamon, let it ftand till it be cold. Then

take

take four eggs, leaving out two of the whites, a little rofe and orange-flower water and fack, with nutmeg and fugar to your palate. Mix them well together, and bake them in cups.

Almond Cuftards.

BOIL a pint of cream in a toffing-pan, with a ftick of cinnamon, a blade or two of mace, and let it ftand to cool. Blanch two ounces of almonds, beat them fine in a marble mortar with fome rofe-water. If you like a ratafia tafte, put in a few apricot kernels, or bitter almonds. Mix them with your cream, fweeten it to your tafte, fet it on a flow fire, and keep ftirring it till it is pretty thick. Bake it in cups.

Orange Cuftards.

BOIL half the rind of a Seville orange till it be tender, beat it very fine in a mortar, and put to it a fpoonful of brandy, a quarter of a pound of loaf fugar, the juice of a Seville orange, and the yolks of four eggs. Beat them all well together for ten minutes, and then pour in by degrees a pint of boiling cream. Keep beating them till they are cold, then put them into cuftard cups, and fet them in an earthen difh of hot water. Let them ftand till they are fet, then take them out, and ftick preferved orange on the top. They may be eaten either hot or cold.

Lemon Cuftards.

FIRST beat the yolks of ten eggs, and ftrain them, and then beat them with a pint of cream. Sweeten the juice of two lemons, boil it with the peel of one, and ftrain it. As foon as it has cooled, ftir it to the cream and eggs; put it on the fire again, ftir it till it nearly boils, grate over it the

the rind of a lemon, and brown with a ſalamander.

Rice Cuſtards.

BOIL a blade of mace and a quartered nutmeg in a quart of cream, and ſtrain it. Then add to it ſome whole rice boiled and a little brandy. Sweeten it, ſtir it over the fire till it thickens, and ſerve it up in cups or a diſh. It may be ſent to table either hot or cold.

CHAP. XX.

To make Creams and Jams.

Orange Cream.

PARE the rind of a Seville orange very fine, and ſqueeze the juice of four oranges. Put them into a ſtewpan with half a pint of water, and eight ounces of ſugar. Beat the whites of five eggs, mix them into it, and ſet them on a ſlow fire. Stir it one way till it grows thick and white, ſtrain it through a gauze, and ſtir it till it is cold. Then beat the yolks of five eggs very fine, and put them into your pan with the cream. Stir it over a gentle fire till it nearly boils, then put it into a baſon, and ſtir it till it is cold, when you may put it into your glaſſes.

Burnt Cream.

BOIL a pint of cream with ſugar and a little lemon-peel ſhred fine. Beat the yolks of ſix, and the whites of four eggs ſeparately, and when the cream

cream is cold, put in your eggs, with a ſpoonful of orange-flower water, and one of fine flour. Set it over the fire, keep ſtirring it till it is thick, and then put it into a diſh. When it is cold, ſift a quarter of a pound of ſugar all over it, and brown it with a hot ſalamander, till it looks like a glaſs plate put over your cream.

Spaniſh Cream.

TAKE three ſpoonfuls of flour of rice ſifted very fine, the yolks of three eggs, three ſpoonfuls of water, two of orange-flower water, and mix them well together. Put to them one pint of cream, and ſet it upon a good fire, ſtirring it till it be of a proper thickneſs. Then pour it into cups.

Piſtachio Cream.

TAKE out the kernels of half a pound of Piſtachio nuts, beat them in a mortar with a ſpoonful of brandy, and put them into a toſſing-pan, with a pint of cream, and the yolks of two eggs finely beaten. Stir it gently over a ſlow fire till it is thick, but do not let it boil. Put it into a China ſoup-plate, and when it is cold, ſtick ſome kernels, cut longways, all over it, and ſend it to table.

Whipt Cream.

BEAT the whites of eight eggs well, and mix them with a quart of thick cream, and half a pint of ſack. Sweeten it to your taſte with double-refined ſugar. Whip it up with a whiſk, and ſome lemon-peel tied in the middle of the whiſk. Take the froth with a ſpoon, and lay it in your glaſſes or baſons. This does well over a tart.

Ice Cream.

PARE, ſtone, and ſcald twelve ripe apricots, and beat them fine in a marble mortar. Put to them ſix ounces of double refined ſugar, and a pint of of ſcalding cream, and work it through a hair ſieve. Put it into a tin that has a cloſe cover, and ſet it in a tub of ice broken ſmall, and a large quantity of ſalt put among it. When you ſee the cream grows thick round the edges of your tin, ſtir it, and ſet it again till it grows quite thick. When your cream is all frozen up, take it out of the tin, and put it into the mould you intend it to be turned out of. Then put on the lid, and have ready another tub, with ice and ſalt in it as before. Put your mould in the middle, and lay your ice under and over it. Let it ſtand four or five hours, and dip your tin in warm water when you turn it out; but, if it be ſummer time, do not turn it out till the very inſtant you want it. If you have not apricots, any other fruit will anſwer the purpoſe, provided you take care to work them very fine in the mortar.

Hartſhorn Cream.

BOIL four ounces of hartſhorn ſhavings in three pints of water till it is reduced to half a pint, and run it through a jelly-bag. Put to it a pint of cream and four ounces of loaf ſugar, and juſt boil it up. Put it into cups or glaſſes, and let it ſtand till it is cold. Dip your cups or glaſſes in ſcalding water, and turn them out into your diſh. Stick ſliced almonds on them. It is generally eaten with white wine and ſugar.

Pompadour Cream.

BEAT the whites of five eggs into a ſtrong froth, and put them into a toſſing-pan with two ounces of ſugar, and two ſpoonfuls of orange-flower water. Stir it gently three or four minutes, and then pour it into a diſh with melted butter over it. Send it up hot to table.

Coffee

Coffee Cream.

PUT an ounce of coffee roasted hot into a pint and half of boiling cream. Boil these together a little; then take it off, and put in two dried gizzards. Cover this close, let it stand one hour, and sweeten it with double refined sugar. Pass it two or three times through a sieve with a wooden spoon, put it into a dish with a tin on the top; set the dish on a gentle stove, put fire over and under it, and when it has taken, set it by. This must be sent up cold to table.

Goosebery Cream.

PUT two quarts of goseberries into a saucepan, just cover them with water, scald them till they are tender, and then rub them through a sieve with a spoon to a quart of pulp. Have ready six eggs well beaten, make your pulp hot, and put in one ounce of fresh butter. Sweeten it to your taste, put it over a gentle fire till they are thick; but take care that they do not boil. Then stir in a gill of the juice of spinach, and when it is almost cold, stir in a spoonful of orange-flower water or sack. Pour it into basons, and serve it up cold.

Clouted Cream.

IN the evening, take four quarts of milk from the cow, put it into a broad earthen pan, and let it stand till the next day. Then put the dish over a very slow fire, and another dish over it to keep out the dust. Make it sufficiently hot to set the cream, and then set it aside to cool. Then take the cream off into a bowl, and beat it well with a spoon. This is very proper to put over pies and tarts.

Snow

Snow and Cream.

BOIL a quart of new milk with a ſtick of cinnamon, a little lemon peel, two or three laurel leaves, and ſweeten it with ſugar to your taſte. Beat up the whites of four eggs, and the yolks of ſix, very fine. Mix the milk and eggs well together, and ſtrain all through a fine ſieve into a ſtewpan. Put it over a ſlow fire, and ſtir it one way till it is thick. Then put it into a deep diſh to cool, and, when cold, beat the whites of ſix eggs to a high froth. Put ſome milk and water into a broad ſtewpan, and when it boils, take the froth off the eggs, and put it on the milk and water. Boil it up once, then with a ſlice take it carefully off, and lay it on your cuſtard.

To make black Currant Jam.

HAVING gathered your currants when they are full ripe, pick them clean from the ſtalks, bruiſe them well in a bowl, and to every pound of currants put a pound and half of loaf ſugar, finely beaten. Put them into a preſerving pan, boil them half an hour, ſkim and ſtir them all the time, and then put them into pots.

Cherry Jam.

TAKE ſome cherries, boil and break them. Take them off the fire, and let the juice run from them. To three pounds of cherries, boil together half a pint of red currant juice, and half a pound of loaf ſugar. Put in the cherries as they boil, ſift in three quarters of a pound of ſugar, and boil the cherries very faſt for more than half an hour. Put on brandy-paper when they are properly cooled.

Goosberry Jam.

CUT into halves and take out the seeds of some large full grown gooseberries, but not too ripe. Put them into a pan of cold spring water, lay some vine leaves at the bottom, then some gooseberries, then vine leaves, till all the fruit is in the pan. Cover it very close that no steam can evaporate, and set them on a very slow fire. When they are scalding hot, take them off, then set them on again, and so on. They must be thus treated till they are of a good green. Then lay them on a sieve to drain, and beat them in a marble mortar with their weight in sugar. Take a quart of water, and a quart of gooseberries, boil them to a mash, and squeeze them. To every pint of this liquor put a pound of fine loaf sugar, and boil and skim it. Then put in the green gooseberries, and let them boil till they be thick and clear, and of a good green.

Apricot Jam.

CUT some fine rich apricots into thin pieces, and infuse them in an earthen pot till they are tender and dry. Put a pound of double refined sugar, and three spoonfuls of water, to every pound and an half of apricots. Then boil your sugar to a candy height, as hereafter directed in the chapter of candying, and put it upon your apricots. Set them over a slow fire, and stir them till they appear clear and thick, but take care that they do not boil. Then put them into your glasses.

Red Raspberry Jam.

RASPBERRIES for this purpose must be gathered when they are ripe and dry. Pick them very carefully from the stalks and dead ones, and crush them in a bowl with a silver or wooden spoon, as pewter is apt to turn them of a purple colour. Having crushed them, strew in their own weight of loaf sugar, and half their weight of currant juice, baked and strained as for jelly. Then boil them half an hour over a clear slow fire, skim them well, and keep stirring them all the time. Then put them into pots or glasses, with brandy paper over them, and keep them for use. As soon as you have got your berries, remember to strew in your sugar; do not let them stand long before you boil them, and it will preserve their flavour.

CHAP. XXI.

To make Blanc Mange, Flummery Ornaments, Jellies and Syllabubs.

To make Blanc Mange.

PUT two ounces of isinglass, a stick of cinnamon, a little lemon-peel, a few coriander seeds, and two or three laurel leaves, into a stew-pan, with a quart of new milk, and sweeten it to your palate. Add to it six bitter almonds cut in slices. Boil it gently till the isinglass is dissolved, and then strain it through a fine sieve into a bowl. Let it stand till it is half cold, and then pour it off from the settlings into another bowl. Let your moulds be ready, fill them, and let them stand to be cold. When they are thoroughly cold, raise them with your fingers from the sides, dip the bottom of the mould into warm water, and turn them out into a dish. Garnish with jellies of different colours, or currant jelly, Seville oranges cut in quarters, flowers, or any thing else you fancy. When

When you want to colour your blanc mange green, juſt when it is done, put in a little ſpinach juice, but take care that it does not boil after it is put in, as that will curdle and ſpoil the whole. If you wiſh to have it red, put in a little bruiſed cochineal; if yellow, a little ſaffron; if violet colour, a little ſyrup of violets; and thus you may have different colours in the diſh, ſuch as plain white, green, yellow, red, and violet. Let your mould for the white be deeper than the reſt; put it in the middle of the diſh, and the others round it.

Another Method.

CUT a calf's foot into ſmall pieces, and put it into a ſaucepan with a quart of water, an ounce of iſinglaſs, a little lemon peel, and a ſtick of cinnamon. Boil it gently, and ſkim it well, till it is of a very ſtrong jelly, which you may know by putting a little into a ſpoon to get cold. Then ſtrain it off, put it into a ſtewpan with a few coriander ſeeds, and two or three laurel leaves. Blanch and beat an ounce of ſweet almonds very fine, and put them in, with two bitter almonds alſo beaten fine. Sweeten it with ſugar to your taſte, and let it boil up. Then put in a pint of good thick cream, and boil it again. Strain it into a bowl, and proceed as before.

Another Method.

PUT two ounces of iſinglaſs, with a ſtick of cinnamon, a little lemon-peel, a few coriander ſeeds, and two or three laurel leaves, into a ſtewpan, with a quart of ſweet cream. Sweeten it with ſugar to your palate, and boil it gently till the iſinglaſs is diſſolved. Blanch an ounce of ſweet almonds, and two bitter almonds. Beat them fine in a mortar, and put them in. Stir it well about, then ſtrain it through a fine ſieve into a bowl, and proceed as before directed.

Hartſhorn

Hartſhorn Flummery.

PUT four ounces of hartſhorn ſhavings into a ſaucepan with two quarts of ſpring water, and let it ſimmer over the fire till it is reduced to a pint; or put it into a jug, and ſet it in the oven with houſehold bread. Strain it through a ſieve into a ſtewpan, blanch and beat half a pound of ſweet almonds with a little orange-flower water, mix a little of your jelly in it, and fine ſugar enough to ſweeten it. Then ſtrain it through a ſieve to the other jelly, mix it well together, and when it is blood warm put it into moulds or half pint baſons. When it is cold, dip the moulds or baſons in warm water, and turn them into a diſh. Mix ſome white wine and ſugar together, and pour them into the diſh. If you pleaſe, you may ſtick almonds in them.

French Flummery.

BEAT an ounce of iſinglaſs fine, put it into a quart of cream, and boil it gently for a quarter of an hour, but keep ſtirring it all the time. Then take it off, ſweeten it with fine powder ſugar, put in a ſpoonful of roſe and another of orange-flower water, ſtrain it through a ſieve, and ſtir it till half cold. Put it into a mould or baſon, and when cold, turn it into a diſh, and garniſh with currant jelly.

Eggs and Bacon in Flummery.

PUT two ounces of iſinglaſs and a quart of new milk into a ſtewpan. Boil it gently till the iſinglaſs is diſſolved, ſweeten it with ſugar, and ſtrain it through a ſieve. Colour a quarter of a pint of it red with cochineal, and have ready a tin mould about four inches long, two broad, and one deep.

Put a little of the red at the bottom, and let it be cold; then put on ſome white, then red, and treble the thickneſs of white at the top, always obſerving to let one be cold before you put on the other, and that only blood warm. Then take five tea-cups and fill them half full with white flummery, and let all ſtand till the next morning. Turn them out, and cut that of the tin moulds into thin ſlices, and lay them in your diſh. Then turn them out of the cups, and put them over the others. Cut a hole in the tops, and lay in half a preſerved apricot, which will appear like the yolk of an egg. Garniſh the diſh with currant jelly, or any thing elſe you think proper.

Orange Butter.

BEAT well the yolks of ten eggs, and put them into a ſtewpan, with half a pint of Rheniſh, ſix ounces of powder ſugar, and the juice of three China oranges. Set them over a gentle fire, and ſtir them one way till they are thick. When you take it off, ſtir in a piece of butter as big as a walnut, put it into a diſh, and ſerve it up when cold.

Solomon's Temple in Flummery.

TAKE a quart of ſtiff flummery, and divide it into three parts. Make one part of a pretty thick colour, with a little cochineal bruiſed fine, and ſteeped in French brandy. Scrape an ounce of chocolate very fine, diſſolve it in a little ſtrong coffee, and mix it with another part of your flummery, which will make it of a light ſtone colour. The laſt part muſt be white. Then wet your temple mould, and fit it in ſomething to make it ſtand even. Fill the top of the temple with red flummery for the ſteps, and the four points with white. Then fill it up with chocolate flummery, and let it ſtand till the next day. Then looſen it round with a pin,

pin, and ſhake it looſe very gently; but do not dip your mould in warm water, as that will take off the gloſs, and ſpoil the colour. When you turn it out, ſtick a ſmall ſprig of flowers down from the top of every point, which will not only ſtrengthen it, but alſo give it a pretty appearance. Lay round it rock candy ſweetmeats.

Jellies for Moulds, &c.

JELLIES for this purpoſe requiring to be made much ſtronger than thoſe for glaſſes, the materials neceſſary muſt in courſe be ſtronger. Take two calves feet and one neat's foot, take out the large bones, and cut them in ſmall pieces. You may uſe two ounces of iſinglaſs, inſtead of the neat's foot, if you like it better. Put it into a large ſaucepan or pot, with a gallon of water, a lemon peel cut thin, and a ſtick of cinnamon. Boil it gently till it is reduced to three pints or leſs. As it boils, ſkim it well, try it with a ſpoon, and if you find it ſtrong enough, ſtrain it off, and let it ſettle half an hour. Then ſkim the top, and pour it from the ſettlings into a ſtewpan. Put in half a pint of white wine, ſweeten it with loaf ſugar, ſqueeze ſix lemons, ſtraining the juice to keep out the ſeeds, and put in a little lemon peel. If you want it quite clear and bright, do not put in any ſaffron. If you want it an amber colour, put in a little ſaffron; if a very high colour, put in a little cochineal bruiſed. Boil it up ten minutes. Beat the whites of ten eggs up to a high froth, mix them with the jelly well together, and boil it up ten minutes. Then take it off the fire, cover it, and let it ſtand for five minutes. Have your bag ready with a bowl under, pour your jelly in gently, and as it runs through pour it into the bag again, till it is as bright as you want it. When it is all run through, fill your moulds, and let them ſtand till they are cold. Then

loofen

loofen the fides with your fingers, dip the mould into warm water, and turn it out on your difh. You may garnifh it according to your fancy.

Calf's Feet Jelly.

TAKE out the large bones of two calves feet, cut the meat in fmall pieces, and put them into a faucepan with three quarts of water, a little lemon peel, and a ftick of cinnamon. Boil it gently till it is reduced to a quart, and remember to try it with a fpoon, in order to fee when it is ftrong enough. Strain it off, and let it fettle half an hour. Then fkim it very clean, and pour it from the fettling into a ftewpan. Put in half a pint of mountain or Lifbon wine, fweeten it to your tafte with loaf fugar, fqueeze four lemons, or two lemons and two Seville oranges, ftrain the juice to keep out the feeds, and put it in with a lemon peel, and a very little faffron. Boil it up a few minutes, then beat up the whites of eight eggs to a high froth, and mix them well together with the jelly. Then boil it up for five minutes. Have your bag ready with a bowl under it, pour your jelly gently in, that it may run pretty faft through at the firft, and as it runs pour it in again feveral times, till it is as clear as you would have it. When it is all run off, fill your glaffes with a fpoon.

Hartfhorn Jelly.

PUT three quarts of water and half a pound of hartfhorn fhavings into a faucepan, with a lemon peel, and a ftick of cinnamon. Boil it gently till it is a ftrong jelly, which you may know by taking a little out in a fpoon, and let it cool, as before directed. Then ftrain it through a fine fieve into a ftewpan, put in a pint of Rhenifh wine, fweeten it with loaf fugar to your palate, fqueeze in the juice of four lemons, or two lemons and two Seville oranges, ftrain ſtrain the juice to keep out the ſeeds, put them in, with a little ſaffron, and boil it up. Beat up the whites of eight eggs to a high froth, mix them well in the jelly and boil it up for five minutes. Then take it off the fire, and proceed in the ſame manner as before directed. Remember to put your ſugar and lemon in, to make it palatable, before you put your eggs in; for by putting in ſugar and lemon afterwards you will prevent its clearing properly.

Orange Jelly.

PUT two quarts of ſpring water into a ſaucepan, with half a pound of hartſhorn ſhavings, or four ounces of iſinglaſs, and boil it gently till it becomes a ſtrong jelly. Take the juice of three Seville oranges, three lemons, and ſix China oranges, the rind of one Seville orange, and one lemon, pared very thin. Put them to your jelly, ſweeten with loaf ſugar to your taſte, beat up the whites of eight eggs to a froth, mix them well in, and boil it for ten minutes. Then run it through a jelly-bag till it is very clear, put it into your moulds, and let it ſtand till it is thoroughly cold. Then dip your moulds in warm water, and turn them into a China diſh, or flat glaſs. You may make uſe of flowers for your garniſh.

Fruit in Jelly.

TAKE ſome mould jelly, made as before directed, and procure a mould, either long or round, about three inches deep. Put ſome jelly at the bottom of the mould, about a quarter of an inch thick. As ſoon as it is cold, put in ripe peaches, grapes, or any ſort of ripe fruit, or preſerved fruit, or China oranges cut in quarters, or in any ſhape you fancy. Put in a little jelly blood warm, and let it ſtand till it is cold, to faſten your fruit in its

its place, otherwife it will rife up. Then fill up your mould with blood-warm jelly, let it ftand till it is thoroughly cold, then turn it into a difh, and garnifh it to your fancy. Thefe jellies look exceedingly well in a difh, if you take care to put in your fruit nicely, fo as to fhew it to advantage, and your jelly be very clear.

Savoury Jelly.

HAVING cut fix thin rafhers of lean ham, put them at the bottom of a foup-pot. Cut the fhank end of a knuckle of veal, with a pound of lean veal, in flices. Put them into the pot with half a pint of water, fix blades of mace, a few cloves, a carrot cut in flices, and cover the pot clofe. Set it over a flow fire, and fweat it gently for fifteen minutes. Then pour in a gallon of boiling water, and as it boils up, fkim it well. Put in a fpoonful of falt, and ftew it gently for fix hours. Then try with a fpoon, whether the jelly is ftrong enough. As foon as it is fufficiently ftrong, ftrain it off into a pan, and let it fettle. Then fkim the fat clean off, pour it clean from the fettlings into a ftewpan, and put in a gill of elder or common vinegar. Beat up the whites of twelve eggs to a high froth, and mix it with the jelly well together. If you want it of a high colour, bruife a little cochineal, and put it in. Boil it up till the eggs become a fine white froth at the top, then take it off the fire, cover it up, and let it ftand ten minutes. Pour it gently into your bag, and as it runs, put it into the bag again, till it is quite clear. When it has all run through, you may then proceed to ufe it as before directed.

Chicken in Jelly.

BONE a nice chicken, and cut off the pinions; make a forcemeat with the flefh of a fowl, fome ſome lean veal, beef marrow, beef ſuet, ſweet herbs, bread crumbs, &c. Fill your chicken with this, and truſs it as for boiling. Put it into a ſaucepan, cover it with veal broth, and put in a bundle of ſweet herbs, a few cloves, a little mace, and all-ſpice. Boil it gently till it is tender, then take it out, and let it ſtand to cool. Put ſome ſavoury jelly, made as above directed, into an oval mould, and cover the bottom to the depth of a quarter of an inch. When it is cold, put in the chicken, breaſt downwards. Then put in a little jelly blood warm, to faſten it, and when it is cold fill your mould with blood-warm jelly. Let it ſtand all night, and the next day turn it into a diſh. You may make uſe of ſlices of Seville orange or lemon for garniſh. Partridges, or any other ſmall birds, may be put into ſavoury jelly, but you need not bone them.

Turkey in Jelly.

TREAT a turkey in the ſame manner as above directed for a chicken. As ſoon as it is cold, put it on the diſh, on which you intend to ſend it to table, and pour over it ſome ſavoury jelly blood-warm. Garniſh with flowers and curled parſley, and ſtick a ſprig of myrtle on the breaſt, or ornament it with ſome coloured jelly.

Hen's Neſt in Jelly.

FILL ſome egg moulds with blanc mange, and when they are cold, turn them out; but if you have no moulds, break holes in the thick ends of ſix or ſeven eggs, and pour out the yolks and whites as clear as you can. Set them on one end in ſalt, and with a funnel fill them with ſtrong blanc mange. When they are cold, very carefully break the ſhells, and take them off the blanc mange. Put a little jelly at the bottom of a round a round mould, or China bowl. Lay the eggs on it, and put on a little jelly to fix them to their places. When it is cold, put in more jelly blood-warm, till it is even with the eggs. Then lay ſome vermicelli over and round them, to make it look like a neſt. When it is cold, fill the mould or bowl quite full, ſet it aſide all night, the next day turn it out into a diſh, and garniſh with flowers, ſweetmeats, or what you pleaſe.

Ribband Jelly.

TAKE out the great bones of four calves feet, and cut the fleſh ſmall. Put it into a pot with ſix quarts of water, four ounces of iſinglaſs, a little lemon-peel, and a ſtick of cinnamon. Boil it gently for ſix hours, ſkim it well, and try a little in a ſpoon to ſee if it be ſtrong enough. As ſoon as it is, ſtrain it off into a clean pan, and let it ſettle an hour. If there be any fat at the top, ſkim it off, and pour it from the ſettlings into a ſtewpan. Put in a pint of white wine, the juice of ſix lemons, and ſweeten it with ſugar to your taſte. Beat up the whites of ten eggs, ſtir them well in, and boil it up gently for ten minutes. Then take it off the fire, and let it ſtand five minutes. Run it through your bag till it is as clear as you would have it. Then colour ſome of it red with cochineal, green with ſpinach juice, yellow with ſaffron, blue with ſyrup of violets, white with thick cream, and ſome of its own colour. Then put your jelly into high glaſſes, and run every colour a quarter of an inch thick. One colour muſt be thoroughly cold before you put on the other, and that you put on muſt be but blood-warm, for fear they ſhould mix together. Or you may take a tin mould, ſix inches long, one broad, and one deep. Fill it in the ſame manner, and when cold turn it

out;

out, cut it with a thin knife in ſlices, and lay it on a diſh. Garniſh to ſuit your fancy.

Gold Fiſh in Jelly.

HAVING filled two or three ſmall fiſh moulds with very ſtrong blanc mange, let them ſtand till they be cold, and then turn them out. Gild the fiſh with leaf gold, and let them ſtand for an hour, that the gold may dry on. Then take a mould, put a little mould jelly at the bottom of it. When it is cold, lay in the gold fiſh back downwards; put in ſome jelly blood-warm to faſten them to their places. When it is cold, fill up the moulds with blood-warm jelly, and let them ſtand all night. The next day turn them out into a diſh, and garniſh with any thing you like.

Green Melon in Jelly.

COLOUR a pint of blanc mange of a light green with the juice of ſpinach. Put it into a melon mould, and when it is cold turn it out. Have a deep mould, with a little cold jelly at the bottom. Put your melon in, and put in ſome jelly blood-warm. Let it be cold, then fill up your mould with blood-warm jelly, let it ſtand all night, and the next morning turn it into a diſh. Garniſh it with ſweetmeats, flowers, or any thing elſe you like.

Black Currant Jelly.

GATHER your currants when they are full ripe, on a dry day, and ſtrip them of the ſtalks. Put them into an earthen pan, and to every ten quarts put in a quart of ſpring water. Tie paper over them, and ſet them in the oven for two hours. Then ſqueeze out the juice through a fine cloth, and to every pint of juice put a pound of loaf ſugar broken to pieces. Stir it and boil it gently

gently for half an hour, and ſkim it well all the time. While it is hot put it into gallipots, put brandy papers over it, tie another paper over that, and keep it in a cool dry place.

Red Currant Jelly.

GATHER your currants as above directed, and to every gallon of red put a quart of white. Put them into a preſerving pan, cover them cloſe, and ſet them over a ſlow fire; ſtirring them to prevent their burning at the bottom, till the juice is out. Or you may put them into an earthen pan, tie a paper over them, and ſet them in a warm oven for an hour. Then put them into a flannel bag, and when the juice is all run out, to every pint put a pound of loaf ſugar broken into ſmall pieces. Put it over a gentle fire, and ſtir it till the ſugar is melted, or it will burn at the bottom. Skim it well, and boil it gently half an hour. While it is hot, put it into your gallipots or glaſſes, and when it is cold, put brandy papers over it, and tie another paper over that. Put them in a cool and dry place.

A Trifle.

PUT a gill of white wine into a quart of thick cream; put in alſo the juice of a lemon or Seville orange, grate in the rind of a lemon, ſweeten it with powder ſugar, whip it with a whiſk, or mill it with a chocolate mill, and as the froth riſes take it off, and put it on a hair ſieve to drain. Put a quarter of a pound of macaroon cakes, and ratafia drops, into a deep diſh, and juſt wet them with ſweet wine. Boil a pint of milk or cream, ſweeten it with ſugar, beat up the yolks of four eggs, and mix them with it. Put it over a ſlow fire, and ſtir it till it is thick. Then put it on the cakes, and when cold put the froth on as high as you can, and

ſtrew

ſtrew it over with nonpareils of different colours, which are to be bought of the confectioners. Garniſh according to your taſte.

An Everlaſting Syllabub.

PUT three pints of good thick cream into an earthen pan, with half a pint of Rheniſh, half a pint of ſack, the juice of two large Seville oranges, the rind of three lemons grated, and a pound of double-refined ſugar pounded and ſifted. Put in a ſpoonful of orange-flower water, beat it well together with a whiſk for half an hour, then with a ſpoon take off the froth, and lay it on a ſieve to drain, and then fill your glaſſes. This will keep a week. The beſt way to whip ſyllabubs is to have a fine large chocolate mill, which you muſt keep on purpoſe, and a large deep bowl or pan to mill them in, it being done quicker and the froth ſtronger. For the thin that is left at the bottom, have ready ſome calves feet jelly thus made. Cut two calves feet into ſmall pieces, put them into a ſaucepan, with two quarts of water, and a little lemon-peel. Boil it gently till it is reduced to a pint and a half, then ſtrain it off, and then let it ſtand half an hour to ſettle. Skim it well, pour it into a ſtewpan from the ſettlings, beat up the whites of ſix eggs, and put them in, and boil it gently for ten minutes. Then run it through a flannel bag, and mix it with the clear that you ſaved from the ſyllabubs. Sweeten it to your taſte, give it a boil, then pour it into your moulds, and when it is cold, turn it into a diſh.

A ſolid Syllabub.

PUT a pint of mountain to a quart of rich cream, the juice of two lemons, the rind of one grated, and ſweeten it with powder ſugar to your taſte. Whip it well, take off the froth as it riſes,

lay

lay it on a hair ſieve, and put it in a cool place till next day. Then make your glaſſes better than half full with the thin, and with a ſpoon put on the froth as high as you can. It will look clear at the bottom, even after it has been kept ſeveral days.

A Lemon Syllabub.

RUB a quarter of a pound of loaf ſugar in one piece on the rind of two lemons till you have got all the eſſence out of them. Then put the ſugar into a pint of cream and a gill of mountain wine, ſqueeze in the juice of both the lemons, and let it ſtand for two hours. Then whip it with a whiſk, or mill it with a chocolate mill, and as the froth riſes take it off, and put it on a ſieve to drain. Let it ſtand all night, then put the clear into the glaſſes, and with a ſpoon put on the froth as high as it will bear it.

A Syllabub under the Cow.

HAVING put a bottle of red or white wine, ale or cyder, into a China bowl, ſweeten it with ſugar, and grate in ſome nutmeg. Then hold it under the cow, and milk into it till it has a fine froth on the top. Strew over it a handful of currants cleaned, waſhed and picked, and plumped before the fire.

A Floating Iſland.

SET a pretty deep glaſs on a China diſh, proportioned in ſize to the quantity you intend to make. Make a quart of the thickeſt cream you can get pretty ſweet with fine ſugar. Pour in a gill of ſack, grate in the yellow rind of a lemon, and mill the cream till it is of a thick froth. Then carefully pour in the thin from the froth into a diſh or glaſs. Take a French roll, if one be ſufficient

for

for the quantity you intend to make, and cut it as thin as you can. Put a layer of that on the cream as lightly as poſſible, then a layer of currant jelly, after that a very thin layer of roll, then hartſhorn jelly, and then French roll. Over that whip the froth you ſaved off the cream, very well milled up, and put on the top as high as you can heap it. As to the rim of the diſh, ſet it round with fruit or ſweetmeats, according to your taſte. This has a very pretty appearance in the middle of a table, with candles round it. You may make it of as many different colours as you pleaſe, according to the jellies, jams, or ſweetmeats, you may have at hand.

CHAP. XXII.

Candying and Drying.

To prepare Sugar for candying.

FRUIT intended for candying muſt be firſt preſerved, and dried in a ſtove, or before the fire, that none of the ſyrup may remain in it. Sugar intended for the uſe of candying muſt be thus prepared. Put into a toſſing-pan a pound of ſugar with half a pint of water, and ſet it over a very clear fire. Take off the ſcum as it riſes, boil it till it looks fine and clear, and take out a little in a ſilver ſpoon. When it is cold, if it will draw a thread from your ſpoon, it is boiled high enough for any kind of ſweetmeat. Then boil your ſyrup, and when it begins to candy round the edge of your pan, it is candy height. It is a great miſtake to put any kind of ſweetmeat into too thick a ſyrup, eſpecially

eſpecially at the firſt, as it withers the fruit, and the beauty and flavour are thereby both deſtroyed.

To candy Melons.

HAVING quartered your melons, take out all the inſide, and put into it as much thin ſyrup as will cover the coat. Let it boil in the ſyrup till it is thoroughly tender, and then put it away in the ſyrup for two or three days, but mind that the ſyrup covers it, and that it may penetrate quite through. Then take it out, and boil your ſyrup to a candy height; dip in your quarters, and lay them on a ſieve to dry either before the fire, or in a ſlow oven.

Lemon and Orange Peel candied.

CUT your oranges or lemons lengthways, and and take out all the pulp and inſide ſkins. Put the peels into hard water and ſtrong ſalt for ſix days, and then boil them in ſpring water till they are tender. Take them out, and lay them on a ſieve to drain. Make a thin ſyrup with a pound of loaf ſugar to a quart of water, and boil them in it for half an hour, or till they look clear. Make a thick ſyrup of double-refined ſugar, with as much water as will wet it. Put in your peels and boil them over a ſlow fire till you ſee the ſyrup candy about the pan and the peels. Then take them out, and ſprinkle fine ſugar over them. Lay them on a ſieve, and dry them before the fire, or in a cool oven.

Caſſia candied.

POUND a little muſk and ambergreaſe with as much of the powder of caſſia as will lie on two ſhillings. Having pounded them well together, take a quarter of a pound of fine ſugar, and as much water as will wet it, and boil it to a candy height.
Then

Then put in your powder, and mix them well together. Butter ſome pewter ſaucers, and when it is cold turn it out.

Angelica candied.

GATHER your angelica in April, cut it in lengths, and boil it in water till it becomes tender. Having put it on a ſieve to drain, peel it, and dry it in a clean cloth, and to every pound of ſtalks take a pound of double-refined ſugar finely pounded. Put your ſtalks into an earthen pan, and ſtrew the ſugar over them. Cover them cloſe, and let them ſtand two days. Then put it into a preſerving-pan, and boil it till it is clear. Then put it into a cullender to drain, ſtrew it pretty thick over with fine powder ſugar, lay it on plates, and dry it in a cool oven, or before the fire.

Ginger candied.

PUT into a toſſing-pan an ounce of race ginger finely grated, with a pound of loaf ſugar beat fine, and as much water as will diſſolve it. Put them over a ſlow fire, and ſtir them well till the ſugar begins to boil. Then ſtir in another pound of fine ſugar well beaten, and keep ſtirring it till it grows thick. Then take it off the fire, and drop it in cakes upon earthen diſhes. Set them to dry in a warm place, when they will become hard and brittle, and have a white appearance.

To dry Plums green.

HAVING dipped the ſtalks and leaves in boiling vinegar, put them on a ſieve to dry. Give them a ſcald in a ſtrong ſyrup, and with a pin very carefully take off the ſkin. Boil your ſyrup to a candy height, and dip in your plums. Then take them out, and hang them by the ſtalks to dry on any thing you conveniently can. Dry them in a cool oven, and they will look finely tranſparent.

To dry Cherries.

PUT a pound of loaf ſugar to four pounds of cherries, and put as much water as will wet the ſugar. When it is melted, make it boil. Stone your cherries, put them in, and make them boil. Having ſkimmed it two or three times, take them off, and let them ſtand in the ſyrup two or three days. Then take them out of the ſyrup, boil it up, and pour it over the cherries; but do not boil the cherries any more. Let them ſtand three or four days longer, then take them out, lay them on a ſieve to dry, and put them in the ſun, or in a ſlow oven. When they are dry, lay ſome white paper at the bottom of a ſmall box, then a row of cherries, then paper, till they are all in, and covered with paper.

Another Method.

TAKE a pound of fine powder ſugar and eight pounds of cherries. Stone the cherries, and lay them one by one in rows in a deep baſon or glaſs, and ſtrew a little ſugar over them. Proceed in this manner till your baſon or glaſs is full, and let them ſtand till next day. Then put them into a preſerving-pan, ſet them over the fire, and let them boil faſt for rather more than a quarter of an hour. Then pour them into your baſon again, and let them ſtand two or three days. Then take them out of the ſyrup, and lay them one by one on hair ſieves, and ſet them in the ſun, or put them into the oven till they are dry, turning them every day on dry ſieves. Put them into boxes with white paper between them.

To

To dry Damſons.

MAKE a thin ſyrup, boil and ſkim it well, and then put in ſome of the fineſt damſons you can get. Take out the ſtones, and give them a boil, and let them ſtand in the ſyrup till next day. Then make a rich ſyrup with double-refined ſugar, and as much water as will wet it. Boil it to a candy height. Then take your damſons out of the other ſyrup, and put them into this. Give them a ſimmer, and put them away till the next day. Then put them one by one on a ſieve, and dry them in a cool oven or ſtove, or before the fire, and mind to turn them twice every day. When dry, put them in a box with white paper between them, and keep them in a place that is cool and dry.

To dry Peaches.

PARE ſome of the cleareſt and ripeſt peaches you can procure, and put them into pure water. Take their weight in double-refined ſugar, and of one half make a very thin ſyrup. Then put in your peaches, and boil them till they look clear. Then ſplit and ſtone them, boil them till they are very tender, and put them on a ſieve to drain. Boil the other half of the ſugar almoſt to a candy, then put in your peaches, and let them lay all night. Then lay them in a glaſs, and ſet them in a ſtove till they are dry. If they be ſugared too much, wipe them a little with a wet cloth, and put them between paper into boxes.

To dry Apricots.

PARE ſome fine ripe apricots very thin, and ſtone them. Put them into a preſerving-pan, and to every pound of apricots allow a pound of double-refined ſugar pounded. Strew ſome among them, and lay the reſt over them. Let them ſtand twenty-four hours, and turn them three or four times

times in the ſyrup. Then boil them pretty quick till they are clear, and put them away in the ſyrup till they are cold. When they are cold, put them on glaſſes, and dry them in a cool oven or ſtove, turning them often. When they are properly dried, put them in boxes as before directed.

To dry Plums.

TAKE ſome fine and clear-coloured large pear plums, weigh them, ſlit them up the ſides, put them into a broad ſtewpan, and fill it full of ſpring water. Set them over a very ſlow fire, and take care that the ſkins do not come off. When they are tender, take them up, and to every pound of plums put a pound of powdered ſugar. Strew a little at the bottom of a large bowl, then lay your plums in one by one, and ſtrew the reſt of the ſugar over them. Set them into your ſtove all night, and the next day, with a moderate fire, heat them, and ſet them into your ſtove again. Let them ſtand two days more, turning them every day. Then take them out of the ſyrup, lay them to dry, and treat them as above directed. Any other ſort of plums may be dried in the ſame manner.

CHAP XXIII.

To make all Sorts of Preſerves, &c.

To preſerve Gooſeberries whole.

PICK off the black eyes, but not the ſtalks, from the largeſt preſerving gooſeberries you can procure. Set them over the fire in a pot of water to ſcald, cover them very cloſe, but do not

let

let them either boil or break, and when they are tender, take them up; and put them into cold water. To a pound of gooseberries take a pound and a half of double-refined ſugar. Clarify the ſugar with water, a pint to a pound of ſugar, and when the ſyrup is cold, put the gooſeberries ſingle in your preſerving pan, put the ſyrup to them, and ſet them on a gentle fire. Let them boil, but not ſo faſt as to break them; and when they have boiled, and you perceive that the ſugar has entered them, take them off, cover them with white paper, and ſet them by till the next day. Then take them out of the ſyrup, and boil the ſugar till it begins to be ropy. Skim it, and put it to them again. Then ſet them on a gentle fire, and let them ſimmer gently till you perceive the ſyrup will rope. Then take them off, and ſet them by till they are cold. Cover them with paper; then boil ſome gooſeberries in fair water, and when the liquor is ſtrong enough, ſtrain it out. Let it ſtand to ſettle, and to every pint take a pound of double-refined ſugar; then make a jelly of it, put the gooſeberries in glaſſes when they are cold, cover them with the jelly the next day, paper them wet, and then half dry the paper that goes in the inſide, as it cloſes down better, and then white paper over the glaſs. Set it in a dry place, or a ſtove.

Currants preſerved for Tarts.

PUT any quantity of currants you pleaſe into a preſerving-pan, with a pound of ſugar to every pound and a quarter of currants, and a ſufficient quantity of currant juice to diſſolve the ſugar. Skim it as ſoon as it boils, put in your currants, and boil them till they are very clear. Put them into a jar, cover them with brandy-paper, and keep them in a dry place.

Red Currants preſerved in Bunches.

HAVING ſtoned your currants, tie them in bunches to bits of ſticks, ſix or ſeven together. Allow the weight of currants in ſugar, which make into a ſyrup. Boil it high, put in the currants, give them a boil, ſet them by, and the next day take them out. When the ſyrup boils, put them in again, give them a boil or two, and then take them out. Boil the ſyrup as much as is neceſſary, and when cold, put it to the currants in glaſſes. You muſt take care that the currants be equally diſperſed.

Barberries preſerved for Tarts

ADD to any quantity of barberries their weight in ſugar, put them into a jar, and ſet them in a kettle of boiling water till the ſugar is melted, and the barberries are become quite ſoft. The next day put them into a preſerving-pan, and boil them a quarter of an hour. Then put them into the jars, and keep them in a cool and dry place.

To preſerve Golden Pippins.

HAVING pared and ſliced your pippins, boil them in water to a maſh, and run the liquor through a jelly-bag. Put two pounds of loaf ſugar into a pan, with almoſt one pint of water, boil and ſkim it, put in twelve pippins pared and cored with a ſcoop, and the peel of an orange cut thin. Let them boil faſt till the ſyrup is thick, taking them off when they appear to part, and putting them on the fire again when they have ſtood a little time. Then put in a pint of the pippin juice, boil them faſt till they are clear, and then take them out. Boil the ſyrup as much as is neceſſary with the juice of a lemon. The orange-peel muſt be firſt put into water for a day, and then boiled, in order that all its bitterneſs may be extracted,

To

To preserve Codlings all the Year.

FOR this purpofe, the codlings muft be gathered when they are about the fize of a walnut, with the ftalk and a leaf or two remaining on each. Put fome vine leaves into a pan of fpring water, and cover them with a layer of codlings, then another of vine leaves, and thus proceed till the pan is full. Set it on a flow fire, having firft covered it to keep the fteam in. As foon as they become foft, take off the fkins with a penknife, and then put them in the fame water with the vine leaves. Take care that the water is cold, otherwife it may crack them. Put in a little roach alum, and fet them over a flow fire till they look green, which will be the cafe in three or four hours. Then take them out, and lay them on a fieve to drain. Make a good fyrup, and give them a gentle boil once a day for three days. Then put them into fmall jars, and cover them clofe with brandy paper.

Apple Marmalade.

PUT fome apples into water, fcald them till they are tender, and then drain them through a fieve. Put three quarters of a pound of fugar to a pound of apples; put them into a preferving-pan, let them fimmer over a gentle fire, fkimming them all the time. Put them into pots or glaffes, as foon as you find them of a proper thicknefs.

Quince Marmalade.

TAKE a pound of double-refined fugar, and a pound and a half of quinces. Make it into a fyrup, boil it high, and then pare and flice the fruit. When it begins to look clear, pour in half a pint of quince juice, or pippins, if quinces be fcarce. Boil it thick, and take off the fcum. To make a juice, pare the quinces or pippins, cut them from

from the core, beat them in a ſtone mortar, and ſtrain the juice through a thin cloth. To every half pint, put more than a pound of ſugar, and let it ſtand at leaſt four hours before it be uſed.

To preſerve green Apricots.

APRICOTS for this purpoſe muſt be gathered before the ſtones are hard. Put them into a pan of hard water, with plenty of vine leaves, and ſet them over a ſlow fire till they are quite yellow. Then take them out, and rub them in a flannel and ſalt, to take off the lint. Put them into the pan with the ſame water and leaves, cover them cloſe, ſet them at a great diſtance from the fire till they are of a fine light green, and then take them carefully up. Pick out all that are bad-coloured and broken, boil the reſt gently two or three times in a thin ſyrup, and let them be quite cold every time. When they look plump and clear, make a ſyrup of double-refined ſugar, but not too thick. Give your apricots a gentle boil in it, and then put them into pots or glaſſes, dip paper into brandy, lay it over them, and keep them for uſe. Take out all the broken and bad-coloured ones, and boil them in the firſt ſyrup for tarts.

Apricot Marmalade.

BOIL ſome ripe apricots in ſyrup till they will maſh, and then beat them in a marble mortar. Add half their weight of ſugar, and as much water as will diſſolve it. Boil and ſkim it well, boil them till they look clear, and the ſyrup like a fine jelly. Then put them into your ſweetmeat glaſſes.

To preſerve Almonds dry.

TAKE half a pound of double-refined ſugar, half a pound of Jordan almonds blanched, and half a pound not blanched. Beat the white of an

egg

egg well, pour it on the almonds, and wet them well with it. Then boil the ſugar, dip in the almonds, ſtir them all together that the ſugar may hang well on them, and then lay them on plates. Put them in the oven after the bread is drawn, let them ſtay all night, and they will keep good for twelve months.

Tranſparent Marmalade.

CUT into quarters ſome very pale Seville oranges, take out the pulp, and put it into a baſon. Pick the ſkins and ſeeds out, put the peels in a little ſalt and water, and let them ſtand all night. Then boil them in a good quantity of ſpring water till they are tender, cut them in very thin ſlices, and put them to the pulp. To every pound of marmalade, put a pound and a half of double-refined ſugar finely pounded, and boil them together gently for twenty minutes. If it be not clear and tranſparent, boil it five or ſix minutes longer, keep ſtirring it gently all the time, and take care you do not break the ſlices. When it is cold, put it into jelly or ſweetmeat glaſſes, and tie them down cloſe with brandy paper.

To preſerve Damſons.

HAVING picked the ſtalks from your damſons, prick them with a pin, put them into a deep pot, and with them half their weight of loaf ſugar pounded. Set them in a moderate oven till they are ſoft, then take them off, give the ſyrup a boil, and pour it upon them. Do this two or three times, then take them carefully out, and put them into the jars, in which you intend to keep them. Pour over them rendered mutton ſuet, tie a bladder over them, and put them into a cool place to keep for uſe.

To preſerve Strawberries.

YOUR ſtrawberries, which for this purpoſe muſt be of the fineſt ſcarlet ſort, muſt be gathered on a dry day, with their ſtalks on, before they are too ripe. Lay them ſeparately on a China diſh, beat and ſift twice their weight of double-refined ſugar, and ſtrew it over them. Then take a few ripe ſcarlet ſtrawberries, cruſh them, and put them into a jar, with their weight of double-refined ſugar finely pounded. Cover them cloſe, and let them ſtand in a kettle of boiling water till they are ſoft, and the ſyrup is come out of them. Then ſtrain them through a muſlin rag into a toſſing-pan, boil and ſkim it well, and when it is cold put in your whole ſtrawberries, and ſet them over the fire till they are milk warm. Then take them off, and let them ſtand till they are quite cold. Then ſet them on again, and make them a little hotter, and repeat the ſame till they look clear; but take care not to let them boil, as that will take off their ſtalks. When the ſtrawberries are cold, put them into jelly glaſſes, with the ſtalks downwards, and fill up your glaſſes with the ſyrup. Tie them down cloſe, with brandy paper over them.

Syrup of Quinces.

HAVING grated your quinces, extract their juice by preſſing their pulp in a cloth. Set the juice in the ſun to ſettle, or before the fire, in order to clarify it. Put a pound of ſugar boiled brown to every four ounces of the juice. If the putting in the juice of the quinces ſhould check the boiling of the ſugar too much, give the ſyrup ſome boiling till it becomes pearled. Then take it off the fire, and when it is cold, put it into your bottles.

To preſerve Raſpberries.

RASPBERRIES intended for this purpoſe muſt be gathered on a dry day, when they are juſt turned red, with their ſtalks on about an inch in length.

length. Lay them one by one on a diſh, and ſtrew over them their weight of double-refined ſugar pounded and ſifted. Put a quart of red-currant jelly juice, with its weight of double-refined ſugar, to every quart of raſpberries. Boil and ſkim it well, then put in your raſpberries, and give them a ſcald. Then take them off, and let them ſtand two hours. Set them on again, and make them a little hotter. Proceed in this manner two or three times till they look clear; but be careful that they do not boil, as that will take off the ſtalks. When they are tolerably cool, put them into jelly-glaſſes, with the ſtalks downwards. White raſpberries are preſerved in the ſame manner, only that inſtead of red you muſt uſe white-currant jelly.

To preſerve Walnuts green.

HAVING gathered your walnuts, which muſt be done when they are not much larger than a common-ſized nutmeg, wipe them very clean, and lay them for twenty-four hours in ſtrong ſalt and water. Then take them out, and wipe them very clean. Then throw them into a ſtewpan of boiling water, and, having let them boil a minute, take them out, and lay them on a coarſe cloth. Take three pounds of loaf ſugar, put it into your preſerving-pan, ſet it over a charcoal fire, and put as much water as will juſt wet the ſugar. Let it boil, and then have ready ten or twelve whites of eggs ſtrained and beat up to a froth. Cover your ſugar with froth as it boils, and ſkim it; then boil it and ſkim it till it is as clear as cryſtal. Then juſt give your walnuts a ſcald in the ſugar, take them up, and lay them to cool. Put them into your preſerving pot, and pour your ſyrup over them.

To

To preserve Walnuts white.

PARE your walnuts till the whites appear, throw them as faſt as you do them into ſalt and water, and let them lie till your ſugar is ready, which muſt be prepared in the ſame manner as directed in the preceding articles. Juſt give them a boil in the ſugar, till they are tender, then take them out, and lay them in a diſh to cool. As ſoon as they are cool, put them in your preſerving-pan, and when the ſugar is as warm as milk, pour it over them. When quite cold, tie them down with brandy paper.

To preserve Walnuts black.

PUT your walnuts, which muſt be of the ſmaller kind, into ſalt and water, and change the water every day for nine days. Then put them into a ſieve, and let them ſtand in the air till they begin to turn black. Put them into a jug, pour boiling water upon them, and let them ſtand till the next day. Then put them into a ſieve to drain, ſtick a clove into each end of them, put them into a pan of boiling water, and let them boil five minutes. Then take them out, make a thin ſyrup, and ſcald them in it three or four times a day, till your walnuts are black and bright. Make a thick ſyrup, with a few cloves, and a little ginger cut in ſlices. Skim it well, put in your walnuts, boil them five or ſix minutes, and then put them into jars. Lay brandy-paper over them, and tie them down cloſe with a bladder. As their bitterneſs goes off with time, they will eat better the ſecond year of keeping than in the firſt.

To preserve Eringo Roots.

THEY muſt be parboiled till they are tender; then peel and waſh them, dry them with a cloth, and

and cover them with clarified ſugar. Boil them gently till they are clear, and the ſyrup ſeems to be thickiſh. Put them up when half cold.

To preſerve Cucumbers.

TAKE ſome ſmall cucumbers, and large ones that will cut in quarters; but let them be as green and as free from ſeeds as you can get them. Put them into a narrow-mouthed jar in ſtrong ſalt and water, with a cabbage leaf to keep them from riſing. Tie a paper over them, and ſet them in a warm place till they are yellow. Then waſh them out, and ſet them over the fire in freſh water, with a little ſalt, and a freſh cabbage leaf over them. Cover the pan very cloſe, but be ſure that you do not let them boil. If they are not of a fine green, change your water, which will help them; then make them hot, and cover them as before. When you find them of a good green, take them off the fire, and let them ſtand till they are cold. Then cut the large ones into quarters, take out the ſeeds and ſoft parts, put them into cold water, and let them ſtand two days; but change the water twice a day to take out the ſalt. Put a pound of ſingle refined ſugar into a pint of water, and ſet it over the fire. When you have ſkimmed it clean, put in the rind of a lemon, and an ounce of ginger, with the outſide ſcraped off. Take your ſyrup off as ſoon as it is pretty thick, and as ſoon as it is cold, wipe the cucumbers dry, and put them into it. Boil the ſyrup once in two or three days for three weeks, and ſtrengthen the ſyrup, if required, for the greateſt danger of ſpoiling them is at firſt. When you put the ſyrup to your cucumbers, take care that it be quite cold.

To

To preserve Fruit green.

TAKE ſome green pippins, pears, plums, apricots, or peaches, and put them into a preſerving pan. Cover them with vine leaves, and then with clear ſpring water. Put on the cover of the pan, and ſet them over a very clear fire. Take them off as ſoon as they begin to ſimmer, and take them carefully out with a ſlice. Then peel and preſerve them as other fruit.

To preserve white Citrons.

CUT ſome white citrons into pieces, put them into ſalt and water, and let them remain there four or five hours. Then take them out, and waſh them in clean water. Boil them till they be tender, drain them, and cover them with clarified ſugar. Having let them ſtand twenty-four hours, drain the ſyrup, and boil it ſmooth. When it is cold, put in the citrons, and let them ſtand till the next day. Then boil the ſyrup quite ſmooth, and pour it over the citrons. Boil all together the next day, and put them into a pot, either to be candied, or into jellies.

To preserve Lemons.

PARE very thin the fineſt and cleareſt lemons you can procure, cut a ſmall round hole at the top, and take out the pulp and ſkins. Rub them in ſalt, and lay them in ſpring water as you do them, which will prevent their turning black. Let them lie in it five or ſix days, and then boil them a quarter of an hour in freſh ſalt and water. Having made a thin ſyrup of a quart of water and a pound of loaf ſugar, boil them in it five minutes for five or ſix days, and then put them in a large jar. Let them ſtand ſix or eight weeks, when they will look clear and plump. Then take them out of that ſyrup, or they will mould. Make a ſyrup with fine powder ſugar, put as much ſpring water to it as will diſ-

ſolve

ſolve it, boil and ſkim it well, then put in your lemons, and boil them gently till they are clear. Put them into a jar, cover them with brandy paper, and tie them down cloſe.

To preſerve Oranges.

HAVING procured ſome of the cleareſt and largeſt Seville oranges, cut out a ſmall hole at the ſtalk end, ſcoop out all the pulp very clean, tie them ſingly in muſlin, and lay them two days in ſpring water, change the water twice a day, and boil them in the muſlin till they be tender. Be careful to keep them covered with water. Before you ſcoop the oranges, weigh them, and to every pound add two pounds of double refined ſugar pounded, and a pint of ſpring water. Boil the ſugar and water with the orange juice to a ſyrup, ſkim it well, and let it ſtand till it be cold. Take the oranges out of the muſlin, and put them into a ſyrup. Put them over a ſlow fire, boil them till they are clear, and put them by till they are cold. Then pare and core ſome green pippins, boil them in water till it is ſtrong of the pippins. Do not ſtir them, but put them down gently with the back of a ſpoon, and ſtrain the liquor through a jelly-bag till it is clear. Put to every pint of liquor a pound of double-refined ſugar pounded, and the juice of a lemon ſtrained as clear as you can. Boil it to a ſtrong jelly, drain the oranges out of their ſyrup, and put them in glaſs or white ſtone jars of the ſize of the orange, and pour the jelly over them. Cover them with brandy-paper, and tie them down cloſe.

Marmalade of Oranges.

CHINA oranges muſt be made uſe of for this purpoſe. Cut them into quarters, and ſqueeze out the juice. Take off the hard parts at both ends, and boil them in water till they are quite tender.

der. Squeeze them to extract the water, and pound them in the water to a marmalade to sift. Mix it with an equal weight of raw sugar, and boil it till it turns to syrup. One pound of marmalade will require two pounds of sugar.

To preserve Morella Cherries.

HAVING gathered your cherries when they are full ripe, take off the stalks, and prick them with a pin. Put a pound and a half of loaf sugar to every pound of cherries. Beat part of your sugar, strew it over them, and let them stand all night. Dissolve the rest of your sugar in half a pint of the juice of currants, set it over a slow fire, and put in the cherries with the sugar. Having given them a gentle scald, take them carefully out, boil your syrup till it is thick, and then pour it on your cherries.

Cherries preserved with the Leaves and Stalks green.

MAKE some vinegar boiling hot, and dip into it the stalks and leaves of your cherries, then stick the sprigs upright in a sieve till they be dry. In the mean time, make a syrup of some double-refined sugar, and dip the cherries, stalks, and leaves, into the syrup, and just let them scald. Lay them on a sieve, and boil the sugar to a candy height. Then dip in the cherries, stalks, leaves, and all. Then stick the branches in the sieves, and dry them like other sweetmeats. They make a very pretty appearance in a desert by candle-light.

To preserve Green-gage Plums.

PLUMS for this purpose must be of the finest sort, and gathered just before they are ripe. Put them into a pan with a layer of vine leaves under them and over them; then a layer of plums on that, and proceed in this manner till your pan is almost full. Then fill it with water, and ſet them on a ſlow fire. When they are hot, and the ſkins begin to riſe, take them off, take off the ſkins carefully, and put them on a ſieve as you do them. Then put them into the ſame water, with a layer of leaves as before. Cover them cloſe, that no ſteam may get out, and hang them a conſiderable diſtance from the fire till they appear green, which will require five or ſix hours. Then take them up carefully, and lay them on a hair ſieve to drain. Make a good ſyrup, and boil them gently in it twice a day for two days. Then take them out, and put them in a fine clear ſyrup. Cover and ſecure them as you do other things of this nature.

To preſerve Pine Apples.

MAKE a ſtrong ſalt and water, and put into it ſome ſmall pine apples before they are ripe, and let them lie in it for five days. Then put a handful of vine leaves in the bottom of a large ſaucepan, and put in your pine apples. Fill your pan with vine leaves, and then pour on the ſalt and water they were ſoaked in. Cover them up very cloſe, ſet them over a ſlow fire, and let them ſtand till they are of a fine light green. Make a thin ſyrup of a quart of ſpring water and a pound of double-refined ſugar. When it is almoſt cold, put it into a deep jar, and put in the pine apples with their tops on. Let them ſtand a week; but take care that they are well covered with the ſyrup. When they have ſtood a week, boil your ſyrup again, and pour it carefully into your jar, that you may not break off the tops of your pine apples. Let them ſtand eight or ten weeks, and during that time give the ſyrup two or three boilings to keep it from moulding. Let your ſyrup ſtand till it is nearly cold before you put it in, and when your pine apples look quite full and green, take them out of the ſyrup,

ſyrup, and make another thick ſyrup of three pounds of double refined ſugar, with as much water as will diſſolve it. Boil and ſkim it well, and put into it a few ſlices of white ginger. When it it is nearly cold, put your pine apples into clean jars, and pour the ſyrup over them. They will keep ſeveral years, if tied down cloſe with a bladder.

Conſerve of Red Roſes, or any other Flowers.

PICK your roſe buds, or any other flowers, of which you intend to make a conſerve, cut off the white part from the red, and ſift them in a ſieve to take out the ſeeds. Then weigh them, and to every pound of flowers take two pounds and a half of loaf ſugar. Beat the flowers very fine in a marble mortar, then by degrees put the ſugar to them, and beat it well till they are properly incorporated together. Then put it into gallipots, properly ſecure it from the air, and it will keep ſome years.

Conſerve of Orange Peel.

HAVING grated the rinds of ſome Seville oranges as thin as you can, weigh them, and to every pound of orange rind add three pounds of loaf ſugar. Pound the orange rind well in a marble mortar, mix the ſugar by degrees with them, and beat all well together. Put it into gallipots, and tie it down ſo as properly to prevent the air getting to it.

Syrup of Citron.

TAKE ſome citrons, pare and ſlice them, and lay them in a china bowl with layers of fine ſugar. The next day pour off the liquor into a glaſs, and clarify it over a gentle fire. Then bottle it up for uſe.

Syrup

Syrup of Peach Bloſſoms.

INFUSE peach bloſſoms in as much hot water as will cover them. Cover them cloſe, and let them ſtand in a moderate heat for twenty-four hours. Then ſtrain the liquor from the flowers, and put in freſh flowers. Let them ſtand to infuſe as before, then ſtrain them out, and to the liquor put freſh peach bloſſoms a third time, and, if you pleaſe, a fourth time. Then to every pound of your infuſion put two pounds of double-refined ſugar, and ſet it in a moderate heat.

It may not be improper, before we quit this chapter of preſerving, to give the young practitioner a few neceſſary hints. When you make your ſyrups for preſerves, always pound your ſugar, and let it diſſolve in the ſyrup before you put it on the fire, as that will occaſion the ſcum to riſe, and make your ſyrup of a better colour. You muſt be careful not to boil any kind of jellies or ſyrups too high, as that will make them dark and cloudy. Be ſure not to keep green ſweetmeats longer in the firſt ſyrup than directed, or they will loſe their colour. The ſame care is required for oranges or lemons. When you preſerve fruits with their ſtones, render mutton ſuet, and pour it over them, tie a bladder over the top, and thick paper over that, to keep out the air; for if the air get to them, it will turn them ſour, which you may know by the ſyrup's fretting and riſing above the ſuet. Wet or dry ſweetmeats ſhould be kept in a dry cool place, as a hot place will deprive them of their virtue, and a damp place will turn them mouldy. Be ſure to let the ſyrup be above the fruit, and cut writing paper in the ſhape of your pot or glaſs, notch it all round the edges, dip it into brandy, lay it cloſe on the

the top of your ſweetmeats, then tie a thick paper over that, and take all the care you poſſibly can to exclude the air.

CHAP. XXIV.

To prepare Pickles of all Sorts.

The Preparation of Vinegars.

VINEGAR being an indiſpenſable ingredient in the buſineſs of pickling, we ſhall endeavour to give the cleareſt and conciſeſt directions for making it; but before we proceed to that buſineſs, it may not be improper to give a word or two of advice to the young practitioner. Pickles being a very neceſſary article in all families, it is proper that the houſekeeper ſhould always make her own, in order to avoid buying them at ſhops, where they are often very improperly prepared, and ingredients made uſe of, which, though they may make the pickles pleaſing to the eye, are often very deſtructive to the conſtitution. Well glazed ſtone jars are beſt to keep in all ſorts of pickles, and though they are more expenſive on the firſt purchaſe, yet, from their uſefulneſs and durability, they are in the end much cheaper than earthen veſſels, it having been found from experience, that ſalt and vinegar will eſcape through earthen veſſels, and thereby leave the pickles dry. Never put in your fingers to take out any pickles, but make uſe of a wooden ſpoon kept clean for that purpoſe. Be careful that your pickles are at all times covered with

with vinegar, and tie them close down after you take any out.

White Wine Vinegar.

THOUGH it should seem by the name given to this vinegar, that it is made from white wine only, yet the following directions for preparing it will shew the contrary. When you brew in the month of March or April, take as much sweet wort of the first running as will be necessary to serve you the whole year. Boil it without hops for half an hour, and then put it into a cooler. Put some good yeast upon it, and work it well. When it is done working, break the yeast into it, and put it into a cask; but be careful to fill the cask, and set it in a place where the sun has full power on it. Put no bung in the bung-hole, but put a tile over it at night, and when it rains. Let it stand till it is quite sour, which will be in the beginning of September. Then draw it off from the settlings into another cask, let it stand till it is fine, and then draw it off for use. If you have any white wine that is tart, put it into a cask, and treat it in the same manner; or you may do cyder the same way. A cask of ale turned sour, makes ale vinegar in the same manner; but none of these are fit for pickles to keep long, except the white wine vinegar first mentioned.

Elder Vinegar.

PUT two gallons of white wine vinegar, and the like weight of the pips of elder flowers, into a stone jar. Let them steep, and stir them every day for a fortnight. Then strain the vinegar from the flowers, press them close, and let it stand to settle. Pour it from the settlings, and put a piece of filtering paper in a funnel, and filter it through. Then put it in pint bottles, cork it close, and keep it for use.

Tarragon

Tarragon Vinegar.

TAKE ſome green tarragon, and pick the leaves off the ſtalks, juſt before it goes into bloom. Put a pound weight to every gallon of white wine vinegar, and treat it in the ſame manner as elder vinegar.

Sugar Vinegar.

MAKE this vinegar in the month of March or April in the following manner. To every gallon of ſpring water you uſe, add a pound of coarſe Liſbon ſugar; boil it, and keep ſkimming it as long as the ſcum will riſe. Then pour it into a cooler, and when it is as cold as beer to work, toaſt a large piece of bread, rub it over with good yeaſt, and let it work as long as it will. Then beat the yeaſt into it, put it into a caſk, and ſet it in a place where the rays of the ſun have full power on it. Put a tile over the bung-hole when it rains, and alſo every night; but take it off in the day-time, and when it is fine weather. When you find it is ſour enough, which will be in the month of Auguſt, (but if it is not ſour enough, let it ſtand till it is) draw it off, put it into a clean caſk, and throw in a handful of iſinglaſs. Let it ſtand till it is fine, and then draw it off for uſe.

To pickle Cucumbers.

TAKE the ſmalleſt cucumbers you can get, but let them be as free from ſpots as poſſible. Put them into ſtrong ale and water for nine or ten days, or till they become yellow, and ſtir them at leaſt twice a day, or they will grow ſoft. Should they become perfectly yellow, pour the water from them, and cover them with plenty of vine leaves. Set your water over the fire, and when it boils, pour it upon them. Proceed in this manner till you

you perceive they are of a fine green, which they will be in four or five times. Be careful to keep them well covered with vine leaves, with a cloth and diſh over the top, to keep in the ſteam, which will help to green them the ſooner. When they are greened, put them in a hair ſieve to drain, and then prepare the following pickle. To every two quarts of white wine vinegar, put half an ounce of mace, ten or twelve cloves, an ounce of ginger cut into ſlices, an ounce of black pepper, and a handful of ſalt. Boil them together for five minutes, pour it hot upon your pickles, and tie them down with a bladder for uſe. You may pickle them with ale vinegar, or diſtilled vinegar, and three or four cloves of garlic or ſhalots may be added.

Cucumbers pickled in Slices.

SLICE ſome large cucumbers, before they are too ripe, of the thickneſs of crown pieces. Put them into a pewter diſh, and to every twelve cucumbers ſlice two large onions thin, and ſo on till you have filled your diſh, with a handful of ſalt between each row. Then cover them with another pewter diſh, and let them ſtand twenty-four hours. Then put them into a cullender, and let them drain well. Put them into a jar, cover them over with white wine vinegar, and let them ſtand four hours. Pour the vinegar from them into a ſauce-pan, and boil it with a little ſalt. Put to the cucumbers a little mace, a little whole pepper, a large race of ginger ſliced, and then pour on the boiling vinegar. Cover them cloſe, and when they are cold, tie them down. In two or three days, they will be fit to eat.

To pickle Walnuts white.

THE largeſt nuts you can procure, juſt before the ſhell begins to turn, are the propereſt for this purpoſe. Pare them very thin till the white appears, and throw them into ſpring water, with a handful of ſalt as you pare them. Let them lie in the ſalt and water ſix hours, and lay on them a thin board to keep them down. Then ſet a ſtewpan on a charcoal fire, with clean water. Take your nuts out of the other water, and put them into the ſtewpan. Let them ſimmer, but not boil, four or five minutes. Have ready a pan of ſpring water, with a handful of white ſalt in it, and ſtir it with your hand till the ſalt is melted. Then take your nuts out of the ſtewpan with a wooden ladle, and put them into the cold water and ſalt. Let them ſtand a quarter of an hour, and put the board on them, as before; for if they are not kept under the liquor they will turn black. Then lay them on a cloth, and cover them with another to dry. Carefully wipe them with a ſoft cloth, put them into your jar or glaſs, with ſome blades of mace, and nutmeg ſliced thin. Mix the ſpice between your nuts, and pour diſtilled vinegar over them. When your glaſs is full of nuts, pour mutton fat over them, and tie them down cloſe with leather, that no air may get to them.

To pickle Walnuts green.

CHOOSE your walnuts in the ſame manner as before directed. Pare them as thin as you can, and as you pare them, throw them into a tub of ſpring water. Put into the water a pound of bay ſalt, and let them lie in it twenty-four hours, when you muſt take them out. Put them into a ſtone jar, and between every layer of walnuts put a layer of vine leaves, as alſo at the bottom and top.

Fill

Fill it up with cold vinegar, and let them ſtand all night. Then pour that vinegar from them into a ſaucepan, put into it a pound of bay ſalt, and ſet it on the fire. Let it boil, then pour it hot on your nuts, tie them over with a woollen cloth, and let them ſtand a week. Then pour that pickle away, rub your nuts clean with a piece of flannel, and put them again into your jar, with vine leaves, as above, and boil freſh vinegar. To every gallon of vinegar put a nutmeg ſliced, cut four large races of ginger, a quarter of an ounce of mace, the ſame of cloves, and a quarter of an ounce of whole black pepper. Then pour your vinegar boiling hot on your walnuts, and cover them with a woollen cloth. Let them ſtand three or four days, and repeat the ſame two or three times. When cold, put in half a pint of muſtard-ſeed, and a large ſtick of horſe radiſh ſliced. Tie them down cloſe with a bladder, and then with a leather. They will be fit to eat in a fortnight. Stick a large onion with cloves, and lay it in the middle of the pot. If you pickle your walnuts for keeping, do not boil your vinegar; but then they will not be fit to eat under ſix months. After they have ſtood one year, you may boil the pickle, and they will keep good and firm two or three years.

To pickle Walnuts black.

TAKE large full-grown nuts before they are hard, lay them in ſalt and water, and let them continue in it two days. Then ſhift them into freſh water, and let them lie two days longer. Shift them again, and let them lie three days longer. Then take them out of the water, and put them into your pickling jar. When the jar is half full, put in a large onion ſtuck with cloves. To an hundred of walnuts, put in half a pint of muſtard-ſeed, a quarter of an ounce of mace, half an ounce of black

black pepper, half an ounce of allſpice, and a ſtick of horſe-radiſh. Then fill your jar, and pour boiling vinegar over them, cover them with a plate, and when they are cold tie them down with a bladder and leather, and they will be fit to eat in two or three months. The next year, if any remain, boil up your vinegar again, and ſkim it. When cold, pour it over your walnuts. This is by much the beſt pickle for uſe. If you pickle a great many walnuts, and eat them faſt, make your pickle for an hundred or two; keep what you do not at firſt pickle, in a ſtrong brine of ſalt and water, boiled till it will bear an egg, and as your pot empties, fill them up with thoſe in the ſalt and water; but take care that the pickle covers them.

To pickle Onions.

PEEL ſome ſmall onions, and put them into ſalt and water. Shift them once a day for three days, and then ſet them over the fire in milk and water till they be ready to boil. Dry them, and pour over them the following pickle, when it has boiled, and ſtood to be cold. Take double-diſtilled vinegar, ſalt, mace, and one or two bay leaves. If you uſe any other vinegar, they will not look white.

Another Method.

PUT a ſufficient number of very ſmall onions into ſalt and water for nine days, obſerving to change the water every day. Then put them into jars, and pour freſh boiling ſalt and water over them. Let them ſtand cloſe covered till they are cold, then make ſome more ſalt and water, and pour it boiling hot upon them. When it is cold, put your onions into a hair ſieve to drain, then put them into wide-mouthed bottles, and

and fill them up with diſtilled vinegar. Put into every bottle a ſlice or two of ginger, a blade of mace, and a large teaſpoonful of eating oil, which will keep the onions white. Secure them properly.

To pickle Mangoes.

YOU muſt procure cucumbers of the largeſt ſort, and taken from the vines before they are too ripe, or yellow at the ends. Cut a piece out of the ſide, and with an apple ſcraper or teaſpoon take out the ſeeds. Then put them into very ſtrong ſalt and water for eight or nine days, or till they are very yellow. Stir them well two or three times each day, and put them into a pan, with a large quantity of vine leaves both over and under them. Beat a little roach-alum very fine, and put it into the ſalt and water they came out of. Pour it on your cucumbers, and ſet it upon a very ſlow fire for four or five hours, till they are pretty green. Then take them out, and drain them in a hair ſieve, and when they are cold, put to them a little horſe-radiſh, ſome muſtard ſeed, two or three heads of garlic, a few pepper corns, a few green cucumbers ſliced in ſmall pieces, then horſe-radiſh, and the ſame as before, till you have filled them. Then take the piece you cut out, and ſew it on with a large needle and thread, and do all the reſt in the ſame manner. Make the following pickle. To every gallon of allegar, put an ounce of mace, the ſame of cloves, two ounces of ſliced ginger, the ſame of long pepper, Jamaica pepper, and black pepper, three ounces of muſtard-ſeed tied up in a bag, four ounces of garlic, and a ſtick of horſe-radiſh cut in ſlices. Boil them five minutes in the allegar, then pour it upon your pickles, and tie them down ſo as to prevent the air getting to them.

To

To pickle French Beans.

GATHER your beans of a middling ſize, pour ſome boiling-hot water over them, and cover them cloſe. The next day drain, them and dry them. Then pour over them a boiling-hot pickle of white wine vinegar, Jamaica pepper, black pepper, a little mace, and ginger. Repeat this two or three days, or till the French beans look green. Then put them carefully by for uſe.

To pickle Red Cabbage.

HAVING ſliced your cabbage croſsways, put it on an earthen diſh, and ſprinkle a handful of ſalt over it. Cover it with another diſh and let it ſtand twenty-four hours. Then put it into a cullender to drain, and lay it in your jar. Take enough white wine vinegar to cover it, a little cloves, mace, and allſpice; put them in whole, with a little cochineal finely bruiſed. Then boil it up, and pour it either hot or cold on your cabbage. Cover it cloſe with a cloth till it is cold, if you pour on the pickle hot, and tie it up cloſe, ſo that no air can get to it.

To pickle Gerkins.

TAKE five hundred gerkins, and have ready a large earthen pan of ſpring water and ſalt. To every gallon of water put two pounds of ſalt; mix it well together, and throw in your gerkins. Waſh them out in two hours, put them to drain, let them be drained very dry, and put them into a jar. In the mean time, get a bell-metal pot, with a gallon of the beſt white wine vinegar, half an ounce of cloves and mace, one ounce of allſpice, one ounce of muſtard-ſeed, a little ſtick of horſe-radiſh cut in ſlices, ſix bay leaves, a little dill, two or three races of ginger cut in pieces, a nutmeg cut in pieces, and a handful of ſalt. Boil it up in the pot all together, and put it over the gerkins. Co-

ver

ver them close down, and let them stand twenty-four hours. Then put them into your pot, and simmer them over the stove till they are green; but be careful not to let them boil, as that will spoil them. Then put them into your jar, and cover them close down till they are cold. Then tie them over with a bladder, and leather over that, and put them in a cool dry place.

To pickle Peaches.

PEACHES for this purpose must be gathered when at their full growth, and just before they begin to ripen; but take great care that they are not bruised. Take a quantity of spring water, as much as you think will cover them, and put in an equal quantity of bay and common salt till it is strong enough to bear an egg. Then put in your peaches, and lay a thin board over them to keep them down. Having let them remain three days, take them out, wipe them very carefully with a fine soft cloth, and lay them in your glass or jar. Take as much white wine vinegar as will fill your glass or jar, and to every gallon put one pint of the best well-made mustard, two or three heads of garlic, a good deal of ginger sliced, half an ounce of cloves, mace, and nutmeg. Mix your pickle well together, and pour it over your peaches. Tie them up close, and they will be fit to eat in two months. You may, if you choose it, cut them across with a fine penknife, take out the stones, fill them with mustard-seed, garlic, horse-radish, and ginger, and tie them together. In the same manner you may pickle nectarines and apricots.

To pickle Asparagus.

HAVING procured some of the largest and finest asparagus, cut off the white ends, and wash the

the green ends in ſpring water. Then put them into another clean water, and let them lie in it two or three hours. Take a large broad ſtewpan full of ſpring water, with a large handful of ſalt. Set it on the fire, and when it boils put in the graſs, not tied up, but looſe, and not too many at a time, for fear you ſhould break the heads. Juſt ſcald them, and no more. Take them out with a broad ſkimmer, and lay them on a cloth to cool. Make a pickle, according to your quantity of aſparagus, of a gallon, or more, of white wine vinegar, and one ounce of bay ſalt. Boil it, and put your aſparagus in your jar. To a gallon of pickle put two nutmegs, a quarter of an ounce of mace, the ſame of white pepper, and pour the pickle hot over them. Cover them with a linen cloth three or four times double. Let them ſtand a week, and then boil the pickle. Let them ſtand a week longer, then boil the pickle again, and pour it on hot as before. Cover them cloſe with a bladder and leather as ſoon as they are cold.

To pickle Radiſh Pods.

MAKE a pickle ſtrong enough to bear an egg, with ſpring water and bay ſalt. Put your pods into it, and lay a thin board on them to keep them under the pickle. Let them ſtand ten days, then drain them in a ſieve, and lay them on a cloth to dry. Take as much white wine vinegar as you think will cover them, boil it, and put your pods in a jar, with ginger, mace, cloves, and Jamaica pepper. Pour your vinegar boiling-hot on them, cover them with a coarſe cloth three or four times double, that the ſteam may come through a little, and let them ſtand two days. Repeat this two or three times. When it is cold, put in a pint of muſtard-ſeed, and ſome horſe-radiſh, and cover them as before directed.

To pickle Muſhrooms white.

CUT off the ſtalks of ſome ſmall buttons, rub off the ſkins with flannel dipped in ſalt, and throw them into milk and water. Drain them out, and put them into a ſtewpan, with a handful of ſalt over them. Cover them cloſe, and put them over a gentle ſtove, for five minutes, to draw out all the water. Then put them on a coarſe cloth to drain till they are cold.

To pickle Muſhrooms brown.

CLEAN them with a flannel and cloth as above directed, throw them into milk and water, and lay them on a cloth to drain. When drained, put them into a jar. Boil enough of white wine vinegar to cover them, with ſpices in it, as directed for radiſh pods. Pour it over them boiling hot; and when they are cold, tie down or cork the bottles tight.

To make Muſhroom Pickle.

PUT a gallon of the beſt vinegar into a cold ſtill, and to every gallon of vinegar put half a pound of bay ſalt, a quarter of a pound of mace, a quarter of an ounce of cloves, and a nutmeg cut into quarters. Keep the top of the ſtill covered with a white cloth, and as the cloth dries, put on a wet one; but do not let the fire be too large, leſt you burn the bottom of the ſtill. Draw it as long as it taſtes acid, and no longer. When you fill your bottles, put in your muſhrooms, here and there put in a few blades of mace, and a ſlice of nutmeg. Then fill the bottles with pickle; melt ſome mutton fat, ſtrain it, and pour over it. You muſt put your nutmeg over the fire in a little vinegar, and give it a boil. While it is hot, you may ſlice it as you pleaſe; when it is cold, it will crack to pieces inſtead of ſlicing.

To

To pickle Samphire.

PUT ſome green ſamphire into a clean pan, throw over it two or three handfuls of ſalt, and cover it with ſpring water. Let it lie twenty-four hours, then put it into a ſaucepan, throw in a hand-ful of ſalt, and cover it with good vinegar. Cover the pan cloſe, and ſet it over a ſlow fire. Let it ſtand till it is juſt green and criſp, and then imme-diately take it off, for ſhould it remain till it be ſoft, it will be ſpoiled. Put it into your pickling pot, and cover it cloſe. As ſoon as it is cold, tie it down with a bladder and leather, and keep it for uſe.

To pickle Capers.

THE tree that bears capers is called the caper ſhrub or buſh, of which they are the flower-buds. They are common in the weſtern parts of Europe, and we have them in ſome of our gardens; but Toulon is the principal place for them. Some are ſent us from Lyons; but they are flatter, and not ſo firm. Some come from Majorca; but they are ſalt and diſagreeable. They gather the buds from the bloſſoms before they open, then ſpread them upon the floor of a room, where no ſun en-ters, and there let them lie till they begin to wither. They then throw them into a tub of ſharp vinegar, and, after three days, they add a quan-tity of bay ſalt. When this is diſſolved, they are fit for packing for ſale, and are ſent to all parts of Europe. The fineſt capers are thoſe of a mode-rate ſize, firm, and cloſe, and ſuch as have the pickle highly flavoured. Thoſe are of little value, which are ſoft, flabby, and half open.

To pickle Cauliflowers.

THE largeſt and the cloſeſt you can get muſt be procured for this purpoſe. Pull them into ſprigs, put them in an earthen diſh, and ſprinkle ſalt over them. Let them ſtand twenty-four hours to draw out all the water. Then put them into a jar, and pour ſalt and boiling water over them. Cover them cloſe, and let them ſtand till the next day. Then take them out, and lay them on a coarſe cloth to drain. Put them into glaſs jars, and put in a nutmeg ſliced, and two or three blades of mace in each jar. Cover them with diſtilled vinegar, and ſecure them from the air as before directed. In a month's time they will be fit for uſe.

To pickle Beet Roots.

THESE roots are generally uſed as a garniſh for made diſhes, and are thus pickled. Having firſt boiled them tender, peel them, and, if agreeable, cut them into ſhapes. Pour over them a hot pickle of white wine vinegar, a little pepper, ginger, and ſliced horſe-radiſh.

To pickle Codlings.

CODLINGS uſed for this purpoſe muſt be about the ſize of a large French walnut. Put a quantity of vine leaves at the bottom of a pan, and then put in your codlings. Cover them well with vine leaves and water, and ſet them over a very ſlow fire till you can peel the ſkins off. Then take them carefully up in a hair ſieve, peel them with a penknife, and put them into the ſaucepan again, with the vine leaves and water as before. Cover them cloſe, and ſet them over a ſlow fire till they are of a fine green. Drain them through a hair ſieve, and when they are cold, put them into diſ-

tilled

tilled vinegar. Secure them properly in jars from the air.

To pickle Barberries.

GATHER your barberries before they are too ripe. Take care to pick out the leaves and dead ſtalks, and then put them into jars, with a large quantity of ſtrong ſalt and water, and tie them down with a bladder. When you ſee a ſcum over your barberries, put them into freſh ſalt and water; for they require no vinegar, their own natural ſharpneſs being ſufficient to preſerve them.

To make Mock Ginger.

CUT off the flowers from the ſtalks of the largeſt cauliflowers you can get. Peel the ſtalks, and throw them into ſtrong ſpring water and ſalt for three days. Then drain them in a ſieve pretty dry, and put them into a jar. Boil white wine vinegar with cloves, mace, long pepper, and allſpice, each half an ounce; forty blades of garlick, a ſtick of horſe-radiſh cut in ſlices, a quarter of an ounce of chyan pepper, a quarter of a pound of yellow turmeric, and two ounces of bay ſalt. Pour it boiling over the ſtalks, and cover it down cloſe till the next day. Then boil it three times more, at different times, and when it is cold, tie it down cloſe.

To make Walnut Ketchup.

GRIND half a buſhel of green walnuts, before the ſhell is formed, in a crab-mill, or beat them in a marble mortar. Then ſqueeze out the juice through a coarſe cloth, and wring the cloth well to get all the juice out. To every gallon of juice, put a quart of red wine, a quarter of a pound of anchovies, the ſame of bay ſalt, one ounce of allſpice, two of long and black pepper, half an ounce of of cloves and mace, a little ginger, and horſe-radiſh cut in ſlices. Boil all together till reduced to half the quantity, and then pour it into a pan. When it is cold, bottle it, cork it tight, and it will be fit for uſe in three months. If you have any pickle left in the jar after your walnuts are uſed, to every gallon of pickle put in two heads of garlic, a quart of red wine, and of cloves, mace, long, black, and Jamaica pepper, each an ounce. Boil them all together till it is reduced to half the quantity. Pour it into a pan, and the next day bottle it for uſe.

To make Muſhroom Ketchup.

GATHER a buſhel of the large flaps of muſhrooms when they are dry, and bruiſe them with your hands. Put ſome at the bottom of an earthen pan, ſtrew ſome ſalt over them, then muſhrooms, then ſalt, till you have done. Put in half an ounce of beaten cloves and mace, the ſame of allſpice, and let them ſtand five or ſix days, remembering to ſtir them up every day. Then tie a paper over them, and bake them four hours in a ſlow oven. When you have ſo done, ſtrain them through a cloth to get all the liquor out, and let the liquor ſtand to ſettle. Then pour it clear from the ſettlings; to every gallon of liquor add a quart of red wine, and, if not ſalt enough, a little ſalt, a race of ginger cut ſmall, half an ounce of cloves and mace, and boil it till about one third is reduced. Then ſtrain it through a ſieve into a pan; the next day pour it from the ſettlings, and bottle it for uſe.

To make Muſhroom Powder.

CUT off the root end and peel ſome of the largeſt and thickeſt button muſhrooms you can procure. Wipe them clean with a cloth, but do not waſh them. Spread them on pewter diſhes, and put

put them in a ſlow oven to dry. Let the liquor dry up in the muſhrooms, as it will make the powder much ſtronger. When they are dry enough to powder, beat them in a mortar, and ſift them through a ſieve, with a little chyan pepper and pounded mace. Put the powder into ſmall bottles for uſe. Be careful to cork them tight.

To pickle Artichoke Bottoms.

BOIL ſome artichokes till you can pull off the leaves, then take off the chokes, and cut them from the ſtalk. Take great care that you do not let the knife touch the top. Throw them into ſalt and water for an hour, then take them out, and lay them on a cloth to drain. Put them into large wide-mouthed glaſſes, and put a little mace and ſliced nutmeg between them. Fill them either with diſtilled vinegar, or ſugar vinegar and ſpring-water. Cover them with mutton fat, and tie them down cloſe.

To pickle Naſturtium Buds.

GATHER the little nobs as ſoon as the bloſſoms are gone off, and put them into cold ſalt and water. Shift them once a day for three days ſucceſſively, then make a cold pickle of white wine vinegar, a little white wine, ſhalot, pepper, cloves, mace, nutmeg quartered, and horſe-radiſh. Then put in your buds, and tie them up cloſe.

To make Peccadillo, or Indian Pickle.

TAKE a cauliflower and a white cabbage, and quarter them. Take alſo cucumbers, melons, apples, French beans, plums, all or any of them, and lay them on a hair ſieve: ſtrew over them a large handful of ſalt, and ſet them in the ſun for three or four days, or till they are very dry. Put them into a ſtone jar with a pickle thus made. Put

a pound

a pound of race ginger into ſalt and water, the next day ſcrape and ſlice it, ſalt it, and dry it in the ſun. Slice, ſalt, and dry a pound of garlic. Put theſe into a gallon of vinegar, with two ounces of long pepper, half an ounce of turmeric, and four ounces of muſtard ſeed bruiſed. Stop the pickle cloſe, then prepare the cabbage, &c. If you make uſe of fruit, it muſt be put in green. The jar need not be emptied, but add freſh vinegar, and put in things as they come into ſeaſon.

To make Caveach.

THIS is made of mackarel, which you muſt cut into round pieces, and divide into five or ſix. To ſix large mackarel, you may take one ounce of beaten pepper, three large nutmegs, a little mace, and a handful of ſalt. Mix your ſalt and beaten ſpice together; then make two or three holes in each piece, and thruſt the ſeaſoning into the holes with your finger. Rub each piece all over with the ſeaſoning, fry them brown in ſweet oil, and let them ſtand till they are cold. Put them into a jar, cover them with vinegar, and pour ſweet oil over them. They are very delicious, and if well covered, they will keep a long time.

To make Mock Anchovies.

TAKE two pounds of common ſalt, a quarter of a pound of bay ſalt, one pound of ſaltpetre, two ounces of ſal prunella, a little bole armoniac, and pound all in a mortar. Take a peck of ſprats, put them into a ſtone pot, a row of ſprats, a layer of your compound, and ſo on to the top alternately. Preſs them hard down, and cover them cloſe. Let them ſtand ſix months, and they will be fit for uſe. Take care that your ſprats are very freſh, and do not waſh or wipe them, but take them as they firſt come out of the water.

To

To pickle Salmon.

SCALE, gut, and waſh your ſalmon very clean. Put your fiſh into a kettle of ſpring water boiling, with a handful of ſalt, a little allſpice, cloves and mace. If it be ſmall, three quarters of an hour will boil it; but if it be large, it will take an hour. Then take out the ſalmon, and let it ſtand till it is cold. Strain the liquor through a ſieve, and when it is cold, put your ſalmon very cloſe in a tub or pan, and pour the liquor over it. When you want to uſe it, put it into a diſh, with a little of the pickle, and uſe fennel for your garniſh.

To pickle Oyſters.

PUT into a pan one hundred of the fineſt and largeſt rock oyſters you can procure, with all their liquor with them; but take care that you do not ſpoil their beauty by cutting them in opening. Waſh them clean out of the liquor ſeparately, put the liquor into a ſtewpan, and give it a boil. Then ſtrain it through a ſieve, and let it ſtand half an hour to ſettle. Then pour it from the ſettlings into a ſtewpan, and put in half a pint of white wine, half a pint of vinegar, a little ſalt, half an ounce of cloves and mace, a little allſpice and whole pepper, a nutmeg cut in thin ſlices, and a dozen bay leaves. Boil it up five minutes, then put in your oyſters, and give them a boil up for a minute or two. Put them into ſmall jars, and when they are cold, put a little ſweet oil at the top, and tie them down with a bladder and leather. Keep them in a cool dry place, and when you uſe them, untie them, ſkim off the oil, put them in a diſh with a little of the liquor, and garniſh them with green parſley. If you want oyſter ſauce, take them out, and put them into good anchovy ſauce, with a ſpoonful of the pickle. For fiſh, or poultry,

poultry, put them into a white ſauce, having firſt waſhed them in warm water.

To pickle Smelts.

BEAT very fine half an ounce of pepper, half an ounce of nutmeg, a quarter of an ounce of mace, half an ounce of ſaltpetre, and a quarter of a pound of common ſalt. Waſh and clean a hundred of fine ſmelts, gut them, and lay them in rows in a jar, and between every layer of ſmelts ſtrew the ſeaſoning, with four or five bay leaves. Then boil ſome red wine, and pour it over them. Cover them with a plate, and when they are cold, tie them down cloſe. Anchovies are not near ſo good as ſmelts done in this manner.

To pickle Sturgeon.

CUT a ſturgeon into handſome pieces, waſh it well, and tie it up with baſs. Make a pickle of half ſpring water and half vinegar; make it pretty ſalt, with ſome cloves, mace, and allſpice in it. Let it boil, and then put in your ſturgeon, and boil it till it is tender. Then take it up, and let it ſtand till it is cold. Strain the liquor through a ſieve, and then put your ſturgeon into a pan or tub as cloſe as you can. Pour the liquor over it, and cover it cloſe. When you uſe it, put it into a diſh, with a little of the liquor, and garniſh it with green fennel or parſley. Take care that you faſten it down ſo cloſe, as not to let in any air.

CHAP.

CHAP. XXV.

The Preparation of Hams, Tongues, Bacon, &c.

To cure Pork Hams.

HAVING killed your hog, cut the leg and part of the hind loin in ſuch a manner as to appear a handſome ham. Rub it well with common ſalt, and let it lie on a board twenty-four hours. For every ham take four ounces of bay ſalt, two ounces of ſaltpetre, and two ounces of ſal prunella; beat them fine, and mix them with half a pound of coarſe ſugar, and two pounds of common ſalt. Rub the hams well with it, and lay them in a ſalting pan, or hollow tray. Rub them with the brine every day for a fortnight, then take them out, and wipe them dry with a cloth. Smoke them with a ſaw-duſt fire, mixed with three or four handfuls of juniper berries, till they are thoroughly dry. Then hang them in a cold dry place; but take care not to let them touch the wall, nor each other. Neats tongues may be cured in the ſame manner, and boiled out of the pickle, or dried and ſmoked.

To cure Beef Hams.

THE leg of a ſmall fat Scotch or Welſh ox is beſt for this purpoſe; it muſt be cut ham faſhion. Beat fine four ounces of bay-ſalt, two ounces of ſaltpetre, and two ounces of ſal prunella. Mix them with half a pound of coarſe ſugar, two pounds of common ſalt, and a handful of juniper berries bruiſed. This quantity will be ſufficient for about fifteeen pounds of beef; but if your joint be large, you muſt increaſe the quantity in proportion. Rub the

the ingredients well into it, and turn it every day for a month. Then take it out, and rub it with bran or ſawduſt. Dry it in the ſame manner you do pork hams, and hang it in a cool dry place. You may either cut a piece off for boiling, or cut it into raſhers, as you have occaſion for it.

To pickle Tongues.

SCRAPE and dry your tongues clean with a cloth, and ſalt them well with common ſalt, and half an ounce of ſaltpetre, to every tongue. Lay them in a deep pan, and turn them every day for a week or ten days. Salt them again, and let them lie a week longer. Then take them out, dry them with a cloth, flour them, and hang them up.

To pickle Pork.

CUT your pork into pieces of a ſize proportioned to your powdering tub, and rub them all over with ſaltpetre. Then mix two thirds of common ſalt with one third of bay ſalt, and rub every piece well with it. Lay the pieces in your tub as cloſe as poſſible, and throw over them a little common ſalt.

To make Hung Beef.

HANG up the navel piece of beef in your cellar as long as it will keep good, and till it begins to be a little ſappy. Then take it down, and waſh it in ſugar and water, one piece after another, for you muſt divide it into three pieces. Dry and pound very ſmall a pound of ſaltpetre, and two pounds of bay ſalt. Mix with them two or three ſpoonfuls of brown ſugar, and rub it well into every part of your beef. Then ſtrew a ſufficient quantity of common ſalt all over it, and let the beef lie cloſe till the ſalt is diſſolved, which will be the caſe in about ſix or ſeven days. Then turn it every other

other day for a fortnight, and after that hang it up in a warm, but not in a hot place. It may hang a fortnight in the kitchen, and when you want it, boil it in bay ſalt and pump water till it is tender. It will keep, when boiled, two or three months, rubbing it with a greaſy cloth, or putting it two or three minutes into boiling water, to take off the mouldineſs.

To make Yorkſhire Hung Beef.

CUT a buttock or ribs of beef in two, and bruiſe fine half a pound of bay ſalt, four ounces of ſaltpetre, four ounces of ſal prunella, and two handfuls of juniper berries. Mix them with a pound of coarſe ſugar, and three pounds of common ſalt, which will be a ſufficient quantity for twenty pounds weight. Rub the beef well with theſe ingredients, lay it in a hollow tray or pan, and turn and rub it with the pickle every day for a fortnight. Then take it out, dry it with a cloth, and hang it up to the kitchen cieling, or in a chimney where a moderate fire is kept, till it is properly dried. You may boil part of it when occaſion requires, or you may cut it into raſhers and broil it; but remember to dip it firſt into warm water, which will make it eat much better.

To make Dutch Beef.

RUB well with coarſe ſugar the lean part of a fine buttock of beef, and let it lie in a pan or tray two or three hours, obſerving to turn and rub it two or three times. Take half a pound of bay ſalt, two ounces of ſaltpetre, two of ſal prunella, a handful of juniper berries bruiſed fine, and a pound of common ſalt. Rub it well with them, and turn and rub it with the pickle for a fortnight. Then roll it tight in a coarſe cloth, put it in a cheeſe-preſs for twenty-four hours, and then hang

it

it to dry in a wide chimney. When you boil it, put it into a cloth.

To make Bacon.

HAVING rubbed the flitches well with common ſalt, let them lie ſo that the brine may run from them. In about a week, rub off all the ſalt, and put them into a tub. Rub the flitches with one pound of ſaltpetre, pounded and heated, and the next day rub them with ſalt, dry and hot. Having let them lie a week, often rubbing them, turn them, and let them lie three weeks or a month in all, rubbing them well. Then dry them, and hang them up for uſe.

Another Method.

HAVING taken off all the inſide fat of a ſide of pork, lay it in ſuch a poſition that the blood may run away from it. Then rub it well with good ſalt on both ſides, and let it lie in that ſtate one day. Then take a pint of bay ſalt, and a quarter of a pound of ſaltpetre, and beat them fine. To theſe add two pounds of coarſe ſugar, and a quarter of a peck of common ſalt. Obſerve to wipe off all the old ſalt before you put it into the pickle, and never keep bacon or hams in a hot kitchen, or in a room where the ſun comes, as it will make them ruſty. Lay your pork in ſomething that will hold the pickle, and rub it well with the above ingredients. Lay the ſkinny ſide downwards, and baſte it every day with the pickle for a fortnight. Then hang it in a wood ſmoke, and afterwards hang it in a dry place, but not hot. Hams and bacon ſhould not hang againſt a wall, but quite clear from every thing.

To

To make Weſtphalia Bacon.

TAKE a gallon of pump water, two pounds of bay ſalt, the ſame quantity of white ſalt, a pound of ſaltpetre, a pound of coarſe ſugar, and an ounce of ſocho tied in a rag. Boil theſe well together half an hour, and let it ſtand till it is cold. Then put into it the ſide of a fine hog, and let it lie in the pickle for a fortnight. Then take it out, rub it over with ſawduſt, and dry it in the ſame manner as before directed for hams. You may make Weſtphalia hams the ſame way, and you may prepare tongues in the ſame pickle; but remember to put them in pump water for ſix or eight hours; and before you put them into the pickle, waſh them well out, and dry them with a cloth.

To make Fine Sauſages.

PICK part of a leg of pork or veal clean from ſkin or fat, and to every pound, add two pounds of beef ſuet. Shred both very fine, and mix them well with ſage leaves finely chopped, pepper, ſalt, nutmeg, pounded cloves, and a little grated lemon-peel. Put this cloſe down in a pot. When you want it for uſe, mix it with the yolk of an egg, a few bread crumbs, and roll it into lengths.

To make Oxford Sauſages.

TAKE a pound of young pork, fat and lean, free from ſkin or griſtle, a pound of lean veal, and the ſame quantity of beef ſuet, all chopped fine together. Put in half a pound of grated bread, half the peel of a lemon ſhred fine, a nutmeg grated, ſix ſage leaves waſhed and chopped very fine, a tea-ſpoonful of pepper, two of ſalt, ſome thyme, ſavory, and marjoram, ſhred fine. Mix theſe well together, and put it cloſe down in a pan. When you uſe it, roll it out the ſize of a common ſauſage, and fry them of a fine brown in freſh butter, or broil them over a clear fire.

To make common Saufages.

CHOP very fine three pounds of nice pork, fat and lean together, but free from fkin and grif-tles. Seafon it with two teafpoonfuls of falt, one of beaten pepper, fom fage fhred fine, about three teafpoonfuls, and mix them well together. Clean fome guts very nicely, and fill them, or put them down in a pot.

To make fham Brawn.

RUB well with faltpetre the belly piece and head of a young porker. Let it lay three or four days, and then wafh it clean. Boil the head, take off all the meat, and cut it into pieces. Boil four neats feet tender, take out the bones, cut the flefh in thin flices, and mix it with the head. Lay it in the belly piece, roll it up tight, bind it round with a fheet of tin, and boil it four hours. Take it up, and fet it on one end, put a trencher on it, and within the tin, and a large weight upon the trencher, and let it ftand all night. In the morning take it out, and bind it with a fillet. Put in fpring water and falt, and it will be fit for ufe. When you ufe it, cut it in flices like brawn, and garnifh with parfley. Take care to change the pickle every four or five days, and it will keep a great while.

CHAP. XXVI.

Directions for Carving.

To cut up a Hare.

THOUGH carving may not be confidered as the indifpenfable province of a cook, yet it is certainly of the houfekeeper, who is often obliged to take her place at the head of the table, where every eye is upon her, who never fail either to applaud or condemn her, according to the manner in which fhe difcharges that office. We fhall therefore lay down a few general rules, accompanied with practical obfervations, which we hope will not fail of making this difficult matter very eafy and familiar. The beft way of cutting up a hare, fee No. 1. is to put the point of the knife under the fhoulder at *g*, and cut through all the way down to the rump, on one fide of the back bone, in the line *g*, *h*. When you have done thus, cut it in the fame manner on the other fide, at an equal diftance from the back bone, by which means the body will be nearly divided into three. You may now cut the back through the fpine or back bone, into feveral fmall pieces, more or lefs, in the lines *i*, *k*. The back is by far the tendereft part, fulleft of gravy, and confidered as the moft delicate. The flefh of the leg is next in eftimation to the back, though the meat is firmer, clofer, and lefs juicy. The fhoulder muft be cut off in the circular dotted line *e*, *f*, *g*. Put the head on a clean pewter plate, fo as to have it under your hand, and turning the nofe to you, hold it fteady with your fork, fo that it may not flip from under the knife. You muft then put the point of the knife into the fkull, and

thus

thus the head may be eafily divided into two. Remember, when you help a perfon to any part of a hare, to give with it a fpoonful of pudding. The method of cutting up a hare as above directed, can only be done when the hare is young. If it be old, the beft method is, to put your knife pretty clofe to the back-bone, and cut off the leg; but, as the hip-bone will be in your way, turn the back of the hare towards you, and endeavour to hit the joint between the hip and the thigh-bone. When you have feparated one, cut off the other, and then cut a long narrow flice or two on each fide of the back-bone, in the direction *g*, *h*. Then divide the back-bone into as many parts as you pleafe; all which may be eafily acquired by a little attention and practice.

A Goofe. See plate No. 2.

PUT the neck end of the goofe before you, and begin by cutting two or three long flices, on each fide of the breaft, in the lines *a*, *b*, quite to the bone. Then take off the leg, by turning the goofe up on one fide, putting the fork through the fmall end of the leg-bone, and preffing it clofe to the body, which, when the knife has entered at *d*, will eafily raife the joint. Then pafs the knife under the leg, in the direction *d*, *e*. If the leg hangs to the carcafe at the joint *e*, turn it back with the fork, and, if the goofe be young, it will eafily feparate. Having thus taken off the leg, proceed to take off the wing, by paffing the fork through the fmall end of the pinion, preffing it clofe to the body, and entering the knife at *c*, and paffing it under the wing in the direction *c*, *d*. This is a nice thing to hit, and can be acquired only by practice. When you have taken off the leg and wing on one fide, do the fame on the other. Then cut off the apron in the line *f*, *e*, *g*; hav-

having done which, take off the merry-thought in the line *i*, *h*. All the other parts are to be taken off in the ſame manner as directed for a fowl in the following article, which ſee. A gooſe is ſeldom quite diſſected, like a fowl, unleſs the company be very large. The parts of a gooſe moſt eſteemed are, ſlices from the breaſt; the fleſhy part of the wing, which may be divided from the pinion; the thigh-bone, or drumſtick, as it is called; the pinions; and the ſide-bones. If ſage and onion be put into the body of the gooſe, which is not now ſo much in faſhion as formerly, when you have cut off the limbs, draw the ſtuffing out with a ſpoon from whence the apron is taken, and mix it with the gravy, which ſhould firſt be poured hot into the body of the gooſe.

A Roaſted Fowl. See Plate, No. 3.

THE fowl is here repreſented as laying on its ſide, with one of the legs, wings, and neck-bone taken off. A boiled fowl is cut up in the ſame manner as one roaſted. In a boiled fowl, the legs are bent inwards, and tucked into the belly; but previous to its being ſent to table, the ſkewers are withdrawn. The moſt convenient method of cutting up a fowl, is to lay it on your plate, and, as you ſeparate the joints, in the lines *a*, *b*, *d*, put them into the diſh. The legs, wings, and merry-thought, being removed in the ſame manner as directed for cutting up a gooſe, the next thing is to cut off the neck-bones. This is done by putting in the knife at *g*, and paſſing it under the long broad part of the bone in the line *g*, *b*, then lifting it up, and breaking off the end of the ſhorter part of the bone, which adheres to the breaſt-bone. All the parts being thus ſeparated from the carcaſe, divide the breaſt from the back, by cutting through the tender ribs on each ſide, from

from the neck quite down to the vent or tail. Then lay the back upwards on your plate, fix your fork under the rump, and placing the edge of the knife in the line *b*, *e*, *c*, and preſſing it down, lift up the tail, or lower part of the back, and it will readily divide, with the help of your knife, in the line *b*, *e*, *c*. In the next place, lay the lower part of the back upwards in your plate, with the rump from you, and cut off the ſide-bones, or ſideſmen, as they are generally called, by forcing the knife through the rump-bone, in the line *e*, *f*, when your fowl will be completely cut up.

A Pig. See Plate, No. 4.

IT is not the cuſtom at preſent to ſend a pig up to table whole, but is uſually cut up by the cook, who takes off the head, ſplits the body down the back, and garniſhes the diſh with the chops and ears. Before you help any one at table, firſt ſeparate the ſhoulders from the carcaſe, and then the legs, according to the direction given by the dotted line *c*, *d*, *e*. The moſt delicate part of the pig is that about the neck, which may be cut off in the line *f*, *g*. The next beſt parts are the ribs, which may be divided in the line *a*, *b*, &c. and the others are pieces cut from the legs and ſhoulders. A pig, indeed, produces ſuch a variety of delicate bits, that the palate of almoſt every one may be ſuited.

A Pheaſant. See Plate, No. 5.

THE bird appears, in the repreſentation here given, in a proper ſtate for the ſpit, with the head tucked under one of the wings. When laid in the diſh, the ſkewers drawn, and the bird carried to table, it muſt be thus carved. Fix your fork in that part of the breaſt where the two dots are marked, by which means you will have a full command

mand of the bird, and can turn it as you think proper. Slice down the breaſt in the lines *a*, *b*, and then proceed to take off the leg on one ſide, in the direction *d*, *e*, or in the circular dotted line *b*, *d*. This done, cut off the wing on the ſame ſide, in the line *c*, *d*. When you have ſeparated the leg and wing on one ſide, do the ſame on the other, and then cut off, or ſeparate from the breaſt-bone, on each ſide of the breaſt, the parts you before ſliced or cut down. Be very attentive in taking off the wing. Cut it in the notch *a*; for if you cut too near the neck, as at *g*, you will find yourſelf interrupted by the neck-bone, from whence the wing muſt be ſeparated. Having done this, cut off the merry-thought, in the line *f*, *g*, by paſſing the knife under it towards the neck. With reſpect to the remaining parts, they are to be cut up in the ſame manner as directed for a roaſt fowl. The breaſt, wings, and merry-thought, are the parts moſt admired in a pheaſant.

A Partridge. See No. 6.

THIS is a repreſentation of a partridge as juſt taken from the ſpit; but before it be ſerved up, the ſkewers muſt be drawn out of it. It is cut up in the ſame manner as a fowl. The wings muſt be taken off in the lines *a*, *b*, and the merry-thought in the line *c*, *d*. The prime parts of a partridge are the wings, breaſt, and merry-thought. The wing is conſidered the beſt, and the tip of it reckoned the moſt delicate morſel of the whole.

Pigeons. See No. 7 *and* 8.

THESE are the repreſentations of two pigeons, the one with the back, the other with the breaſt uppermoſt. Pigeons are ſometimes cut up in the ſame manner as chickens; but as the lower part, with the thigh, is in general moſt preferred,

red, and as, from its ſmall ſize, half a one is not too much for moſt appetites, they are ſeldom carved now, otherwiſe than by fixing the fork at the point *a*, entering the knife juſt before it, and dividing the pigeon into two, cutting away in the lines *a*, *b*, and *a*, *c*, No. 7, at the ſame time bringing the knife out at the back, in the direction *a*, *b*, and *a*, *c*, No. 8.

A Fore Quarter of Lamb. See No. 9.

A FORE quarter of lamb is always roaſted, and when it comes to table, before you can help any one, you muſt ſeparate the ſhoulder from the breaſt and ribs, by paſſing the knife under, in the direction *c*, *g*, *d*, *e*. The ſhoulder being then taken off, the juice of a lemon, or Seville orange, ſhould be ſqueezed upon the part it was taken from, a little ſalt added, and the ſhoulder replaced. The griſtly part muſt then be ſeparated from the ribs, in the line *f*, *g*, and then all the preparatory buſineſs to ſerving will be done. The ribs are generally moſt eſteemed, and one, two, or more may be eaſily ſeparated from the reſt, in the line *a*, *b*; but to thoſe who prefer the griſtly part, a piece or two may be cut off in the line *h*, *i*, &c. If your quarter be graſs lamb, and runs large, you may put the ſhoulder into another diſh, and carve it in the ſame manner as a ſhoulder of mutton uſually is.

A Haunch of Veniſon. See Plate, No. 10.

CUT down to the bone, in the line *b*, *c*, *a*. Then turn the diſh, with the end *d* towards you, put in the point of the knife at *c*, and cut it down as deep as you can, in the direction *c*, *d*, ſo that the two ſtrokes will then form the reſemblance of the letter T. Having cut it thus, you may cut as many ſlices as are neceſſary, according to the number

ber of the company, cutting them either on the right or left. As the fat lies deeper on the left, between *d* and *a*, to those who are fond of fat, as is the case with most admirers of venison, the best flavoured and fattest slices will be found on the left of the line *c*, *d*, supposing the end *d* turned towards you. In cutting the slices, remember that they must not be either too thick or too thin. With each slice of lean, add a proportion of fat, and put a sufficient quantity of gravy into each plate. Currant jelly should always be served up with venison, as most people in general like it.

We might enlarge this chapter considerably, by describing the different methods of carving the various joints of butcher's meat; but, as we suppose every housekeeper is well acquainted with that business, we shall here omit it, and pass on to matters of more consequence.

CHAP. XXVII.

Directions for Marketing.

To choose Turkies.

THE shortness of the spur, and the smoothness and blackness of the legs, is the certain sign of a cock turkey being young. The feet will also be limber and moist, and the eyes full and bright. It will however be very necessary to observe, that the spurs are not cut or scraped, in order to deceive you, which is an artifice too often made use of. If the turkey be stale, the eyes will be sunk, and the

the feet dry. The ſame rules will enable you to judge of a hen turkey, with this difference, that if ſhe be old, her legs will be rough and red; if with egg, the vent will be ſoft and open; but if ſhe has no eggs, the vent will be hard and cloſe.

Cocks and Hens.

IF they be ſtale, the vents will be open; but, if freſh, cloſe and hard. The ſpurs of a young cock are ſhort; but the ſame precaution muſt here be attended to as juſt given in the choice of turkies. Hens are always beſt when full of eggs, and juſt before they begin to lay. The combs and legs of an old hen are rough, but ſmooth in a young one. The comb of a good capon is very pale, its breaſt remarkably fat, and has a large rump and a thick belly.

To chooſe Geeſe.

THE bill and feet of a young gooſe are yellow, with very few hairs upon them; but, if they be old, both will look red. The feet will be limber, if it be freſh, but ſtiff and dry if ſtale. Green geeſe are in ſeaſon from May or June, and till they are three months old. A ſtubble gooſe will be in good order till it is five or ſix months old. Green geeſe ſhould be ſcalded before they are picked; but ſtubble geeſe ſhould be picked dry.

To chooſe Ducks.

THE legs of a freſh-killed duck are limber, and if it be fat, the belly will be hard and thick; but the feet of a ſtale duck are dry and ſtiff. The feet of a tame duck are inclining to a duſky yellow, and are thick; but thoſe of a wild-duck are ſmaller than thoſe of a tame one, and are of a reddiſh colour. Ducklings ſhould be ſcalded before they are picked, but ducks ſhould be picked dry.

Pheaſants.

Pheaſants.

PHEASANTS, as well as woodcocks and partridges, are not expoſed to ſale in the markets, ſo that all choice is out of the queſtion; but, as many of them are ſometimes ſent as preſents to different families in London, it may not here be improper to inform the cook, by what means they may diſtinguiſh the better from the worſe. The cock pheaſant has ſpurs, but the hen has none. The ſpurs of a young cock pheaſant are ſhort and blunt, or round; but they are long and ſharp when he is old. If the vent of the hen be open and green, ſhe is ſtale, and when rubbed hard with the finger, the ſkin will peel. The vent will be ſoft, if ſhe be with egg.

Partridges.

THE legs of partridges will be yellowiſh, and the bill of a dark colour, if the birds are young. The vent will be firm, if they be freſh; but it will look greeniſh, and the ſkin will peel when rubbed with the finger, if they be ſtale. The bill will be white, and the legs blue, if they are old.

Woodcocks.

THESE, being birds of paſſage, are to be procured only in the winter. They are beſt about a fortnight or three weeks after their firſt appearance, when they have reſted after their long flight over the ocean. If they feel firm and thick, it is a proof they are fat and in good condition. The vent will alſo be thick and hard, and a vein of fat will run by the ſide of the breaſt; but a lean one will feel thin in the vent. If the bird be newly killed, its feet will be limber, and the head and throat clean; but, if it be ſtale, every thing will have a contrary appearance.

To

To choose Pigeons.

PIGEONS, when new, are full and fat at the vent, and limber-footed; but if the toes be harsh, the vent loose, open, and green, it is a sure sign they are stale; and the legs will be large and red, if old. The tame pigeon is generally preferred to the wild, and should be large in the body, fat and tender; but the wild pigeon is not so fat. Wood pigeons are much larger than either wild or tame; but like them in other respects. The same rules will hold good in the choice of other small birds, such as plovers, field-fares, larks, &c.

To choose a Hare.

IF the claws are blunt and rugged, the ears dry and tough, and the cleft wide and large, it is a sign that the hare is old; but, if the claws be smooth and sharp, the ears tear easily, and the cleft in the lip is not much spread, you may then presume that it is a young one. The body will be stiff, and the flesh pale, if newly killed; but, if the flesh be turning black, and the body limber, it has every appearance of being stale. Hares, however, are not always considered the worse for being kept till they begin to smell. The chief distinction between a hare and a leveret is, that the leveret should have a knob, or small bone, near the foot, on its fore leg, which a hare has not. A hare should be kept, before dressing, as long as it will remain sweet, and no longer; for no food can be wholesome that is in a state of putrefaction.

To choose Rabbits.

THE claws will be very rough and long, and gray hairs well be intermixed with the wool, if the rabbit be old; but, in a young one, the wool and claws will be smooth. The flesh will look blueish, with

with a kind of ſlime upon it, and the body limber, if it be ſtale; but, if the body be ſtiff, and the fleſh white and dry, you may conclude it is freſh.

To chooſe Beef.

IF the meat of ox-beef be young, it will have a fine, ſmooth, open grain, a pleaſing carnation red colour, and will feel tender. The fat ſhould look rather white then yellow; for the meat is ſeldom good, when the fat is of a deep yellow. The ſuet ſhould alſo be perfectly white. In order properly to diſtinguiſh between ox, cow, and bull-beef, take the following rules. The grain of cow-beef is cloſer, and the fat whiter, than that of ox-beef; but the lean is not of ſo bright a red. The grain of bull-beef is ſtill cloſer, the fat hard and ſkinny, the lean of a deep red, and gives a ſtrong and rank ſcent; but ox-beef is the reverſe of all this.

To chooſe Mutton.

SQUEEZE the fleſh with your finger and thumb, and if it be young, it will feel tender; but, if it be old, it will feel hard, be wrinkled, and the fat will be fibrous and clammy. The fleſh of ewe-mutton is paler than that of the wether, and the grain cloſer. The grain of ram-mutton is likewiſe cloſer, the fleſh of a deep red, and the fat ſpongy.

To chooſe Lamb.

THAT is good lamb, in which the eyes appear bright and full in the head; but if they be ſunk and wrinkled, it is a ſign it is ſtale. Another method of judging is, if the rein in the neck of the fore-quarter appears of a fine blue colour, it is freſh; but if green or yellow, it is undoubtedly ſtale. If you find a faint diſagreeable ſcent from the kidney in the hind quarter, or if the knuckle feels

feels limber on your touching it with your fingers, you may conclude it is not good.

To choose Veal.

THE fillet of a cow calf is generally preferred to that of a bull. The eyes will appear plump, if the head be fresh; but they will be sunk and wrinkled, if stale. If the vein in the shoulder be not of a bright red, the meat is stale, and if there be any green or yellow spots, you may then conclude it is very bad. A good neck and breast will be white and dry; but if they be clammy, and look green or yellow at the upper end, have nothing to do with them. The kidney in the loin is soonest apt to be infected, and if it be stale, it will be soft and slimy. If the leg be white and firm, you may conclude it is good; but you may be assured it is bad, if the flesh be flabby.

To choose Pork.

THE lean of young pork, on being pinched with the finger and thumb, will break, and the skin dent. If the rind be thick, rough, and cannot be easily impressed with the finger, it is old. When it is fresh, the flesh will be cool and smooth; but if it be clammy, it is tainted, and in this case, the knuckle is always the worst. What is called measly pork is very unwholesome to eat; but this may be easily discovered by the fat being full of little kernels, which in good pork is never the case.

To choose Bacon.

THE fat of good bacon will feel firm, and have a red tinge, and the lean will be of a good colour, and stick close to the bone; but if there be any yellow

yellow ſtreaks in the lean, it either is or will be very ſoon ruſty. When bacon is young, the rind is thin, but thick when it is old.

To chooſe Hams.

STICK a knife under the bone of the ham, and on ſmelling at the knife, if the ham be good, it will have a pleaſant flavour; but reject it as a bad one, if it be daubed and ſmeared, and has a diſagreeable ſcent. Hams ſhort in the hock generally turn out the beſt.

To chooſe Brawn.

THE rind of young brawn will feel moderately tender; but it will be thick and hard if old. The rind and fat of barrow and ſow brawn are very tender.

To chooſe Veniſon.

THE fat of veniſon muſt generally direct your choice of it. If the fat be thick, bright, and clear, the cleft ſmooth and cloſe, it is young; but you may be aſſured it is old, if the cleft is very wide and tough. The haunches and ſhoulders are the places veniſon will firſt change at: therefore, in order to judge of its ſweetneſs, run a knife into thoſe parts, and the newneſs or ſtaleneſs will be diſcovered by its ſweet or rank ſcent. You may be ſure it is tainted, if it looks greeniſh, or is inclined to have a very black appearance. Veniſon, like hares, is often kept till it acquires a rank ſmell, and has what the French call the *haut goût*; but it is not generally liked in that ſtate, nor can it be wholeſome.

To

To choose Eggs.

PUT the greater end of the egg to your tongue, and if it feels warm, it is new; but if cold, it is ſtale; and according to the degree of heat or cold there is in the egg, you will judge of its ſtaleneſs or newneſs. Another method is, to hold it up againſt the ſun or a candle, and if the yolk appears round, and the white clear and fair, it is a mark of its goodneſs; but if the yolk be broken, and the white cloudy or muddy, the egg is a bad one. Some people, in order to try the goodneſs of an egg, put it into a pan of cold water: in this caſe, the freſher the egg is, the ſooner it will ſink to the bottom; but if it be addled or rotten, it will ſwim on the ſurface of the water. The beſt method to preſerve eggs is to keep them in meal or bran; though ſome place them in wood aſhes with their ſmall ends downwards. When neceſſity obliges you to keep them for any conſiderable time, the beſt way is to bury them in ſalt, which will preſerve them in almoſt any climate; but the ſooner an egg is uſed, the better.

To choose Butter.

GREAT precaution is neceſſary in the purchaſing of this article in order not to be deceived. Do not truſt to the taſte the ſeller gives you, as they will frequently give you to taſte of one lump, and ſell another of inferior quality. If you buy ſalt butter, put a knife into it, and apply it to your noſe, when the ſmell will direct you much better than the taſte. If the butter be in a caſk, have it unhooped, and thruſt in your knife, between the ſtaves, into the middle of it; for, by the artful mode of package, and the ingenuity of thoſe who ſend it from the country, the middle of the caſk is frequently

frequently a different ſort from that put at the top of it.

To chooſe Cheeſe.

IN the purchaſing of this article, pay particular attention to the coat or rind. If the cheeſe be old, and has a rough and ragged coat, or dry at top, you may expect to find little worms or mites in it. If it be moiſt, ſpongy, or full of holes, it probably is maggoty. Wherever you ſee any periſhed places on the outſide, obſerve to probe the bottom of them; for, though the hole in the coat may be but ſmall, it may be of conſiderable dimenſions within the cheeſe.

To chooſe Salmon.

BEFORE we proceed to give directions for chooſing a ſalmon, it may not be improper to make a few obſervations on the choice of fiſh in general. In order to know whether they be freſh or ſtale, take notice of the colour of the gills, which ſhould be of a lively red; whether they are hard or eaſily to be opened; the projection or indention of their eyes, the ſtiffneſs or limberneſs of their fins, and by the ſcent from their gills. We now proceed to the choice of the ſalmon. Its fleſh, when new, is of a fine red, and particularly ſo at the gills. The ſcales ſhould be bright, and the fiſh very ſtiff. The ſpring is the proper ſeaſon for the ſalmon, which is of a fine, rich, and pleaſant flavour.

To chooſe a Turbot.

THIS fiſh will be thick and plump, if good, and the belly of a yellowiſh white; but, if they appear thin and blueiſh, they are bad. This fiſh is in ſeaſon during the greateſt part of the ſummer, and is in high eſtimation.

To

To choose Trout.

THE beſt ſort of this beautiful and excellent freſh-water fiſh are red and yellow. The females, which are moſt in eſteem, are diſtinguiſh by having a ſmaller head, and deeper body, than the male. They are in high perfection the latter end of June, and their freſhneſs may be aſcertained by the general rules we have given in the article of ſalmon.

To choose Cod.

A COD ſhould be very thick at the neck, and, if it be perfectly fine and freſh, the fleſh will be white and firm, and of a bright clear colour, with red gills. When they are ſtale they will appear flabby, and will not retain their proper flavour. From Chriſtmas to Lady-day is their proper ſeaſon.

To choose Tench.

TENCH ſhould be dreſſed alive, in order to be eaten in perfection; but, if they be dead, examine the gills, which ſhould be red, and hard to open. If freſh, the eyes will be bright, and the body firm and ſtiff. They are generally covered with a kind of ſlimy matter, which, if clear and bright, is a proof of their being good. Rubbing them with a little ſalt will eaſily remove this ſlimy matter.

To choose Soles.

WHEN ſoles are good, they are thick and firm, and the belly of a fine cream colour; but if they are flabby, or incline to a blueiſh white, they are not good. Midſummer is the proper ſeaſon for this fiſh.

To choose Flounders.

WHEN these fish are fresh and fine, they are stiff, their eyes bright and full, and their bodies thick. They are inhabitants of both salt and fresh water, and should be dressed as soon as possible after they are dead.

To choose Eels.

THE Thames silver eel is generally esteemed the best, and the worst are brought by the Dutch, and sold at Billingsgate market. They should be dressed alive, and are in season all the year, excepting the very hot summer months.

To choose Smelts.

IF smelts be fresh, they will be of a fine silver hue, very firm, and have a peculiarly strong smell, greatly resembling that of a pared cucumber.

To choose Skate.

WHEN this fish is perfectly good and sweet, the flesh will look exceedingly white, and be thick and firm. This fish has a peculiar inconvenience, which is, if it be too fresh, it will eat very tough; and, if stale, they have a strong and disagreeable scent. Some judgment is therefore necessary to know the proper time of dressing them.

To choose Sturgeon.

THE flesh of this fish is very white, and has a few blue veins, the grain even, the skin tender, good-coloured, and soft. All the veins and gristles should be blue; for when they are brown or yellow, the skin harsh, tough, and dry, the fish is not good. When in perfection it has a pleasant smell, but a very disagreeable one when it is bad. It should also cut firm without crumbling. The females are as full of row as a carp, which is taken out, and ſpread upon a table, beat flat, and ſprinkled with ſalt; it is then dried in the air and ſun, and afterwards in ovens. It ſhould be of a reddiſh-brown colour, and very dry. This is eaten with oil and vinegar, and is called Caviare.

To chooſe Oyſters.

OF the various ſpecies of oyſters, thoſe called the native Milton are the moſt eſteemed, they being the fatteſt and whiteſt; but ſome prefer the Colcheſter, Pyfleet, and Milford oyſters. When they are alive, and in full vigour, they will cloſe faſt upon the knife on opening, and let go as ſoon as they are wounded in the body.

To chooſe Lobſters.

THE tail of a lobſter will be ſtiff, and pull up with a ſpring, if it be freſh; but, if it be ſtale, the tail will be flabby, and have no ſpring in it. This rule, however, concerns lobſters that are boiled; but it is more adviſeable to buy them alive, and boil them yourſelf, taking care that they are not ſpent by too long keeping. If they have not been long taken, the claws will have a quick and ſtrong motion on ſqueezing the eyes, and the heavieſt are eſteemed the beſt. The cock lobſter is known by the narrow back part of his tail. The two uppermoſt fins within his tail are ſtiff and hard; but thoſe of the hen are ſoft, and the tail broader. The male, though generally ſmaller than the female, has the higher flavour, the fleſh is firmer, and the body of a redder colour, when boiled.

To chooſe Prawns and Shrimps.

WHEN theſe fiſh are in perfection, they afford an excellent ſcent, are very firm, with the tails turning ſtiffly inwards. They have a very bright colour

colour when fresh; but when stale their tails grow limber, the brightness of their colour goes off, and they become pale and clammy.

To choose Herrings.

THE gills will be of a fine red, and the whole fish stiff and very bright, if they be fresh; but if the gills be of a faint colour, and the fish limber and wrinkled, you may be assured they are stale. Pickled herrings when good are fat, fleshy, and white; and red herrings, if good, will be large, firm, and dry. The latter should be full of row or melt, and the outsides of a fine yellow. Those that have the skin or scales wrinkled on the back, will turn out preferable to those whose scales are very broad, the distinction between which is sufficiently obvious.

CHAP. XXVIII.

The Preparation of Made Wines.

To make Smyrna Raisin Wine.

TO an hundred pounds of raisins put twenty-four gallons of water, let it stand about fourteen days, and then put it into your cask. After it has continued there six months, put a gallon of brandy to it, and bottle it as soon as it is fine.

Common Raisin Wine.

PUT two hundred weight of raisins, stalks and all, into a hogshead. Having filled the cask with water, let the raisins steep a fortnight; but observe to to ftir them every day. Then pour off all the liquor, and prefs the fruit. Put both liquors together in a nice clean veffel, juft big enough to hold it; for it muft be full. Let it ftand till it is done hiffing, or making the leaft noife. Then ftop it clofe, and let it ftand fix months. You may then peg it, and if you find it quite clear, rack it off into another veffel, ftop it clofe, and let it ftand three months longer. Then bottle it, and rack it off into a decanter when you ufe it.

Red Currant Wine.

YOU muft gather your currants when they are full ripe, and choofe a fine dry day for that purpofe. Strip them, put them into a large pan, and bruife them with a wooden peftle. Let them ftand in a tub twenty-four hours to ferment, then run it through a hair fieve, but do not let your hand touch the liquor. To every gallon of this liquor put two pounds and a half of white fugar, ftir it well together, and put it into your veffel. To every fix gallons, put in a quart of brandy, and let it ftand fix weeks. If it be then fine, bottle it; if it be not, draw it off as clear as you can into another veffel, or large bottles, and put it into fmall bottles in a fortnight.

Grape Wine.

BRUISE the grapes, and to every gallon of ripe grapes put a gallon of foft water. Let them ftand a week without ftirring, and then draw the liquor off fine. To every gallon of wine, put three pounds of lump fugar. Put it into a veffel; but do not ftop it till it has done hiffing. Then ftop it clofe, and it will be fit to bottle in fix months.

Orange Wine.

PUT into fix gallons of fpring water twelve pounds of the beft powdered fugar, with the whites of of eight or ten eggs well beaten. Boil it three quarters of an hour; and when cold, put into it ſix ſpoonfuls of yeaſt, and the juice of twelve lemons, which, being pared, muſt ſtand with two pounds of white ſugar in a tankard. In the morning, ſkim off the top, and then put it into the water. Then add the juice and rinds of fifty oranges, but not the white part of the rinds, and let it work all together two days and two nights. Then put to it two quarts of Rheniſh or white wine, and put it into your caſk.

Orange Wine with Raiſins.

PICK and chop ſmall thirty pounds of good Malaga raiſins. Then take twenty large Seville oranges, ten of which you muſt pare as thin as for preſerving. Boil about eight gallons of ſoft water till a third be waſted, let it cool a little, and then put five gallons of it hot upon your raiſins and orange peel. Stir it well together, cover it up, and when it is cold, let it ſtand five days, ſtirring it once or twice a day. Then paſs it through a hair ſieve, and with a ſpoon preſs it as dry as you can. Put it in a caſk that will juſt hold it, and put to it the rind of the other ten oranges, cut as thin as the firſt. Then make a ſyrup of the juice of twenty oranges, with a pound of white ſugar, ſtir it well together, and ſtop it cloſe. This muſt be done the day before you tun it up. Let it ſtand two months to clear, and then bottle it up, and it will keep good three years.

Elder Wine.

THESE berries muſt be picked when they are full ripe, and on a dry day. Put them into a ſtone jar, and ſet them in the oven, or in a kettle of boiling water, till the jar is hot through. Then take them out, and ſtrain them through a coarſe

coarſe cloth, wringing the berries. Put the juice into a clean kettle, and to every quart of juice put a pound of fine Liſbon ſugar. Let it boil, and ſkim it well. When it is clear and fine, pour it into a jar. As ſoon as it is cold, cover it cloſe, and keep it till you make raiſin wine. Then, when you tun your wine, to every gallon of wine, put half a pint of the elder ſyrup.

Elder Flower Wine, in Imitation of Frontiniac.

PUT twelve pounds of white ſugar, and ſix pounds of raiſins of the ſun chopped, to ſix gallons of ſpring water, and let them boil one hour. Then take the flower of elders that are falling, and rub them off to the quantity of half a peck. When the liquor is cold, put them in; and, the next day, put in the juice of three lemons, and four ſpoonfuls of good ale yeaſt. Let it ſtand covered two days, then ſtrain it off, and put it in a veſſel fit for it. To every gallon of wine put a pint of Rheniſh, and put your bung lightly on for a fortnight: then ſtop it down cloſe, let it ſtand ſix months, and bottle it off, if it be then fine.

Mead Wines.

THERE being ſeveral ſorts of mead wines, it will be neceſſary to mention three of them ſeparately. *White or Sack Mead* is made in the following manner. Put a gallon of the beſt honey to every five gallons of water. Set it on the fire, and boil it well one hour, remembering to ſkim it well. Then take it off the fire, and ſet it by to cool. Take two or three races of ginger, a ſtick of cinnamon, and two nutmegs. Bruiſe theſe a little, put them into a Holland bag, and let them ſtand in the hot liquor till it is nearly cold. Then put as much ale yeaſt to it as will make it work, keep it in a warm place, as they do ale, and when it it has worked well, put it into a caſk that will juſt hold it. In two or three months you may bottle it off: cork it well, and keep it for uſe.

Walnut Mead.

PUT ſeven pounds of honey to every two gallons of water, and boil it three quarters of an hour. To every gallon of liquor put about twenty-four walnut leaves, pour your liquor boiling hot over them, and let it ſtand all night. Then take out the leaves, and pour in a cupful of yeaſt. Let it work two or three days, and then make it up. After it has ſtood three months, bottle it, cork it tight, and keep it for uſe.

Cowſlip Mead.

PUT twenty-four pounds of the beſt honey to ten gallons of water, and boil it till near one gallon is waſted, obſerving to ſkim it well. Cut ten lemons in halves, and put them to three quarts of the hot liquor. Put the reſt of the liquor into a tub, with five pecks of cowſlips, and let them ſtand all night. Then put in the liquor, with the lemons, ſix large ſpoonfuls of good ale yeaſt, and a handful of ſweetbrier. Stir them all well together, and let them work three or four days. Then ſtrain the liquor from the ingredients, and put it into a caſk. Let it ſtand ſix months, and then bottle it for uſe.

Gooſeberry Wine.

GOOSEBERRIES for this purpoſe muſt be gathered when they are half ripe, and in dry weather. Pick the fineſt, and bruiſe a peck in a tub with a wooden mallet. Then take a horſe-hair cloth, and preſs them as much as poſſible, without breaking the ſeeds. When you have preſſed out all the juice, to every gallon of gooſeberries put three

three pounds of fine dry powder fugar, and ftir it all together till the fugar is diffolved. Then put it into a veffel juft big enough to hold it. If it be ten or twelve gallons, let it ftand a fortnight; if a twenty-gallon cafk, five weeks. Set it in a cool place, then draw it off from the lees, clear the veffel of the lees, and pour in the liquor clear again. If it be a ten-gallon cafk, let it ftand three months; and if a twenty-gallon, four months. Then bottle off, as before directed.

Mountain Wine.

PICK all the ftalks out of fome fine Malaga raifins, chop them very fmall, and put ten pounds of them to every two gallons of fpring water. Let them fteep three weeks, ftirring them frequently during that time. Then fqueeze out the liquor, and put it into a veffel that will juft hold it, but do not ftop it till it has done hiffing. Then bung it up clofe, and it will be fit for ufe in about fix months.

Cherry Wine.

GATHER your cherries when they are full ripe, pull them off the ftalks, and prefs them through a hair-fieve. Put two pounds of lump fugar finely beaten to every gallon of liquor. Stir it together, and put it into a veffel juft big enough to hold it. When it has done working and making a noife, ftop it clofe for three months, and then bottle it off for ufe.

Black Cherry Brandy.

PROCURE eight pounds of the fineft black moroon cherries, and eight pounds of fmall black cherries. Pick them, and bruife them in a mortar, or you may ufe them whole, if you pleafe. Put them into a cafk, and pour fix gallons of brandy

brandy over them. Put in two pounds of loaf ſugar broken to pieces, a quart of ſack, ſtir all well together, and let it ſtand two months. Then draw it off into pint bottles, cork it tight, and keep it for uſe. It is much finer when made with Morella cherries.

Birch Wine.

THE proper ſeaſon for extracting the liquor from the birch tree is the beginning of March, while the ſap is riſing, and before the leaves ſhoot out; for when the ſap is come forward, and the leaves appear, the juice being long digeſted in the bark, grows thick and coloured, which before was thin and clear. The method of extracting the juice is by boring holes in the body of the tree, and putting in foſſets, which are commonly made of the branches of elder, the pith being taken out. You may, without hurting the tree, if it be large, tap it in ſeveral places, four or five at a time; and by thoſe means procure from different trees ſeveral gallons every day. If you have not enough in one day, the bottles in which it drops muſt be corked cloſe, and roſined or waxed. At any rate, however, make uſe of it as ſoon as you can. Take the ſap and boil it as long as any ſcum riſes, ſkimming it all the time. To every gallon of liquor put four pounds of good ſugar, and the thin peel of a lemon. Boil it afterwards half an hour, ſkimming it well. Then pour it into a clean tub, and when it is almoſt cold, ſet it to work with yeaſt ſpread upon a toaſt. Let it ſtand five or ſix days, ſtirring it often. Then take a caſk juſt big enough to hold the liquor. Fire a large match dipped in brimſtone, throw it into the caſk, and ſtop it cloſe till the match is extinguiſhed. Tun your wine, and lay the bung on lightly, till you find

find it has done working. Stop it close, keep it three months, and then bottle it for use.

Apricot Wine.

HAVING boiled six pounds of loaf sugar in six quarts of water, and skimmed it well, put in twelve pounds of apricots pared and stoned, and boil them till they are tender. Then strain the liquor from the apricots, put it into a stone bottle, and bottle it as soon as it is fine. Cork it well, and keep it in a cool cellar for use.

Balm Wine.

BOIL twenty pounds of lump sugar in four gallons and a half of water one hour gently, and put it into a tub to cool. Bruise two pounds of the tops of green balm, and put them into a barrel with a little new yeast, and when the liquor is nearly cold pour it on the balm. Stir it well together, and let it stand twenty-four hours, stirring it frequently. Then bung it up, and let it stand six weeks. Then bottle it off, put a lump of sugar into each bottle, cork it tight, and the longer it is kept, the better it will be.

Quince Wine.

QUINCES for this purpose must be gathered when dry and full ripe. Wipe twenty large quinces clean with a coarse cloth, and grate them with a large grater or rasp as near the core as you can, but none of the core. Boil a gallon of spring water; throw in your quinces, and let them boil softly a quarter of an hour. Then strain them well into an earthen pan, on two pounds of double-refined sugar. Pare two large lemons, throw in the peel, and squeeze the juice through a sieve, and stir it about till it be quite cool. Then toast a very thin piece of bread very brown, rub a lit-

tle

tle yeaſt on it, and let it ſtand cloſe covered twenty-four hours. Then take out the toaſt and lemon-peel, put the liquor up in a keg, keep it three months, and then bottle it. If you make a twenty-gallon caſk, let it ſtand ſix months before you bottle it. When you ſtrain your quinces, you muſt wring them hard in a coarſe cloth.

Raſpberry Wine.

BRUISE ſome fine raſpberries with the back of a ſpoon, then ſtrain them through a flannel bag into a ſtone jar. To each quart of juice put a pound of double-refined ſugar, ſtir it well together, and cover it cloſe. Let it ſtand three days, and then pour it off clear. To a quart of juice, put two quarts of white wine; then bottle it off, and it will be fit to drink in a week.

Raſpberry Brandy.

PICK two gallons of raſpberries clean from the ſtalks, bruiſe them with your hands, and put them into a caſk. Put to them eight gallons of good brandy, two pounds of loaf ſugar finely beaten, and a quart of ſack. Stir all well up together, and let it ſtand a month. Then draw it off clear into another caſk, and when it is fine, bottle it: cork the bottles well, and keep it for uſe.

Orange Shrub.

TAKE twenty gallons of water, and break into it, in ſmall pieces, one hundred pounds of loaf ſugar. Boil it till the ſugar be melted, ſkim it well, and put it in a tub to cool. When cold, put it into a caſk, with thirty gallons of good Jamaica rum, and fifteen gallons of orange juice; but mind to ſtrain all the ſeeds out of the juice. Mix them well together, then beat up the whites of ſix eggs very well, ſtir them well in, let it ſtand a week to fine, and then

then draw it off for uſe. The ſame rules will hold good for the making of any quantity you pleaſe.

Damſon Wine.

HAVING gathered your damſons on a fine day, and when they are ripe, weigh them, and bruiſe them. Put them into a ſtone ſtein that has a cock in it, and to ſixteen pounds of fruit boil two gallons of water. Skim it, pour it over the fruit ſcalding hot, and let it ſtand two days. Then draw it off, and put it into a veſſel, and to every two gallons of liquor put five pounds of fine ſugar. Fill up the veſſel, and ſtop it cloſe. Keep it in a cool cellar for twelve months, then bottle it, and put a ſmall lump of ſugar into each bottle. Cork them well, and it will be fit for uſe in two months after.

Cowſlip, or Clary Wine.

PUT twelve pounds of ſugar, the juice of ſix lemons, and the whites of four eggs well beaten, into ſix gallons of water. Let it boil half an hour, and ſkim it well. Take a peck of cowſlips, (if they be dry, half a peck will do) and put them into a tub with the thin peelings of ſix lemons. Then pour on the boiling liquor, and ſtir them about. When almoſt cold, put in a thin toaſt, baked dry, and rubbed with yeaſt, and let it ſtand two or three days to work. If you put in, before you tun it, ſix ounces of ſyrup of citron, or lemons, with a quart of Reniſh wine, it will be a great addition. The third day ſtrain it off, and ſqueeze the cowſlips through a coarſe cloth; then ſtrain it through a flannel bag, and tun it up. Lay the bung looſe two or three days, to ſee if it works; and, if it does not, bung it down tight, let it ſtand three months, and then bottle it for uſe.

Turnip

Turnip Wine.

PARE, ſlice, and put a good many turnips into a cyder preſs, and preſs out all the juice. Put three pounds of lump ſugar to every gallon of juice, put your juice into a veſſel juſt big enough to hold it, with half a pint of brandy to every gallon of juice. Lay ſomething over the bung for a week, to ſee if it works. As ſoon as it has done working, ſtop it cloſe for three months, and draw it off into another veſſel. When it is fine, bottle it off.

Blackberry Wine.

PUT your berries when full ripe into a veſſel of wood or ſtone, with a ſpicket in it, and pour upon them as much boiling water as will juſt appear upon the top of them. As ſoon as it is cool enough to permit you to put your hand in, bruiſe them till all the berries are broken. Let them ſtand, cloſe covered, till the berries are well wrought up to the top, which is uſually in three or four days. Then draw off the clear juice into another veſſel, and add to every ten quarts of the liquor one pound of moiſt ſugar. Stir it well in, and let it ſtand to work in another veſſel, like the firſt, a week or ten days. Then draw it off at the ſpicket, through a jelly bag, into a large veſſel. Take four ounces of iſinglaſs, ſteep it twelve hours in a pint of white wine, and then boil it till it is diſſolved over a ſlow fire. Then take a gallon of your blackberry juice, put in the iſinglaſs, give it a boil, and put it hot to the reſt. Put it into a veſſel, ſtop it up cloſe till it has purged and ſettled; then bottle it, cork it tight, put it into a cool cellar, and it will be fit to drink in three months.

CHAP.

CHAP. XXIX.

The Preparation of Cordial Waters.

Cordial Poppy Water.

BEFORE we proceed to the preparation of cordial waters, it may not be amiſs to premiſe a few particulars. If you make uſe of a limbec, be careful to fill the top with cold water, when you ſet it on, make a paſte of flour and cold water, and cloſe the bottom of your ſtill with it. Be particularly careful not to let your fire be ſo hot as to endanger its boiling over, as that will weaken the ſpirit of your water. The water on the top of your ſtill ſhould be frequently changed, and never ſuffered to be ſcalding hot, which will prevent your ſtill dropping gradually. If you uſe a hot ſtill, when you put on the top, dip a cloth in white lead and oil mixed together, and lay it well over the edges of your ſtill, and a coarſe cloth over the top. Make a ſlow fire under it, but mind and keep it very clear; and when your cloth is dry, dip it in cold water, and lay it on again. If your ſtill be very hot, wet another cloth, and lay it round the top. When you uſe a worm-ſtill, keep your tub full to the top with water, and change it often, to prevent its growing hot. When the young practitioner has ſtrongly fixed theſe preliminaries in his mind, he may then proceed to the preparation of Cordial Poppy Water, and the other articles mentioned in this chapter. Put a peck of poppies, and two gallons of very good brandy, into a wide-mouthed glaſs, and let them ſtand forty-eight hours. Then ſtrain out the poppies, take a pound of raiſins

ſins of the ſun ſtoned, an ounce of coriander ſeeds, and an ounce of liquorice ſliced. Bruiſe them all together, and put them into the brandy, with a pound of good powder ſugar. Let them ſtand four or eight weeks, ſhaking it every day, and then ſtrain it off and bottle it cloſe for uſe.

To make Milk Water.

TAKE of rue, carduus, and wormwood, each two large handfuls; four handfuls of mint, as much balm, and as much angelica. Cut theſe a little, and put them into a cold ſtill, and put to them three quarts of milk. Let your fire be quick till your ſtill drops, and then ſlacken it. You may draw off two quarts: the firſt quart will keep all the year.

Another Method.

TAKE of each of the following herbs three handfuls: fumitory, endive, agrimony, water creſſes, white nettles, elder-flowers, balm, bank-creſſes, and ſage; of eyebright, brook-lime, and celendine, each two handfuls; of the roſes of yellow dock, red madder, fennel, horſe-radiſh, and liquorice, each three ounces; one pound of ſtoned raiſins; nutmeg ſliced, winter-bark, turmerick, galingal, of each two drams; carraway and fennel ſeed three ounces; and one gallon of milk. Diſtil all with a gentle fire in one day.

To make Walnut Water.

BRUISE a peck of fine green walnuts in a large mortar, put them into a pan with a handful of balm bruiſed, put to them two quarts of good French brandy, cover them cloſe, and let them lie three days. The next day diſtil them in a cold ſtill. You may, in the courſe of one day, draw three quarts from this quantity.

To

To make Aqua Mirabilis.

TAKE cloves, mace, nutmeg, cinnamon, galingal, cubebs, and cardamums, of each four drams; put to them two pints of the juice of celendine, one pint of the juice of ſpearmint; the juice of balm, flowers of melilot, cowſlip, roſemary, borrage, bugloſs, and marygolds, of each ſix drams; ſeeds of carraway, coriander, and fennel, of each four drams; four quarts of the beſt ſack, and two quarts of white wine; the ſtrongeſt brandy, angelica water, and roſe-water, of each a quart. Bruiſe the ſpices and ſeeds, and ſteep them with the herbs and flowers in their juices, waters, ſack, white wine and brandy, all night. In the morning, diſtil it in a common ſtill paſted up; and from this quantity you may draw off two gallons at leaſt. Sweeten it to your taſte with ſugar-candy, bottle it up, and keep it in a cool place.

To make Treacle Water.

TAKE four pounds of the juice of green walnuts; balm, marygold, rue, and carduus, of each three pounds; half a pound of roots of butter bur; one pound of roots of burdock; angelica and maſtic wort, of each half a pound; leaves of ſcordium ſix handfuls; Venice treacle and mithridates, of each half a pound; old Canary wine two pounds; white wine vinegar, ſix pounds; and juice of lemon, the ſame quantity. Diſtil this in an alembic.

Lady Monmouth's Treacle Water.

TAKE three ounces of hartſhorn ſhaved, and boiled in borrage water, or ſuccory, wood-ſorrel, or reſpice water, or three pints of any of theſe waters boiled to a jelly. Put the jelly and hartſhorn both into the ſtill, and add a pint more of theſe waters. When you put it into the ſtill, take the

roots

roots of elecampane, gentian, cypreſs, tuninſal, of each an ounce; ſorrel roots two ounces, bleſſed thiſtle, called carduus, and angelica, each one ounce; balm, ſweet marjoram, and burnet, half a handful of each; lily-comvally flowers, borrage, buglos, roſemary, and marygold flowers, of each two ounces; citron rinds, carduus ſeeds, alkermes berries, and cochineal, of each an ounce. Prepare all theſe ſimples thus: Gather the flowers as they come in ſeaſon, and put them in glaſſes with a large mouth. Put with them as much ſack as will cover them, and tie up the glaſſes cloſe with bladders wet in the ſack, with a cork and leather upon that, adding more flowers and ſack till you have a proper quantity. Put cochineal into a pint bottle, with half a pint of ſack, and tie it up cloſe with a bladder under the cork, and another on the top, wet with ſack. Then cover it up cloſe with leather, and bury it, ſtanding upright in a bed of hot horſe-dung, nine or ten days. Then look at it, and, if it be diſſolved, take it out of the dung; but do not open it till you diſtil. Slice all the roots, beat the ſeeds and berries, and put them into another glaſs. Put no more ſack among them than neceſſary; and when you intend to diſtil, take a pound of the beſt Venice treacle, and diſſolve it in ſix pints of the beſt white wine, and three of red roſe water. Put all the ingredients together, ſtir them, and diſtil them in a glaſs ſtill.

To make Angelica Water.

WASH eight handfuls of the leaves of angelica, cut them, and lay them on a table to dry. As ſoon as they are dry, put them into an earthen pot, and put to them four quarts of ſtrong wine lees. Let it ſtand twenty-four hours, but ſtir it twice in that time. Then put it into a warm ſtill, or alembic, and draw it off. Cover your bottles with a paper, and prick holes in them, and let them ſtand thus

thus two or three days. Then mix all together, and fweeten it; and when it is fettled, bottle it up, and ftop it clofe.

To make Fever Water.

TAKE ten green walnuts, two ounces of carduus feeds and marygold flowers, and three ounces of Virginia fnake-root; carduus water and poppy water, one quart of each, and one ounce of hartf-horn. Slice the walnuts, and fteep all in the waters a fortnight. Then add to it half an ounce of London treacle, and diftil the whole in an alembic pafted up.

Piedmont Water.

BEAT up a pound of all-fpice in a mortar, and put it to two gallons of brandy, and the fame quantity of water. Let it ftand all night, and then draw it off in a worm-ftill.

Red Rofe-bud Water.

TAKE four gallons of rofes, and wet them in near two gallons of water. Then diftil them in a cold ftill. Take the fame ftilled water, and put into it as many frefh rofes as it will wet. Then diftil them again. In the fame manner you may diftil mint, balm, parfley, and pennyroyal waters.

Black Cherry Water.

BRUISE fix pounds of black cherries, and put to them the tops of rofemary, fweet marjorum, fpearmint, angelica, balm, and marygold flowers, of each a handful; dried violets an ounce; anife-feeds and fweet fennel-feeds, of each half an ounce. Bruife the feeds well, and cut the herbs fmall. Mix all together, and diftil them off in a cold ftill.

Stag's Heart Water.

TAKE rofemary flowers, clove gilliflowers dried, rofe-buds dried, and borrage flowers, of each an ounce; four handfuls of balm, and one of fweet marjorum; marygold flowers half an ounce; lemon-peel, two ounces; mace and cardamum, of each thirty grains; of cinnamon, fixty grains; or yellow and white fanders, of each a quarter of an ounce; fhavings of hartfhorn an ounce. Take nine oranges, and put in the peels; then cut them in fmall pieces, and pour upon thefe two quarts of the beft Rhenifh, or the beft white wine. Let it infufe three or four days, clofe ftopped in a cellar or cool place; but it will not be the worfe for infufing nine or ten days. Take a ftag's heart, and cut off the fat, cut it very fmall, and cover it with Rhenifh or white wine. Let it ftand all night clofe covered in a cool place, and the next day add to it all the before mentioned ingredients, mixing them very well together, and adding to it a pint of the beft rofe-water, and a pint of the juice of celandine. If you pleafe you may put in ten grains of faffron. Put it in a glafs ftill, diftilling in water, raifing it well to keep in the fteam both of the ftill and receiver.

Peppermint Water

CUT your peppermint which muft be gathered when it is full grown, and before it feeds, into fhort lengths. Fill your ftill with it, and cover it with water. Then make a good fire under it, and when it is near boiling, and the ftill begins to drop, if your fire be too hot, draw a little from under it, to keep it from boiling over, or your water will be muddy. The flower your ftill drops, the clearer and ftronger your water will be; but do not reduce it too low. Bottle it the next day,

let

let it ſtand three or four days to take off the fiery taſte of the ſtill, then cork it well, and it will keep a long time.

Orange or Lemon Water.

TAKE the outer rinds of fifty oranges or lemons, put them into ſix quarts of brandy and one quart of ſack, and let them ſteep in it one night. The next day diſtil them in a cold ſtill, and draw it off till it begins to taſte ſour. Sweeten it to your taſte with double-refined ſugar, and mix the firſt, ſecond, and third runnings together. If it be lemon water, it ſhould be perfumed with two grains of ambergris, and one of muſk. Grind them fine, tie them in a rag, and let it hang five or ſix days in each bottle, or you may put to them three or four drops of the tincture of ambergris. Take care that you cork it well, and it will remain good a great while.

Nutmeg Water.

PUT one pound of nutmegs beat up in a mortar to two gallons of brandy, and the ſame quantity of water. Let it ſtand all night, and then draw it off in a warm ſtill.

Hyſterical Water.

TAKE ſeeds of wild parſnip, betony, and roots of lovage, of each two ounces; roots of ſingle piony four ounces; of miſletoe of the oak three ounces; myrrh a quarter of an ounce, and caſtor half an ounce. Beat all theſe together, and add to them a quarter of a pound of dried millepedes. Pour on theſe three quarts of mugwort water, and two quarts of brandy. Let them ſtand in a cloſe veſſel eight days, and then ſtill it in a cold ſtill paſted up. You may draw off nine pints of water, and ſweeten it to your taſte. Mix all together, and bottle it up.

Surfeit

Surfeit Water.

TAKE chives, ſage, balm, mint, rue, Roman wormwood, ſcurvy-graſs, brook-lime, and water creſſes, of each one handful; green merery two handfuls; poppies, if freſh, half a peck; but, if they be dry, uſe only half the quantity; cochineal and ſaffron, ſixpennyworth of each; aniſeſeeds, carraway-ſeeds, coriander and cardamum-ſeeds, of each, an ounce; two ounces of ſcraped liquorice; a pound of ſplit figs, the ſame quantity of raiſins of the ſun ſtoned, an ounce of juniper berries bruiſed, an ounce of beaten nutmeg, an ounce of mace bruiſed, and the ſame of ſweet fennel-ſeeds alſo bruiſed, with a few flowers of roſemary, marigold, and ſage. Put all theſe into a large ſtone jar, put to them three gallons of French brandy. Cover it cloſe, and let it ſtand near the fire for three weeks. Stir it three times a week, and be ſure to keep it cloſe ſtopped, and then ſtrain it off. Bottle your liquor, and pour on the ingredients a bottle more French brandy. Let it ſtand a week, ſtirring it once a day, then diſtil it in a cold ſtill, and you will have a fine white ſurfeit water. Though this is beſt made in ſummer, yet you may make it at any time of the year, if you live in London, where the ingredients are always to be had either in a green or dry ſtate.

Roſe Water.

ROSES for this purpoſe muſt be gathered on a fine day, when they are full blown. Pick off the leaves, and to a peck put a quart of water. Then put them into a cold ſtill, make a ſlow fire under it, and the ſlower you diſtil it the better it will be. Then bottle it, and you may cork it after two or three days.

Lavender

Lavender Water.

TAKE two pounds of lavender pips, and put them into two quarts of water. Put them into a cold ſtill, and put a ſlow fire under it. Diſtil it off very ſlowly, and put it into a pot till you have diſtilled all your water. Then clean your ſtill well out, put your lavender water into it, and diſtil it off again ſlowly. Put it into your bottles, and cork it well.

CHAP. XXX.

Directions for brewing Malt Liquors.

THOUGH the Houſekeepers in London are very ſeldom troubled with the buſineſs of brewing, yet it is a very neceſſary article to be properly underſtood by thoſe who reſide much in the country. We ſhall therefore be very particular in this buſineſs, and proceed to lay down ſuch plain and conciſe rules, as may enable every one to become a good brewer of malt liquors. And, firſt, we ſhall deſcribe

On what Principles the Copper ſhould be built.

THE various implements neceſſary for this buſineſs muſt be properly made, and kept clean and in good order. The proper poſition of the copper, and the manner of its being ſet, require very attentive conſideration. The beſt method to be adopted is to divide the heat of the fire by a ſtop; and, if the door and draft be in a direct line, the ſtop muſt be erected from the middle of each outline

line of the grating, and parallel with the centre ſides of the copper. By this method, the middle of the fire will be directly under the bottom of the copper. The ſtop is compoſed of a thin wall in the centre of the right and left ſides of the copper, which is to aſcend half the height of it. On the top muſt be left a cavity, from four to five inches, for a draught for that half part of the fire which is next the door of the copper; and then the building muſt cloſe all round to the finiſhing at the top. By this method the heat will communicate from the outward part of the fire round the outward half of your copper, through the cavity, as will the fartheſt part of the flue, which alſo contracts a conjunction of the whole, and cauſes the flame to glide gently and equally round the bottom of the copper.

Very great are the advantages ariſing from a copper being ſet in this manner, and among theſe conſiderations, the ſaving of fuel is not the leaſt. It has a conſiderable advantage over wheel-draughts; for with them, if there be not particular attendance given to the hops, by ſtirring them down, they are apt to ſtick to the ſides, and ſcorch, which will deprive the liquor of its ſweet and proper flavour. By the method above adviſed, the copper will laſt many years longer than it will by the wheel-draught; for that draws with ſo much violence, that ſhould your liquor be beneath the communication of the fire, your copper will thereby be liable to injury; whereas, by the other method, you may boil half a copper full, without any bad conſequences enſuing.

The proper Management of Veſſels for Brewing.

THE day before you intend to brew, very attentively examine all your veſſels, and ſee that they be thoroughly clean, and in a ſtate proper for

for uſe. Brewing utenſils ſhould never be converted to any other uſe, unleſs for wines; and even then, as ſoon as they are done with, they ſhould be thoroughly cleanſed, and kept in a clean place. Caſks muſt be well cleaned with boiling water; and, if the bung-hole be large enough, ſcrub them well with a ſmall birch broom or bruſh. If you find them bad, and have a muſty ſcent, take out the heads, and let them be ſcrubbed clean with a hand-bruſh, ſand, and fullers earth. When you have done this, put on the head again, and ſcald it well; then throw in a piece of unſlacked lime, and ſtop the bung cloſe. When they have ſtood ſome time, rince them well with cold water, and they will then be in a condition proper to be uſed.

Your coolers alſo require equal attention, they being implements of much conſequence in brewing; for, if they be not properly kept in order, your liquor will contract a diſagreeable flavour, of which nothing can cure it. This often proceeds from wet having infuſed itſelf into the wood, it being ſometimes apt to lodge in the crevices of old coolers, and even infect them to ſuch a degree, that it cannot be removed even after ſeveral waſhings and ſcaldings. One cauſe incidental to this evil is, ſuffering women to waſh in a brewhouſe, which ought never to be permitted, where any other convenience can be had; for nothing can be more hurtful than the remains of dirty ſoap left in veſſels intended for brewing only.

Never let the water ſtand too long in the coolers while you are preparing them, as the water will ſoak into them, and ſoon turn putrid, when the ſtench will enter the wood, and make them almoſt incurable. To prevent theſe ill effects, as well as to anſwer good purpoſes, it has been recommended,

commended, where fixed brewhoufes are intended, that all coolers fhould be leaded. It muft be allowed, in the firft inftance, that fuch are exceedingly cleanly; and, fecondly, that it expedites the cooling of part of your liquor worts, which is very neceffary to forward it for working, as well as afterwards for cooling the whole; for evaporation caufes confiderably more wafte than proper boiling. Your coolers muft alfo be well fcoured two or three times with cold water, which is more proper than hot water to effect a perfect cleaning, efpecially if they be in a bad condition, from the undifcovered filth that may be in the crevices. The application of warm water will drive the infection further; fo that, if your liquor be let into the coolers, and any remain in the crevices, the heat will collect the foulnefs, and the whole will thereby be rendered unwholefome and difagreeable.

Another material point is to keep the mafh-tub clean; the grains muft not be left in the tub any longer than the day after brewing, left the tub fhould be thereby foured; for if there be a four fcent in the brewhoufe before your beer be tunned, it will be apt to infect your liquor and worts. Cleanlinefs in brewing is fo indifpenfable an article, that every attention fhould be paid to it.

The Management of the Mafh-tub and other Utenfils.

IN order to make your mafh-tub more lafting and complete, you muft have a circular piece of brafs or copper, to inlay and line the hole where the penftaff enters, to let the wort run off into the underback. The penftaff fhould be alfo ftrongly ferelled with the fame metal, and both well and taperly finifhed, fo that you may place it properly. By this method you have it run from the finenefs of a thread to the fulnefs of an inch tube, &c. firft dreffing dreſſing your muck-baſket with ſtraw, fern, or ſmall buſhy furze without ſtems, ſix or eight inches in from the bottom of your baſket, and ſet quite perpendicularly over the whole with the penſtaff, through the center of the baſket, and the middle of the furze or fern, and faſtened into the hole of the tub. To ſteady it properly, you muſt have a piece of iron let into a ſtaple faſtened to the tub, at the neareſt part oppoſite to the baſket, and to reach nearly to it; and from that piece another added on a jointed ſwivel, or any other contrivance, ſo as to be at liberty to let round the baſket like a dog's collar, and to enter into the ſtaple formed in the ſame to pin it faſt, and by adding a half-circular turn in the collar, in which you have room to drive in a wedge, which will keep it ſafe down to the bottom, where there can be no danger of its being diſturbed by ſtirring the maſh, which will otherwiſe ſometimes be the caſe. When you let go, you will raiſe the pen-ſtaff to your own degree of running, and then faſten the ſtaff, by the help of two wedges tightened between the ſtaff and the baſket.

The copper-work, like every thing elſe, muſt give way to time, and become defective. When this is the caſe, you may repair the imperfection by the following ſimple method. Work the penſtaff in the braſs ſocket with emery and water, or oil, which will perhaps make it more perfect than when new. The like method is ſometimes taken even with cocks juſt purchaſed, in order to prevent their decaying ſo ſoon as they otherwiſe would.

Underbacks may be made to receive a very material addition, by having a piece of copper to line the hole in the bottom, which may be ſtopped with a cloth put ſingly round a large cock, which will prevent its flying up by the heat. When the liquor is pumped clean out of the back, the cloth round the

the cock will enable you to take out the cock with eafe; and there fhould be a drain below the underback to carry off the water, which will enable you to wafh it very clean without much trouble. This drain fhould be made with a clear defcent, fo that no damp may remain under the back. With the conveyance of water running into your copper, you may be enabled to work that water in a double quantity, your underback being filled by the means of letting it in at your leifure, out of your copper, through a fhoot to the mafh-tub, and fo to the underback. Thus you will have a referve againft the time you wifh to fill your copper, which may be complete in a few minutes, by pumping while the under cock is running. We cannot conclude this article of utenfils, without again recommending cleanlinefs as a moft effential point to be attended to in brewing.

The proper Seafon for Brewing.

MARCH is generally confidered as one of the principal months for brewing malt liquors for long keeping. The reafon of this is, becaufe the air, at that time of the year, is in general temperate, and contributes to the good working or fermentation of the liquor, which principally promotes its prefervation and good keeping. The extremes of heat or cold weather are equally pernicious to the fermentation or working of liquors. Hence, if you brew in very cold weather, unlefs you ufe fome means to warm the cellar while new drink is working, it will never clear itfelf in the manner you would wifh; and the fame misfortune will arife, if in very hot weather, the cellar is not put into a temperate ftate. The confequence of all which will be, that fuch drink will be muddy and four, and in fuch a degree, as to be perhaps paft recovery. Thefe accidents frequently happen, even in in the proper feafon for brewing, and that owing to the badnefs of the cellar; for, if they be dug in fpring grounds, or are fubject to damps in the winter, the liquor will chill, and become vapid or flat. When cellars are in this fituation, it will be much better to brew in March than in October, as you may keep fuch cellars temperate in fummer, which cannot be done in winter. Thus your beer brewed in March, before the cold can any ways materially affect it, will have due time to adjuft and fettle itfelf.

Every cellar, defigned for the keeping of liquors, fhould be formed on fuch a plan, that no external air can get into it; for the variation of the external air, were the free admiffion of it into the cellar, would caufe as many alterations in the liquors, and confequently would keep them in fuch an unfettled ftate, as totally to fpoil them. A regular and temperate air digefts and foftens malt liquors, which makes them agreeable to the tafte; but in cellars, where the heats and colds are irregular, very little good liquor can be expected out of them.

The moft proper Water for Brewing.

REPEATED experiments have proved, that river-water is the moft proper for brewing, as fuch is generally foft, and has received thofe benefits, which are naturally derived from the air and fun, and which permit it eafily to penetrate into the malt, and extract its virtues. Hard waters, on the contrary, aftringe and bind the power of the malt, fo that its virtues are not freely communicated to the liquor. Some people hold it as a maxim, that all water that will mix with foap is fit for brewing, which is the cafe with the generality of river water; and it has been frequently found from experience, that when the fame quantity of malt has been ufed

to

to a barrel of river-water, as to a barrel of ſpring-water, the brewing from the former has exceeded the other in ſtrength above five degrees in the courſe of twelve months keeping. It has alſo been obſerved, that the malt was not only the ſame in quantity for one barrel as for the other, but was the ſame in quality, having been all meaſured from the ſame heap. The hops were alſo the ſame, both in quality and quantity, and the time of boiling equal in each. They were worked in the ſame manner, and tunned and kept in the ſame cellar. This is a proof beyond all contradiction, that the water only could be the cauſe of this difference.

The ableſt brewers have been much puzzled with one circumſtance, which is, that ſeveral country gentlemen in the ſame town have employed the ſame brewer, have had the ſame malt, the ſame hops and water, have brewed in the ſame month, and broached their drink at the ſame time, yet one has had exceedingly fine, ſtrong, and well-taſted beer, while the other has had nothing worth drinking. Three reaſons may be adduced, in order to account for this very ſingular difference. Firſt, it might ariſe from the difference of weather, which might happen at the different brewings in this month, and make an alteration in the working of the liquors. Secondly, the yeaſt, or barm, might be of different ſorts, or in different ſtates, wherewith theſe liquors were worked; and, thirdly, the cellars might not be equally adapted for the purpoſe. The goodneſs of ſuch drink as is brewed for keeping, depends, in ſome meaſure, on the proper form and temperature of the cellars in which it is kept.

Dorcheſter beer, which is generally in much eſteem, is chiefly brewed with chalky water, which is plenty in almoſt every part of that county; and as the ſoil is moſtly chalk, the cellars, being dug in in that dry ſoil, contribute much to the good keeping of their drink, it being of a cloſe texture, and of a dry quality, ſo as to diſſipate damps; for it has been found by experience, that damp cellars are equally injurious to the caſks and the good keeping of liquor.

Where water is naturally of a hard quality, it may, in ſome meaſure, be ſoftened by expoſing it to the air and ſun, and putting into it ſome pieces of ſoft chalk to infuſe; or, when, the water is ſet on to boil, in order to be poured on the malt, put into it a quantity of bran, and it will have a very good effect.

The Quality of the Malt and Hops moſt proper for Brewing.

MALT is generally diſtinguiſhed by two names, high-dried malt, and low-dried malt. Of theſe, the former, when brewed, produces a liquor of a deep-brown colour; and the other, which is the low-dried, produces a liquor of a pale colour. The firſt is dried in ſuch a manner as to be rather ſcorched than dried, and is not ſo wholeſome as the pale malt. It has alſo been found from experience, that brown malt, although it may be well brewed, will ſooner turn ſharp than the pale; ſo that the pale malt is generally in moſt eſteem.

A gentleman, who has made the art of brewing his ſtudy for many years, gives his opinion in theſe words. Brown malt makes the beſt drink when it is brewed with a coarſe river-water, ſuch as that of the Thames about London; and that being brewed with ſuch water it makes very good ale; but that it will not keep above ſix months without turning ſtale, even though he allows fourteen buſhels to the hogſhead. He adds, that he has tried the high-dried malt to brew beer with for keeping, and hopped it accordingly; and yet he could never brew

brew it ſo as to drink ſoft and mellow, like that brewed with pale malt. There is, he ſays, an acid quality in the high-dried malt, which occaſions thoſe who drink it to be greatly troubled with that diſorder called the heart burn.

We have been here ſpeaking only of malt made of barley; for as to wheat malt, pea-malt, or thoſe mixed with barley malt, though they produce a high-coloured liquor, will keep ſome years, and drink ſoft and ſmooth, yet they are ſubject to have the flavour of mum.

High-dried malt ſhould not be brewed till it has been ground ten days or a fortnight, as it will then yield much ſtronger drink than from the ſame quantity ground but a ſhort time before it is uſed. On the contrary, pale malt, which has not received much of the fire, muſt not remain unuſed above a week after it is ground.

The neweſt hops are by far the beſt. Though hops will keep two years, yet after that they begin to decay, and loſe their flavour, unleſs great quantities are kept together, in which caſe they will keep good much longer than in ſmall quantities. They ſhould, with a view to preſerve them the better, be kept in a very dry place; whereas thoſe who deal in them, with a view to encreaſe their weight, keep them as damp as they can.

It is hence evident, that every article for the brewery ſhould be judiciouſly choſen before you commence brewing, otherwiſe you will ſuſtain a loſs, which will be aggravated by your labour being in vain. Be particularly careful to be provided with every neceſſary article before you commence brewing; for bad conſequences muſt enſue when you wait for any thing that ſhould be immediately ready.

The

The practical Part of Brewing.

HAVING properly cleanſed and ſcalded all your utenſils, your malt ground, your water boiling in the copper, and your penſtaff well ſet, you muſt then proceed to maſh, by putting a ſufficient quantity of boiling water into your tub, in which it muſt ſtand until the greater part of the ſteam is gone off, or till you ſee your own ſhadow in it. It will then be neceſſary, that one perſon ſhould pour the malt gently in, while another is carefully ſtirring it, for it is equally as eſſential, that the ſame care ſhould be obſerved when the maſh is thin as when thick. This being properly done, and having a ſufficient reſerve of malt to cover the maſh, to prevent evaporation, you may cover your tubs with ſacks, &c. and leave your malt three hours to ſteep, by which time its virtues will be properly extracted.

Be careful, before you let the maſh run, to be prepared with a pail to catch the firſt fluſh, as that is generally thickiſh, and another pail to be applied while you return the firſt on the maſh, and ſo on for two or three times, at leaſt, till it runs fine. By this time your copper ſhould be boiling, and a convenient tub placed cloſe to your maſh-tub. Let into it, through your ſpout, half the quantity of boiling water you mean to uſe for drawing off your beſt wort; after which you muſt inſtantly turn the cock to fill up again, which, with a proper attention to the fire, will boil in due time. During ſuch time, you muſt ſlop the maſh with this hot water out of the convenient tub, in moderate quantities, every eight or ten minutes, till the whole is conſumed; and then let off the remaining quantity, which will be boiling hot, to the finiſhing proceſs for ſtrong beer.

Having

Having filled your copper, let it boil as quick as poffible for the fecond mafh, whether you intend it either for ale or fmall beer. Being thus far prepared, let off the remaining quantity of water into your tub, as you did for the ftrong beer; but if you would have fmall beer befides, you muft act accordingly, by boiling a proper quantity off in due time, and letting it into the tub as before directed.

As to the quantity of malt, twenty-four bufhels will make two hogfheads of as good ftrong beer as any perfon would wifh to drink, as alfo two hogfheads of very decent ale. The ftrong beer made from this quantity of malt fhould be kept two or three years before it is tapped, and the ale never lefs than one. If your mafh be only for one hogfhead, it fhould be two hours in running off; if two hogfheads, two hours and a half; and three hours for any greater quantity.

Great attention muft be paid to the time of fteeping your mafhes. Strong beer muft be allowed three hours; ale, one hour; and, if you draw fmall beer afterwards, half an hour. By this mode of proceeding your boilings will regularly take place of each other, which will greatly expediate the bufinefs. In the courfe of mafhing, be careful that it is thoroughly ftirred from the bottom, and efpecially round the muck bafket; for, being well fhaken, it prevents a ftagnation of the whole body of the mafh.

The greateft care muft be taken, in the preparation for boiling, to put the hops in with the firft wort, or it will char in a few minutes. As foon as the copper is full enough, make a good fire under it; but be careful in filling it to leave room enough for boiling. Quick boiling is a part of the bufinefs that requires very particular attention. Great caution muft be obferved when the liquor begins to to ſwell in waves in the copper. If you have no aſſiſtant, be particularly attentive to its motions; and being provided with an iron rod of a proper length, crooked at one end, and jagged at the other, then with the crook you are enabled to open the furnace, or copper door, and with the other end puſh in the damper, and thus proportion your fire, as you muſt take care not to have it too fierce.

To aſcertain the proper time the liquor ſhould boil, proceed as follows. Take a clean copper bowl-diſh, dip out ſome of the liquor, and when you diſcover a working, and the hops ſinking, you may then conclude it to be ſufficiently boiled. Long and ſlow boiling both hurts and waſtes the liquor.

As ſoon as your liquor is properly boiled, traverſe a ſmall quantity of it over all the coolers, ſo as to get a proper quantity cold immediately to ſet to work; but if the airineſs of your brewhouſe is not ſufficient to expedite a quantity ſoon, you muſt traverſe a ſecond quantity over the coolers, and then let it into ſhallow tubs. Put theſe into any paſſage where there is a thorough draft of air, but where no rain or other wet can get to it. Then let off the quantity of two baring-tubs full from the firſt one, the ſecond and third coolers, which may be ſoon got cold, to be ready for a ſpeedy working, and then the remaining part that is in your copper may be quite let out into the firſt cooler. In the mean time, mend the fire, and alſo attend to the hops, to make a clear paſſage through the ſtrainer.

As ſoon as the liquor is done running, return to your buſineſs of pumping; but remember, that when you have got four or five pailfuls, you return all the hops into the copper for ale.

By this time, the ſmall quantity of liquor traverſed over your coolers, being ſufficiently cooled, you

you muſt proceed as follows to ſet your liquor to work. Take four quarts of barm, and divide half of it into ſmall veſſels, ſuch as clean bowls, baſons, or mugs, adding thereto an equal quantity of wort, which ſhould be almoſt cold. As ſoon as it ferments to the top of the veſſels, put it into two pails, and when that works to the top, put one into a baring-tub, and the other into another. When you have half a baring-tub full together, you may put the like quantity to each of them, and then cover them over, until it comes to a fine white head. This may be perfectly completed in three hours, and then put thoſe two quantities into the working guile. You may now add as much wort as you have got ready; for, if the weather be open, you cannot work it too cold. If you brew in cold froſty weather, keep the brewhouſe warm; but never add hot wort to keep the liquor to a blood heat, that being a bad practice.

Take care that your barm be not from foxed beer, that is, beer heated by ill management in its working; for, in that caſe, it is likely to carry with it the contagion. If your barm be flat, and you cannot procure that which is new, put to it a pint of warm ſweet wort, of your firſt letting off, the heat to be about half the degree of milk-warm. Then give the veſſel that contains it a ſhake, and it will ſoon gather ſtrength, and be fit for uſe. As to the quantity of hops neceſſary to be uſed, remember, that half a pound of good hops is ſufficient for a buſhel of malt.

Tunning is the laſt and moſt ſimple operation in the buſineſs of brewing, the general methods of doing which are, either by having it carried into the cellar on mens ſhoulders, or conveying it thither by means of leathern pipes uſed for that purpoſe. Your caſks being perfectly clean, ſweet, and dry, and placed on the ſtand ready to receive the

the liquor, firſt ſkim off the top barm, then proceed to fill your caſks quite full, and immediately bung and peg them cloſe. Bore a hole with a tap-borer near the ſummit of the ſtave, at the ſame diſtance from the top as the lower tap-hole is from the bottom, for working through that upper-hole, which is a more clean and effectual method than working it over the caſk; for, by the above method, being ſo cloſely confined, it ſoon ſets itſelf into a convulſive motion of working, and forces itſelf fine, provided you attend to the filling of your caſks five or ſix times a day. New caſks are apt to give liquor a bad taſte, if they be not well ſcalded and ſeaſoned ſeveral days ſucceſſively before they are uſed; and old caſks are apt to grow muſty, if they ſtand any time out of uſe.

The proper Management of Malt Liquors.

TO keep ſtrong beer in a ſtate of perfection, having once broached the veſſel, attention muſt be paid to the time in which it may be expended; for, if there happen to be a quick draught for it, it will in that caſe laſt good to the bottom; but, if there is likely to be but a ſlow draught, then do not draw off quite half before you bottle it; otherwiſe it will grow flat, dead, or ſour.

The time requiſite for beer to ripen, depends on the quantity of liquor contained in the caſk. A veſſel that contains two hogſheads of beer, will require twice as much time to perfect itſelf as one of a hogſhead; and it is found by experience, that no veſſel ſhould be uſed for ſtrong beer intended for keeping, leſs than a hogſhead.

Small beer ſhould be made tolerably good in quality; for, if it be not good, ſervants, for whom it is principally calculated, will be feeble in ſummer-time, incapable of ſtrong work, and ſubject to various diſorders. Beſides, when the beer is bad, a great a great deal will be thrown away; whereas, on the contrary, good wholeſome drink will be valued, and conſequently taken care of. It is adviſeable, therefore, where there is good cellaring, to brew a ſtock of ſmall beer in March or October, or in both months, to be kept, if poſſible, in hogſheads. The beer brewed in March ſhould not be tapped till October, nor that brewed in October till the March following.

Some people, who brew with high-dried barley malt, in order to fine their beer, put a bag, containing about three pints of wheat, into every hogſhead of liquor, which has had the deſired effect, and made the beer drink ſoft and mellow. Others have put about three pints of wheat malt into a hogſhead, which has produced the ſame effect.

Malt liquors may be ſpoiled by bad cellaring, be ſubject to ferment in the caſk, and conſequently turn thick and ſour. When this happens, the beſt way of bringing the liquor to itſelf is, to open the bung-hole of the caſk for two or three days; and, if that does not ſtop the fermentation, then put in about two or three pounds of oyſter-ſhells, waſhed, dried well in an oven, and then finely pounded. After you have put it in, ſtir it a little, and it will ſoon ſettle the liquor, make it fine, and take off the ſharp taſte. When you find this effected, draw it off into another veſſel, and put a ſmall bag of wheat, or wheat malt, into it, in proportion to the ſize of the veſſel.

In ſome country places remote from principal towns, it is a practice to dip whiſks into yeaſt, then beat it well, and hang up the whiſks, with the yeaſt in them, to dry; and if there be no brewing till near two months afterwards, the ſtirring and beating one of theſe whiſks in new wort, will ſoon raiſe a working or fermentation. It is a rule, that all liquor ſhould be well worked in the tun, before it is put into the veſſel, otherwiſe it will not eaſily grow fine.

The properest Method to bottle Malt Liquors.

THE firſt attention to be paid is to your bottles, which muſt be well cleaned and dried; for wet bottles will ſpoil your liquor by making it turn mouldy. Though the bottles may be clean and dry, yet, if the corks be not new and ſound, the liquor will be liable to be damaged; for, if the air can penetrate the bottles, the liquor will grow flat, and never riſe. Many, who have flattered themſelves of a ſaving knowledge, by uſing old corks on this occaſion, have ſpoiled as much liquor as ſtood them in four or five pounds, in order to ſave three or four ſhillings. If bottles be corked properly, it will be difficult to draw the cork without a ſcrew; and to ſecure the drawing of the cork without breaking, the ſcrew ought to go through the cork, and then the air muſt neceſſarily find a paſſage where the ſcrew has paſſed. If a cork has once been in a bottle, though it has not been drawn with a ſcrew, yet that cork will turn muſty as ſoon as expoſed to the air, and will communicate its ill flavour to the bottle into which it is next put, and thereby ſpoil the liquor. In the choice of corks, take thoſe that are ſoft and clean from ſpecks. You may alſo obſerve, in the bottling of liquor, that the top and middle of the hogſhead are the ſtrongeſt, and will ſooner riſe in the bottles than the bottom. When you begin to bottle a veſſel of any liquor, do not go about any thing elſe till the whole of that buſineſs is completed.

As ſoon as a veſſel of liquor begins to grow flat whilſt it is on tap, bottle it, and into every bottle put a piece of loaf ſugar about the ſize of a walnut,

nut, which will make it riſe and come to itſelf; and to forward its ripening, you may ſet ſome bottles in hay in a warm place; but ſtraw will do nothing towards its ripening.

If you ſhould have the opportunity of brewing a good ſtock of ſmall beer in March and October, ſome of it may be bottled at the end of ſix months, putting into every bottle a lump of loaf ſugar, which, in the ſummer, will make a very pleaſant and refreſhing drink. Or, if you happen to brew in ſummer, and are deſirous of having briſk ſmall beer, as ſoon as it has done working, bottle it as before directed.

Should your cellars not happen to be properly calculated for the preſervation of your beer, you may uſe the following expedient. Sink holes in the ground, put into them large oil jars, and fill up the earth cloſe about the ſides. One of theſe jars will hold about two dozen bottles, and will keep the liquor in proper order; but great care muſt be taken, that the tops of the jars are kept cloſe covered. In winter time, when the weather is froſty, ſhut up all the lights or windows of your cellars, and cover them cloſe with horſe-dung, which will keep your beer in a proper and temperate ſtate.

To keep Yeaſt good for ſeveral Months.

IN order to preſerve a large ſtock of yeaſt, which will keep and be of uſe for ſeveral months, either for brewing, or to make bread or cakes, proceed as follows. When you have plenty of yeaſt, and are apprehenſive of a future ſcarcity, take a quantity of it, ſtir and work it well with a whiſk until it becomes liquid and thin. Then get a large wooden platter, cooler, or tub, clean and dry, and with a ſoft bruſh lay a thin layer of yeaſt on the tub, and turn the mouth downwards, that

no

no duſt may fall upon it, but ſo that the air may get under to dry it. When that coat is very dry, then lay on another, and ſo on till you have a ſufficient quantity, even two or three inches thick, always taking care that the yeaſt is very dry in the tub before you lay any more on, and this will keep good for ſeveral months. When you have occaſion to uſe this yeaſt, cut a piece off, and lay it into warm water; then ſtir it together, and it will be fit for uſe. If it be for brewing, take a large handful of birch tied together, dip it into the yeaſt, and hang it up to dry. In this manner you may do as many as you pleaſe; but take care that no duſt comes to it. When your beer is fit to ſet to work, throw in one of theſe, and it will make it work as well as if freſh yeaſt had been uſed.

CHAP. XXXI.

Directions for baking Bread.

The proper Form of an Oven.

EVERY new oven ſhould be built round, and not lower from the roof than twenty inches, nor higher than twenty-four inches. The mouth ſhould be ſmall, with an iron door to ſhut quite cloſe; by which means it will require leſs fire, and keep in the heat much better than a long and high-roofed oven, and in courſe bake every thing better.

The

The London Method of making Bread.

PUT a bufhel of good flour, which has been ground about five or fix weeks, in one end of your trough, and make a hole in the middle of it. Take nine quarts of warm water, which the bakers call liquor, and mix it with one quart of good yeaft. Put it into the flour, and ftir it well with your hands. Let it lie till it rifes as high as it will go, which will be in about an hour and twenty minutes. Mind and watch it when it is at the height, and do not let it fall. Then make up your dough with eight quarts more of warm liquor, and one pound of falt. Work it well with your hands, and then cover it over with a coarfe cloth or a fack. Put your fire into the oven, heat it well, and by the time your oven is hot, the dough will be ready. Then make your dough into loaves of about five pounds each, fweep out your oven clean, and put in your loaves. Shut it up clofe, and two hours and a half will bake them. Then open your oven, and draw them out. In fummer, let your liquor be juft blood-warm, in winter a litte warmer, and in hard frofty weather as hot as you can bear your hand in it; but not fo hot as to fcald the yeaft, for that will fpoil the whole batch of bread. A larger or fmaller quantity may be made in the fame proportion.

To make French Bread.

LAY half a bufhel of the beft Hertfordfhire white flour at one end of the trough, and make a hole in the middle of it. Mix a pint of good fmall-beer yeaft with three quarts of warm liquor, put it in, and mix it up well till it is tough. Put a flannel over it, and let it rife as high as it will; but mind and watch it that it does not fall. When it is at the height, take fix quarts of fkimmed

med milk blood-warm, the bluer the better, provided it is ſweet, and a pound of ſalt; but be ſure not to put any milk with the yeaſt at firſt, as that will prevent the yeaſt from riſing, as any thing greaſy will. Then, inſtead of working it with your hands, as you would dough for Engliſh bread, put the ends of your fingers together, and work it over your hands till it is quite weak and ropey, and then cover it over with a flannel. Put your fire into the oven, and make it very hot, by which time your dough will be ready. Lay your dough on the dreſſer, and, inſtead of a common knife, have one made like a chopping knife to cut it with. Then make it up into bricks, or rolls, as you chooſe. The bricks will take an hour and a half baking, and rolls half an hour. Then draw them out, and either raſp them with a raſp, or chip them with a knife, as you pleaſe. You may, if you think proper, break in two ounces of butter, when you work it up with the ſecond liquor.

To make Bread without Yeaſt, by the Means of a Leaven.

TAKE about two pounds of dough of your laſt making, which has been made with yeaſt; keep it in a wooden veſſel, and cover it well with flour. This is your leaven. The night before you intend to bake, put the leaven to a peck of flour, and work them well together with warm liquor. Let it lie in a dry wooden veſſel, well covered with a dry linen cloth, alſo a blanket over the cloth, and keep it in a warm place. This dough kept warm will riſe again the next morning, and will be ſufficient to mix with two or three buſhels of flour, being worked up with warm liqour, and a pound of ſalt to each buſhel of flour. When it is well worked up, and thoroughly mixed with all the flour, let it be well covered with wtih the linen and blanket, until you find it rise. Then knead it well, and work it up into loaves and bricks, making the loaves broad, and not so thick and high as is done for bread made with yeast. Then put it into your oven, and bake it as before directed. Always keep by you two pounds of the dough of your last baking, well covered with flour, to make leaven to serve from one baking day to another. The more leaven is put to the flour, the lighter and spongy the bread will be; and the fresher the leaven, the less sour will be the bread.

To make Muffins and Oat-Cakes.

PUT a bushel of Hertfordshire white flour into your trough, three gallons of milk-warm liquor, and mix in a quart of mild ale, or good small-beer yeast, and half a pound of salt. Stir it well about a quarter of an hour, then strain it into the flour, mix your dough as high as you can, and let it lie one hour to rise. Then with your hand roll it up, and pull it into little pieces as big as a large walnut. Roll them with your hand like a ball, lay them on a table, and as fast as you do them lay a flannel over them; and be sure to keep your dough covered with flannel. When you have rolled out all your dough, begin to bake the first, and by that time they will be spread out in the right form. Lay them on your plate, and as the bottom begins to change colour, turn them on the other side. Take great care that they do not burn. If the middle of your plate be too hot, put a brick or two into the middle of the fire to slacken the heat. The plate you bake on must be thus fixed. Build a place, as if you were going to build a copper, of a piece of cast iron, all over the top, fixed in form just the same as the bottom of a copper, or iron pot, and make your fire under with coal, as under a copper. Oat-cakes are made the

the ſame way, only uſe fine ſifted oatmeal inſtead of flour, and two gallons of water inſtead of three. When you pull them to pieces, roll them out with a rolling-pin with a good deal of flour, cover them with a piece of flannel, and they will riſe to a proper thickneſs; and, if you find them either too big or too little, you muſt roll your dough accordingly. Before you eat either muffins or oatcakes, toaſt them criſp on both ſides, but do not burn them. Then pull them open with your fingers, and they will be like a honey-comb. Lay in as much butter as you chooſe, then clap them together again, and put them before the fire; but uſe a knife only when you cut them into pieces. Some flour will take a quart more liquor than other flour; but practice will make theſe things familiar.

C H A P. XXXII.

The Breeding, Rearing, and Management of Poultry.

THE buſineſs of this chapter is certainly ſuch as is neceſſary to be known by every houſekeeper. Many families reſide in the country only for a limited time, while others make it their conſtant abode, and prefer the peace and tranquility of a country life to the noiſe and buſtle of the metropolis and other capital cities.

The firſt conſideration is the proper choice of ſuch fowls as are the beſt calculated for breeding. Thoſe of a middling age are the more proper for ſitting, and the younger for laying. Six hens to a cock is the uſual proportion; and, in order to make

make them familiar, feed them always at one place, and at a particular hour.

From two years old to five is the beſt age to ſet a hen, and the beſt month February, though any month will anſwer the purpoſe between that and Michaelmas. A hen ſits twenty days, and ducks and turkies thirty days.

In the mixture of fowls for breeding, the nature of the hen ſhould be as nearly equal as poſſible with that of the cock, and ſhe ſhould be vigilant and induſtrious both for herſelf and her chickens. Thoſe of the largeſt ſize are the beſt, and they muſt be in every reſpect proportioned to the cock, only, inſtead of a comb, ſhe ſhould have upon her crown a high tuft of feathers. Hens that crow are neither good breeders nor good layers. Never chooſe a hen that is fat, as ſhe will not anſwer the purpoſe of either ſitting or laying. If you ſet a fat hen, ſhe will forſake her neſt; the eggs ſhe lays will be without ſhells, and ſhe will grow ſlothful and indolent.

A hen lays the beſt eggs when ſhe is about a year and a half or two years old, at which time, if you would have large eggs, give them plenty of victuals, and ſometimes oats. To prevent your hens eating their own eggs, which they ſometimes will, lay a piece of chalk ſhaped like an egg in their way, at which they will often be pecking, and thus finding themſelves diſappointed, they will not afterwards attempt it. When you find your hens inclinable to ſet, which you will know by their clucking, do not diſappoint them, nor put more than ten eggs under each. It is a vulgar notion, and founded only in caprice, that a hen ſhould always be ſet with an odd egg, as nine, eleven, or thirteen.

The beſt time for ſetting a hen is in the month of February, when the moon has turned the full, that

ſhe

ſhe may diſcloſe the chickens in the increaſe of the next new moon; for a brood of this month is preferable to that of any other. Hens may, however, ſet from this time to October, and have good chickens till then, but not afterwards.

If you ſet a hen upon the eggs of ducks, geeſe, or turkies, you muſt ſet them nine days before you put her own eggs to her. Before you put the eggs under the hen, it will be neceſſary to make ſome particular mark on one ſide of them, and to obſerve whether ſhe turns them from that to the other; if ſhe does not, you muſt take the opportunity, when ſhe is off her neſt, to turn them yourſelf. Be careful that the eggs you ſet her with are new, which may be known by their being heavy, full, and clear. Do not chooſe the largeſt, as they ſometimes have two yolks, and in that caſe they will diſappoint you, as ſuch eggs cannot be good for any thing.

The hen muſt not be diſturbed while ſhe is ſitting, as that will make her entirely forſake her neſt. In order to prevent this, put her meat and water near her during the time ſhe is ſitting, that her eggs may not cool while ſhe is gone in queſt of food. If at any time ſhe is abſent from the neſt, ſtir up the ſtraw gently, make it ſoft, and lay the eggs in the ſame order you found them.

Your hen-houſe muſt be large and ſpacious, with a high roof, and ſtrong walls. There ſhould be windows on the eaſt ſide, that they may enjoy the benefit of the riſing ſun, and theſe muſt be ſtrongly lathed and cloſe ſhut. Round about the inſide of the walls, upon the ground, ſhould be made large pens, three feet high, for geeſe, ducks, and large fowls, to ſet in, and near the roof of the houſe ſhould be long perches, reaching from one ſide to the other. At one ſide of the houſe, at the darkeſt part, over the ground pens, ſhould be placed ſeve-

ral

ral ſmall hampers of ſtraw, not only for the uſe of the fowls to make their neſts, but likewiſe for them to lay their eggs in; but when they ſit to hatch chickens, let them ſit on the ground. There muſt be pins ſtuck in different parts of the walls, for the convenience of the fowls getting up to their perches.

The floor of the hen-houſe muſt not be paved, but made of earth quite ſmooth. A hole ſhould be made at one end for the ſmaller fowls to go in and come out at when they pleaſe, otherwiſe they will ſeek out rooſt in other places; but, for the larger fowls, you may open the door every night and morning.

One eſſential point is to keep your hen-houſe free from vermin, and contrive your perches ſo as not to be over each other. Wherever poultry is kept, various kinds of vermin will naturally come; for which reaſon it will be proper to ſow wormwood and rice about your hen-houſe. You may alſo boil wormwood, and ſprinkle the floor with the liquor, which will not only contribute to keep away vermin, but alſo aſſiſt much to keep your poultry in health.

When your chickens are hatched, if any are weaker then the reſt, wrap them in wool, and let them receive the benefit of the fire. The chickens firſt hatched may be kept in a deepiſh ſieve till the reſt are diſcloſed, for they will not eat for two days. Some ſhells being harder than others, they will require ſo much more time in opening; but unleſs the chickens are weak, or the hen unkind, it will not be improper to let them continue under her, as they will thereby receive the greater nouriſhment.

When the chickens have been hatched two days, give them very ſmall oatmeal, ſome dry, and ſome ſteeped in milk, or elſe crumbs of white bread.

When

When they have gained ſtrength, you may give them curds, cheeſe parings, white bread, cruſts ſoaked in milk, or the like ſoft meat that is ſmall, and will be eaſily digeſted. They muſt be kept in the houſe a fortnight, before they are ſuffered to go abroad with the hen. Take care that their water is quite clean, for if it be dirty it will perhaps give them the pip.

In order to fatten your chickens, confine them in coops, and feed them with barley meal. Put a ſmall quantity of brick-duſt with their water, which will not only give them an appetite to their meat, but will facilitate their fattening. All fowls, and other birds, have two ſtomachs: the one is their crop, which ſoftens their food, and the other their gizzard, which macerates it. In the laſt are generally found ſmall ſtones and ſharp bits of ſand, which help to do that office, and without them, or ſomething of that kind, a fowl will be wanting of its appetite; for the gizzard cannot macerate or grind the food faſt enough to diſcharge it from the crop without ſuch aſſiſtance, and therefore, in this caſe, the brick-duſt thrown into the water is of great ſervice.

Sitting hens are ſometimes troubled with lice and vermin, for the cure of which, waſh them with a decoction of wild lupines. Fowls in general are ſubject to a diſorder called the pip, which ariſes from a white thin ſcale growing on the tip of the tongue, and will prevent their feeding. This is eaſily diſcerned, and generally proceeds from drinking puddle water, or want of water, or eating filthy food. This, however, may be cured, by pulling off the ſcale with your nail, and then rubbing the tongue with ſalt.

Ducks.

Ducks.

FEBRUARY is the month in which ducks begin to lay; and if your gardener be diligent in picking up ſnails, grubs, caterpillers, worms, and other inſects, and lay them in one place, it will make your ducks familiar, and is the beſt food they can have for a change. If parſley be ſown about the ponds they frequent, it will give their fleſh an agreeable taſte; and be ſure always to have one certain place for them to retire to at night. Partition off their neſts, and make them as near the water as poſſible. Always feed them there, as it will make them love home; for ducks are very apt to ramble.

You muſt every day take away their eggs till you find them inclined to ſit, and then leave them in the place where they have laid them. Little attendance is required while they ſit, except to let them have ſome barley or offal corn and water near them, that they may not hurt their eggs by ſtraggling from the neſt.

It is much better, in winter time, to ſet a hen upon the duck eggs, than any kind of duck whatever; becauſe the latter will lead them, when hatched, too ſoon to the water, where, if the weather be cold, ſome of them will very likely be loſt. The number of eggs to ſet a duck on is about twelve or thirteen. The hen will cover as many of theſe as of her own, and will bring them up as carefully.

If the weather be tolerably moderate at the time the ducklings be hatched, they will require very little attendance; but if they happen to be produced in a wet ſeaſon, it will be neceſſary to take them under cover, eſpecially during night; for though a duck naturally loves water, it requires the aſſiſtance of of its feathers, and is eaſily hurt by the wet till it is ſtrengthened by age.

Ducks are fattened in the ſame manner, let their age be what it will. They muſt be put into a retired place, and kept in a pen, where they muſt have plenty of corn and water. Any ſort of corn will anſwer the purpoſe, and by this treatment alone, in a fortnight or three weeks, they will ſufficiently fatten themſelves.

Geeſe.

GEESE require very little attendance or expence, as they will live upon commons, or any ſort of paſture, provided they have plenty of water. The largeſt geeſe are the moſt eſteemed, and they ſhould be either of a white or grey colour, as the pyed are not ſo profitable, and the darker coloured are the leaſt in eſteem.

A gooſe generally ſits thirty days; but, if the weather be fair and warm, ſhe will hatch three or four days ſooner. She muſt be carefully ſupplied with food, ſuch as ſhag oats and bran ſcalded. When the goſlings are hatched, you muſt keep them in the houſe ten or twelve days, and feed them with curds, barley meal, bran, and ſuch like food. One gander is a proper proportion for four or five geeſe.

In order to fatten green geeſe, you muſt ſhut them up when they are about a month old, and they will be fat in about a month more. Older geeſe are fattened when they are about ſix months old, in or after harveſt, when they have been in the ſtubble fields, from which food ſome kill them; but thoſe who are deſirous of having them very fat, ſhut them up for a fortnight or three weeks, and feed them upon oats, ſplit beans, barley meal, or ground malt mixed with milk.

Turkies.

THESE birds are of a very tender conſtitution, and, while young, muſt be carefully watched and kept warm; for the hens are ſo negligent, that while they have one to follow them, they will never take any care of the reſt. Turkies are great feeders on corn, and, if kept on it, will conſume a prodigious quantity; but, if left to their own liberty when grown up, they will get their own living, by feeding on herbs, ſeeds, and what they can pick up.

As they are very apt to wander, they will often lay their eggs in ſecret places, and in courſe muſt be well watched, and compelled to lay at home. They begin to lay in March, and will ſit in April; but they muſt not have more than twelve eggs put under them.

Having hatched their brood, which will be in twenty-five or thirty days, you muſt take great care to keep the young ones warm, as the leaſt cold will kill them. They muſt be fed either with curds, or green freſh cheeſe cut in ſmall pieces, and their drink muſt be new milk, or milk and water. They muſt be often fed, for the hen will not take much care of them, and when they have got ſome ſtrength, feed them in the open air in a cloſe-walled place, from whence they cannot wander. You muſt not let them out till the dew be off the graſs, taking care to have them in again before night, the dew being very prejudicial to their health.

When you intend to fatten turkies, give them ſodden barley or ſodden oats for the firſt fortnight, and for another fortnight cram them with the following. Take a quantity of barley meal properly ſifted, and mix it with new milk. Make it into a good ſtiff dough paſte; then make it into long crams or rolls, big in the middle, and ſmall at both

both ends. Then wet them in lukewarm milk, give the turkey a full gorge three times a day, morning, noon, and night, and in a fortnight it will be ſufficiently fattened.

Pigeons.

MAY or Auguſt are the beſt months to provide yourſelf with pigeons, as at thoſe times they are young and in good condition. Tame pigeons generally produce but two young ones at a brood; but they make ſome amends for the ſmallneſs of the number by the frequency of their hatching: if they be well fed, and properly looked after, they will have young ones twelve or thirteen times in a year.

Though they make a great deal of dirt, yet they are not fond of it, and muſt therefore be kept clean. Their beſt food is tares, or white peas, and they ſhould have ſome gravel ſcattered about their houſe, and clean water ſet in different places. They muſt be carefully preſerved from vermin, and their neſts from the ſtarlings and other birds, as the latter will ſuck their eggs, and the former entirely deſtroy them. The common, or dovecote pigeon, has the advantage of many other kinds, as they are very hardy, and will live in the ſevereſt weather. If the breed ſhould be too ſmall, it may be mended by putting in a few tame pigeons of the moſt common kind, and the leaſt conſpicuous in their colours, that the reſt may the better take to them from their being more like themſelves. Good management is required in proportioning the ſexes among pigeons; for there is nothing ſo hurtful as having too many cocks, eſpecially if you keep the larger or tame kind. An abundance of cocks will thin the dovecote; for they will grow quarrelſome, and beat others away, ſo that a good dovecote mav be thereby ſpoiled.

The

The beſt and moſt eaſy method of making a dovecote, is to build the walls with clay mixed with ſtraw. They may be made four feet or more in thickneſs, and while they are wet it is eaſy to cut holes in them with a chiſſel or other inſtrument. But of whatever materials the cote is erected, it ſhould be frequently white-waſhed on the outſide, which will make the building more conſpicuous.

As pigeons are very fond of ſalt, they ſhould have a large heap of clay laid near the dovecote, and let the brine done with in the family be frequently beaten among it. It is beſt to make it thin, and keep it ſo by often mixing brine with it. The uſe of ſalt is of much more advantage to pigeons than merely the pleaſing them, for nothing will recover them ſo readily from ſickneſs, a mixture of bay ſalt and cummin-ſeed being with them an univerſal remedy for moſt diſeaſes they are ſubject to.

Pigeons are ſometimes apt to be ſcabby on the backs and breaſts, which will kill the young, and make the old ones ſo faint, that they cannot take their flights. In order to remove this diſorder, take a quartern of bay-ſalt, and as much common ſalt, a pound of fennel ſeed, a pound of dill-ſeed, as much cummin-ſeed, and an ounce or two of aſſafætida; mix all theſe together with a little wheat flour, and ſome fine worked clay. When it is well beaten together, put it into two pots, and bake them in an oven. When they are cold, lay them longways on the ſtand or table in the dovehouſe, and the pigeons will ſoon be cured by pecking it.

Rabbits.

FEW animals are more fertile than tame rabbits, bringing forth young every month. As ſoon as the doe has kindled, ſhe muſt be put to the buck, otherwiſe ſhe will deſtroy her young. The beſt food for them is the ſweeteſt hay, oats and bran, ſowthiſtle,

ſowthiſtle, parſley, cabbage leaves, and ſuch like, always freſh. They muſt be carefully kept clean, otherwiſe they will not only poiſon themſelves, but every one who comes near them.

CHAP. XXXIII.

The Management of the Dairy.

THE dairy requires a great ſhare of care and attention, of which cleanlineſs is not the leaſt. As its productions are eſſentially neceſſary in a family, the houſekeeper ſhould entruſt the care of it to one, who is well converſant in thoſe matters; and that the houſekeeper may judge when things are done properly, we ſhall proceed to deſcribe the moſt eſſential points.

Next to obſerving that every thing is perfectly clean and neat, the cows muſt be milked at a regular hour; for the detention of the milk will not only contribute to ſpoil the cows, but keep the animals in great pain. They ſhould not be milked later than five in the evening, that they may have time to fill their bags by the next morning, and their udders ſhould always be properly emptied every time they are milked.

As ſoon as the milk is brought into the dairy, it ſhould be well ſtrained, and emptied into clean pans. White ware pans are the beſt, as they are of a ſuperior cleanlineſs, the brown ſort being very porous, and ſcarcely any ſcalding will be ſufficient properly to cleanſe them.

To

To make Butter.

BUTTER cannot be wholeſome unleſs it be very freſh, and free from rancidity, otherwiſe it will hurt digeſtion, render it difficult and painful, and introduce much acrimony into the blood. As ſoon as you have churned your butter, open the churn, and with both hands gather it well together, take it out of the butter-milk, and lay it in a very clean bowl, or earthen pan. If the butter is deſigned to be uſed freſh, fill the pan with clear water, and work the butter in it to and fro, till it is brought to a firm conſiſtence of itſelf, without any moiſture. When you have done this, ſcotch and ſlice it over with the point of a knife, every way as thick as poſſible, in order to draw out the ſmalleſt hair, bit of rag, ſtrainer, or any thing that may have happened to fall into it. Then ſpread it thin in a bowl, and work it well together with ſuch a quantity of ſalt as you think fit, and then make it up in what form you like beſt.

If the milk of any cow ſhould happen to be foul and corrupt, owing to the teats being injured by ſome accident, it muſt by no means be mixed with the ſweet milk, but given to the pigs. In the hot ſummer months, the cream ſhould be ſkimmed from the milk before the dairy gets warm from the influence of the ſun; nor ſhould the milk at that ſeaſon ſtand longer in the pans than twenty-four hours, nor be ſkimmed in the evening till after ſun-ſet. In winter, milk may remain unſkimmed for thirty-ſix or forty-eight hours.

The cream ſhould be depoſited in a deep pan, which ſhould be kept, during the ſummer, in the cooleſt part of the dairy, or in a cool cellar, where a free air is admitted, which is much better. You muſt not omit to churn at leaſt twice a week in the hot weather, and this buſineſs ſhould be done very

early

early in the morning, taking care to fix the churn in a free draught of air.

More labour will be required to churn butter in winter than in ſummer. The butter-milk, which remains after the butter is churned, is eſteemed excellent food in ſpring for thoſe who are inclined to be conſumptive.

To make Cheeſe.

CHEESE differs in quality according to the manner in which it is made. It may be made from new or ſkimmed milk, from the curd which ſeparates of itſelf upon ſtanding, or that which is more ſpeedily produced by the addition of rennet. In making cheeſe, as ſoon as the milk is turned, ſtrain the whey carefully from the curd. Break the curd well with your hands, and when it is equally broken, put it by degrees into the vat, carefully breaking it as you put it in. The vat ſhould be filled an inch or more above the brim, that when the whey is preſſed out, it may not ſhrink below the brim; for, in that caſe, the cheeſe will be ſpoiled. But before the curd be put in, a cheeſe-cloth or ſtrainer ſhould be laid at the bottom of the vat; and this ſhould be ſo large, that when the vat is filled with the curd, the end of the cloth may turn again over the top of it.

When this is done, it ſhould be taken to the preſs, and there remain for the ſpace of two hours. It ſhould then be turned, and have a clean cloth put under it, and turned over as before. It muſt then be preſſed again, and remain in the preſs ſix or eight hours, when it ſhould again be turned, and rubbed on each ſide with ſalt. After this it muſt be preſſed again for the ſpace of twelve or fourteen hours more, when, if any of the edges project, they ſhould be pared off. It may then be put on a dry board, and regularly turned every day.

The beſt method of preparing the rennet is as follows. Take the maw or rennet-bag of a calf, and take care that it be perfectly ſweet; for if it be the leaſt tainted, the cheeſe can never be good. Take three pints or two quarts of ſoft water, clean and ſweet, put into it ſome ſalt, ſome ſweet-briar, roſe-leaves, cinnamon, mace, cloves, and almoſt every ſort of ſpice and aromatic that can be procured. Boil theſe gently in two quarts of water till the liquor is reduced to three pints, and be careful it is not ſmoaked. Strain the liquor clear from the ſpices, &c. and when it has ſtood till it is no warmer than milk from the cow, pour it upon the calf's maw. You may then ſlice a lemon in it, and let it ſtand a day or two; after which it muſt be again ſtrained, and then put into a bottle. Cork it quite cloſe, and it will keep good a twelvemonth. It will ſmell like perfume, and a ſmall quantity of it will turn the milk, and give the cheeſe a pleaſing flavour.

To make Cream Cheeſe.

PUT twelve quarts of new milk and a quart of cream together, with rennet juſt ſufficient to turn it, and let the milk and cream be juſt warm. When it has ſtood till the curd has come, lay a cloth in the vat, which muſt be made of a ſize proportionate to the cheeſe. Cut out the curd with a ſkimming-diſh, and put it into the vat till it is full, turning the cheeſe-cloth over it, and as the curd ſettles, lay more on, till you have laid on as much as will make one cheeſe. When the whey is drained out, turn the cheeſe into a dry cloth, and then lay upon it a pound weight. At night turn it out into another cloth, and the next morning ſalt it a little. Then having made a bed of nettles or

aſh-leaves

ash-leaves to lay it on, cover it with the same, shifting it twice a day, for about ten days, when it may be brought to table.

To make Sage Cheese.

TAKE the tops of young red sage, and bruise them in a mortar, till you can press the juice out of them. Bruise likewise some leaves of spinach, and having squeezed out the juice, mix it with that of the sage, in order to give it an agreeable green colour, which the juice of the sage alone will not accomplish, and this will also contribute to deprive the sage of its bitter taste.

The juice being thus prepared, put the rennet to the milk, and at the same time mix it with as much of the sage and spinach juice as will give the milk the green colour you desire, putting in more or less, according as you would have the cheese taste stronger or weaker of the sage. When the curd is come, break it gently, and when it is all equally broken, put it into the cheese vat or mote, and press it gently, which will make it eat tender and mellow. When it has stood in the press about eight hours, it must be salted, turned every day, and in about a month it will be fit for use.

To make Marygold Cheese.

POUND in a mortar some of the freshest and best coloured marygold leaves you can procure, and strain out the juice. Put this into your milk at the same time you put in the rennet, and stir them together. The milk being set, and the curd come, break it as gently and as equally as you possibly can, put it into the cheese vat, and press it with a gentle weight, there being at the bottom of the vat a number of holes sufficient easily to let out the whey. The management afterwards must be the same as with other cheeses.

To imitate Cheſhire Cheeſe.

THE milk being ſet, and the curd being come, do not break it with a diſh, as is cuſtomary in making other cheeſes, but draw it together with your hands to one ſide of the veſſel, breaking it gently and regularly; for if it be preſſed roughly, a great deal of the richneſs of the milk will go into the whey. Put the curd into the cheeſe vat or mote as you gather it, and when it is full, ſalt it at different times, and preſs it and turn it often.

The thickneſs of theſe cheeſes muſt be about ſeven or eight inches, and they will be fit to cut in about twelve months. You muſt turn and ſhift them frequently upon a ſhelf, and rub them with a dry coarſe cloth. At the year's end, you may bore a hole in the middle, and pour in a quarter of a pint of ſack, then ſtop the hole cloſe with ſome of the ſame cheeſe, and ſet it in a wine cellar for ſix months to mellow; at the expiration of which you will find the ſack all loſt, and the hole in a manner cloſed up. If this cheeſe be properly managed, its flavour will be pleaſant and grateful, and it will eat exceedingly fine and rich.

CHAP. XXXIV.

The Management of the Kitchen Garden.

THOUGH the buſineſs to be done in the Kitchen and Fruit Gardens do not fall to the lot of the houſekeeper, yet it is abſolutely neceſſary that ſhe ſhould know what is to be expected from the gardener, that the family may be regularly

regularly ſupplied with thoſe vegetables and fruits the different months of the year produce. We will venture to affirm, that, by the aſſiſtance of the few following pages, the houſekeeper will be enabled to give ſuch directions, as will fully anſwer her purpoſe, in ſupplying the kitchen, every month of the year, with every neceſſary ſpecies of the vegetable creation. To thoſe ſmall families, where the garden is made a principal amuſement, as well from ſaving principles, as for the promotion and preſervation of health, the following remarks will be of ſingular utility. We ſhall treat the buſineſs of every month ſeparately, with all the ſimplicity and perſpicuity the nature of the ſubject, and the limits of this work, will admit of.

January.

VEGETATION makes very little progreſs in the garden during this month; but there are now many things neceſſary to be attended to for the production of vegetables in the ſucceeding months. Sowing and planting may now be moderately performed, ſome in natural grounds, and ſome in hot-beds. Radiſhes, ſpinach, lettuce, carrots, peas, beans, parſley, cauliflowers, cabbages, muſhrooms, kidney-beans, aſparagus, ſmall ſallading, &c. Theſe may be ſown in natural grounds, but muſt be in the warmeſt corners, and gently covered every night with warm mats, and, when the weather is ſevere, they muſt likewiſe be covered in the day.

Cucumbers may be ſown in a hot-bed any time this month, to produce early fruit in March, April, and May. For this purpoſe be well prepared with hot dung. Make the hot-bed a yard high, for one or two light frames, and earth it ſix inches thick with rich mould. Sow ſome early prickly cucumber-ſeed half an inch deep, and when the plants have come up, and the ſeed leaves

leaves are half an inch broad, prick them in ſmall pots, four in each, and put them into the earth of the hot-bed, obſerving from the beginning to have proper air by tilting the lights at top, one or two fingers breadth. Cover the glaſſes every night with mats, give them occaſionally watering, and, when you find the heat of the bed decreaſed, line the ſides of it with hot dung. When your cucumbers are advanced in growth, with the rough or proper leaves, one or two inches broad, tranſplant them to a larger hot-bed, there to remain for fruiting.

Earth up your full-grown crops of celery, and tie up ſome of your endive every week to blanch. Towards the latter end of the month, ſow a little carrot-ſeed, and plant horſe-radiſh, by cuttings from the off-ſet roots of the old ones. Set them in rows two feet diſtant, and about fifteen inches deep, that they may obtain long ſtrait ſhoots. Artichokes muſt now be earthed up, digging between them, and laying the earth along the rows cloſe about the plants.

Radiſhes, and other tender plants, ſown in borders, muſt be conſtantly covered with ſtraw till they come up, and afterwards every night, eſpecially if the weather be froſty.

February.

MUCH attention muſt be paid to the kitchen garden this month, it being the commencement of the early efforts of vegetation. All the vacant ground muſt now be dunged, digged, and trenched, and made ready for ſowing and planting.

On ſouth borders, ſow early crops, and ſome main crops in the open quarters, ſuch as radiſhes, peas, beans, ſpinach, lettuce, onions, leeks, cabbages, carrots, parſnips, beets, coleworts, ſavoys, brocoli, ſmall ſallading, parſley, chervil, borrage, fennel,

fennel, dill, marygolds, burnet, clary, creffes, muftard, rape, &c.

Sow full crops of peas at the beginning, and towards the latter end of the month, of the beft bearers, or fuch as are moft efteemed. Alfo beans, of different forts, in rows, a yard diftant from each other. Sow cauliflower-feeds in a hot-bed, or in a warm border, or under a frame, to plant out in April or May, to fucceed the winter plants.

If the weather be mild, begin fowing the firft main crop of carrots, in an open fituation, in light rich ground trenched two fpades deep, fcatter the feed moderately thin, and rake it in regularly. Sow alfo parfnips, onions, leeks, fpinach, and beet.

Tranfplant fome of the ftrongeft cabbage plants into an open quarter of good ground, in rows, one, two, and three feet diftant, to cut young, and at half and full growth. Plant cabbage plants of the fugar-loaf and early kinds, in rows a foot diftant.

Sow parfley for a main crop, both of the plain leaved and curled forts, either in a fingle drill, along the edge of borders or quarters, or in continued drills eight or nine inches afunder.

Give air to plants in hot-beds, as alfo thofe under frames and glaffes, by either tilting the glaffes two or three inches, or, on mild and dry days, drawing them up or down half way; but cover them up again towards night.

March.

THIS is a bufy month, in which all dunging, digging, and trenching, fhould be completed. Now prepare for the main crops of onions, leeks, carrots, parfnips, red beet, green beet, white beet, fpinach, lettuce, cabbage, favoys, cauliflowers, brocoli, borecole, colewort, afparagus, beans, peas, kidney-

kidney-beans, turnips, parſley, celery, turnip-cabbage, turnip radiſh; and of ſallads and ſweet herbs, creſſes, muſtard, rape, radiſh, marjorum, naſturtium, borrage, marygolds, chervil, thyme, ſavory, coriander, corn ſallad, clary, fennel, angelica, dill, and ſome others.

Great care ſhould be taken that the ſeeds are quite freſh, which is a matter of great importance, and for want of which many are diſappointed in their principal crops, when too late to ſow again. When you ſow your different crops, let it be in dry weather, and while the ground is freſh dug, or levelled down, or when it will admit of raking freely without clogging.

Cauliflower plants, that have ſtood the winter in frames or borders, ſhould now be planted out, if the weather be mild, in well-dunged ground, two feet and a half diſtant, and draw earth to thoſe remaining under the glaſſes. Give air to theſe, and your melon and cucumber plants; but cover the glaſſes every night with mats.

Towards the end of this month, plant potatoes for a full crop, in lightiſh good ground, ſome of the early kind for a forward crop in ſummer, and a large portion of the common ſorts for the general autumn and winter crops. Plant your main crop of ſhalot by off-ſets, or the ſmall or full roots, ſet in beds ſix inches apart. Sow a ſucceſſional and full crop of ſpinach twice this month, of the round-leaved kind, in an open ſituation; or it may be ſown occaſionally between two rows of beans, cabbages, cauliflowers, horſeradiſh, artichokes, &c.

As this month the weeds will begin to ſpring up apace, you muſt be careful to deſtroy them either by hand or hoe, or they will ruin all your crops.

April

April.

IF you omitted to finiſh your planting or ſowing at the latter end of laſt month, do it at the beginning of this. Sow the main crop of the red and green borecole, in an open ſituation, to plant out in May and June, for autumn, winter, and the ſupply of the following ſpring. Sow likewiſe ſome of the purple and cauliflower ſorts of brocoli, to plant out in ſummer, for the firſt general autumn crop.

Kidney beans of the early dwarf kinds ſhould now be ſown in a warm border, as alſo ſome ſpeckled dwarfs, and a large ſupply in the open quarters, in drills two feet, or two and a half diſtant. Sow different kinds of lettuce two or three times this month, for ſucceeding crops.

Great care muſt now be taken of your melons in hot beds. Train the vine regular, give them air daily, with occaſional moderate waterings. Cover the glaſſes every night, and keep up a good heat in the beds, by linings of hot dung.

Sow full crops of peas for a ſucceſſion of marrowfats once a fortnight, and alſo of other large kinds. Sow the ſeed for all ſorts of pot-herbs, and plant aromatic herbs, ſuch as mint, ſage, balm, rue, roſemary, lavender, and ſuch like, either by young or full plants.

Continue ſowing ſucceſſional crops of radiſhes every fortnight, in open ſituations, in order to have an eligible variety, young and plentiful. Sow a principal crop of ſavoys in an open ſituation, detached from walls, hedges, or any other impediment, that the plants may be ſtrong and robuſt for planting out in ſummer, to furniſh a full crop well cabbaged in autumn, and for the general winter ſupply, till next ſpring, this being a moſt valuable cabbage in autumn and winter.

May.

May.

TO ſow and plant ſeveral ſucceſſion crops of plants that are of ſhort duration, and others of a more durable ſtate, is the principal buſineſs of this month. Weeding, hoeing, and watering, muſt now be properly attended to. Top your early beans that are in bloom; alſo the ſucceeding crops as they come in flower, to make the pods ſet ſoon and fine.

Thin your carrots, and cleanſe them from weeds, either by hand-weeding or ſmall hoeing, leaving thoſe intended to draw young in ſummer four or five inches apart, but the main crops muſt be thinned ſix or eight inches. Likewiſe hoe between your cauliflowers, and draw the earth to their ſtems. Alſo between rows of beans, peas, kidney-beans, and oll other plants in rows.

Thin the ſpring-ſowed crop of lettuces, and plant out proper ſupplies of the different ſorts at a foot diſtance. Weed the ſpring-ſowed crop of onions, and thin them where too thick. Continue ſowing once a fortnight marrowfats, and other large kinds of peas; alſo ſome of the beſt hotſpurs, or other ſorts in eſteem, to furniſh a regular ſucceſſion of the different kinds. You may likewiſe continue to ſow radiſhes in open ſituations, once a week or fortnight, in moderate quantities, for ſucceſſion crops this and the following month.

Sow ſallading of the different ſorts, as lettuce, creſſes, muſtard, radiſh, rape, and purſlane, to have a proper ſucceſſion to cut while young. Plant out ſome of the ſtrongeſt early ſavoy plants, in an open ſituation, two feet and a half aſunder, for autumn and winter. Continue to ſow ſome round-leaved ſpinach in open ſituations.

Moſt new-planted crops will now require frequent watering, both at planting, and occaſionally fionally afterwards in dry weather, till they have taken root. Alfo water the feed-beds of fmall crops lately fowed, or young plants, in very dry weather. Your weeding muft be very diligently attended to both by hand and hoe; for as weeds will be advancing numeroufly among all crops, it will become a principal bufinefs to eradicate them before they fpread too far. Nothing is a greater difcredit to a gardener than to have his ground over-run with weeds.

June.

MANY fucceffional and main crops muft ftill be fown or planted for autumn and winter; and as to the crops now advancing, or in perfection, the bufinefs of hoeing, weeding, and occafional watering, will demand no fmall fhare of attention.

In the open ground plant cabbage, brocoli, borecole, favoys, coleworts, celery, endive, lettuce, cauliflowers, leeks, beans, kidney-beans, and various aromatic and pot herbs, by flips, cuttings, or young plants. Showery weather is by far the beft either for fowing or planting; and when it occurs, lofe no time in putting in the neceffary crops wanting.

Hoe your artichokes, and keep your afparagus beds very clean from weeds. Plant fucceffional crops of beans in the beginning, middle, and latter end of this month, fome Windfors, long pods, white bloffom, and Mumford kinds.

The firft main crops of celery muft now be planted in trenches to blanch. The trenches to be three feet diftance, a foot wide, and dig the earth out a fpade deep, laying it equally to each fide in a level order. Then dig the bottom, and if poor, add rotten dung, and dig it in. Draw up fome of the ftrongeft plants, trim the long roots and tops, plant a row along the bottom of each trench four or five inches diſtance, and finiſh with a good watering.

Every day give plenty of air to the cucumbers in hot beds, and water them two or three times a week, or oftener, if the weather be hot; but ſtill continue the glaſſes over them all this month. Shade them from the mid-day ſun, and ſtill cover them on nights with mats. In the beginning of the month, ſow a full crop of them in the natural ground to produce picklers, and for other late purpoſes in autumn.

Sow the main crops of the green curled endive, alſo a ſmall ſupply of the white curled, and large Batavia endive; each thin in open ground, to plant out for autumn and winter. Sow more marrowfat peas, and ſome hotſpurs or rouncivals, and other large kinds. Hoe your potatoes, looſen the ground, and draw the earth to the bottom of the plants.

Thin all cloſe crops now remaining to tranſplant at proper diſtances. Many ſorts will now require it, as carrots, parſnips, onions, and ſuch like; all which may be done by hand or ſmall hoeing.

July.

THE buſineſs of ſowing and planting this month will be more ſucceſsful if done in moiſt or ſhowery weather; or on the approach of rain, or immediately after, eſpecially for ſmall ſeeds, and young ſeedling plants. Several ſucceſſional crops are required to be ſown this month for the ſupply of autumn, and ſome main crops for winter conſumption. Many principal crops will now be arrived to full perfection, and ſome mature crops all gathered. When the latter is the caſe, the ground ſhould be cleared for ſucceeding crops, or for ſome general autumn and winter crops, as turnips, cabbages, ſavoys, brocoli, celery, and ſeveral other articles of that claſs.

This

This is the time to gather aromatic herbs, for drying and diſtilling, as ſpearmint, peppermint, balm, pennyroyal, and ſuch like, moſt of which, when juſt coming into flower, are in beſt perfection for gathering. The fennel, dill, and angelica, ſhould remain till they are in ſeed.

Plant the laſt crop of beans, for the late production in autumn. Let them be of the ſmaller kind, as they are moſt ſucceſsful in late planting, ſuch as white bloſſom, green nonpareils, ſmall long pods, &c. putting in a few at two or three different times in the month; and alſo ſome larger kinds, to have the greater chance of ſucceſs and variety. If it be dry weather, ſoak the beans in ſoft water ſix or eight hours, plant them thin, and water the ground along the rows.

Plant a main crop of the purple and white brocoli, in good ground, two feet and a half aſunder, to produce full heads the end of autumn and the following ſpring. Cauliflowers, that were ſown in May, muſt be now planted out in rich ground, two feet and a half diſtant from each other for the Michaelmas or autumn and winter crop. Earth up celery plants to blanch; alſo the ſtems of young cabbages, ſavoys, brocoli, borecole, beans, peas, kidney beans, &c. to ſtrengthen their growth.

Sow the principal late crops of kidney beans, of the dwarf kind, for autumn ſupply, and more for later ſucceſſional production in September, &c. Sow them all in drills at two feet or two feet and a half diſtance. If the weather be very hot and dry, either ſoak the beans, or water the drills well before you ſow them. Continue to plant out different ſorts of lettuces at a foot or fifteen inches diſtance from each other. Plant them in ſmall ſhallow drills, to preſerve the moiſture longer, and water them well at the time you plant them.

Dig

Dig up ſome of the early crops of potatoes for uſe, but take no more at a time than is wanted; for, as they are not at their full growth, they will keep but a few days. Radiſhes may be ſown for an autumn crop to draw next month.

Auguſt.

IN the courſe of this month you muſt ſow the winter and the next ſpring and early ſummer crops, as cabbages, cauliflowers, onions, carrots, ſpinach, and ſome principal crops planted for late autumn and winter ſupplies. All new planted articles muſt be watered, and due attention paid to the deſtruction of the weeds before they grow large or come to ſeed.

Artichokes will now be in full perfection. Earth up the former planted crops of celery, repeating it every week according as the plants advance in growth. Cucumbers in frames may now be fully expoſed by removing the glaſſes. Picklers, or thoſe in the open ground, will now be in full perfection. Gather thoſe for pickling while young two or three times a week. Daily water the plants, while the weather continues hot; and in dry weather, hoe various crops in rows, to kill weeds, looſening the earth about, and drawing ſome to the ſtems of the plants to encourage their growth.

Onions being now full bulbed, and come to their mature growth, ſhould be pulled up in dry weather, and ſpread in the full ſun to dry and harden, for a week or fortnight, frequently turning them to ripen and harden for keeping. Then clear them from the groſs part of the ſtalks and leaves, bottom fibres, any looſe ſkins, earth, &c. and then houſe them on a dry day.

Sow winter onions both of the common bulbing and Welch kinds, for the main crops to ſtand the winter, to draw young and green, ſome for uſe in

that

that ſeaſon, but principally for ſpring ſupply; and ſome of the common onions alſo to ſtand for early bulbing in ſummer. The common onion is mildeſt to eat, but more liable to be cut off by the froſt than the Welch onion. This never bulbs, and is of a ſtronger hot taſte than the other, but is ſo hardy as to ſtand the ſevereſt weather.

Sow an autumn crop of radiſhes, both of the common ſhort top and ſalmon kinds. Likewiſe turnip-radiſhes, both of the ſmall white, and the red, for autumn, and the principal crop of black Spaniſh for winter.

The prickly-ſeeded, or triangular leaved ſpinach, muſt now be ſown, for the main winter crop, and for next ſpring, that ſort being the hardieſt to ſtand the winter. Sow ſome in the beginning, but none towards the latter end of the month, in dry-lying rich ground expoſed to the winter ſun.

Gather ripe ſeeds in dry weather, when at full maturity, and beginning to harden. Cut up or detach the ſtalks with the ſeeds thereon, and place them on a ſpot, where the ſun has the greateſt power, for a week or two. Then beat or rub out the ſmall ſeeds on cloths, ſpread them in the ſun to harden, then cleanſe them, and put them by for uſe.

September.

WITH this month muſt end all the principal ſowing and planting neceſſary this year, ſome for ſucceſſional ſupply the preſent autumn and beginning of winter, others for general winter ſervice, and ſome to ſtand the winter for next ſpring and ſummer.

Artichokes require no particular culture now, but only to break down the fruit ſtem cloſe, according as the fruit is gathered, and hoe down the weeds among them. Aſparagus now requires only

only the large weeds cleared out till next month, when the ſtalks muſt be cut down, and the beds winter dreſſed. Cauliflowers of laſt month's ſowing, intended for next year's early and main ſummer crops, ſhould now be pricked out in beds, three or four inches diſtance, watered, and to remain to October, then ſome of them to be planted out under hand-glaſſes, &c.

Plant out more celery in trenches, and earth up all former planted crops, repeating it once a week, two, three, or four inches high or more. Plant out likewiſe full crops of the two laſt months ſowing of coleworts, a foot diſtance, for winter and ſpring ſupply. Alſo endive for ſucceſſional crops, in a dry warm ſituation, a foot diſtance.

Potatoes will now be advanced to tolerable perfection for taking up in larger ſupplies than heretofore, but not any general quantity for keeping; for they will continue improving in growth till the latter end of next month.

Muſhroom beds muſt now be made for the principal ſupply at the end of autumn and winter, this being a proper ſeaſon for obtaining plenty of good ſpawn, which is found in all places where horſe dung and litter has been of any long continuance, and moderately dry, as in horſe-rides, under cover in livery ſtable yards, in horſe-mill tracks, where horſes are employed in manufactories, &c. in working machines and mills under cover, and under old hay-ſtacks; in all which places the ſpawn is found in cakes or lumps, abounding with ſmall white fibres, which is the ſpawn. The bed muſt be thus formed and ſituated: Mole it in a dry ſheltered ſituation in the full heat of the ſun. Let it be four or five feet wide at bottom, in length from ten, twenty, or thirty, to forty or fifty feet or more, and four or five feet high, narrowing on each

each ſide gradually till they meet at top in form of the roof of a houſe, that it may more readily ſhoot off the falling wet, and keep it in a dryiſh temperature. In a fortnight or three weeks, more or leſs, when the great heat of the bed is reduced, and become of a very moderate warmth, the ſpawn is then to be planted, in ſmall lumps, inſerted into both ſides of the bed juſt within the dung, five or ſix inches diſtance, quite from bottom to top, beating it down ſmoothly with the back of a ſpade, then earth the ſurface of the bed all over with fine light mould, an inch or two thick. Cover it with dry ſtraw or litter, after it has ſtood a week, to defend the top from rain. Let it be covered only half a foot thick at firſt, and increaſe it by degrees till it is double that thickneſs. This will finiſh the buſineſs, retaining the covering conſtantly on the bed night and day. In a month or ſix weeks it will begin to produce muſhrooms, which will be ſoon followed by plenty.

October.

SOWING is this month required in only three articles for early production next ſpring and ſummer, and thoſe are peas, lettuces, and radiſhes, and ſmall ſallading for the preſent ſupply. Cut down the ſtems of the aſparagus in the beds of laſt ſpring, hoe off the weeds, dig the alleys, and ſpread ſome of the earth over the beds.

Your main ſpring-ſowed crop of carrots being now arrived at full growth, take them up towards the latter end of the month, for keeping in ſand all winter. Cut the tops off cloſe, cleared from earth, and when quite dry, let them be carried under cover, and placed in dry ſand, or light dry earth, a layer of ſand and carrots alternately. Young carrots of the autumn ſowing in July and

 Auguſt,

Auguſt, muſt now be cleared from weeds, and thinned where too cloſe.

Manure your ground where it is required, with the rotten dung of old hot-beds, &c. eſpecially where the hand-glaſs crop of cauliflowers, and early cabbages, are intended to be placed. Continue to tie up full-grown plants of endive, in dry weather, every week to blanch. Plant endive for the laſt late crop, in a warm border, to ſtand till ſpring.

Your horſe-radiſh is now at full growth, to be dug up for uſe as wanted. Parſnips being now at their full growth, dig up a quantity, and lay them in ſand, in the ſame manner as directed for carrots. Potatoes, which are now arrived at their full growth, may be all dug up, and houſed in ſome dry cloſe place, thickly covered with ſtraw, from the air and moiſture, to keep all winter, till ſpring or ſummer.

Seed plants of ſeveral ſorts ſhould now be planted, as cabbages, ſavoys, diveſted of the large leaves, and put in by trenching them down to their heads, two feet diſtance; as alſo carrots, parſnips, turnips, and red beet, all of full growth, cutting the tops off near the crown, and planting them two feet diſtance, with the heads one or two inches under the ſurface of the earth. Alſo the largeſt dried onions planted in rows, at the ſame diſtance, and three or four inches over the crown.

November.

DIGGING and dunging the ground muſt now be attended to for the benefit of future crops. Aromatic plants, in beds and borders, ſhould now, if before omitted, have the laſt thorough cleaning from weeds and litter, and the beds dreſſed to remain in decent order for the winter. Earth up the

the different crops of celery when dry, and let thofe of full growth be earthed up almoft to the top.

Dig vacant ground one or two fpades deep, and if dunged, dig it in a fpade deep, laying the ground in rough ridges to improve by the weather, till wanted for fowing and planting with future crops. Dig up fome roots of horfe-radifh to preferve in fand, that it may be ready for ufe when that in the ground is frozen up. Do the like by Jerufalem artichokes, which are now in their full perfection.

Defend your mufhroom beds night and day with dry ftraw, or long dry ftable litter a foot thick, and put mats over all as a fecurity againft rain and cold. Sow fome early fhort-topped radifhes on a fouth border. Cover it with ftraw two inches thick till they come up, afterwards on nights, and in frofty weather, to have the chance of drawing a few early. Sow likewife fmall fallading, as creffes, muftard, and rape, under glaffes, or in a hot-bed.

Finifh deftroying weeds, in all parts, by hand and hoe. Carefully hand-weed beds of fmall plants, as onions, &c. In other compartments, eradicate them by hoe in dry days, and rake or fork off the large weeds after hoeing, or let them be beat about and loofened off effectually, fo as not to grow again.

December.

DUNGING and digging the ground is the principal bufinefs to be done in the kitchen garden this month, and laying it in ridges to enrich for fowing and planting after Chriftmas with fome principal and early crops, for the enfuing fpring and fummer. Drefs your artichoke beds by firft cutting down any remaining ftems, and the large leaves clofe.

Pay

Pay diligent attention to your asparagus hot-beds, to keep up the heat of the beds by linings of hot dung, and to admit air in mild days to the plants come up, by opening the glasses two or three inches behind; but shut them close on night, and cover the glasses with mats. Take up your red-rooted beet on a dry day, and let them be placed in sand, &c. under cover, for use, in case of hard frosts. Hoe earth to the stems of your borecole and brocoli on a dry day.

In all moderate weather, give air to your cauliflowers in frames and hand-glasses. Pick off all the decayed leaves, and destroy slugs, if any infest the plants. Whatever vacant ground you have, dig it in ridges trench ways two spades aside, and one or two spades deep. If dunged, dig in the dung, but one spade, laying each trench in a rough ridge, to remain for future cropping, that it may improve by the weather, and be ready for levelling down expeditiously for the reception of seeds and plants.

CHAP. XXXV.

The Management of the Fruit Garden.

January.

THE business to be done this month in the fruit garden and orchard consists in preparing for and planting such fruit trees as are intended, pruning and nailing wall and espalier trees in general, and standard trees where necessary, and in preparing

preparing to force fruit trees on hot walls for early fruit.

The proper ages for trees to be planted are when they are one, two, or three years old, and theſe may be had at public nurſeries, as well as thoſe more advanced and trained to a bearing ſtate for immediate bearers. Particular attention muſt be paid to their being taken up with their full ſpread of roots as entire as poſſible. Prune broken parts and long ſtragglers, and any very irregular branch in the head. When you plant them, dig a wide aperture two or three feet over, and one deep, or more or leſs according to the ſize of the roots. Fill the earth in regularly about them from three or four to five or ſix inches over the uppermoſt roots, and tread it evenly and gently thereto, firſt round the outſide, then gradually towards the middle, and cloſe round the ſtem of the tree.

You muſt now prune peaches, nectarines, apricots, and other wall fruit. They bear moſtly on the young wood produced the preceding year, and of which a general ſupply of the moſt regularly-placed muſt now be every where retained at proper diſtances, for ſucceſſional bearers, or for new wood, occaſionally for multiplying the branches. When pruned, nail them to the wall, four or five inches aſunder.

Prune vines, which bear only on the young wood, the laſt ſummer ſhoots being the proper bearers. Take out moſt of the laſt year's bearers, and all the naked old wood. Shorten the reſerved ſhoots, the ſmaller to three or four joints, and the ſtronger to five or ſix. Nail the vines to the wall as ſoon as pruned, arranging the general branches and ſhoots from eight to ten or twelve inches diſtance.

Prune your apples, pears, plums, and cherries, on walls and eſpaliers, and alſo currants and gooſeberries.

goofeberries. Cut away any crofs-placed or too crouded branches, decayed wood, and worn out bearers. Prune alfo your orchard trees, cutting out crofs-growing and confufed branches; thin fuch as grow too clofe together, and reduce the very long branches to moderate lengths.

February.

THE ground muft now be prepared for planting, by proper digging and trenching, and improving it with dung, frefh loam, or compoft, where required. A compoft of good loam, common earth, and rotten dung together, is excellent for fruit-tree borders. General planting of fruit-trees may be now performed in open mild weather, but particularly thofe forts moft required.

Standard-tree planting, in any kind of fruit-trees, may now be performed in open weather, in gardens or orchards, principally of apples, pears, plums, and cherries, for the main collection, efpecially moft of the two former, for family fupply during the courfe of the year. Plant the trees from twenty or thirty to forty or fifty feet diftance; the moderate growers, clofer in proportion, fuch as the codlin, common cherry tree, plum, &c. Dwarf ftandards, with low ftems, from one to two or three feet, may be planted in borders, fifteen or twenty feet diftance, in different fpecies and varieties.

Let all fruit-trees for planting be dug up with full roots, and at planting, prune any long ftraggling roots, and broken or bruifed fhoots from the ftems of the trees; and in young trees, having their firft fhoots of but a year old from grafting or budding entire, leave them in that ftate till next month, then to be headed. In thofe more advanced with trained or fuller heads, cut away only any ill-grown or crofs-planted branches or fhoots,

or

or prune thinner any that are too numerous and crouded, or any very luxuriant productions; and from the wall and espalier tree kinds, prune out all fore-right or projecting shoots.

Your vines must now be pruned and nailed, as directed last month. Prune gooseberries and currants, where required, to keep the heads moderate, and the branch thin to obtain large fruit. Prune raspberries in proper order, and make new plantations of them where required. Plant cuttings and suckers of gooseberries and currants, for new plants.

March.

IN the earliest part of this month finish the principal planting and pruning of all kinds of fruit-trees, as the trees will now be advancing in their blossoms and buds. In planting the different fruit-trees, observe the proper distances for wall-trees, espaliers, and standards; and give each a good watering to the earth, to settle it close about the roots and fibres, and to promote their taking fresh root.

In frosty weather, shelter wall-trees in blossom of apricots, peaches, the early, and some principal kinds, by nailing up large mats on nights before the trees; or occasionally on days, when the frost is severe, and no sun, to protect the young fruit now in embrio, and its generative organs in the center of the flower.

Train young wall and espalier trees, now in their first or second years shoots, pruning out fore-right and cross-placed shoots. In peaches, nectarines, apricots, and vines, shorten the remaining shoots more or less, to obtain a further supply of wood and shoots for bearers. But in apples, pears, plums, cherries, if well furnished with second and third years branches, leave most entire, only cutting

ting ſhort any middle ſhoots in the vacancies, to force out laterals in ſummer to ſupply the deficiencies; and as ſoon as pruned, train in all the branches horizontally to the wall, and eſpaliers at regular diſtances.

Propagate fig-trees by layers, cuttings, and ſuckers of the young ſhoots. Plant vine cuttings of the young ſhoots, two or three joints long, inverted in the ground to the uppermoſt eye or bud. Plant ſuckers and cutlings of the ſeveral ſorts of fruit-trees that produce them, for new plants and ſtocks to bud and graft upon. Perform grafting now on apples, pears, plums, cherries, quinces, and medlars, this being the proper ſeaſon for that operation.

April.

WATER new-planted trees in dry weather moderately, about once a week. Diveſt young budded and grafted trees of all ſhoots from the ſtock, below the bud or graft.

If any webs of caterpillars now appear on any fruit trees, clear them off before they ſpread, to prevent the inſects from devouring the advancing leaves. Defend early wall-trees now in bloſſom and young fruit, particularly apricots, peaches, nectarines, and others of the principal kinds, continuing to nail up mats in froſty nights. Rub off uſeleſs buds in early-ſhooting wall-trees, as peaches, nectarines, and apricots. Their ſhoots will now be advancing: rub off cloſe the fore-right ones, and others where too numerous, and ſuch as are ill placed, or where not wanted.

May.

THE moſt principal part of the buſineſs of this month in the fruit garden is to commence the ſummer pruning, by diſbudding early all the fore-right

right and other ill-placed and evidently unneceſſary ſhoots, and to thin the young fruit where ſet in cluſters. The new-planted trees muſt now be watered in dry weather.

The operation of ſummer pruning, at this early period, is performed without a knife: the buds being tender, the uſeleſs growths are more eaſily diſbudded, or detached with the finger and thumb, by rubbing them off cloſe to the old wood. Go over peaches, nectarines, and apricots, and rub off all the fore-right and other ill-placed ſhoot buds of the year. Likewiſe diſplace, in a thinning order, part of the ſuperfluous ſhoots, where evidently too numerous in any parts of the trees, and the remaining ſhoots, when of due length, train in cloſe and regular. Vines likewiſe, which will be now advancing in numerous ſhoots, go over early, and diſplace all the improper and ill-placed ſhoots of the year, particularly thoſe omitted from the old wood, where not wanted, and the weak and unfruitful ſtraggling ſhoots in all parts.

Wall-trees defended when in bloſſom and ſetting their fruit, ſhould now have all the covering diſcontinued, and removed away. Thin wall-fruit, as apricots, nectarines, and peaches, where ſet too thick, or in cluſters, retaining the moſt promiſing fruit at moderate diſtances, from three or four to five or ſix inches aſunder.

Water new-planted fruit-trees in hot dry weather, giving each about a watering pot of water once a week or fortnight, during this month, or till they have taken good root.

June.

SUMMER pruning or nailing the fruit-trees comprehends the principal buſineſs of this month. Begin the ſummer pruning of the earlieſt ſhooting kinds of wall-trees, as peaches, nectarines, apricots,

cots, vines, cherries, plums, pears, apples, &c. to diſplace the fore-right and other ill-placed ſhoots, and nail in all the regular placed ſide or terminal ſhoots to the wall.

From fig-trees, advanced in the preſent year's ſummer ſhoots, prune out the ill-placed branches, and nail the ſide ſhoots and terminal ones to the wall. Thin apricots, peaches, and nectarines, where too thick or in cluſters, thinning out the ſmalleſt, and leaving the moſt promiſing ſingly, at moderate diſtances, ſaving the apricots, and nectarines thinned off for tarts. Currants trained againſt walls, and eſpaliers, &c. muſt now be diveſted of all ſuperabundant ſhoots to admit the ſun to the fruit. Gooſeberries and currant buſhes in ſtandard, if very crouded with ſhoots of the year, prune where thickeſt, to admit the ſun to ripen the fruit with proper flavour. Defend the fineſt ſort of cherry-trees in ripe fruit from the birds, by the aſſiſtance of nets.

July.

THE buſineſs of this month will continue to require great attention to the ſummer pruning and nailing in all wall and eſpalier trees, both in continuance of the former regulations, and more particularly in thoſe not done, to regulate the numerous ſhoots of the year, by diſplacing thoſe improper and ſuperfluous, and to nail and train the young wood in regular order to the wall and eſpalier, and according as they advance in length to train them along cloſe, always at their full length all ſummer. Where the above regulations were commenced in May or June, very little will be required at this time but to faſten along the regular ſhoots in their proper places.

Thin apricots, peaches, and nectarines, if they be ſtill too cloſe. Regulate and nail vines, and prune and nail fig-trees, theſe having now made numerous ſtrong ſhoots. Prune apples, pears, plums, cherries, and currants; and defend ripe wall-fruit from birds and inſects: the former by nets, and the latter by placing phials of ſtrong liquor and water, or water ſugared, to emit an odorous ſmell, to decoy waſps and flies from the fruit.

Keep raſpberries cleared from all ſtraggling ſuckers of the plants, between the rows, or at a diſtance from the main ſtools, and hoe down weeds. Go over wall-trees, &c. every week, to diſplace with your knife uſeleſs after-ſhoots, and nail the proper ſupply cloſe as they ſhoot in length.

Auguſt.

THIS month will require great attention to be paid to the wall and eſpalier trees. Diſplace all uſeleſs young wood that may prevent the ſun ripening the fruit, which will be now getting to a ſtate of maturity. Gather ripe apricots before they become too ſoft and mealy-taſted.

Train and faſten in all the requiſite ſupply of proper ſhoots cloſe to the wall and eſpalier in regular order, and as they advance in length without ſhortening, both to preſerve the neceſſary regularity of the trees, to admit the ſun and free air to improve the ſupply of young wood to perfection, and for the advanced fruit to have all poſſible benefit of the ſun to accelerate its ripening in a regular manner, in the fulleſt ſtate of perfection and richneſs of flavour. Purſue the ſame method with the eſpaliers of apples, plums, and all other trees in that order of training.

Defend the choiceſt ſorts of wall-fruit, that are now ripening, from birds and inſects; the former, by hanging nets before the trees, and the latter by placing phials of ſweetened water, &c. to decoy and drown them, ſuch as waſps and flies. If annoyed

noyed with ants, place cuttings of common or Spanifh reed, hollowed elder, or any thing of a hollowed pipe-like kind, in which they will harbour, and may be deftroyed.

September.

THE principal fummer pruning in wall and efpalier trees being by this time completed, nothing material of that operation will now be wanted, except adjufting any diforderly fhoots that project from the wall, or have fprung from their places, or training along any that have extended in length, or to reduce others that have overtopped the walls, or run confiderably out of their limited fpace, fo as to keep the whole in perfect regularity, and that the full fun may be admitted to ripen the fruit of the feafon, now in moft forts advanced to near or full growth.

Vines muft be particularly attended to, it being the principal ripening feafon of the grapes, which in this country demand every poffible affiftance of the fun, by ftill keeping the vines cleared from all improper fhoots, and nailing the others along clofe and regular to the wall, to admit the fun's warmth in full power, equally to the ripening grapes, that they may acquire perfection before the cold and wet in autumn commence, and ripen with their particular richnefs and flavour. Such grapes as are fully ripe muft be guarded from wafps or birds, by putting fome of the beft bunches into bags of fine paper, or rather of thin gauze or crape, that will admit the fun, and keep off birds and infects.

Fruit in general will now be ripe on all walls, efpalier, and ftandard trees, which be careful to gather when in beft perfection before too ripe, efpecially of fome particular forts, as peaches, nectarines, plums, pears, &c. for prefent ufe.

October.

October.

THE moſt material buſineſs of this month is to give proper attention to the gathering of all winter fruits, particularly apples and pears for keeping; and the ſeveral autumnal fruits, for preſent ſupply, according as they ripen, and in late wall-fruits, keeping all the ſhoots nailed cloſe to admit the full ſun, eſpecially grapes.

Gather apples and pears now of full growth, both of the autumnal eating, and winter keeping kinds, all on dry days. All the autumnal kinds, and thoſe deſigned for keeping, ſhould be gathered by hand. Apples are proper both for preſent uſe, and to keep ſeveral months; but of the winter pears few are fit for immediate eating, only for ſtewing, &c. They ripen to perfection as they lie in the houſe, ſooner or later, according to the different ſorts, from next month and December, till March and April, and thoſe late ripeners will ſometimes keep till May or June.

November.

THE gathering of any fruits that are ſtill out muſt now be finiſhed, and all intended planting of fruit-trees forwarded, being an eligible ſeaſon for tranſplanting moſt ſorts, walls, eſpaliers, and ſtandards; alſo for the general operation of winter pruning and nailing, which ſhould now be performed at all opportunities.

Wall-tree planting may now be forwarded in apricots, peaches, nectarines, plums, cherries, vines, figs, pears; likewiſe any deſirable apples, to ripen earlier with an approved flavour; alſo occaſionally mulberries, to obtain larger fruit and ſooner ripe, with an improved flavour, generally allotting a principal ſupply for ſouth walls, particularly of the peaches, nectarines, apricots, figs, and

and vines; alſo of the others in a ſmaller portion: others on ſouth-weſt and eaſterly walls, and ſome on north expoſures, as morello and other cherries, plums, and pears.

Standard planting may now be performed in all the hardy fruits in their different varieties, as apples, pears, plums, cherries, mulberries, medlars, quinces, ſervices, filberts, all the hazle nut tribe, barberries, bullaces, damſons, almonds, walnuts; likewiſe the Breda and Bruſſels apricot in a warm ſituation; all which may be planted in kitchen gardens, pleaſure-grounds, orchards, &c. always allotting the fulleſt ſupply of the moſt uſeful kinds, as apples, pears, cherries, plums, &c. and planted from twenty or thirty, to forty or fifty feet diſtance.

Winter pruning ſhould now be forwarded in all kinds of fruit-trees, particularly wall-trees, and eſpaliers in the general annual regulation, both among the young and old branches; which general pruning is indiſpenſibly neceſſary in all wall and eſpalier trees every year in winter, any time from this month till March, to preſerve their requiſite regularity within the limited bounds, and their proper fruitfulneſs. As to the ſtandard-tree pruning, the trees having full ſcope for their heads to branch freely all round and above, they only need pruning occaſionally, to regulate any ill-growing branches, and for which now, or any time in the winter, is the proper ſeaſon.

Prune gooſeberries and currants, thinning the branches where too crouded, cutting out thoſe that are croſs-placed and decayed. Raſpberries may now be planted in full ſupply of both the red and white kinds, in rooted young ſtems of the laſt ſummer, in rows four feet and a half diſtance by a yard in the row, as in the ſpring months.

December.

December.

THE bufinefs of this month in the fruit-garden is principally the fame as in the laft; that is, if the weather be open, to prepare ground, where neceffary, to plant with any kind of fruit-trees that may be wanted, or intended for planting this, or the two following months when the weather admits; but for fear of a fevere froft, it is adviseable to finifh the principal planting early in the month, at leaft all that is intended before Chriftmas. As to pruning it may be continued, when convenient, all this month.

Standard-tree planting may be now forwarded in open weather. Plant orchard trees where intended, as apples, pears, plums, and cherries, in full ftandards, thirty, forty, or fifty feet fquare, to form ftraight ranges each way. Likewife occafionally plant half ftandards, grafted on dwarf ftocks, in fmall orchards, at lefs diftances. Efpalier-tree planting may be performed in apples, or pears, fifteen or twenty feet diftance; plums, cherries, quinces, or medlars, at fifteen feet diftance.

Fruit put by for keeping, fuch as apples, pears, and quinces, muft be occafionally examined, in order to remove what are decayed or rotten, and keep the whole clofely covered with ftraw, at leaft a foot thick, in order to exclude the damps.

CHAP. XXXVI.

Articles omitted in the preceding Part of the Work.

To preſerve Dripping.

THIS is a very uſeful article at ſea, and in order to be kept properly for that purpoſe, muſt be managed in the following manner. Take ſix pounds of good beef dripping, boil it in ſome ſoft water, ſtrain it into a pan, and let it ſtand till it is cold. Then take off the hard fat, and ſcrape off the gravy which ſticks to the inſide. Do this eight times, and when it is cold and hard, take it off clean from the water, and put it into a large ſaucepan, with ſix bay leaves, twelve cloves, half a pound of ſalt, and a quarter of a pound of whole pepper. Let the fat be all melted, and juſt hot enough to ſtrain through a ſieve into a ſtone pot. Then let it ſtand till it is quite cold, and cover it up. In this manner you may do what quantity you pleaſe. It is a very good method to keep the pot upſide down, to prevent its being deſtroyed by the rats. It will keep good any voyage, and make as fine puff-paſte cruſt as the beſt butter.

To keep and dreſs dried Fiſh.

THE generality of fiſh, except ſtock-fiſh, are either ſalted and dried in the ſun, as the moſt common way, or in preparing-kilns, and ſometimes by the ſmoak of wood fires, in chimney-corners; and, in either caſe, they require to be ſoftened and freſhened, in proportion to their bulk, nature, or dryneſs. The very dry ſort, as cod-fiſh, or whiting, and ſuch like, ſhould be ſteeped in lukewarm milk and water, and the ſteeping kept as nearly as poſſible to an equal

degree

degree of heat. The largeſt fiſh ſhould be ſteeped twelve hours; the ſmaller, as whitings, &c. about two hours. The cod muſt, therefore, be laid to ſteep in the evening; the whitings, &c. in the morning of the day they are to be dreſſed. After the time of ſteeping, they are to be taken out, and hung up by the tails until they are dreſſed. The reaſon of hanging them up is this, that they ſoften equally as in the ſteeping, without extracting too much of the reliſh, which would make them inſipid. When thus prepared, the ſmall fiſh; as whitings, tuſk, and ſuch like, muſt be floured and laid on the gridiron, and when a little hardened on the one ſide, muſt be turned, and baſted with oil upon a feather; and when baſted on both ſides, and heated through, take them up, always obſerving, that as ſweet oil ſupplies the fiſh with a kind of artificial juices, ſo the fire draws out theſe juices and hardens them. Be carefnl, therefore, not to let them broil too long; but no time can be preſcribed, becauſe of the difference of fires, and various ſizes of the fiſh. A clear charcoal fire is much the beſt, and the fiſh kept a good diſtance to broil gradually. The beſt way to know when the fiſh are enough is, that they will ſwell a little in the baſting, and you muſt not let them fall again. To thoſe who like ſweet-oil, the beſt ſauce is oil, vinegar, and muſtard, beat to a conſiſtence, and ſerved up in ſaucers. If your fiſh be boiled, as thoſe of a large ſort uſually are, it ſhould be in milk and water, but not properly to ſay boiled, as it ſhould only juſt ſimmer over an equal fire. In this way, half an hour will do the largeſt fiſh, and five minutes the ſmalleſt. Some people broil both ſorts after ſimmering, and ſome pick them to pieces, and then toſs them up in a pan with fried onions and apples. They are very good either way, and the choice depends on the weak or ſtrong ſtomach of the eaters. Dried ſalmon muſt be managed in a different manner: for, though a large fiſh, it does not require more ſteeping than a whiting, and ſhould be moderately peppered when laid on the gridiron. Dried herrings ſhould be ſteeped the ſame time as a whiting, in ſmall beer, inſtead of milk and water; and to which, as to all kinds of broiled ſalt-fiſh, ſweet oil will always be found the beſt baſting, and no ways effect even the delicacy of thoſe who are not fond of it.

To make Panada.

TAKE a blade of mace, a large piece of crumb of bread, and put them into a ſaucepan, with a quart of water. After it has boiled two minutes, take out the bread, and bruiſe it very fine in a baſon. Mix as much water as you think it will require, pour away the reſt, and ſweeten it to your palate. Put in a piece of butter about the ſize of a walnut; but do not put in any wine, as that will ſpoil it. Grate in a little nutmeg.

To make ſweet Panada.

HAVING ſliced the crumb of a penny loaf very thin, put it into a ſaucepan with a pint of water, and boil it till it be very ſoft and looks clear. Then put in a glaſs of Madeira wine, grate in a little nutmeg, and put in a lump of butter about the ſize of a walnut, and ſugar to your taſte. Beat it exceedingly fine, and put it into a deep ſoup-diſh.

To make Beef Tea.

TAKE a pound of lean beef, cut it into very thin ſlices, and put it into a jar. Pour a quart of boiling water over it, cover it cloſe that the ſteam

may

may not get out, and let it ſtand by the fire. This is ſtrongly recommended by phyſicians for weak conſtitutions, and ſhould be drank milk warm.

To make Water Gruel.

PUT a large ſpoonful of oatmeal to a pint of water, ſtir them well together, and let it boil up three or four times, ſtirring it often; but take care not to let it boil over. Then ſtrain it through a ſieve, ſalt it to your palate, put in a good piece of freſh butter, brew it with a ſpoon till the butter be all melted, and it will be fine and ſmooth.

Barley Gruel.

PUT a quarter of a pound of pearl barley, and a ſtick of cinnamon, into two quarts of water, and let it boil till it be reduced to one quart. Add a pint of red wine and ſugar to your taſte. You may add two or three ounces of currants, if you pleaſe.

To make Barley Water.

BOIL a quarter of a pound of pearl barley in two quarts of water, ſkim it well, boil it half away, and then ſtrain it. Sweeten it, but not too much, and put to it two ſpoonfuls of white wine. It muſt be drank a little warm.

To make Orgeat.

BEAT to a paſte two pounds of almonds, with thirty bitter almonds. Mix it with three quarts of water, and ſtrain it through a fine cloth. Having added orange and lemon juice, with ſome of the peel, ſweeten it to your taſte.

To make Lemonade.

PARE two Seville oranges and ſix lemons very thin, and ſteep the parings four hours in two quarts

quarts of water. Put the juice of ſix oranges and twelve lemons upon twelve ounces of fine ſugar, and when the ſugar is melted, put the water to it. Add a little orange-flower water, and more ſugar, if neceſſary. Paſs it through a bag till it be fine.

To make Sack Poſſet.

BEAT well and ſtrain the yolks and whites of fifteen eggs. Then put three quarters of a pound of white ſugar into a pint of canary, and mix it in a baſon with your eggs. Set it over a chafing-diſh of coals, and keep continually ſtirring it till it is ſcalding hot. In the mean time, grate ſome nutmeg into a quart of milk, and boil it; then put it into your eggs and wine, they being ſcalding hot. Hold your hand very high as you pour it, and let ſomebody ſtir it all the time you are pouring in the milk. Then take it off the chafing-diſh, ſet it before the fire half an hour, and it will be fit for uſe.

To make Wine Poſſet.

PUT the crumb of a penny loaf into a quart of milk, and boil it till it be ſoft. Then take it off the fire, grate in half a nutmeg, and ſweeten it to your taſte. Put it into a China bowl, and by degrees add to it a pint of Liſbon wine. Send it up to table with toaſt and butter on a plate.

To make Ale Poſſet.

PUT a little white bread into a pint of milk, and ſet it over the fire. Then put ſome nutmeg and ſugar into a pint of ale, warm it, and when your milk boils, pour it upon the ale. Let it ſtand a few minutes to clear, and the curd will riſe to the top.

To make an Orange Poſſet.

GRATE the crumb of a penny loaf very fine, and put it into rather more than a pint of water, with

with half the peel of a Seville orange grated, or ſugar rubbed upon it to take out the eſſence. Boil all together till it looks thick and clear, and then beat it well. Take a pint of Mountain wine, the juice of half a Seville orange, three ounces of Jordan almonds, and one ounce of bitter, finely beat, with a little French brandy and ſugar to your taſte. Mix it well, put it into your poſſet, and ſerve it up. A lemon poſſet is made in the ſame manner.

To make White Wine Whey.

PUT half a pint of white wine and half a pint of ſkimmed milk into a baſon. Let it ſtand a few minutes, and then pour over it a pint of boiling water. Let it ſtand a little, and the curd will gather in a lump, and ſettle to the bottom. Then pour your whey into a China bowl, and put in a lump of ſugar, a ſprig of balm, or a ſlice of lemon.

To make Capillaire.

TAKE fourteen pounds of loaf ſugar, three pounds of coarſe ſugar, ſix eggs beaten in with the ſhells, and three quarts of water. Boil it up twice, ſkim it well, and then add to it a quarter of a pint of orange-flower water. Strain it through a jelly-bag, and put it into bottles. When it is cold, mix a ſpoonful or two of this ſyrup, as it is liked for ſweetneſs, in a draught of warm or cold water.

To mull Wine.

GRATE half a nutmeg into a pint of wine and ſweeten it to your taſte with loaf-ſugar. Set it over the fire, and when it boils, take it off to cool. Take the yolks of four eggs well beaten, add to them a little cold wine, and then mix them carefully with your hot wine, a little at a time. Pour it backwards and forwards ſeveral times till it looks fine

fine and bright. Then ſet it on the fire, and beat it a little at a time for ſeveral times, till it is quite hot, and pretty thick, and pour it backwards and forwards frequently. Then put it into chocolate cups, and ſerve it up with dry toaſt cut in long narrow pieces.

To make Gooſeberry Fool.

PUT two quarts of gooſeberries into about a quart of water, and ſet them on the fire. When they begin to ſimmer, turn yellow, and to plump, throw them into a cullender to drain out the water, and with the back of a ſpoon carefully ſqueeze the pulp through a ſieve into a diſh. Make them pretty ſweet, and let them ſtand till they are cold. In the mean time, take two quarts of milk, and the yolks of four eggs beaten up with a little grated nutmeg. Stir it ſoftly over a ſlow fire, and when it begins to ſimmer, take it off, and by degrees ſtir it into the gooſeberries. Let it ſtand till it be cold, and then ſerve it up. If you make it with cream, you need not put any eggs.

To make a White Pot.

PUT eight eggs, and half the whites, beat up with a little roſe-water, a nutmeg; and a quarter of a pound of ſugar, to two quarts of milk. Cut a penny loaf in very thin ſlices, and pour the milk and eggs over them. Put a little piece of butter on the top, and bake it half an hour in a ſlow oven.

A Rice White Pot.

HAVING boiled a pound of rice in two quarts of milk till it be tender and thick, beat it in a mortar with a quarter of a pound of ſweet almonds blanched. Then boil two quarts of cream, with a few crumbs of white bread, and two or three blades

of

of mace. Mix it with eight eggs, and a little rofe-water, and fweeten to your tafte. Cut fome candied orange or citron peels thin, and lay it in. It muft be baked in a flow oven.

To make Sago.

PUT a large fpoonful of fago to three quarters of a pint of water; ftir it, and boil it foftly till it is as thick as you would have it. Then put in wine and fugar, with a little nutmeg, to your palate.

To make Rice Milk.

PUT half a pound of rice into a quart of water, with a little cinnamon, and let it boil till the water is wafted; but take care that it does not burn. Then add three pints of milk, and the yolk of an egg beat up. Keep ftirring it, and when it boils, take it up and fweeten it.

To make Salop.

TAKE a large tea-fpoonful of this powder, which is fold at the chemifts, and put it into a pint of boiling water. Keep ftirring it till it becomes a fine jelly, and then add wine and fugar to your tafte.

To make White Caudle.

MIX four fpoonfuls of oatmeal, a blade or two of mace, and a piece of lemon-peel, with two quarts of water. Let it boil a quarter of an hour, ftirring it often; but be careful not to let it boil over, and then ftrain it through a coarfe fieve. When you ufe it, fweeten it to your tafte, grate in a little nutmeg, and put in what wine you think proper.

To make brown Caudle.

MAKE your gruel as above, with fix fpoonfuls of oatmeal, and ftrain it. Then put to it a quart of of ale that is not bitter. Boil it, and ſweeten it to your palate, and add half a pint of white wine or brandy. When you do not put in white wine or brandy, let it be half ale.

To fricaſſee Chickens.

HAVING ſkinned your chickens, and cut them into ſmall pieces, waſh them in warm water, and dry them very clean with a cloth. Seaſon them with pepper and ſalt, and put them into a ſtewpan with a little water, and a good piece of butter, a little lemon pickle, or half a lemon, a glaſs of white wine, an anchovy, a little mace and nutmeg, an onion ſtuck with cloves, a bunch of lemon-thyme, and ſweet-marjoram. Let theſe ſtew together till your chickens are tender, and then lay them on your diſh. Thicken the gravy with flour and butter, and ſtrain it. Beat the yolks of three eggs a little, and mix them with a large teacupful of rich cream, and put it into your gravy. Shake it over the fire, but do not let it boil, and pour it over your chickens.

To fricaſſee Rabbits white.

CUT up your rabbits, put them into a toſſing-pan, with a pint of veal gravy, a tea-ſpoonful of lemon-pickle, an anchovy, a ſlice of lemon, a little beaten mace, chian pepper, and ſalt, and ſtew them over a ſlow fire. When they are enough, thicken your gravy with flour and butter, and ſtrain it. Then add the yolks of two eggs mixed with a large teacupful of cream, and a little nutmeg grated in it. Take care not to let it boil; as that will ſpoil it.

To fricaſſee Rabbits brown.

HAVING cut them as for eating, fry them of a light brown in butter, and put them into a toſſing-pan,

pan, with a pint of water, a tea-ſpoonful of lemon pickle, an anchovy, a ſlice of lemon, a large ſpoonful of muſhroom catchup, the ſame of browning, with chian pepper, and ſalt to your taſte. Stew them over a ſlow fire till they be enough; thicken your gravy and ſtrain it, diſh up your rabbits, and pour the gravy over them.

To fricaſſee Tripe.

GET ſome nice white tripe, cut it into ſlips, put it into ſome boiled gravy with a little cream, and a bit of butter mixed with flour. Stir it till the butter be melted, and add a little white wine, lemon-peel grated, chopped parſley, pepper, ſalt, and pickled muſhrooms, or lemon-juice. Shake all together, and give it a gentle ſtew.

To fricaſſee Ox Palates.

HAVING well cleaned your palates, put them into a ſtew-pot, cover them with water, and ſet them in the oven for three or four hours. When they come from the oven, ſtrip off the ſkins, and cut them in ſquare pieces. Seaſon them with mace, nutmeg, chian, and ſalt. Mix a ſpoonful of flour with the yolks of two eggs, dip in your palates, fry them of a light brown, and then put them in a ſieve to drain. Have ready half a pint of veal gravy, with a little caper liquor, a ſpoonful of browning, and a few muſhrooms. Thicken it well with flour and butter, pour it hot on your diſh, and lay in your palates. Garniſh with barberries and fried parſley.

To fricaſſee Pigeons.

CUT your pigeons in the ſame manner as chickens for fricaſſeeing, fry them of a light brown, put them into ſome good mutton gravy, and ſtew them near half an hour. Put in half an ounce of morels, a ſpoonful of browning, and a ſlice of lemon.

mon. Take up your pigeons, and thicken your gravy; ſtrain it over your pigeons, lay round them forcemeat balls, and garniſh with pickles.

To fricaſſee Eggs.

HAVING boiled your eggs pretty hard, ſlice them. Take a little veal gravy, a little cream and flour, and a bit of butter, nutmeg, ſalt, pepper, chopped parſley, and a few pickled muſhrooms. Boil this up, and pour it over the eggs. Put a hard yolk in the middle of the diſh, with toaſted ſippets.

A

CATALOGUE

OF THE

Various ARTICLES in Season in the different MONTHS of the YEAR.

JANUARY.

MEAT.

BEEF	Veal	Pork
Mutton	House-Lamb	

POULTRY, &c.

Pheasant } Game	Woodcocks	Pullets
Partridge } Game	Snipes	Fowls
Hares	Turkeys	Chickens
Rabbits	Capons	Tame Pigeons

FISH.

Carp	Soles	Smelts
Tench	Flounders	Whitings
Perch	Plaice	Lobsters
Lampreys	Turbot	Crabs
Eels	Thornback	Prawns
Craw-fish	Skate	Oysters
Cod	Sturgeon	

VEGETABLES, &c.

Cabbage	Lettuces	Sage
Savoys	Cresses	Parsnips
Coleworts	Mustard	Carrots
Sprouts	Rape	Turnips
Brocoli, purple and white	Radish	Potatoes
	Turnips	Scorzonera
Spinach	Tarragon	Skirrets

Ff

Cardoons

Cardoons
Beets
Parſley
Sorrel
Chervil
Celery
Endive

Mint
Cucumbers in hot houſes
Thyme
Savory
Pot-Marjoram
Hyſop

Salſifie
To be had, though not in Seaſon
Jeruſalem Artichokes
Aſparagus
Muſhrooms

FRUIT.

Apples
Pears
Nuts

Almonds
Services

Medlars
Grapes

FEBRUARY.

MEAT.

Beef
Mutton

Veal
Houſe-Lamb

Pork

POULTRY, &c.

Turkeys
Capons
Pullets
Fowls

Chickens
Pigeons
Pheaſants
Partridges

Woodcocks
Snipes
Hares
Tame Rabbits

FISH.

Cod
Soles
Sturgeon
Flounders
Plaice
Turbot
Thornback

Skate
Whitings
Smelts
Lobſters
Crabs
Oyſters
Prawns

Tench
Perch
Carp
Eels
Lampreys
Craw-fiſh

VEGETABLES, &c.

Cabbage
Savoys
Coleworts
Sprouts
Brocoli, purple and white

Muſtard
Rape
Radiſhes
Turnips
Tarragon
Mint

Aſparagus
Kidney Beans
Carrots
Turnips
Parſnips
Potatoes

Cardoons
Beets
Parſley
Chervil
Endive
Sorrel
Celery
Chard Beets
Lettuces
Creſſes

Burnet
Tanſey
Thyme
Savory
Marjoram

Alſo may be had

Forced Radiſhes
Cucumbers

Onions
Leeks
Shalots
Garlick
Rocombole
Salſifie
Skirret
Scorzonera
Jeruſalem Artichokes

FRUIT.

Pears
Apples
Grapes

MARCH.

MEAT.

Beef
Mutton
Veal
Houſe-Lamb
Pork

POULTRY, &c.

Turkeys
Pullets
Capons
Fowls
Chickens
Ducklings
Pigeons
Tame Rabbits

FISH.

Carp
Tench
Turbot
Thornback
Skate
Eels
Mullets
Plaice
Flounders
Lobſters
Soles
Whitings
Crabs
Craw-fiſh
Prawns

VEGETABLES.

Carrots
Turnips
Parſnips
Jeruſalem Artichokes
Onions
Garlick
Shalots
Brocoli
Cardoons
Beets
Parſley
Fennel
Celery
Endive

Tanſey	Turnips	Burnet
Rape	Tarragon	Thyme
Radiſhes	Mint	Winter-Savory
Coleworts	Muſhrooms	Pot-Marjoram
Borecole	Lettuces	Hyſop
Cabbages	Chives	Fennel
Savoys	Creſſes	Cucumbers
Spinach	Muſtard	Kidney-Beans

FRUIT.

Pears	Apples	Forced Straw-berries.

APRIL.

MEAT.

Beef Mutton Veal Lamb

POULTRY, &c.

Pullets	Ducklings	Rabbits
Fowls	Pigeons	Leverets
Chickens		

FISH.

Crabs	Salmon	Smelts
Chub	Turbot	Herrings
Tench	Soles	Lobſters
Trout	Skate	Prawns
Craw-fiſh	Mullets	

VEGETABLES.

Coleworts	Young Onions	Lettuces
Sprouts	Celery	All ſorts of ſmall Sallad
Brocoli	Endive	
Spinach	Sorrel	Thyme
Fennel	Burnet	All ſorts of Pot-Herbs
Parſley	Tarragon	
Chervil	Radiſhes	

FRUIT.

Apples	Forced Cherries and	Apricots for Tarts.
Pears		

MAY.

MAY.

MEAT.

Beef	Mutton	Veal	Lamb

POULTRY, &c.

Pullets	Green Geeſe	Rabbits
Fowls	Ducklings	Leverets
Chickens	Turkey Poults	

FISH.

Carp	Salmon	Lobſters
Tench	Soles	Craw-fiſh
Eels	Turbot	Crabs
Trout	Herrings	Prawns
Chub	Smelts	

VEGETABLES, &c.

Early Potatoes	Barley	Savory
Carrots	Mint	All other ſweet Herbs
Turnips	Purſlane	
Radiſhes	Fennel	Peaſe
Early Cabbages	Lettuces	Beans
Cauliflowers	Creſſes	Kidney Beans
Artichokes	Muſtard	Aſparagus
Spinach	All ſorts of ſmall Sallad Herbs	Tragopogon
Parſley		Cucumbers, &c.
Sorrel	Thyme	

FRUIT.

Pears	And Melons	Gooſeberries
Apples	With Green Apricots	And Currants for Tarts
Strawberries		
Cherries		

JUNE.

MEAT.

Beef	Veal	Buck Veniſon
Mutton	Lamb	

POULTRY, &c.

Fowls	Ducklings	Wheat-Ears
Pullets	Turkey Poults	Leverets
Chickens	Plovers	Rabbits
Green Geeſe		

FISH.

Trout	Salmon	Herrings
Carp	Soles	Smelts
Tench	Turbot	Lobſters
Pike	Mullets	Craw-fiſh
Eels	Mackarel	Prawns

VEGETABLES, &c.

Carrots	Aſparagus	Rape
Turnips.	Kidney Beans	Creſſes
Potatoes	Artichokes	All other ſmall Sallading
Parſnips	Cucumbers	
Radiſhes	Lettuces	Thyme
Onions	Spinach	All ſorts of Pot-Herbs
Beans	Parſley	
Peaſe	Purſlane	

FRUIT.

Cherries	Apricots	Nectarines
Strawberries	Apples	Grapes
Gooſeberries	Pears	Melons
Currants	Some Peaches	Pine Apples

JULY.

MEAT.

Beef	Veal	Buck Veniſon
Mutton	Lamb	

POULTRY, &c.

Pullets	Ducklings	Pheaſants
Fowls	Turkey Poults	Wheat-Ears
Chickens	Ducks	Plovers

Pigeons

Pigeons	Young Partridges	Leverets
Green Geese		Rabbits

FISH.

Cod	Herrings	Skate
Haddocks	Soles	Thornback
Mullets	Plaice	Salmon
Mackarel	Flounders	Carp
Tench	Eels	Prawns
Pike	Lobsters	Craw-fish

VEGETABLES, &c.

Carrots	Cabbages	All sorts of small Sallad Herbs
Turnips	Sprouts	Mint
Potatoes	Artichokes	Balm
Radishes	Celery	Thyme
Onions	Endive	All other Pot-Herbs
Garlick	Finocha	Pease
Rocombole	Chervil	Beans
Scorzonera	Sorrel	Kidney Beans
Salsifie	Purslane	
Mushrooms	Lettuce	
Cauliflowers	Cresses	

FRUIT.

Pears	Nectarines	Strawberries
Apples	Plumbs	Raspberries
Cherries	Apricots	Melons
Peaches	Gooseberries	Pine Apples

AUGUST.

MEAT.

Beef	Veal	Buck Venison
Mutton	Lamb	

POULTRY, &c.

Fowls	Ducklings	Pheasants
Pullets	Leverets	Wild Ducks

Chickens	Rabbits	Wheat-Ears
Green Geeſe	Pigeons	Plovers
Turkey Poults		

FISH.

Cod	Mullets	Eels
Haddock	Mackarel	Lobſters
Flounders	Herrings	Craw-fiſh
Plaice	Pike	Prawns
Skate	Carp	Oyſters
Thornback		

VEGETABLES, &c.

Carrots	Beans	Finocha
Turnips	Kidney Beans	Parſley
Potatoes	Muſhrooms	Lettuces
Radiſhes	Artichokes	All ſorts of ſmall Sallad
Onions	Cabbage	Thyme
Garlick	Cauliflowers	Savory
Shalots	Sprouts	Marjoram
Scorzonera	Beets	All ſorts of ſweet Herbs
Salſifie	Celery	
Peaſe	Endive	

FRUIT.

Peaches	Pears	Strawberries
Nectarines	Grapes	Gooſeberries
Plums	Figs	Currants
Cherries	Filberts	Melons
Apples	Mulberries	Pine Apples

SEPTEMBER.

MEAT.

Beef	Mutton	Pork
Veal	Lamb	Buck Veniſon

POULTRY.

POULTRY, &c.

Geeſe	Pullets	Chickens
Turkies	Fowls	Ducks
Teals	Hares	Pheaſants
Pigeons	Rabbits	Partridges
Larks		

FISH.

Cod	Skate	Tench
Haddock	Soles	Pike
Flounders	Smelts	Lobſters
Plaice	Salmon	Oyſters
Thornbacks	Carp	

VEGETABLES.

Carrots	Kidney Beans	Finocha
Turnips	Muſhrooms	Lettuces, and all ſorts of ſmall Sallads
Potatoes	Artichokes	Chervil
Shalots	Cabbages	Sorrel
Onions	Sprouts	Beets
Leeks	Cauliflowers	Thyme, and all ſorts of Soup Herbs
Garlick	Cardoons	
Scorzonera	Endive	
Salſifie	Celery	
Peaſe	Parſley	
Beans		

FRUIT.

Peaches	Walnuts	Lazaroles
Plums	Filberts	Currants
Apples	Hazel Nuts	Morello Cherries
Pears	Medlars	Melons
Grapes	Quinces	Pine Apples

OCTOBER.

MEAT.

Beef	Lamb	Pork
Mutton	Veal	Doe Veniſon

POULTRY,

POULTRY, &c.

Geefe	Rabbits	Larks
Turkies	Wild Ducks	Dotterels
Pigeons	Teals	Hares
Pullets	Widgeons	Pheafants
Fowls	Woodcocks	Partridges
Chickens	Snipes	

FISH.

Dorees	Gudgeons	Salmon Trout
Holobets	Pike	Lobfters
Bearbet	Carp	Cockles
Smelts	Tench	Mufcles
Brills	Perch	Oyfters

VEGETABLES.

Cabbages	Scorzonera	Chard Beets
Sprouts	Leeks	Corn Sallad
Cauliflowers	Shalots	Lettuces
Artichokes	Garlick	All fortsof young Sallad
Carrots	Rocombole	Thyme
Parfnips	Celery	Savory
Turnips	Endive	All forts of Pot-Herbs
Potatoes	Cardoons	
Skirrets	Chervil	
Salfifie	Finocha	

FRUIT.

Peaches	Quinces	Filberts
Grapes	Black and white Bullace	Hazle-Nuts
Figs	Walnuts	Pears
Medlars		Apples
Services		

NOVEMBER.

MEAT.

Beef	Veal	Doe Venifon
Mutton	Houfe-Lamb	

POULTRY,

POULTRY, &c.

Geefe	Wild Ducks	Dotterels
Turkies	Teals	Hares
Fowls	Widgeons	Rabbits
Chickens	Woodcocks	Partridges
Pullets	Snipes	Pheafants
Pigeons	Larks	

FISH.

Gurnets	Salmon Trout	Gudgeons
Dorees	Smelts	Lobfters
Holobets	Carp	Oyfters
Bearbet	Pike	Cockles
Salmon	Tench	Mufcles

VEGETABLES, &c.

Carrots	Rocombole	Cardoons
Turnips	Jerufalem Arti-chokes	Parfley
Parfnips		Creffes
Potatoes	Cabbages	Endive
Skirret	Cauliflowers	Chervil
Salfifie	Savoys	Lettuces
Scorzonera	Sprouts	All forts of fmall Sallad Herbs
Onions	Coleworts	
Leeks	Spinage	Thyme, and all other Pot Herbs
Shalots	Chard Beets	

FRUIT.

Pears	Chefnuts	Medlars
Apples	Hazle-Nuts	Services
Bullace	Walnuts	Grapes

DECEMBER.

MEAT.

Beef	Veal	Pork
Mutton	Houfe-Lamb	Doe Venifon

POULTRY,

POULTRY, &c.

Geeſe
Turkeys
Pullets
Pigeons
Capons
Fowls

Chickens
Hares
Rabbits
Woodcocks
Snipes
Larks

Wild Ducks
Teals
Widgeons
Dottrels
Partridges
Pheaſants

FISH.

Turbot
Gurnets
Sturgeon
Dorees
Holobets
Bearbet

Smelts
Cod
Codlings
Soles
Carp

Gudgeon
Eels
Cockles
Muſſels
Oyſters

VEGETABLES, &c.

Cabbages
Savoys
Brocoli, purple and white
Carrots
Parſnips
Turnips
Lettuces
Creſſes
All ſorts of ſmall Sallad

Potatoes
Skirrets
Scorzonera
Salſifie
Leeks
Onions
Shalots
Cardoons
Forced Aſparagus

Garlick
Rocombole
Celery
Endive
Beets
Spinach
Parſley
Thyme
All ſorts of Pot-Herbs

FRUIT.

Apples
Pears
Medlars

Services
Cheſnuts
Walnuts

Hazle-Nuts
Grapes

to face p. 320

A Hare
N°1
N°5
A Pheasant
N°6
A Partridge
A Goose
N°2
Wing
Roast Fowl
N°3
Leg
N°8
Pigeon
N°7
Pigeon
Neck
Bone
A Pig
N°4
N°9
A Quarter of Lamb
N°10
A Haunch of Venison

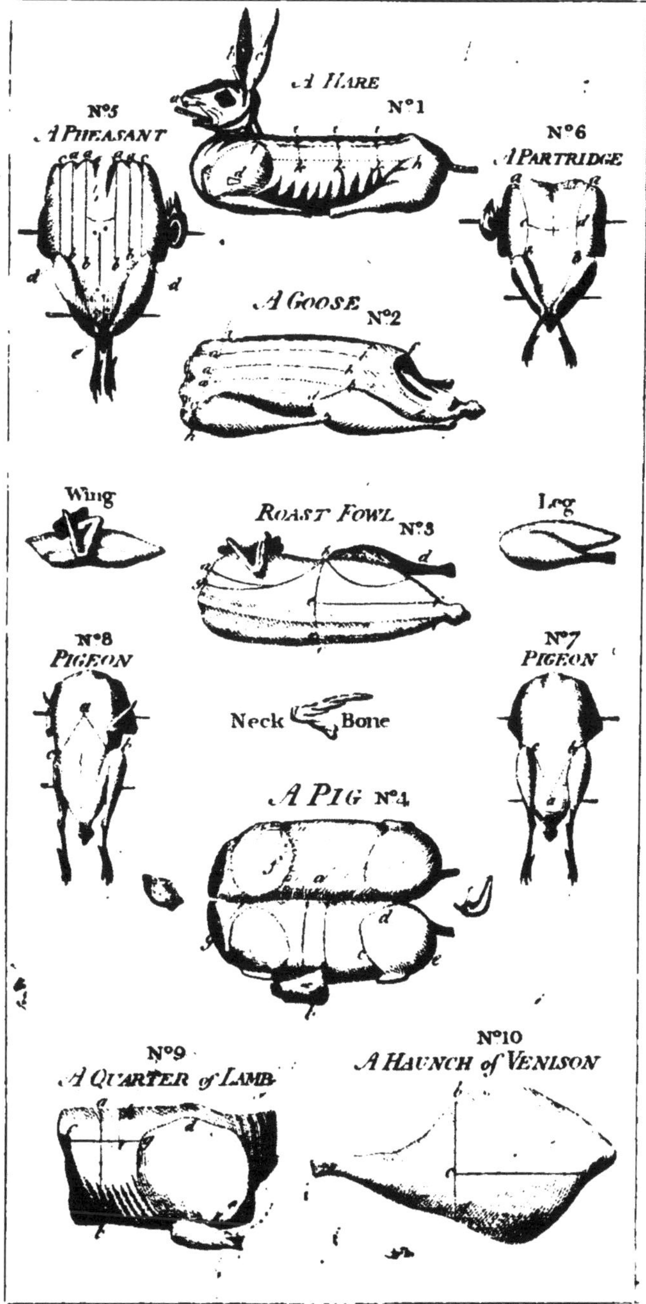

You may also be interested in these titles:

Townsends is please to make available a growing list of rare and valuable books from the 18th and early 19th centuries, including those listed below. Be sure to visit our website for a complete list of titles.

Cookbooks

The Art of Cookery by Hannah Glasse (1765)

The Domestick Coffee-Man by Humphrey Broadbent (1722)
and ***The New Art of Brewing Beer*** by Thomas Tyron (1690)

The Complete Housewife by Eliza Smith (1730)

The Universal Cook by John Townshend (1773)

The Practice of Cookery by Mrs. Frazer (1791 & 1795)

The London Art of Cookery by John Farley (1787)

The Complete Confectioner by Hannah Glasse (1765)

A New and Easy Method of Cookery by Elizabeth Cleland (1755)

The English Art of Cookery by Richard Briggs (1788)

18th & Early 19th-Century Brewing by multiple authors

The Lady's Assistant by Charlotte Mason (1777)

The Experienced English Housekeeper by Elizabeth Raffald (1769)

The Professed Cook by B. Clermont (1769)

The Cook's and Confectioner's Dictionary by John Nott (1723)

The Modern Art of Cookery Improved by Ann Shackleford (1765)

The Country Housewife's Family Companion by William Ellis (1750)

A Collection of Above Three Hundred Receipts by Mary Kettelby (1714)

England's Newest Way in All Sorts of Cookery by Henry Howard (1726)

Biographies & Journals

The Hessians by multiple authors

Travels Through the Interior Parts of North-America in the Years 1766, 1767, and 1768 by Jonathan Carver (1778)

The Women of the American Revolution, Volumes 1, 2, & 3 by Elizabeth Ellet (1848)

The Backwoods of Canada by Catharine Parr Traill (1836)

Travels into North America by Peter Kalm (1760)

New Travels in the United States of America. Performed in 1788 and ***The Commerce of America and Europe*** by J.P. Brissot De Warville (1792 & 1795)

The Journal of Nicholas Cresswell, 1774–1777 by Nicholas Cresswell (1924)

An Account of the Life of the Late Reverend Mr. David Brainerd by Jonathan Edwards (1765 & 1824)

Travels for Four Years and a Half in the United States of America During 1798, 1799, 1800, 1801, and 1802 by JohnDavis (1909)

Travels through North and South Carolina, Georgia, East and West Florida by William Bartram (1792)

A Tour in the United States of America, Volumes 1 & 2 by John F. Smyth Stuart (1784)

Made in the USA
Columbia, SC
13 April 2019